YOUR
ASTROLOGICAL
MOON
SIGN

YOUR ASTROLOGICAL MOON SIGN

WEREWOLF, ANGEL, VAMPIRE, SAINT

Discover Your Hidden Inner Self

DAVID WELLS

HAY HOUSE

Australia • Canada • Hong Kong • India
South Africa • United Kingdom • United States

First published and distributed in the United Kingdom by:
Hay House UK Ltd, 292B Kensal Rd, London W10 5BE. Tel.: (44) 20 8962 1230;
Fax: (44) 20 8962 1239. www.hayhouse.co.uk

Published and distributed in the United States of America by:
Hay House, Inc., PO Box 5100, Carlsbad, CA 92018-5100. Tel.: (1) 760 431 7695 or (800)
654 5126; Fax: (1) 760 431 6948 or (800) 650 5115. www.hayhouse.com

Published and distributed in Australia by:
Hay House Australia Ltd, 18/36 Ralph St, Alexandria NSW 2015. Tel.: (61) 2 9669 4299;
Fax: (61) 2 9669 4144. www.hayhouse.com.au

Published and distributed in the Republic of South Africa by:
Hay House SA (Pty), Ltd, PO Box 990, Witkoppen 2068. Tel./Fax: (27) 11 467 8904.
www.hayhouse.co.za

Published and distributed in India by:
Hay House Publishers India, Muskaan Complex, Plot No.3, B-2, Vasant Kunj, New Delhi –
110 070. Tel.: (91) 11 4176 1620; Fax: (91) 11 4176 1630. www.hayhouse.co.in

Distributed in Canada by:
Raincoast, 9050 Shaughnessy St, Vancouver, BC V6P 6E5. Tel.: (1) 604 323 7100;
Fax: (1) 604 323 2600

© David Wells, 2012

The author of this book does not dispense medical advice or prescribe the use of any
technique as a form of treatment for physical or medical problems without the advice of
a physician, either directly or indirectly. The intent of the author is only to offer information
of a general nature to help you in your quest for emotional and spiritual wellbeing. In the
event you use any of the information in this book for yourself, which is your constitutional
right, the author and the publisher assume no responsibility for your actions.

A catalogue record for this book is available from the British Library.

ISBN 978-1-84850-584-1

Printed and bound by CPI Group (UK) Ltd, Croydon CR0 4YY

For Jenni Shell, a teacher and friend.

'Begin at the beginning; end at the end.'

CONTENTS

ACKNOWLEDGEMENTS

Writing a book takes lots of things, but most of all it takes you away from friends and family as you ponder this word or that and gaze into the distance over Sunday lunch as you wonder what a Cancer Moon would make of it all and what's the best way of saying something challenging without hurting a sensitive Scorpio Moon. There but not present.

So, thank you to: Lee Fadden, Jarvis Cresdee, Diane Carter and Mark Symonds for seeing less of me. I am sure it was better than seeing the grumpy me!

To Gill Benning for her support and common sense, and Karen Martone for her non-sense and cakes.

To my mum – a Cancer mum, just the best you can get.

To my little sister, for matronly advice.

And to Hay House for the idea and support, especially Michelle, Jo Lal and Jo Burgess.

WHY THE MOON?

When you were little, did you ever gaze up at the Moon in awe and wonder? She truly is a wonderful sight – her ever-changing face gazing down at us, linking us all through her presence.

The first clue to how we feel about the Moon is in that second sentence. *She* – we assume the Moon to be a female energy, and in western astrology that is most definitely the case, with only the Moon and Venus, of all the planets, carrying that gender.

However, the Moon isn't even a planet. She's a light, a guiding light, a luminary – a title she shares only with the Sun, and rightly so, because she actually has no light of her own but reflects the light of the Sun.

Old friend.

She has been worshipped in her time. Some still do worship her, and always in ways that are associated with feminine principles. It's safe to say that her 28-day (27.32 if you want to be precise) cycle is more than likely where this sprang from, as it echoes a woman's menstrual cycle – or is that the other way round?

When I was a wee boy I remember watching cowboy and Indian movies and running off afterwards to play in the woods, always wanting to be the Indian so I could say, 'Many moons have passed since our last meeting.' Perhaps playing in the woods talking

Moon talk was a sign of things to come? That and the feathers in my hair…

The Moon is definitely embedded in our collective subconscious. Her symbolism instantly conjures up words like 'feminine', 'emotional', 'cycles', 'habits', 'feelings', 'madness', 'time passing', 'magik', 'ritual', 'witchcraft', 'mother', 'sister', 'family', 'intuition', 'home', 'lunacy', 'werewolves', 'howling', 'memory' and 'silver'. When you see the Moon, she invokes them all and many more. She draws you in…

Moon Cycles

The Moon waxes and wanes, grows bigger and shrinks, moving from new to full and back again – a constant cycle that we all observe. Anyone will tell you that when there's a full Moon there's an increase in lunacy. Is it true? I'm not so sure myself – perhaps it's just an excuse for bad behaviour? Though some studies suggest there may be a link.

Before we get into Moon cycles, let's talk about how astrology affects us. What are the mechanics? In my very, very humble opinion, astrology is a divination tool. It's a system that can help us understand ourselves and our place in the universe and show us our talents as well as what we might need to work on.

Some will suggest that as the Moon has a gravitational pull, all the planets exert some magical force on us. We are, after all, 60 per cent water, and if the Moon can turn tides, surely she affects us when she's full…? And that means Jupiter does the same, and so does Pluto. But whilst we can see the Moon affecting the tides, we can't see Pluto reshaping anything as he moves closer to and further away from Earth. Or can we?

Astrologically, we can. Pluto's recent move into Capricorn, for example, has caused some interesting times, with old ways of doing things falling apart and governments throughout the world definitely having their bottoms kicked, just as astrologers predicted. But that was down to divination, not a wave of magical energy coming from Pluto. So when we look at the Moon in our own chart, it's from that viewpoint: as a divination tool.

Back to new and full. Because if the Moon is full in your sign, have a look at what you want to get rid of – or is that who? Use this powerful time to clear away old habits and to face up to what you know needs to be done. And if the Moon is new in your sign, it's a great time to start something new. Hardly rocket science.

How do you know where the Moon is and what she's doing? By getting yourself a Moon app on your phone, or checking a Moon calendar, or here's an easier way: if the Moon is new, she's always in the sign that's celebrating its birthday; if she's full, she's in the sign seven along, counting the one that's celebrating. So if it's Aries' birthday time and the Moon is new, she's in Aries, and if she is full, you go: 1. Aries, 2. Taurus, 3. Gemini, 4. Cancer, 5. Leo, 6. Virgo and end up at 7. Libra. So, when Aries is getting spoiled silly, the Moon is full in Libra.

Notes on the Nodes

The Nodes of the Moon are also shown in an astrological chart, but they aren't planets, they are points calculated using the relationship between the Sun, the Moon and Earth at the time of birth. They sit opposite each other in your chart and the South Node looks at the skills you have brought into this life, while the North Node is about what lessons in particular you want to work on.

The Nodes therefore hold the keys to much past-life memory and future life direction. This book doesn't cover past lives, but the cover covers it! In the word 'your' you will see this symbol: ☊ This is the symbol for the South Node of the Moon. Through the skills you have brought with you, it refers back to your past lives, something your astrological chart can help you reveal. If you're interested in knowing more, my own book *Past, Present and Future* (Hay House, 2007) covers this subject. It's fascinating, but for another time perhaps.

Back to the here and now.

Ms Moon and her Influence

The purpose of this book is to give you an idea of just how the Moon may be affecting you in your current incarnation and some of the challenges she may have put your way – or *you* have put your way really, for she is only highlighting them.

The influence of Ms Moon is subtle. She could be behind many decisions you make without you even realizing it. Often seen as an emotional planet (and she is), she brings things to your attention through an emotional response. What you do with that is up to you. Actually what you do with that is probably a learned response, from this life or another, from your parents, your teachers, your peers, your memory banks… those memory banks that are astrologically governed by the one and only Moon.

So, read on. The next section will give you some basics about each of the Moon signs. As you learn more about your own Moon sign, of course you'll be fascinated, but don't take it all too seriously. Consider whether you do react in that way, and how that is affected by your Sun sign (what you might call your star sign), and then look more closely at the good things the Moon brings you and aim to work on the challenges.

Check out your mates' Moon signs, your mum's, your significant other's and even the cat's if you like. Become familiar with the principles and you will have gained a little more astrological information that could help you along the way.

Finding your Moon Sign

So how do you find your Moon sign? That's kind of important.

There are several ways:

- Probably the easiest right now while you are holding this book is to use the tables at the back. Just find your birthday (hopefully you know your time of birth too), see where the Moon was at that point in time and there you go. (Times shown are GMT. If you were born outside the UK, please readjust your time of birth to GMT.)
- If you want, you can go to a search engine on the internet and type in 'What's my Moon sign?' You will find lots of Moon sign calculators on there.
- Or you can get an app for your phone, then when your mates don't know, you can type in their details, tell them what Moon sign they are and look really clever as you explain what that means for them. Or try it out on that person you fancy – you get a great chat-up line *and* their Moon sign to see if it's worth carrying on talking or not. Perfect.

What if you don't know your time of birth?

You should be OK – the Moon is in a sign for about two days and a bit, so it may be that your whole birthday falls into one section. If not, read the sign behind or ahead, whichever seems closer to you, and it will usually be obvious where your Moon is.

The Technical Stuff

Or technical stuff-*ish*.

Each astrological sign has a gender – masculine or feminine.

Each is associated with an Element – Earth, Air, Fire or Water.

And each has a quality – cardinal, fixed and mutable – which indicates whether the sign is easily persuaded to change, prefers to dig in or feels happiest lording it up over everyone.

Sign	Gender	Element	Quality
Aries	Masculine	Fire	Cardinal
Taurus	Feminine	Earth	Fixed
Gemini	Masculine	Air	Mutable
Cancer	Feminine	Water	Cardinal
Leo	Masculine	Fire	Fixed
Virgo	Feminine	Earth	Mutable
Libra	Masculine	Air	Cardinal
Scorpio	Feminine	Water	Fixed
Sagittarius	Masculine	Fire	Mutable
Capricorn	Feminine	Earth	Cardinal
Aquarius	Masculine	Air	Fixed
Pisces	Feminine	Water	Mutable

Gender

This is the gender of the sign, not you – whether it acts with more masculine principles or feminine. It's pretty straightforward. As you can see, all Earth and Water signs are feminine, whilst all Fire and Air are masculine.

Now consider the Moon. Will she be happier in a feminine sign or a masculine one? And if she is in a masculine sign, will she have to fight to be heard more? Will her natural nurturing tendencies perhaps be a little compromised?

Element

It's elemental, the Moon in the elements.

Fire: Aries, Leo and Sagittarius

Here we have enthusiasm and creativity, an urge to act quickly and to be at the front of the pack, and anyone who can't keep up will cause frustration, resulting in a sharp bark as the Aries, Leo or Sagittarius Moon encourages them on. These people love to start things but may not be so great at finishing them, and when they get bored they will often just walk away.

The Moon is watery, so she may not feel too comfortable here. An initial head of steam to get things moving could very soon wane to a little wisp.

Earth: Taurus, Virgo and Capricorn

People with the Moon here are practical, and whilst they may be slow to start, there's something to be said for taking it steady. When others try to hurry them along, they can get stubborn and dig in, and they aren't easy to budge. They work hard, however, and keep good routines that enable them to reach their goals.

When the Moon is in an Earth sign, her watery nature nurtures the Earth, resulting in growth. Emotional support is essential for these Moon signs and they are very family-oriented.

Air: Gemini, Libra and Aquarius

Can you feel a cool breeze blowing when this lot walk in? Logical and able to solve the conundrums that others can't, they are thinkers who are not necessarily touchy-feely. They may even suffer from short arms and long pocket syndrome.

When the Moon is in an Air sign, the cool winds freeze her Water, but below the ice she's still there waiting to be discovered and the right soul can thaw her out!

Water: Cancer, Scorpio and Pisces

This element is a natural place for the Moon to be in, but sometimes over-familiarity can bring out too much emotion. This is a highly sensitive placement for the Moon, bringing a psychic, intuitive side, but whilst that sounds great it also means that people with the Moon here pick up the emotions of others and the atmosphere of their surroundings very easily and can be affected by them.

The Moon is at home here, but that can cause issues, as outlined above. She also wants to stay at home, so getting those with this Moon placement out and about may be a struggle.

Quality

Quality counts.

Cardinal: Aries, Cancer, Libra and Capricorn

Perhaps life has bigger things in store for this lot. Big opportunities are often presented to them, but do come with some disruption. This teaches them to react quickly and that there's nothing they can't overcome, making it difficult to tell them what to do. Not easy employees, they will do things their own way.

Fixed: Taurus, Leo, Scorpio and Aquarius

As the name suggests, these can be set in their ways. They learn how things should be done early on in life and if that's how it is, that's how it is. They can have difficult childhoods and find the memories hard to release. They like stuff; it validates their success.

Mutable: Gemini, Virgo, Sagittarius and Pisces

These Moon signs throw themselves on the altar of someone else's ego. They can give up what they want to do for the sake of what someone else thinks they should. They may change their mind, too, sometimes at the last minute, causing disruption.

That's just for starters. Intrigued? Even if you just want to see if Bob the Builder can fix it for you, what you will discover is there's more to the astrology, to the Moon and to you than you first thought. I hope. Enjoy.

MOON SIGNS

ARIES MOON

'She was a lovely girl. Our courtship was fast and furious
— I was fast and she was furious.'

Max Kauffmann

Archetype

The warrior. Able to step up and say what's on their mind and in their heart, Aries Moon types won't shy away from a fight but are just as swift to make sure peace is restored afterwards and things move on. There will be no grey areas with them — they are ready for a fight, but for a cause.

ARIES MOON ♈

So you have an Aries Moon. Are you excited? You probably are. In fact you're probably so excited that you have one of the passionate and creative Moons rather than a wishy-washy watery number that you're telling your mates with great pride, 'I'm an Aries Moon!' It's like letting them know you're the hunter-gatherer back with plenty of meat to feed the whole village, the one everyone should be looking at, admiring just how big and butch you are. And some of the men are just as butch…

Yes, you are indeed born under a brave Moon, one whose fearlessness will get you into trouble as you rush in where angels fear to tread — the pound shop, for example. You don't care what people think; what you do care about is being first with the bargain, first with the information, first to date that hot number from Packing and first to let everyone know what happened on the date.

Women with an Aries Moon aren't going to be ruled by men – or anyone, in fact – and that's fine, why should you be, but just to be sure, you're going to make that clear before anyone has even mentioned whether you want to 'love, honour and obey'. No doubt that will be changed to 'love, be superior to and do exactly what I want when I want, and if you don't like it, tough'! It's impossible to suppress your inner rebel, but oddly enough that's the very thing that has some men hot under the collar and you top of their list.

You're not good with ditherers, Aries Moon, and want problems to be solved instantly. If they aren't, you're first in there with a rousing cheer to chivvy others along, and if they don't get the urgency, you're likely to take their job away from them and do it yourself – not something that does your energy any good at all! Keeping your temper with such folks would work better. Explaining what you need from them will save you energy in the long run.

Energy – like a new puppy you run around, run around, run around and sleep. Then it's run around, run around, run around and sleep again, but if the last part is interrupted, you change from puppy to bear – you get grizzly, and anything anyone does from then on is going to annoy you. Better to admit when you're over-tired and seek somewhere to get some rest.

A cardinal Moon sign gives you a restless quality – you want to be constantly on the move and seeking new and challenging things to do. You could seek things that are exciting but have an element of risk. I know an Aries Moon who turned up on the roof of his home to help his father repair it. Aged six. This fearlessness is a good thing if used wisely, but if foolish ideas become fixed in your mind, you choose to ignore the risks, and that can lead to trouble, so *calculated risk* is the way to go. Learn to step back and think for a moment before putting your foot on any ladders.

You're not fazed by the opinions of others – if they don't like it, they can lump it, and rather than just saying that and worrying about things in private, you do actually mean it! You can throw yourself into the most amazing activities, and when others are worrying about their hair or whether their knickers are showing, you won't care much as long as you're doing what you think is right or having some fun!

Fun is to be enjoyed with absolute abandonment, of course. There really is no point in going on a funfair ride and worrying about whether or not the bolts are on tight enough; you want to throw your hand in the air like you just don't care – mostly because you don't.

Your humour may not be to everyone's taste – it can be blunt and most definitely shocking – and when you laugh it's from the bottom of your stomach, a hearty laugh produced from the Fire of your Moon. Happily, you can laugh at yourself. With that hair, you need to.

Secretive sorts are never going to be your BFF. You can't deal very well with having to dig around to find out what's going on. 'For goodness' sake, will you just come out and say it?!' is more your style. If you do happen to come across someone who is keeping things from you, they may perceive you as being pushy, intrusive or even rude, but all you really want is to move a situation along with some honesty, and frankly their opinion of you isn't much of a concern. All fine, unless of course there are good reasons for their secrets being secrets, in which case you could just pick at a scab that will pop in your face. Nice. Know when to stop.

This isn't about being insensitive, though. When seeking a shoulder to cry on, you're one shoulder I would seek, as you offer not just the usual support but also ideas to help someone out of a corner, but if that someone doesn't act on those words of wisdom and comes back with the same troubles time and time again, they're going to lose your sympathy and get the full-blown horoscope according to Aries Moon.

Having such a hot Moon means having a lot of energy, and you need to get rid of it somehow. Sport is one thing I can think of, and of course sex is the one you're probably thinking of. With an Aries Moon, you have to be fired up, be active and keep yourself fit and healthy. Don't underestimate your ability to make trouble for yourself by over extending yourself. You could end up having to be untangled from your yoga teacher whilst trying to perform the downward-facing dog as he shows you his one-legged king pigeon.

Aerobic workouts are safer, but truth is you don't want safe, you want mountain-biking on a cold sunny morning over cold sunny actual mountains, and sports with risk do suit you better. As for sex, cold sunny mountains might be about the only thing that will keep the heat down! You're passionate and need that within a relationship to make it work for you. Doesn't everyone? Nope, your Moon sign does, but for others it's not so important. Seriously, not joking.

Life in the country with a couple of cats and a lovely cottage where you could make your own jam and do a bit of gardening does sound great to you – for about ten minutes. What you want is noise, stuff to do, things going on, places to be seen at, new discoveries to make. You want to be first to eat at the hottest restaurant in town, first to see that new movie, first to wear those latest trainers and… you get it by now: first, first, first. And you can't do that if you're out of the loop. Sitting with a cat on your lap whilst knitting a scarf for the postman isn't for you.

Rather than cats and scarves, your home could easily be full of DIY projects that haven't quite been completed, so try GSE (Get Someone Else) to sort things out, because as much as you like knocking down a wall or two, you don't like constant reminders of when things go wrong. As for *décor*, you don't do frou-frou, and chintz is not your friend; you prefer clean lines that allow you to move about with freedom and get out quickly if you're in need of some excitement.

Love Life

One of your lessons in this life is to learn to nurture, to show others how you feel, and to do it in a way that actually goes against your natal Moon and reaches out to her opposite sign of Libra. You need to learn to relate rather than dominate. So put that whip away, even if it is a Walnut Whip, and think about how you can be less pushy, princess.

Whilst most of us would deliver a hug when our other half was in need, you would be likely to punch them on the arm, tell them to get on with it and suggest they go and tell someone what they think of them. It works for you, doesn't it?

You're not being unsympathetic to your other half here. Far from it. You're just doing it your way. But the trick to any relationship is to do things the other person's way – at least some of the time. So read their Moon sign and see if you can try to relate to their way. And don't hold back from showing your softer side now and again.

Partners can do many things, however, and you will just get on with it. They can tell you that your backside does indeed look huge in those jeans, that you've got egg on your chin and even that your hairdo is much more of a hair don't, but woe betide them if they ever whine in your presence. Anyone who whinges or whines 'Can't do this', 'What about that?', 'I am scared of…' will last about a week.

Good humour is an aphrodisiac to you, and those who can laugh at themselves are appealing to you. In fact the more they can take the Mickey out of themselves (and take it from you), the better. You want to be free to be yourself and sometimes you are irreverent – quite a lot of times in fact. The last thing you need is someone you have to be careful you don't upset. But remember that there will be times when you do have to put your pint of lager down and have a heart-to-heart without using rugby club rules. You too, boys.

Also remember that routine in a relationship is to be avoided. Keep things interesting by avoiding steak Fridays and visiting Auntie Vera every Monday.

You're probably attracted to those who can bring you stability, are good with money and provide those structures you're so good at ignoring. Accountants, not werewolves, in other words. But if you're looking for fun, wolf boy will suit you until the next full Moon...

Sexually, you're the one on top, the one driving things forward, the one who has enough front to go into that dodgy-looking shop and come out with what can only be described as fun until someone gets hurt. (But you thought that was the point!) Barry White on in the background and a box of milk chocolates on the sofa aren't going to get you going. You want to hear the results of your hard work and carrying on an informative conversation in the bedroom is more interesting than the Walrus of Love singing in your ear.

You are impatient generally, and in the bedroom you can switch off very quickly, so any would-be partners need to know what they are doing and that waiting for the computer to download position number 103 isn't going to impress you. Taking charge of the situation is what you're about and whilst you might like the idea of being dragged off to a cave by Brad Pitt in a bearskin, once you're in there you want him to shut up and do what he's told.

Partnering an Aries Moon

They need excitement in their life, a rush of adrenalin that gets their heart rate up and interest piqued, so make sure you feed that need.

If you're trying to attract an Aries Moon, remember they will be drawn to active sorts, sporty types and those in uniform, but above all to those with the ability to laugh at themselves as well as to be slightly irreverent to them.

Best fit Sun signs are Aries, Leo, Libra and Sagittarius.

Career

You will need a job where there is an element of being your own boss. You don't do boring routine or being told exactly what to do all the time. Your energy is likely to see you get promoted, and hard work will prevail very quickly for you, but don't be led astray by those who will tempt you into doing something for a laugh. Jokes will inevitably be at the expense of your otherwise hard work.

You will give your boss your opinions freely and without holding anything back, which is a good thing, but doing this when they ask is better than doing it halfway through lunch with the managing director. Watch your timing.

Using your creativity and initiative is important to you, and if you don't have free rein to do this, you're going to feel stifled and very quickly seek to move on. Creative pursuits like marketing or something artistic that shows off your talents and allows you to embrace new techniques and ways of working will suit you better.

Although the Moon isn't usually used to define actual career paths, you could seek roles in the military, 999 services, teaching, marketing, IT, design and sport.

Parents and Family

The feminine Moon with the masculine energy of Aries isn't an easy mix and can result in family dynamics being volatile. As a child, your need to express yourself and be seen as an individual could have been at odds with your parents' need for you to fit in and comply with their ideals, not yours. Inevitably that could have led to a desire to leave the family home early, seeking independence as soon as it was possible.

An Aries Moon can often describe tough times with Dad, seeing him as a hero but having some kind of distance from him. Mum may have been a very busy woman with lots going on. Seeking her attention could have involved competing with all of her tasks, but hindsight will show she was busy making sure you were provided for. She could, in some cases, have been absent for a while. No matter the reason, the lesson for you was one of self-determination and gaining the ability to look after your own needs.

Early childhood could have been a time where you were moved around a lot, perhaps as the child of someone serving in the armed forces or with another kind of job that meant everyone upping sticks at a few months' notice. Whilst disruptive, this would have taught you to make friends quickly and adapt to new situations quicker than most.

You may have fought with any siblings on a regular basis as you tried to establish not only your own identity but that of pack leader, regardless of age. In fact if you were the youngest child, you're likely to have been even feistier!

In turn, you will want to teach your own children independence and remind them they are their own people. That's a healthy perspective for anyone, but your parenting skills could be erratic. Changing direction and ideas will make things interesting, but routine and structure could suffer as a consequence. Stability needn't be boring, though, and seeing that could help you make the most of your wonderful energy whilst still maintaining strong foundations. That said, never lose your sense of excitement and enthusiasm, for a child with an Aries Moon mum or dad will know they can have a go at anything!

Health

Aries rules the head, and when emotional drama occurs, headaches will follow.

Your need to be first, to be at the top, to be out there when everyone else has given in, could also lead to bumps, bruises and breaks, so maybe learning to slow down when you find yourself rushing around would be a good idea. You think? Go on, use your need for sport to keep fit and healthy rather than prove to the world that you're number one.

Life Skills

It should be clear by now that you're a positive upbeat Moon sign who needs to have things your way, an initiator who has a lot to offer but might need to learn to pull back now and again. Learning to get your ideas out there won't be a problem, but get into the habit of taking a step back before signing any deals or committing to things you won't be able to get out of. A pause now could prevent embarrassment or even disaster later.

You do well where courage is required and risks need to be taken, and where winning is the only option, you can be the hero others are looking for to lead the way.

Stumbling Blocks

When you're at the end of your emotional fuel you can get angry. Not 'I've spilled my drink' angry, full-on volcanic stuff that could have those around you running for safer ground. Your emotions can take over and see you acting before thinking, rushing right in when you know you shouldn't but you're going to anyway and damn the consequences.

When those around you don't respond to your ideas or direction, you might also poke and prod, sometimes without even knowing you're doing it, pushing them into saying or doing things that will lead to confrontation and give you the opportunity to let your full fury out. Your need to be in charge has to be expressed, but finding a way to do it without the need for such confrontation will work better in the long term.

Spiritual Lesson

Past lives spent as a warrior will have brought you much strength and courage, and these are admirable qualities, but remember that peace and love conquer all. Introduce calmness into your life through meditation and gardening, and remember to pause long enough to see the beauty that surrounds you.

SUN SIGN, MOON SIGN

So now you know a little more about your Moon sign, but how does that work with your Sun sign?

Sun Aries, Moon Aries

You really do rush in, get things done and get out, hopefully in one piece. You are a true initiator and always ready to start something, even if someone else might have to finish it! Stirring things up is your natural state of being and that's a great tool when things get stagnant, but make sure everyone is moving at your pace or you could end up so far in front you have to leave someone behind.

Fantastic in a crisis, you can be relied on to help no matter what the dangers are. You are an inspiration to others and that can be a very attractive quality, but being the hero all the time can be tough. There will be days when you want to be rescued, so choose a partner who knows when to cuddle up and when to stand back and let you through.

Being a force to be reckoned with won't be to everyone's taste, so expect there to be people who think you're too hectic. These are commonly known as objects in your rear-view mirror.

Sun Taurus, Moon Aries

An earthy Sun with a fiery Moon will bring conflict. Sometimes you will want to be up and at them, but then getting you off the sofa could take two big lads and a wheelbarrow. If balanced properly, however, you have the perfect Sun sign to complement your Aries Moon, as it will bring some structure and foundations that are strong enough to actually get you to the end of some of your creative processes.

A sensual combination of Sun and Moon, you're loyal in relationships and enjoy the physical side of your love life, indulging yourself and your partner by stimulating all of your senses with massage oils, candles, wine, chocolate, music and the occasional feather.

A strong business sense could bring financial rewards your way, and with your unique creative flair, occupations in fashion and the art world would suit you well.

Although forceful and a highly attractive personality, you might want to watch out for stubbornness and sometimes jealousy. If the latter is present, watch out for its older brother: revenge. But overall, your Taurus Sun uses your Aries Moon to bring it rewards to enjoy.

Sun Gemini, Moon Aries

Not only could you not wait to read about yourself, I bet you couldn't wait to tell someone what it said about you! What? Chatterbox? You? Never.

You're dynamic, that's for sure, but can you calm down long enough to be understood and to have your ideas accepted? Letting others catch up is important; if you don't, they might stop following you, and that's not what you want at all.

Persuading people to join in your quest is easy for you, and a career in the media could be right up your street. Sales and marketing and journalism would suit you too.

Forever young, you're always seeking the latest trends, but at some point you might want to check with mates whether you're actually still down with the kids or the oldest swinger in town. Just saying.

Romantically, you're all for some flirting, and the first flush of a new relationship is where you're at your shiny best, but for it to last a partner needs to keep you interested. To do that they have to be spontaneous and willing to give new things a go.

Sun Cancer, Moon Aries

The intuitive side to your nature can bring you insights that others will miss, giving you a head start in business, love and making sure you get that sale item before anyone else. Sometimes, however, you will be beaten to the finishing line, which is where you have to rely on your warrior Moon to overcome your Sun's tendency to take defeat and harbour it until it becomes moody and even bitter. Come out fighting instead!

In love, you need a close relationship, one you truly want to come home to, and a home you've filled with love and mementoes of shared adventures.

You can capture people's imaginations with both your ideas and your delivery of them, making you a persuasive individual who is sought after to lead and inspire, but look out for those who doubt you. They need more persuasion rather than being allowed to spoil your plans through a belief that they are right and you are wrong. It's only their opinion, so go prove *them* wrong.

Sun Leo, Moon Aries

Shy? Of course you're not, the spotlight is on you and you're ready to perform, so curtain up, let's get on with it!

As a child, you would have been the centre of attention, and if ever you weren't, you would have made it happen using your acting skills, your talent for humour or… perhaps a tantrum or three?

As an adult, the need for applause could shift to the workplace. You are driven by a desire to be the best and be seen to be the best. This is a great way of making sure you are indeed at the top of your profession. Watch out, however, if the applause stops. It may be tempting to try to make what you do bigger and bigger, but it might be better to step back and see if you need a rewrite.

In love, you both make and expect to receive grand gestures. That's all well and good if you remember that 'grand' doesn't have to be 'expensive'. Money could be a tough lesson for you. Living like a queen may not be possible unless you have a princess's income.

Sun Virgo, Moon Aries

It's not easy throwing the rule book away, and even when you know it's good to take a risk now and again, what if you're caught taking two boxes of staples out of the stationery cupboard instead of just one? Doing what's expected when you just want to break the rules and go with your passions could cause you some sleepless nights and the occasional upset stomach, but you're designed to break the rules now and again and those occasions when you do will be defining moments in your life, moments that get you that dream job, the love of your life… or an extra box of staples.

In a relationship, you will also feel the need to conform to traditional roles while wishing that just sometimes you could lose the washing-up, dance the tango in the front room and end up making love attached to the chandelier – and so you should. Just make sure the in-laws aren't round for supper.

Perfection is your thing, but it may not be so easy for others, so watch out for a tendency to point it out in a less than subtle manner.

Sun Libra, Moon Aries

This is a full Moon position, as your natal Sun and Moon sit opposite each other, bringing an opposition of head and heart, of will and emotions. That can bring conflict with it, but also the ability to even it out to find the best way forward. There is a Buddhist saying that suggests there can be no harmony without conflict, and this best describes your Sun and Moon position.

You're one of the most romantic signs in the zodiac and flourish when you're in a relationship, but your Aries Moon will bring a need to maintain your individuality, and that can be at odds with your Libra Sun's desire to give your all. Balance will be found through security within the relationship, good communication with your other half and acceptance that it's OK to do some things without them.

You are absolutely charming, a real joy to be around, but getting out on a Saturday night could be a nightmare of what shoes go with what bag. Making decisions quickly isn't one of your strong points.

Sun Scorpio, Moon Aries

Are you going to break the door down or are you going to sneak around the back and climb in the window? Is it better to be upfront or would a little secrecy and subterfuge work? Are you Ninja or Cat Burglar? You get the picture.

Moving between the two isn't easy, but if you can judge it correctly and know when silence works and when being in someone's face is the only way to go, you can really make this combo work wonders for you. This will attract controversy into your life and inevitably make you stand out. What you need to be aware of is *why* you are standing out. What is it that you have to say that's so important?

With a partner, you're full-blooded, and yes, that is a way of saying you're passionate and like to express it physically, and if you want to coat that in rubber and spank me on Monday, that fits too.

Belief in what you're about is paramount to you, but take care that you allow for the opinions of others and temper how you go about things, or that belief can turn into narcissism.

Sun Sagittarius, Moon Aries

A natural optimist, you're a glass half-full kind of person, seeing the way ahead paved with adventure and good times. Sitting still isn't for you, and that hunger to learn and to embrace new cultures needs to be fed through foreign travel.

That's all well and good, but maintaining a settled home could be a challenge when being out of the home doing stuff is more appealing. You're also good at going on faith, what your gut tells you, and having a vision, but don't forget to incorporate some hard facts in there somewhere too, otherwise you could leap and underestimate the distance.

You throw yourself into love, embracing it with everything you've got, and seek a partner who does the same. Travelling with your other half or spending long nights discussing a book you've read or an experience you've had is the norm for you, but who does the washing-up? Mundane tasks may not be your thing, but they are important and it's important they are shared. Life should be lived large, but after the ecstasy, the washing-up.

Sun Capricorn, Moon Aries

Time to get serious. You're not one to let a little thing like government get in the way of what you think is right and wrong, and you're going to make sure that anyone who stands in your way listens to what you have to say.

Having a cause is important to you and whether it's the latest trade figures or who hasn't put in for the tea-boat at work, you're going to make sure the rules are adhered to – unless of course you don't agree with them, in which case you're going to shout until they are changed.

Highly career-minded, you will find the combination of goat and ram in your natal chart gives you a double set of horns to butt your way through any walls that appear to stand in your way. Taking 'no' for an answer just isn't part of your plan.

Your romantic life could take second place to your career, and this is a choice you can make, but allowing yourself some down-time will help the headaches produced by constantly butting those walls at work.

You may approach love like a business proposal, and a home run like clockwork is the stereotype of your Sun/Moon combination. Of course it needn't be that way. Choose a partner who brings colour into your life as well as knowing that when the whistle blows, it's time for dinner. Only joking. Not.

Sun Aquarius, Moon Aries

One thing that's easy to predict about you is that you're unpredictable! With the independence of your Sun and the spontaneity of your Moon, changing direction could be as common as changing your underwear, so that's once a month at least!

Nonconformity is your reason for living. You see what's classed as normal and you really don't want any part of it, preferring to stand out even if sometimes that can bring emotional moments – usually brought on by the realization that you're different from everyone else! Such is the cantankerous nature of this combination, but the really mad thing is that it works for you.

Anywhere new ideas are needed or a breath of fresh air is required is where you truly excel. Working for social services or a charity appeals to you, as do marketing and sales – anywhere you can be creative and use your maddest ideas to the full.

In love, would-be partners had better hold onto their seats as you take them on a roller-coaster ride then go off for a hot dog and come back three days later because you met a mate who invited you for dinner and then… Try to focus on one thing at a time.

Honesty and fighting for the truth are what you're about. Listening to the truth as *others* see it will bring balance.

Sun Pisces, Moon Aries

A mix of feathers and nails, of angels and imps, you're sweetness and light with a poke in the ribs if someone isn't paying attention. Not an easy combination, as you probably already know. Your need to be heard is buried under a blanket of marshmallows and sometimes all people will see is the sweet exterior. More fool them.

When emotions get you riled up, your inner animal sheds its fluffy layer and out comes the beast, the beast that delivers such an unexpected burst of emotional energy that everyone listens and runs around trying to make sense of what's happening and fulfils your wishes. Neat.

In love, you're romantic and poetic, able to sweep your other half off their feet, and you want the same in return. You can sometimes feel the need to withdraw, however, and that may be tough on a partner. Being direct about your emotional needs will help them understand that sometimes you need space to dream on your own and if you don't get it, Pisceszila is released. Easy.

If you fear you're not being noticed at work, the temptation may be to go over the top and show where everyone is going wrong. Whilst you may have a point, your timing could be off. Your strength lies in your magic, an intuition that knows what to do and how to drive you through this thing called life, so all you need do is listen to it and when the foot goes down too hard on the accelerator, ease it off a bit.

TAURUS MOON

*'All I really need is love, but a little chocolate
now and then doesn't hurt!'*

Lucy Van Pelt (in *Peanuts*, by Charles M. Schulz)

Archetype

The builder. Get that hod of bricks on your broad shoulders, or maybe it's a load of emotional bricks that you're bearing, because you have learned to dig deep and lay strong foundations as a result of your experiences in life.

Even if it sometimes takes you longer to get moving than most, when you do, you don't stop until the job is done.

TAURUS MOON ♉

The Moon is exalted in this sign, which means she is a welcome guest at the feast and only the best will do, so that has to be a good start. The funny thing is you're not likely to want over-fussy. Good quality will do, whether that's food, fabric or emotional bonds with your near and dear. It needn't be trumpet-blowing, banner-waving, 'Look at me!' stuff, just that feeling of contentment, like a warm blanket on a chilly day, that snuggled-up cosy sensation you get after a good Sunday lunch cuddled on the sofa with someone you love. If you get it, everything is OK in Taurus Moon land. But is that sustainable?

Life has a habit of throwing curve balls our way now and again, and being rocked out of your comfort zone upsets you emotionally, so what can you do about it? Whatever you can, Taurus Moon, but one thing that might not work is a harrumph with your name written all over it! 'Stubborn' is of course a big Taurean word, but when attached to the Moon it could prevent you from saying what's really in your heart and that's never a good thing. Ask yourself if pushing down your feelings is strengthening or weakening your foundations at work, rest or play.

Routine will help you maintain things the way you want them, and if that routine revolves around food, drink and socializing in gorgeous places, then so much the better. You want to go where everyone knows your name and chocolate is of the highest quality. You get comfort from it all and when you feel comfortable you are at your best. These things feed your soul and replenish your energy and leave you ready to go out and fight again and deal with change.

Change is something you're unlikely to instigate – you like things to stay as they are – but in a modern world things move, and move fast, and fast is something that may not be your forte. For some that could be frustrating, but going at everyone else's pace could cause you to be a little clumsy and mistakes could be made, so do yourself a favour: let them know you're a Taurus Moon, so you'll be going at your own speed, and if they don't like it, you'll be in the coffee shop at 10.30 having your usual cappuccino if they would like to discuss it further.

And just maybe change would be a good thing…? Sometimes you can stay in a job/relationship/dressing gown for too long and when you look honestly at what's happening, you're comfortable, yes, but are you settling rather than exploring your full potential?

With cash, you like to make sure you know what's coming in and what's going out, and even though you might not feel as if you have much of it, you're actually good with it and won't allow your emotions to go shopping for you, resulting in some completely useless gadget you can't even pass off to a relation as a birthday gift.

Money isn't likely to come your way as if by magic, however. Your best way to cash bonuses is a methodical approach, slowly building your fortune. You may only really reach your full financial potential later in life.

Fashion may not be high on your list of priorities, but good, clean and well-made clothes will be. It needn't be *couture*, but it does have to last and be value for money.

When mates come round, it's fine if they want to take their shoes off and kick back, putting their feet on the coffee table and helping themselves to a coffee and any cake that might have somehow escaped a midnight feast.

Pets are likely to be part of your life and having animals as well as lots of plants around reflects the earthy quality of your Moon sign.

Sofas have to be big and squashy – none of those silly high-backed chairs are allowed, thank you very much – and when it comes to the kitchen, it had better be ready to do some work, as you show your emotions to your friends through good food – well prepared and plenty of it.

Those friends are likely to be well-grounded sorts. People who spend their lives attached to some air balloon floating around in la-la land won't make it to your party shortlist. And your mates will be comfortable enough to tell you what they think without worrying that you will throw a tantrum and storm off in a cloud of chiffon, refusing to speak to them ever again. They do, of course, run the risk of you folding your arms, pulling a face and refusing to budge, even if deep down you know they have a point.

Stubbornness is, you will have noticed, a recurring theme, and the point of astrology isn't to offer an 'I'm a Taurus Moon, that's just how I am' excuse, it's to shed light on the subject and help you recognize a trait that could use some work. Just saying.

Possessions help validate who you are, they offer a way to show people what you have achieved in life, and whilst some signs will go for flashy jewellery or golden hot pants, that's not for you. Understated and elegant but clearly expensive will do just nicely. Of course true wealth comes from the stability you have as an individual, and no matter what your Sun sign, that stability should be what you rely on. In your case, it comes from remembering what's truly important in life.

When you fix on a purpose, you really fix on it, even to the point of doggedly pursuing something that could never happen. Consider someone who wants to be friends, but you know it could be so much more if you just stay the course, it's just that this bloke you fancy is never going to give up his nights out with the boys for you, or his nights in with one bloke in particular... Sometimes no matter how dependable you are, how determined, how loyal and how stubborn, things are never going to go your way, so look around you now and again and have a review.

As a Taurus Moon you're going to be one of the first ports of call for family and friends when they are having a drama and are looking for some straightforward no-nonsense advice. You will be happy to give it to them. Imagine if you could use that magical gift to solve your own problems... You already can, Taurus Moon, already do, but do you *do* anything with your golden advice when it comes to your own stuff?

The Moon shows us many things, including past-life memories and the cycles or habits we have chosen to address in this lifetime. Other people often mirror just what these are, so look at what people bring to you, think about how it reflects your own life and take action, just as you advise others to do.

Also, find something to nurture. Be it your garden, a pet or an idea that helps you blossom personally, you need to help something grow, and you do it so beautifully. You're linked very closely to the elemental kingdoms and can see the magic in your garden, or in a window box if that's all you have. Know that even if they can't speak, those creatures are grateful.

Love Life

You want to build a strong relationship and are dependable and faithful in love, but if things aren't going great you're likely to remain in a relationship for the sake of the kids, the cat or even the person you're not too impressed with.

You can be flirty yourself, and sometimes that Taurus Moon can also cause jealousy to rear its big green head, but normally all you need in a relationship is a routine. And good communication, so that if that routine is affected in any way, you know what's happening, when and why.

If that sounds rather boring, remember that having your Moon in Taurus brings you an appreciation of great food, beautiful music, lovely scents, soft velvet and good firm buttocks – a recipe for a great sex life, wouldn't you say?

You want your love life to be a celebration and respond well to a little effort from your partner. In return you will indulge them with your own sensual journey, which might make the chocolate spread disappear more quickly than it should but will never be dull.

Your flirty nature is of course very useful when you're single, and that coy look and slightly dipped head thing you do is endearing, if somewhat bovine in appearance. Did I just call you a cow? No, I did not, I referenced the ruling creature of Taurus, as it offers an endearing sweetness that shows how charming you can appear to those looking for a mate.

Taking things slowly is how you prefer to approach a new relationship, and that may make your prospective partner think you aren't as interested as you actually are, but once they get to see the effort you put into making them feel comfortable when you're with them they will soon realize that a slow hand and an easy touch are way better than a fumble and a hurried handful.

You don't enter into relationships easily is what's really being said, but when you do, you do it wholeheartedly and you do it wanting to build something special.

Your Taurus Moon is a real blessing in a relationship that works well, as it offers sensuality and dependability, but if things aren't perfect, be aware that that same Moon brings stubbornness and a refusal to instigate change even when it's clearly needed.

Partnering a Taurus Moon

Taurus Moons need their hit of sensuality. They want to be wooed with a good meal, lovely wine, fabulous hotel rooms and a little loving – twice nightly would be ideal. They respond well to routine and don't expect things to change dramatically without some sort of plan or lead-up to it, and the only surprises they need are ones involving spa days, mud baths and a regular trot around the love paddock.

Best fit Sun signs are Taurus, Virgo, Capricorn and Scorpio.

Career

Taurus Sun signs are drawn to roles that involve money, music, art, dance, gardening and of course cooking, and all could apply to you too, but whatever you choose there has to be an aesthetic sense about it – it has to bring beauty into the world.

As an Earth sign Moon, you're a good finisher. Unlike those flighty Air Moon lot or rushy-in Fire sorts, you get the job done, and usually where others would get bored all too easily. The trouble may be you're in a role that your mum said would be good for you, or you have a reliable job but inside you yearn for something more. Give in to your Moon and you'll not only fill your heart with joy but also be likely to find that circumstances will help you along the path to success.

So, be persistent and go for what you want, and if keeping home and hearth well provided for whilst you do that means doing something you're not that interested in for a while, that's fine, but put a time limit on it or it could be all you do.

Parents and Family

As the Moon often represents the mother in our charts, your Taurus Moon could suggest your own mother was a strong individual and that her own background was a difficult one, one where she had to forge her own identity through some very hard work or under tough conditions.

Having the effects of Taurus wrapped around your Moon should have helped her find time for cuddles, to feed you well and to make sure you were comfortable, but sometimes Earth signs forget to express how they are feeling in language, so she showed you how she felt rather than said it.

Your father may have been overshadowed by such a strong mother. This could mean he seemed to be less effective in family decisions and even if that wasn't the case it could have appeared that way to others.

If you are a mum yourself, you will work hard to make sure your children have everything they want and finding time for yourself could be a problem. Make sure you do, as a happy home is dependent on a happy mum! Run a bath, have an at-home spa, stop every now and again to look at what you've built for your children and reward yourself with a bar of chocolate.

Filling your home with creativity is important, and music could be big, either performing with the okey-dokey karaoke machine or something more serious. Encouraging your children to get involved in art and music could be something you're keen on. And if you're holding a secret desire to sing or dance or get to that knitting circle in your local cake shop once a week, give in to it sooner rather than later – you were born to express yourself through creative pursuits.

A lush, sensual feast is the best sort of home for you, and minimalism won't be high on your list. Just make sure that doesn't go too far the other way and clutter takes over. It's a fine line, but with your sense of style, it's one you can walk.

Health

One of the greatest threats to your health with this Moon is a tendency to over-indulge on the food front. Whilst enjoying food is part of who you are, sticking to healthy alternatives is better. Try to eat as well as you can, and if you must indulge, go for high quality and small amounts rather than barrowloads of rubbish. Your appreciation of fine things will help and also in your favour is a tendency to respond very well to exercise: get some.

Your ears, nose and throat are particularly vulnerable areas and may be affected when emotional issues or stress appear in your life.

Life Skills

We all have different things to bring to life's great table and for you it's an ability to get things done. When others fall by the wayside, you're able to keep going, and even if some tasks are really ploddy, you can still get through them. Your ability to do so with good humour and to laugh at yourself even when things are very tough indeed comes from a memory of when things were even tougher and still you managed just fine.

There's an old saying that goes 'Wise is the man who has two loaves and sells one to buy lilies.' That sums you up perfectly: you recognize that you must be fed, but surrounding yourself with beauty feeds the needs of your soul as well.

Stumbling Blocks

When you're out of energy, worn out with the emotions of a situation, you can shut down and go to ground. Sometimes that's the right thing to do, as it allows you space to consider what's next for you. However, there needs to be a limit on how long you dwell there. Recognize when you're thinking things through and when you're in a rut.

You will have noticed the word 'stuff' a lot for your Moon sign and there is no doubt that things are important to you. But being secure isn't about how many toys you have or how big your house is, it's knowing that deep down you can deal with anything, so take time to remind yourself of that fact whilst still enjoying your stuff!

Spiritual Lesson

You probably already realize what your spiritual lesson is: it's letting go of the need for those possessions to validate your life but equally embracing all the pleasures that life has to offer, and by life I mean a life lived through your five senses. Be present in the moment and learn to love it no matter what's going on, secure in the knowledge that you can deal with anything by using your practical approach and ability to build again on strong foundations dug out from your experiences from the past.

SUN SIGN, MOON SIGN

So now you know a little more about your Moon sign, but how does that work with your Sun sign?

Sun Aries, Moon Taurus

You're certain to get stuck right in, and with a Sun–Moon combination that offers both creative spark and the ability to get the job done, you've been given the drive to succeed in life. There's real charm with this union and that certain something that will attract people to you in business as well as for pleasure, but woe betide anyone who crosses you — they won't know what's hit them!

At work, you must be sure to leave room for the rest of the team. Wanting to be at the front isn't the same as winning the race, and you will have to rely on others' support if you want to do that.

Watch your sense of humour – it could be somewhat robust and not everyone will get it. You could also whip it out at an inappropriate moment – never a good thing.

However, the combination of Mars (Aries) and Venus (Taurus) brings real sex appeal, and if you're not too busy this weekend, how do you fancy a coffee?

Sun Taurus, Moon Taurus

With so much Taurus energy, over-indulgence in life's pleasures is a danger. You can easily have too much of good thing rather than just a taste here and there. Balance these pleasures with practical steps to stay healthy.

Business matters can truly ground you and you should be able to make a tidy sum of money with your gift for putting together secure and well-planned projects, with catering, nursing, property and the music industry high on the list.

Friends are likely to use your grounded nature as their rock, but who do *you* turn to? Make sure it isn't a case of everyone leaning on you and you yourself having nobody to lean on. That will wear after a while and could cause you to retreat.

As a partner, you're sensual and love to include massage oil, soft music and the occasional feather duster in your love-making – and why not?

Watch your temper – when it goes, it really goes, but that can be avoided by letting off steam rather than waiting for things to boil over.

Sun Gemini, Moon Taurus

Is it better to get on the bus or should you take the car? The bus is greener and better for the planet, but the car will get you there more quickly, and you do like cars. Sometimes you confuse even yourself when making choices, when all you really need do is stop and ask yourself what you really feel, then convince yourself that following your heart is better than constantly weighing things up with your head.

You're able to use what's around you in an imaginative way and could come up with the most amazing recipes, as well as business solutions that others can't even perceive. And what's more, they work!

In love, you could go for the bad boys or girls, as they offer a challenge, and that's exciting, but you also crave loyalty, and the two may not go together. If you're in a relationship, your partner shouldn't take all that flirting you do with others as a threat – it's just what you do!

Sun Cancer, Moon Taurus

Your home is most definitely your castle, your domain, and nobody, but nobody, is going to rule it other than you. Nobody is going to disagree with that either! The cushions are fabulous and the curtains match perfectly; your home is a dream home where cakes abound and cuddles are mandatory.

Family and friends will gather there for support and great gossip mixed with good food and warm surroundings, but what happens when they are busy elsewhere? Making your home inviting is a good thing and easy for you to do. Learning to live in it on your own may not be quite so simple.

In a secure relationship, you will truly blossom. You are likely to value that relationship above most other things in life, but watch out for a tendency to be over-protective with both partner and family. Sometimes you just have to let them make their own mistakes; 'mother' can turn to 'smother' if you're not careful. Best to open your heart and your ears, listen, bake and make it all better.

Sun Leo, Moon Taurus

A bright shiny character, you want to be the centre of attention, and what better way to do it than by putting on your dancing shoes and giving the world a performance it will never forget: step, two, three. Tapping your troubles away is good for you and even if you don't want to be the next big thing, it's a way of letting out your frustrations and it's far better than having a drama of a whole different sort when things don't go your way.

Did someone say 'drama'? If you don't discuss how you feel, creating a moment when others have no option but to talk about what's going on could be something you do without even recognizing you're doing it. Just saying.

You're fierce in a relationship, and that's meant in the modern way – good at the whole love thing – but then again, maybe the old-fashioned meaning would fit too? Grrr! Reciting poetry whilst wrapped in an exquisite silk scarf sitting beside a lake with a loved one is bliss for this little miss.

Sun Virgo, Moon Taurus

In the land of clipboards and staplers you're ruler of all you survey, and if there's any chance of getting a wall planner up or a flip-chart moment you're at the front of the queue.

Of course that's not all that's on your list – you're far more complex than that – and what you really want is to be of use, to be of service to those who need your organizational skills, and be they family or work colleagues, you hope that they will come to you for help in putting things into boxes, perhaps literally.

Behind the façade of the stationery cupboard, there's lots going on and in a romance your attention to detail is appreciated in a whole different way. This can be a surprise to those who only see the anorak and not what's happening underneath it all.

An eternal student, you don't have to be told something twice. You're a quick learner and you should put that to good use professionally.

Sun Libra, Moon Taurus

A double dose of Venus and her magical powers here, so it's all about love, art, beauty, grace and charm for you. Careers in the beauty industry, interior and fabric design, property development and high-end confectionery suit you well.

Talking of sweet things, you're likely to have a sweet tooth. When you're out for dinner, pudding is way better than the main course. If you can't make up your mind which one to have, you might have to have two. Just one pudding – such a cruel choice to make!

In love, you're a sensual being. You love to be in love, but watch you're not just in love with being in love – that's a whole different bag of bonbons.

If you have children, beware of a tendency to over-indulge them. Practise the art of saying 'no' now and again, and the same goes for shoes. Nice heels.

Sun Scorpio, Moon Taurus

When Water and Earth mix, as they do here, they can offer the potential for some amazing growth or they can go sludgy and turn to mud, so which one is it to be? Do you feel as if you can't get going or are you fertile with new ideas and can't wait for things to grow? Probably both, sometimes in the same day, so how do you get out of the mud when you're in it? Raising your head from the details that may bog you down will help, as will focusing on what you're building rather than how deep the foundations go.

This is a highly charged sexual line-up and you won't be able to hide your feelings when you see someone who warms your cockles. Your flirting techniques and prowess are likely to be legendary, and whatever Scorpio Sun, Taurus Moon wants, it gets. Success comes to you through dogged determination and an incredibly tenacious ability to hang on in there.

Sun Sagittarius, Moon Taurus

You love to go a-wandering, but do you know when it's time to get back home and deal with stuff? Your need to be out in the big wide world, seeing it all and experiencing other cultures, is at odds with a need to maintain strong roots to keep the money coming in so you can go on holiday again.

Yes, you would like to travel forever, but things need to be done. Luckily, this Sun–Moon combination brings you the ability to earn the money, perhaps a lot of money, to facilitate your need for world knowledge.

In a relationship, you're going to want to share your experiences. A big-hearted soul, you're generous with your time, energy and money.

Use your ability to dream up amazing ideas and get the details put in place to fill your coffers and live a life full of adventure.

Sun Capricorn, Moon Taurus

Being successful takes on a whole new meaning with you – your ability to not only build big but build better means you can outshine everyone in your quest to be the big I am. You can deliver on time, on budget and to expectation, be it yours or your employer's, but make sure you don't allow this earthy determination to develop into a dreary plod through life without any time to stop and enjoy the benefits of all your hard work.

Nature is important to you and a walk in the forest will help replenish your energy when you're tired or need to think through an idea. Don't underestimate the power of Mother Nature in your otherwise practical world.

At home, you're ruler of all you survey and are likely to be the main breadwinner. With that comes responsibility, and that may sometimes feel like a burden, so learn to share it early on.

In love, you want an equal in every way – not easy to find, but not impossible.

Learn to be flexible in life – a little flexibility makes things easier for you and those around you.

Sun Aquarius, Moon Taurus

With your gifts, you can not only think outside the box but also build a better box in the process. No academic genius without common sense, you are able to be both inspired and practical.

This combination brings you a natural ability to befriend people really easily, and if that's one person in particular, they will love the fact that you can be spontaneous but also able to provide a solid home environment.

Professionally, you would do well in medicine, but may find complementary medicine more appealing than conventional. Animal husbandry and botanical studies would suit you well too.

Don't assume you're always right – you may be right most of the time, but it's a rare breed that's right all of the time – and taking the time to stop and listen is advised, as is removing the icy blasts you sometimes give off and replacing them with velvety warm hugs.

Sun Pisces, Moon Taurus

You are a dreamer, a poet, an idealist who loves the finer things in life and adores art, but what of life's more practical things? Even though you would prefer to stay at the bottom of the garden with the fairy folk, you know that at some time or other you have to attend to earthly concerns. You're no stranger to those either and recognize that whilst you would prefer things to be perfect, the only way to help them along that path is to make sure the details are dealt with.

You have a canny knack of getting others to help you with very little fuss, and if there is resistance, you're adept at manipulating situations without others even realizing you're doing it.

In love, you want full-on romance. If your partner is willing to give you that, they will be your prince or princess forever!

Overall, you don't want lots of unruly noise or clashing fabrics in your life. It should be pretty, pretty, pretty – and it pretty much will be.

GEMINI MOON

'I've learned that people will forget what you said, people will forget what you did, but people will never forget how you made them feel.'

Maya Angelou

Archetype

Peter Pan. Never growing up has many blessings, including youthful looks that others will envy and the ability to mix with those younger than your years successfully without looking like the oldest swinger in town, but sometimes you may be accused of not taking things seriously and those around you could find that annoying, so know when to play and when to grow up and step up.

GEMINI MOON ♊

Our modern world is an information superhighway and as long as you're on it, you're going to travel to as many places as you can without settling down anywhere in particular, indulging yourself at various buffets along the way rather than staying long enough for a full meal. A little here, a little there, a little anywhere, but never so much that you get bogged down in routine and can't move on.

Some may think you're Jack or Jill of all things but master of none, but that's not the case. You may be an expert in your field, but you never consider yourself to have fully learned everything and will constantly be seeking more information.

As a child, you may have taken things apart, much to the annoyance of your parents, and not been able to put them back together again until you had had several goes. Of course as you learned more, you moved on to the next project. In adulthood, if you keep on learning and growing, you keep on keeping on. Your education in life may not give you a degree from any university, but you will learn, and continue to do so when others give in to daily routines and mind-numbing soap operas.

Having learned lots, you know lots, and knowing lots means you're particularly good at conversations and can form a quick bond with new people as you inevitably have some common ground. Your true opinions might not be easy to gauge – you often take an opposing view just for argument's sake – and some may not know what you really think. If they can't work it out, you're not telling them! Playing games makes you smile inwardly and outwardly, and your mischievous sense of humour will be one of the things that makes you attractive to those who really do get you. To those who don't, you're cantankerous, argumentative and even highly opinionated, but the good news is eventually most people will see the twinkle in your eye and work out what's going on.

If you're a serious Earth Sun sign, Taurus, Virgo or Capricorn, there will be the tendency to keep this lighter side of your nature for those who know you really well. It's an indication to others that they have been let into your inner circle. If they are work colleagues, some may be surprised at just how funny you are when the serious business of your working day is over.

Gadgets could demand a lot of your attention. If it beeps, shines a light or tells you what to have for your tea, it's well worth the price tag. You might even find that nothing gets your heart racing faster than a gadget. Sad but true. Mind you, an old-fashioned pen and notebook could put a smile on your face too, and there may be lots of lovely journals around the house full of good intentions and not a lot else!

You could be a little skittish on occasions, a nervous creature that scampers at the first sign of any emotional drama. You don't really want to get too involved. You can talk about things, and talk and talk and talk, but anything touchy-feely and you're looking at your watch, remarking on how late it is and scrambling for the door. As a consequence you might find you come across a lot of people who love to tell you their problems, and until you realize that you actually can get involved without catching chronic emotional dependency, they are likely to keep on coming. Life shows us lessons through the people we meet and the message they bring us.

As of yet the telephone hasn't been mentioned. Well, I don't know why not – it's your favourite gadget and the perfect way to communicate without the need for hugs and closeness. Your life will be stored on your phone and you'll seldom be without it. Imagine not being able to text, e-mail, social network and chat to everyone you know, usually all at the same time.

You want to be in amongst all the gossip and heaven forbid you're the last one to know anything. I remember a long train journey sitting opposite a young person who boarded the train in Portsmouth and got off at London Waterloo and for the length of the journey, almost two hours, they were on the phone. Nothing wrong with that? They must have called about ten people and every single one got the same drama, the same tale told ten times in a voice loud enough to curl my already harassed cheese and pickle roll. A Gemini Moon? Perhaps.

Driving is something that could come to you very easily and you're likely to have a license when some of your peers are still learning. Having a car gives you independence, the ability to be here, there and everywhere, and all at once if you could. In fact a Tardis might be a better idea. Taking a road trip with mates could also be something that interests you. Just remember you're better at bright lights, big city stuff than quiet locations, and make sure there's internet access, whatever you do.

When you work hard, your energy is easily depleted, and you should take great care to make sure you replenish it, which means good food and lots of fresh air. It's not always easy to gauge energy loss when the work you do involves ideas and communication, but using your mind is just as tiring as physical toil and sometimes more so. Ask yourself why you're so busy. Is it work pressure or are you using it to cover up an emotional issue? Relaxation techniques aren't for theory, they're for practice too!

An avid reader, you may have many books on the go, but when was the last time you finished one? You probably spot the plot way before the end and know whodunnit, or do you? Knowing *yourself* is everything, and so what if you do only read half a book, who cares if occasionally you're a little waspish with someone who can't take a joke and is it really the end of the world if you repeat a conversation ten times? Absolutely not.

What is important to you is to keep learning – about yourself and about those around you – and to keep moving, because if you keep moving, you will stay forever young. Nice tights by the way. Green is so your colour.

Love Life

When you're single, you're hardly likely to take much rest between your flirtier moments. Playing the field is far too much fun, but don't let that label follow you into a relationship. A Gemini Moon is just as likely to stay in a committed relationship as any other Moon sign, but that relationship has to be one that offers diversity, new things happening and not so much of the 'if it's Tuesday, it's curry for tea' thing going on.

You like change, you like things to look forward to and of course you also want things to talk about, so shared experiences with your other half will be essential.

In a romance, you're likely to hold a little bit back. This emotional reserve cushions you should things not go as planned, and whilst nobody else will notice, least of all your partner, a part of you will know that you can pick yourself up quicker than most should things go a bit *EastEnders* on you and end with a duff-duff moment.

Getting the right script is important for you. You want a good dialogue with your other half, and those who look good and have loads of cash or fancy clothes are no good unless they can talk to you and engage in stimulating conversation. Those with a nice car or their own yacht could get your interest for a couple of weeks, mind, but no chat, no future.

You could find you marry late in life, as having some fun is clearly important to you. Don't be persuaded to leap into anything that doesn't feel quite right just because your best friend had a lovely wedding and weren't those bridesmaids adorable?! The idea may sound nice – in fact you will have 1,000 ideas about how a wedding or a relationship should be – but can you see it all working practically and not just in your head?

In amongst those conversations with your other half or potential love squeeze, leave some space for silence, for finding their eyes and feeling the words they say rather than just listening to them. You're seduced by language, but not all language is audible. Think about the other person's body language, think about your own, and remember that eye contact will tell you everything you need to know.

Look for go-getters, action and travel types. Those from another country could also interest you, even to the point of emigrating to be with them. Avoid mummy's boys and anyone who likes to build their own models of warships out of lolly sticks.

Partnering a Gemini Moon

Keep life exciting and make sure they are informed about things you're going to do in the future – that gives them something to look forward to – but please make sure you follow through on those promises or you will hear about it for a very long time.

Confront them on their feelings and talk them out, or you may never truly know what's going on, even if you think you do.

Best fit Sun signs are Gemini, Aquarius, Libra and Sagittarius.

Career

Jobs in the media suit you, and your ability to ask questions is particularly useful in journalism, or perhaps in counselling, where you can debate both sides of an issue with impartiality. The adventure of travel would suit you well – just make sure the company perks give you some cheap deals to exotic locations and take full advantage of it. Airline steward would combine your love of people and travel, but why stop there? Why not move to the front of the cabin and indulge your love of fast-moving means of transport with travel?

Telephone marketing, or even marketing telephones, will suit your chattery style, and when faced with you, few of us can resist your charms, something I am sure you use to your advantage in more than your career.

Take care at work that you don't repeat anything that would be best kept to yourself. Involving yourself in idle chit-chat and gossip is a dangerous pastime. Ask yourself who really benefits from repeating what you overheard whilst you had your ear casually jammed up against the office door? Did you really hear all the conversation or have you made up the bits that were missing?

With this in mind, however, your natural charm and adaptable nature will help you succeed in whichever career you choose.

Parents and Family

Your mother is likely to have been a busy bee, with lots of things to do and lots of people to talk to. She may also have had a career that involved being away for short periods of time or travelling when perhaps you would have preferred she was at home. Certainly a strong work ethic will have been instilled in you by a woman who could get up and get on with it with extraordinary energy.

With your siblings, there might be a higher degree of rivalry than with some signs. As you aim to talk yourself up in their eyes, they will aim to beat you, and so the benchmarks get higher and higher. Whilst competition is a good thing, too much of this sort of jockeying for position could leave some deep-seated resentment, and snappy comments may result in crocodile tears. As you get older, it's better to let go and take the higher ground by using that cool emotional Moon of yours to recognize past cycles and that you no longer have to repeat them. But even in spite of this, your siblings are likely to always be on the phone to you and you to them.

Moving house frequently may be something you do early on. Later, finding a settled and forever home will be a steadying factor in your life and your relationship.

As a parent, you're going to be an exciting ever-youthful one who won't need to ask the kids how the DVD player works or what that button on the phone is for. In fact you might be showing them the new gadgets, and let's face it, you've got more spending power than they have. Really? Pester power is easily learned by children of Gemini Moons. They will work out very quickly that Mummy or Daddy loves those games and gadgets as much as they do and will steer you in the direction of their favourite gizmos.

At home, you will love to be surrounded by people, to have that buzz, but you're also going to love being away from your home. Remember that time spent on holiday or at your caravan by the sea still counts as family time as long as you take the family with you.

Gadgets, books and DVDs are likely to fill your home, offering you an outlet to beat boredom, which is your worst enemy. They may also be a way of introducing you to a hobby that later in life you could turn into something profitable, be it selling collectors' items, writing your own book or starring in your own movie.

Health

Gemini rules the lungs, hands and arms, so pay attention to these areas of your body, with things like asthma and eczema top of the list. Don't panic – it doesn't mean you *will* get these, the Moon just indicates where there may be a weakness.

You're a hectic Moon sign, so illness is usually associated with stress in your life. Remove the stress and you will maintain your optimum health – and yes, that is easier said than done, but not impossible with your changeable temperament.

Life Skills

Clearly one of your main skills is communication. Another is your adaptability and willingness to change. Once you understand why change is necessary, you're highly capable of keeping a cool head whilst you do it.

You like to be where the action is, and putting yourself amongst those who can help you achieve your goals is easy – your charm will have you invited to the best parties with the wittiest sorts who will revel in your quick responses. Noël Coward and Barack Obama share your Moon placement – both talkative and charming in their own way.

The world can come to your door these days – it's easy to have things delivered over the internet and to travel to all sorts of places through electronic media – but do make actual travelling and experiences with people part of your life and use your skills face to face rather than interface to interface.

Stumbling Blocks

It's been one of those days, you've used up all your energy and you really have nothing left to give, but you still have the washing to do and the kids' meals to prepare for the next day. Your emotional responses can get waspish when you're in that place and you can end up saying things you don't necessarily mean. So, get proper amounts of rest and, as boring as it is for you, remember that it is easier to get everything done if you have a schedule.

Finishing projects or making ideas happen may not be the easiest of things for you, but recognizing you're not a finisher is half the battle. Either surround yourself with the Earth signs of Taurus, Virgo and Capricorn to help you complete tasks or force yourself into an end date by publishing your deadlines.

When things aren't going your way, you might bang on about it rather than take any steps to rectify the situation. But one thing in life you can always change, no matter what Sun sign–Moon sign combination you are, is your attitude. Use your mind to change your approach and inevitably the outcome.

Spiritual Lesson

You have chosen your Moon in Gemini to learn how to deal with things objectively. The real lesson here is discrimination, seeing what really needs to be done and ignoring the millions of excuses for not getting on with it. Any message to yourself from the future is likely to include the words: 'Stay focused'.

SUN SIGN, MOON SIGN

So now you know a little more about your Moon sign, but how does that work with your Sun sign?

Sun Aries, Moon Gemini

You're the life and soul of the party, but what if there isn't a party going on? Then start one. If you do start one, it will be the best one, yes, it will… 'So what can I do now, eh, eh, eh?' Calm down, dear – you may be one of the busiest Sun–Moon combinations, but even you might need to find time to wind down at the end of the day, and that could be a challenge.

You're a master of words, controller of who said what to whom and ready to take on anyone who disagrees; in fact the thought of a good old argument gets you excited and you're good at it. Telling it how it is to anyone who will listen is what you're about. Diplomacy may not, however, be your strongest point!

Find a way of anchoring yourself to something or someone who provides solid ground for your thrilling life. That means choosing a partner who can go mountain-biking or paragliding and still find time to get you to sit on the sofa now and again.

Sun Taurus, Moon Gemini

Do you want to stay here and put down roots or would you be happier flying off somewhere with just a good book for company? Part of you wants to settle down whilst the other part wants the adventures you know life has out there waiting for you, but if you stop and think about it, you have great potential to have both. Your Taurus Sun provides the ability to create wealth and security, and your Gemini Moon is then funded to have her wandering, and in five-star luxury too: woo hoo!

You will be able to communicate with people in a way that not only charms them but also warms them to your ideas, but try to stay consistent – a tendency to go slightly Jekyll and Hyde now and again won't win friends and influence people.

In love, you could be a very popular choice, but your too cool for school attitude won't make it easy for anyone to get a ring on your finger and most definitely impossible for them to get one through this particular bull's nose and lead you anywhere you don't want to go.

Sun Gemini, Moon Gemini

Need I really go on? I know *you* can go on, and on, and on and then on some more, so why don't *you* tell *me* what Gemini Sun and Gemini Moon mean together? You're way ahead of most people,

Gemini, and this is an incredible gift that if used wisely and without ego could see you very successful indeed, especially in the writing and communication industries.

Challenge yourself with mind-stretching puzzles that nobody else will get half as fast as you, but also try to use the power of your amazing mind to calm yourself down. Active meditation will save you from burning out your nervous system with too much activity.

In a relationship, you will talk a good game and admirers will be plentiful, but can you deal with the cuddly, fluffy stuff? Find a partner who challenges you to show your emotions and do the physical stuff, otherwise you might as well marry your best friend.

Sun Cancer, Moon Gemini

You have the ability to make an excellent appraisal of someone's character and in record time. And with your natural empathy and mothering instinct, coupled with the ability to help them be at ease with you, you will soon find them opening up to confirm your assessment.

Working in human resource management or any role that puts people to the fore will suit you well, and if you work in a busy environment, you're likely to be the mother hen regardless of your sex. The confidence you give to others is unlikely to be what you feel inside, however, and you will seek to have your own skills validated through the actions and words of those around you. Work on letting go of that need and realize you are much loved.

In a relationship, find a partner with old-fashioned values, one who fulfils your idea of what a relationship should be like and knows that in order to truly know you they will have to give you time to come out of your shell and expose your emotions fully.

Sun Leo, Moon Gemini

You're a creative individual, even if sometimes what you create is mischief! You're charming, as all Gemini Moons are, but perhaps you're one of the most charming, as you're master of the twinkle in the eye, the diamond-bright smile and the ability to portray exactly what's required to make the most of any situation you find yourself in. In short, the perfect actor. But it's not all for show, Leo Sun, as you genuinely believe in your characters and will develop those that work best for you into an Oscar-winning performance getting you that job, love or heavy discount in the designer shop.

In love, you love the first flush, that head-spinning wonderful few days of will he call, does she like me, what costume should I put on to seal the deal? After that it might get more difficult. Be wary of tantrums – they generally lead to dramas, and whilst those *can* get results, are they really the way to go about it? Now don't you pout at me.

Sun Virgo, Moon Gemini

Fake it til you make it! If you don't really know what you're doing, for goodness' sake look as if you do and you will get away with it – and frequently do, I'm sure. Jack of all trades and very nearly master of some? You learn on the job, Virgo Sun, and pushing yourself into a situation where you have chanced your luck and have ended up very successful won't be a one-off for you. It should continue to serve you well, but maybe taking a little time to learn new skills before making those leaps would be even better?

Of course you're great with language, but especially good with the written word, so a career in publishing, journalism or writing advertising copy would suit you well, as would specializing in a medical role, be it human or animal subjects you're interested in.

On the romantic front, you may need to work on showing your emotions, as do most Gemini Moons, but for you this can sometimes manifest as appearing aloof. You're not, but you could give that impression. Think Posh Spice.

Sun Libra, Moon Gemini

A cool breeze blows through with this combination, a breeze that freezes on occasion, and words are your cooling agent. Your ability to either calm a situation or freeze people out with just a few words will be legendary.

You're likely to have lots of relationships with people who like to chatter and when you all get together there can be at least three threads to your conversation going on at the same time and those outside your clique may have great difficulty in following what's going on.

Careers in the law, relationship counselling and the fashion world would suit you, as would any role where your naturally great style and easy manner serve others.

In love, give your partner time to have their say before you go on with what you were saying. This is something they will pick up on early on, and don't be surprised if it's the butt of a few jokes. All done with love. That's L.O.V. E., love.

Sun Scorpio, Moon Gemini

Hiding away will work for a while, but eventually you're going to have to come out into the Sun, and when you do, you will have something to say. Getting in touch with your emotional self will often come with a journey into your own personal hideaway, Scorpio Sun, but if you know that's your process then own it, tell people you will be unavailable for the next ten minutes, two days or whatever works for you, and save yourself the poking and prodding of questions and interruptions.

This ability to look directly into the face of life's bigger questions will help you in roles such as detective, pathologist or exposing the truth whenever you feel things haven't been portrayed correctly.

In love, you're an intense one and no mistake, an individual who can talk a good game and produce results too. In fact, what are you doing Friday night? Dinner at mine?

Sun Sagittarius, Moon Gemini

When you were a child you were probably one of those kids who was constantly asking why, and when you were told why, your next question would be 'Why?'!

As an adult, your ability to say what you can just about get away with could see you sailing pretty close to the wind now and again, and sometimes straight into a storm, but you're a good navigator and will somehow manage to get yourself out of it without too much damage.

You have the ability to lift your mates out of their troubles with a few encouraging words, but equally you could send some folks spiralling the other way with an off-the-cuff remark that formed somewhere in your mind and then forgot to go through the appropriate filter before it hit your mouth.

In love, you're not up for too much of that cuddly nonsense, but show you a partner who has a *Rough Guide to Europe* and a tent, and you're a happy camper, a playful soul who never wants to stop playing – and why should you?

Sun Capricorn, Moon Gemini

Do you do a straight up and down presentation at work or do you introduce a unicycle and a bag of doughnuts to add variety? Your serious side is complemented by your playful nature, and your ability to bring humour to proceedings is usually well judged.

Your words are also calculated and well chosen, with little wastage, and those hoping to indulge in mind-numbing gossip with you are likely to be disappointed. You would make a great teacher, and even if it were double maths, you would find a way to make your lesson interesting for your students.

In a relationship, you're likely to want things well ordered and will need to know that your partner wants precisely the same things as you and is sticking to the plan. And emotionally? You're cool, of course, and able to do just about anything to avoid showing your feelings. Not big; not clever. Just saying.

Sun Aquarius, Moon Gemini

When an Air sign Sun and Moon combine, it's clear there's a lot of chatter going on, but what are you talking about, Aquarius Sun? Anything and everything, and always with a sense of authority, because we all know you're going to be right. Yes, even when you're wrong!

A scientific approach to most things suits you very well; in fact you may choose roles in life that employ your ability to see things from that analytical angle and yet, being the cantankerous and unpredictable individual that you are, you could also use those same skills in other pursuits such as astrology or mysticism.

In love, you don't make it easy to let your other half know what you're feeling and any approach could be met with 'I'm fine', which is of course code for 'Leave me alone.' Fellow Air signs will make that comfortable for you, but if you want a challenge, try a Fire sign: Aries, Leo or Sagittarius.

Sun Pisces, Moon Gemini

When you're sitting at the bottom of the garden talking to the fairy folk, are you also having a conversation that questions whether that's rational or not? Maybe your ethereal Pisces nature fights with the logical side of your Gemini Moon, but there really is no need. Use the combination of Water and Air to bring bubbles into your life, bubbles that help your effervescent nature to shine through.

Your mind is likely to produce a lot of chatter, and a lot of that will involve an almost psychic ability to predict how people are going to react to the situation they find themselves in. The same goes for your own stuff, but will you believe it or talk yourself out of it?

Whatever you tell yourself, you make a great storyteller, especially of children's stories, and if you have kids of your own they will love the tales you make up for them.

A partner may not love your tales quite as much, so be straight-talking in a relationship. And that goes for when you're unhappy with a situation: speak up rather than leave things hanging about in your magical mind to grow into a beast of a problem. Believe in yourself!

CANCER MOON

'If you cannot get rid of the family skeleton,
you may as well make it dance.'

Geoclubrge Bernard Shaw

Archetype

The mother. You're a natural at empathizing with people and they will be drawn to you for comfort and support, and all because they recognize your own vulnerability. But don't be misled – it's not all about mothering other people; you nurture and mother your own ideas and by default your own growth too.

CANCER MOON ♋

Here the Moon is where she wants to be. She is the governess of this sign and that would bring you extra points, wouldn't you think? What she does here is up her dose of lunar treats, but she also increases the challenges she carries in her silver purse, spreading some interesting opportunities to learn on your path.

If you imagine the Moon as a giant mirror, the idea that you too reflect and absorb not only images but also emotions is easier to understand. You are that mirror, so take a look at whom you surround yourself with and first ask what they are seeing in you and then what you are reflecting back at them: it's the same thing. So, a great way for you to recognize things in yourself that may need to change is to look at what you don't like about your mates. And then, to see what you can really work on, look at your mates. You get the picture.

As the mother hen of the group, regardless of your sex, you're the one everyone is going to come to for support and a hefty slice of home-baked cake. They are looking for someone to listen, someone to empathize and someone to point them in the right direction. Letting that turn into *doing* things for them should be the line you refuse to cross. Unless it's your kids.

For your children you would do anything. Most parents would, but you might just get in the car and go to the school and let Mr Brown in Geography know exactly what he can do with his globe. Embarrassing for little Miss Cancer Moon's daughter, who was only having a bad day and really only needed a cuddle and some encouragement. This too could be learned behaviour reflected from your own mum, who was likely to have been very protective, perhaps a real matriarch ruling the family – and perhaps she still does.

The images for Cancer Moon are clearly the mother, the mirror and of course the crab, but the ebb and flow of the sea are also closely connected to the Moon. Does this mean you love the sea? Yes, but I was thinking of going a little deeper than that, if you don't mind? What about the ebb and flow of those moody moments?

Sometimes you can be oversensitive. Hitting a harrumph at 100 miles an hour causes you to close down and take whatever has upset you into your shell to let it fester for a while. A sulk may be the way you work things out or simply the way you get those around you to notice you're hurting. If it's an especially tough one, you could become the hermit crab, the one who sits on the sea bed on its own and rushes out snapping when something wanders past. Oh dear.

Thankfully these are rare days, certainly rarer than the ones when you're ready to open your doors and your heart to anyone who needs your help, so figure out what (or who) the triggers for super-crab are and learn to nip them in the bud. Sorry about that rubbish pun.

At work you're likely to be the United Nations, waving your flag for peace and understanding, and the go-between should Accounts declare war on the Packing Department. By using your natural way with people you can bring them back together like two naughty kids who are best friends really but fight now and again. You're also excellent at wheedling out the truth behind the gossip at work and may be deployed as a truth-seeking missile by those who need to know. Getting things running smoothly is likely to be something you do at work generally, without even recognizing you're doing it. Put it down to your lucky gonk. (Do people still have gonks?)

Nostalgia is something you're likely to be big on too, going on about old black and white movies and how things used to be in the olden days… How old *are* you? And do you have a box of keepsakes from when little Tommy was months old, all the letters your other half wrote when you were first together and any old theatre ticket, chocolate wrapper or lock of hair that holds memories of important times in your life? My mum is a Cancer Sun and has what we call her 'greety box' – 'greeting' being a Scottish term for 'crying' – which she takes out now and again when she feels like getting all wistful over my first pair of Baby Dear shoes. Oddly enough, she doesn't have my size 12 trainers in there. As a Cancer Moon, your past will also be important to you. Remembering it will bring you comfort, and emotionally it can also bring you some solutions.

The Moon holds all your experiences and memories, and some would say she's a key player in past-life memories too. So, if you stop long enough to listen, you will find an answer to most situations within this memory stick you have implanted in your chart.

This brings me to your natural sensitivity, your ability to just 'know' things. A lot of Cancer Moon sign people have a highly developed sixth sense and some go on to make more of it in a professional capacity. It's a great placement for mediumship in particular, so maybe you're not bonkers after all? Then again…

Having such an attractive Moon will inevitably bring you some folks who will see that special quality in you, the light that shines from your Cancer Moon, and not all of them will want to give back as much as you give them. Because of your own past experiences, you will take note early on and very quickly snap them out of their dream world and into the real one, the one where they have to stand on their own two feet.

Your home is of course your sanctuary and what you say goes. Those curtains may not be to everyone's taste, but you love them and that's all that matters. End of.

Children are important to you and you love their company, but when you've had enough of other people's kids being dumped on you because you're so good with them, say something. Babysitting is great, but in small doses, so speak up sooner rather than later or your mates will think they have struck babysitting gold. More about your own children and childhood later.

The sea will be very attractive to you and you could live there or harbour dreams to live there when you're older. For some of you, the draw may be so great you could want to work on or near it. Simply being near the ocean could bring you peace, calm you down and help you come to decisions if you empty your mind of everything but the ebb and flow of the tide, the rhythm of life itself. Poetic guff or practical advice? Try it.

Love Life

Behind your floury apron and kitchen sink kudos lies a whole other creature, one in synch with their senses and sensitivities and ready to throw off the shackles of domesticity and throw on some fluffy handcuffs and a tub of double cream.

As a Water sign Moon, you will want things to be romantic and meaningful rather than a fumble in Waitrose car park on the way back from the chip shop. I still haven't found my mobile phone, by the way. Anyway, back to you. Your home is where you're most comfortable, and with a partner that shows. You're affectionate and want them to know that they complete the perfect home. For you, starting a family could be a really strong drive. The Duke and Duchess of Cambridge are both Cancer Moon, so expect big things there! You want your home and family life to be just perfect and put a lot of effort into it, which I suspect is greatly appreciated by your other half.

Things have to cut both ways, of course, so make sure your other half offers you the protection, nurturing and emotional openness that you are offering them. If you find yourself with someone who isn't very good at showing affection, be it publicly or privately, ask yourself what you're really getting from the relationship. If you do want things to change, you must be prepared to speak up. Hoping your other half will somehow pick up on your needs psychically is a long shot, and even if you think you've dropped enough hints, perhaps hints aren't enough and you need to actually come out of your shell and say something. Perhaps in fact you are trying too hard to be the nurturer and protector within a relationship when all you really want is to be looked after for a change. Just saying.

If you're looking for romance, you're likely to be attracted to someone who reminds you of your father or mother – not physically, you understand (that would just be too odd), but emotionally. Although beware of adding lines like 'Not as good as my mother's apple pie' or 'I'll ask my mum, she'll tell me what to do' to your conversations.

Once you have found your partner, build that perfect home with those kids and those roses round the door if you have to, but make sure it all rests on a foundation of emotional honesty and open communication.

Partnering a Cancer Moon

Being as open as you can about how you feel is a good way of showing them that they can be the same. They will respond to you making the first move, albeit slowly at first. Sometimes your Cancer Moon may seem to power down, to switch off, so give them space to figure out what's really going on and let them know you're there with tomato soup and lots of love when they need you.

In relationships with Cancer Moon males in particular, the mother could be a very strong character, almost overbearing. Just something to bear in mind.

Best fit Sun signs are Cancer, Scorpio, Pisces and Capricorn.

Career

You're suited to careers that make good use of your skills as a nurturer, with jobs in hospitals, schools and catering heading a long list of roles where your ability to put people at ease is a coveted talent. As a sideline, you could also be interested in antiques, something that could bring you some income in either the short or long term.

You could delay following your real goals until later in life. Perhaps earlier on, family life will dictate where you live or how many hours you devote to training, etc., but as children grow up, your opportunities may increase, and you shouldn't consider yourself too old to retrain or change careers completely. Those with a Cancer Moon tend to do very well later in life.

Family business also does well under a Cancer Moon, but be prepared to wear one hat at work and another at home, and make sure all those involved know the rules and stick to them.

If you ever find yourself in a worrying situation at work, ask the right questions of the right people rather than take things back home to go over and over in your mind until you end up creating a monster of a problem that wasn't really there in the first place. You want your work environment to be peaceful – who doesn't? – so treat it as you would your home by talking things out. Just don't throw up a set of hideous curtains, thank you very much.

Parents and Family

A lot has already been said about your home and family life, and there's no doubt that with a Cancer Moon it will be a dominant area of your life.

You're likely to have been brought up in a comfortable home with nurturing parents, and if you have any siblings, you would all have been treated equally.

You may be interested in going further back in your family tree. Asking questions of your parents and grandparents as well as aunts and uncles will help you build a picture of where you came from, and that will provide you with a greater understanding of who you are. In turn, you will be keen to pass that information down to your own children.

Your mum is likely to have been very traditional, perhaps a stay-at-home mum who saw her role as nurturer and homemaker, as essential in making the family unit work. She will have had a very strong work ethic and taken her role very seriously, saving money where possible, making and mending and always providing healthy food for her growing kids. Of course it probably wasn't always that perfect, but your memory has it that way and that provides the model for your own parenting and homemaking skills.

Recognizing you're living in different times from your parents whilst still maintaining your core values, family and career balance in particular might be something you need to work at. Be careful you don't put too much pressure on yourself to live up to the *Family Circle* magazine lifestyle.

As described earlier, you will be very close to your children and would do anything to protect them, but occasionally they might need to skin their knees to learn how to ride a bike, and now and again life will give them lessons that are good for them, just as it did with you.

Providing a comfortable and safe environment for them is important, but what they will really benefit from is your ability to listen to what they have to say without judging and offer ways for them to come up with their own answer — as long as it's the one you subconsciously planted about half an hour before they came up with it!

Your sixth sense goes into overdrive with your family; you will know when they are feeling off, when they are ill or when they just need a hug. Let it guide you, but also know when you need to back off and leave them to come up with their own solutions. Of course you will never be so far away that they can't reach out and you will be there.

Health

Cancer rules the breasts, chest and lungs, so care should be taken around these areas in particular, but remember astrology and health are about prevention, not diagnosis. Suggesting care should be taken isn't suggesting there *will* be a problem.

Generally in fact you have good health. Your good diet will help with that, as will feeding your emotional needs through helping and caring for others.

As a sensitive sign, take care with your work and home environment, though. Lighting, water quality, fresh air, etc., all need to be conducive to good health.

Life Skills

Trusting in your intuition is essential. When you feel things aren't right, it will be because they aren't. Finding a way to bring up your concerns in conversation won't be difficult for you, but you might sometimes worry about upsetting those close to you. Better to have your say than not.

When you're faced with a crowd, you can easily pick out those you could get along with, and if it's a work situation, forming long-lasting bonds with colleagues could lead to you being welcomed into a bigger career-based family and rising through the ranks quicker than most. It's not so much who you know as who you like and who likes you!

Your ability to be a good listener is something that's coveted by most. Acting as a sounding board for your mates as well as your family will make you popular, but try to remember they are there for you too and don't be shy when you have things on your mind.

Old-fashioned values are what you stand for, but that doesn't mean your approach is dusty. Your strong moral code, combined with your intuitive ability, will see you shine in a sometimes grey world.

Stumbling Blocks

Whilst retreating is sometimes an opportunity to regroup, you may use it as a way of grabbing attention, and if that doesn't work, it tips over into avoidance. Avoidance can then turn into bitterness and that can turn into silence of a different sort, the sort that is really difficult to resolve. Being the mother figure means holding the 'family' together, no matter whether that's your work, mates or actual family, and what won't go down well is prolonged silence, so someone has to be the grown-up and it might as well be you. Sometimes it just takes a little gesture for everyone to realize that arguing never really gets anyone anywhere.

Your intuition can pick up when things are right, but your imagination can sometimes then create a story of why they are right that is as far away from the truth as you can get, so trust that intuition but stop there and find out the facts of a situation before you go too far down the Mystic Meg road and tell someone why they should avoid a blue door with the number four on it.

Spiritual Lesson

You have accepted a role in this life that many people would find tough; in fact one of the toughest jobs in the world is being a mother. You are on call all the time, you are expected to be supportive and nurturing and to knock out a chocolate cake in times of drama, and in order to give all that love you must receive love to balance it out. Your lesson is simply that: to receive as much love as you give out. Easy?

SUN SIGN, MOON SIGN

So now you know a little more about your Moon sign, but how does that work with your Sun sign?

Sun Aries, Moon Cancer

So there you are, all fired up with things to do, people to see, ideas to get out there, and then your mum turns up and wants to have a little chat. Bless. No doubt you listen to her, or any waif that comes your way, while looking at your watch until eventually you have to say something and get on with your day. Then you feel bad. That look on the old girl's face as you escorted her to her sad little car!

This fight between obligation and your need for excitement will be an old and familiar one. No matter where it shows itself, use your Cancer Moon to let those who need to know you care that you do indeed care, but use your Aries Sun to lead the way towards a balance between yourself and your commitment to others. That goes for your love life too.

Sun Taurus, Moon Cancer

Earth mother, goddess by any other name, you're the pinnacle of nurturing success and offer cuddles and comfort like no other Sun–Moon combination. And you smell so good too! Then again you could be the 'Elbows off the table!' sort. Rules is rules and you won't get any pudding if you don't eat your dinner up.

Providing security for those you love and care about is a great thing, but make sure it's not the only thing. With great creative skills, especially around food, you could carve out a very successful and fulfilling professional life.

Music around the home will be important to you too and you may have been brought up by parents who instilled the love of a particular genre of music into you.

In relationships, you need a partner who is as committed to building a family life as you are, someone who wants to spend time tending the garden and reading bedtime stories. A partner who is absent from the home isn't ideal for many of us, but for you it could be a deal-breaker.

Sun Gemini, Moon Cancer

An airy Sun with a watery Moon could produce conflict between what you think and what you feel, and sometimes that can move into an ever-decreasing circle that takes you down the plughole of indecision. To avoid this, learn to trust in your intuitive side, which isn't reliant on either your mind or your emotions but sits somewhere in between. Not easy, but once you've mastered it, you will save yourself so much time!

In love, you fall head over heels very quickly and tell all your mates about it, but they all know you're really trying to convince yourself that it's as wonderful as you say it is. Try to slow things down a bit and let a relationship unfold in its own time. Don't go flicking through *Brides* magazine on the second date. No, really.

You make a good reporter and researcher and would do well in any role where you had to write for a living, but don't forget your Cancer Moon's ability to go back into the past – roles where you have to do some forensic work will suit you too.

Sun Cancer, Moon Cancer

A double delight of all those Cancer treats, a double whammy of all those sensitivities and homely gifts! You're extremely emotional and probably have a good cry at the adverts on telly, never mind the movie you're watching. Well, there's nothing wrong with that.

Where it might not work for you is away from your sofa, especially at work, where you could become a little tired and emotional if you don't look after yourself properly. If you need to make a point, give yourself space to think about what you want to say and how you're going to say it, and then come out and do it. You're no shrinking violet, just a little apprehensive about the first flush of engagement, and once you're past that, woe betide anyone who thinks they can get past your snapping claws without giving you what you went in to get.

Brooding about things isn't going to work at home either and your other half is likely to be the sort that points it out. You will have chosen them for that reason – they will reflect back to you strengths that you wish you had, and confrontation is one of them. Learn from them. Even if you find yourself wanting to digest the contents of the fridge whilst wrapped in a duvet rather than talk about what's wrong, talking will do you and your waistline more good.

PS. This is a very psychic configuration, but you knew I was going to say that.

Sun Leo, Moon Cancer

You may want to stay at home, but how will you be famous if you do? How will you reach the audience you crave? Perhaps working from home could satisfy both requirements, and anything artistic would certainly suit you – a home studio perhaps? Most likely getting out and about will win, but once you have used the power of your enormous personality to move and shake your way into the path of those who can help you achieve your goals, make sure you have your sanctuary at the end of the day.

With the Sun and Moon at home in their own signs, you're likely to be very regal, with gold, silver and bright colours surrounding you and a home that will reflect your love of fine things, even if it isn't quite to everyone's taste. So few people can really pull off leopard print.

In love, you are fiercely loyal and will defend your partner even if they are well capable of defending themselves, which they probably are, given you're not going to be attracted to weak individuals. Relationships may have more than their fair share of drama, but that's what makes them work for you, and the partner that can stand up to you and gain your respect for doing so is the one for you.

Sun Virgo, Moon Cancer

'Don't put that glass down without a coaster underneath!' Oh come on, surely it's OK for just five minutes. No? You're probably right, Virgo Sun, and that's the most annoying thing! There's no point in letting it go, either – you would only fester and stew until you were less than subtle with your removal of the glass, wiping of the table and slamming down of the coaster.

You're a stickler for detail, but the Moon in Cancer will bring your nurturing ability to the fore, turning that attention to detail into a bigger force, a force for the betterment of your family as well as humanity as a whole. That sounds like a tall order? Never fear – whether taking on the role of environmental officer at work or nagging your nearest and dearest to do more recycling, you can and will do your bit.

In love, you're very loyal and take good care of your partner and should expect the same in return. If you don't get it, make sure you're leaving them some room to do it and aren't taking over completely.

This is a generous and caring placement with a sense of duty. Admirable, but don't turn duty into servitude.

Sun Libra, Moon Cancer

If there's a party going on for a family celebration, it's either round yours or you're the one who is organizing all the details, especially the theme, colours and those fancy little cakes. And if it is at yours, it'll be in a home that's full of grace and charm, perhaps minimalist but still warm, peaceful and inviting.

Making a decision, especially one that affects your family, may not be the easiest of things for you, as one minute you know what you want and the next you don't, all fed and fuelled by the fact that you will ask for the opinion of others and then open up a debate, even though you thought you had made your mind up already.

One thing that's sure to send you into a moody is injustice. Seeing someone who gets what they absolutely don't deserve will have you incensed, especially if there's nothing you can do about it. What if you can? Stand by to see you at your best: a master debater who can run rings around the competition using a mix of fact and pure emotional power.

In love (and you do love to be in love), you're sensitive to your partner's needs and they should be to yours, but you might push their buttons in order to test their loyalty or commitment to the relationship. Make sure you don't push them too hard. Just saying.

Sun Scorpio, Moon Cancer

Enough Water? Are you drowning in the emotion of it all or are you treading water nicely by making sure you say how you feel and leaving those around you enough time to respond without whipping out your tail to take a swipe? What kind of sea-beast are you? Don't worry, we all know you're really not that bad, but sometimes you can look very scary and never more so than when your Cancer Moon stirs up emotions from your past.

Your ability to look at the darker side of life could prove useful professionally. Roles as a detective, pathologist and crime writer could suit you – anything that helps answer some of your own questions about life, death and the mystery of life and still has you home in time for tea. I know a Scorpio Sun with Cancer Moon who is a forensic officer and in her spare time bakes cakes and sells them at Sunday markets. Perfect.

In love, you're an intense and very sensual lover, but you need a strong emotional connection to really let go. When you do, I hope your partner has taken their vitamins and can take the next day off work to recover.

Sun Sagittarius, Moon Cancer

Whilst you love to get out and about and travel for travel's sake, you need to know those 600-thread-count sheets and electric blanket are waiting for you when you get home. You may be the sort that takes their pillow with them when they travel, as much for the smell of home as for the fact that most hotel pillows are like wafers.

On your travels, and I mean through life in general not just through airports and train stations, you will love to talk to your fellow travellers, listen to their experiences and tell them about yours, reliving your past triumphs as well as the challenges and adventures you've had along the way.

If you don't travel literally, you could travel in your mind through a love of foreign culture, which you are likely to pass on to your children.

In love, you're likely to go for those who will travel with you or, oddly enough, those who prefer to keep the home fires burning, safe in the knowledge they will be there when you get home and your need for familiarity will be met.

Watch your tendency to spend money like it's going out of fashion, especially when you're emotionally challenged. Get a good financial adviser and try to avoid using family in that role, as it could cause arguments.

Sun Capricorn, Moon Cancer

Capricorn and Cancer are opposite numbers and some with this placement will have been born on a full Moon. Don't worry, you're not a werewolf, but you are likely to transform from practical, grounded and highly efficient business type into emotional wreck at the first sign of a puppy with a broken leg.

You're both parents rolled into one – the strict father figure with the gentle mum providing a safe place to understand what's going on. These roles may not always be appreciated by your children at the time, but later in life they will come to see that firm but fair was followed up with support and an environment to grow in.

In relationships, you're likely to be big on old-fashioned values. You're looking for Mr Right, not Mr Right Now. Whilst you do your fair share of flirting, it's probably not for flirting's sake – you only really do it when you feel someone has the potential to become more than a just a passing phase.

Working from home is highly possible for you. That would feed your need for success and your desire to be at the heart of the family, but make sure you have rules. As we all know, you like to stick to them!

Sun Aquarius, Moon Cancer

If charity begins at home, it most definitely begins at your home, and you might find you take in waifs and strays many times as you move through life. It's also about you stepping out of your home too. Even if you would rather not bother, sometimes your need to share your blessings with those less fortunate than you is something for which you're happy to get up from your sofa.

You might take this further and work for a charity full-time. If you do, make sure you have in place mechanisms that will prevent you taking too much of it home or onto your own shoulders when the responsibility clearly ought to be shared.

In love, you're likely to be independent and seek a partner who doesn't mind you doing pretty much what you like when you like. Your Cancer Moon will always bring you home and expect a cup of tea, slice of cake and not too many questions about what you've been up to. If your partner is reading this, perhaps they need to know that the way to keep you close is to appreciate you when you're around, and when you're not, appreciate the space!

Sun Pisces, Moon Cancer

A full-on romantic combo that truly wants perfection in life, complete with roses round the door and two kids playing on a garden swing made from rope and a plank of wood that Granddad made for them. Sweet.

When your children are older, or perhaps in your relationships with friends, you are likely to want to be a part of everything they do, and often can give advice when it wasn't asked for. Tough, they are getting it and that's that. At this point, maybe a rethink wouldn't go amiss, or an outlet for your need to nurture through a job in nursing, social work or teaching.

The arts are important to you, too, and a home full of lovely things, beautiful music and gorgeous smells will bring comfort to all who enter the lair of the bewitching Pisces/Cancer combo.

In love, the worst thing that could happen is a passing hump and dump – not something you go looking for, but life has a way of dishing up things we don't like so we can learn from them and move on. If it does happen, your inner diva is released and a performance worthy of Bridget Jones will actually help you move on, so jim-jams on, ice-cream out...

For you, love is at its finest with a sensitive soul who knows and appreciates your need to nurture and allows you to do just that, but also knows when to say thank you and bring you flowers, and never, ever takes you for granted.

LEO MOON

'Be noble! And the nobleness that lies in other men, sleeping,
but never dead, will rise in majesty to meet thine own.'

JAMES RUSSELL LOWELL

Archetype

The king/queen. A noble Moon that wants to help others as best that it can, a Moon that will be generous with emotional help when those it loves need support… but sometimes that's an act, a way of encouraging others whilst hiding how you are feeling yourself, isn't it? A true ruler will be what their subjects expect of them, but what about when the act is over and you're alone with your confidantes?

LEO MOON ♌

Being royalty, you are faced with expectations. Don't panic, you don't have to plant a tree at precisely 2:30 p.m. in three years' time (and please make sure you're wearing the blue). Imagine your life being that ordered – it just wouldn't suit you. But then again, access to a few jewels would put a smile on your face…

Of course you can't mention the word 'Leo' without thinking of the lion, the king of the jungle, that proud beast. Those qualities, when attached to your Moon, bring you just that, pride, but isn't that something you get just before a fall? That depends on what you've been up to. You want to show yourself as someone to trust, the honourable sort, but what if you succumb to another of this Moon's traits and put yourself in compromising situations because your mates did? Then you can become angry and roar at the injustice of it all. Why are people picking on you? The thing is, when you wear the crown you're going to be the first they see and the one who will inevitably get in the bother whilst the instigators of the drama slink off into the shadows.

You're capable of making sure things get done, and even if you have to stay up all night sewing sequins on by hand, if you've promised your little princess she will be the belle of the ball, the belle of the ball she will be. Kids adore your playful nature and you love the way they just let themselves go, reminding you of your own childhood and encouraging you to approach things with the same ethos.

If you're not sure of someone, you can play your court card and appear aloof and detached and, of course, regal. Although others may initially think you're a bit too far up your own ego, once they get to know you they will realize that's not true and your little act was one of protection rather than aggression. If you're in a social situation where you might have to warm up more quickly, try to find a way of turning off Elizabeth I and going for something slightly less Cate Blanchett.

With the Moon in a fixed sign, you're likely to be able to control your emotions very well; however, as we all know, when you keep a lid on things that aren't all that predictable, the chances are when they do go, they really go. Think home brew – there you are, doing whatever you do with your demijohn, keeping it all under control, and then something changes. Pop! It's all over the place and impossible to get back in the bottle and takes an age to clear up. Just saying.

All these more difficult traits can be helped if you don't bottle things up. Rubbish pun, I do apologize. You could of course do a lot better on the pun front, with a sense of humour that keeps friends and family entertained, and as long as they are laughing, you'll be telling those jokes.

Life needs to be fairly fast-paced for you. You're not one for sitting in doing your knitting and telling tales of the time you went to Bognor and it did nothing but rain. You would prefer to be in Bognor in the rain rather than doing anything involving wool and a pattern for a bobble hat. (If you are actually going for the wool option, maybe you're a Virgo Moon?) Keeping that pace will take its toll on your emotions, though, so make sure you build in some space to relieve the pressure and talk out what you're really feeling, and if that has to be somewhere fabulous with chandeliers and at least three different kinds of sauna, then so be it.

With a partner, life is interesting, as one moment you're the adoring and very romantic lover and the next, well, let's face it, a bit of a princess. The switch is likely to come if your partner doesn't fully appreciate the effort you have gone to to make sure dinner is perfect and the scene is set for a romantic evening. Maybe they are just worn out from a tough day at work? Maybe the cat can't play with the mouse because the mouse is too tired to stand up?

Having said that, sometimes drama is the very thing that keeps your relationship going, and perhaps acknowledging that with your other half could make it even more fun. If you know what you're dealing with and call it by its true name, life is easier. So, be honest, you need *excitement*.

Just like Leo Sun signs, you may be fussy about your hair, your mane. This tops off a tendency to be quite vain about your appearance in general – or is that 'well groomed'? I would go with well groomed, unless of course you glance in every mirror or shop window you pass, and it is definitely vain if you stop to sort out your hair in the reflection of an estate agent's window whilst everyone looks back at you. Frankly, of course, you couldn't care less.

The Moon's reflective quality will shine back on you by bringing people into your life who are similar to you as well as people you aspire to be like. The latter are probably people who have power in some way, shape or form as well as all the trappings that success can bring. Having aspirations is a good thing, but remember the Moon will also show you the emotional cost of these things. What about time spent with family, partner or friends? Are you prepared to push those emotional buttons to get what you want?

If you do want it all, and why shouldn't you, find a way to balance family and home with those aspirations. Perhaps the only way to do that is to work out who brings drama your way and get off that particular stage. What you need are people who support your role and understand what you're about and, when faced with your sometimes emotional eruptions, remain calm and listen to what you have to say instead of fanning the flames.

Generally, you are a playful Moon sign, one that has a pleasant disposition unless riled, and perhaps that's no bad thing. To keep things on as even a keel as possible, make sure you take plenty of breaks and holidays, preferably somewhere warm and sunny where you can show off your new clothes, swish your dreamy hair and be adored by all and sundry.

When you do come home, it's likely to be to a home that is luxurious and the hub of your friends' and family's social life. In fact if there's a party, it's going to be at yours, where you can play the perfect host and keep everyone entertained with your sparkling wit and elegance. No chippie tea on your lap in front of 'Enders for you.

Love Life

Are you really high maintenance? Not really. All you need is to be appreciated. All those things you do to make your partner happy and to bring excitement and passion into their life should be noticed. It's really not much to ask.

If a partner does ignore your efforts, intentionally or not, you're not likely to respond well. A huffy with your name on it could be on its way. Find a way to let your partner know you're feeling a little unloved without turning it into a drama. Perhaps you could use humour? I have a Leo Moon friend who has a stuffed lion. She turns it to face the wall when she's feeling left out, so with humour, without a big fuss and without saying anything, she lets her husband know she's around and feeling hurt. Nine times out of ten it works. The other time Mr Lion can fly. Amazing.

When choosing a partner, you might think the sensible one is someone you need to keep you calm, but frankly that might not work. What you really need is someone to play with without tipping over into wild child. Find the balance.

Sexually, you are a big cat waiting for some playtime, and like any kitten you need to be teased with treats dangled for you to reach up and grab. Your partner would do well to know that love is a game for you and if they play it well they will be rewarded handsomely. Finding suitable partners won't be difficult; keeping them might be tougher if they haven't got the energy reserves you have. Fire signs suit you best, or those with lots of planets in Fire.

It's not all arms, legs and swinging from the chandelier – you want the nice dinner, the romantic walk and five-star hotel too, and time to let your partner understand your true passions is important as well. They should be prepared to share in your goals for the future and, let's face it, they should be rich enough, hot enough and well-connected enough to make your friends jealous.

You need support from a partner on all levels and will see yourselves very much as a team that has to work – that's work at making sure that team Leo Moon is the best team around that dinner table when you get together with friends and family. Competitive? You? Maybe just a bit.

Partnering a Leo Moon

Time and energy – two things you must have in abundance if you're to keep them satisfied, and not just in the obvious way.

Understanding them is a lifetime's work, but it can be the most amazing job in the world and you will never, ever be bored. Learn to swing from a trapeze and make sure you come with a dressing-up box with at least ten different outfits for date night.

Best fit Sun signs are Leo, Aries, Sagittarius and Aquarius.

Career

At school you may have spent so long in the naughty corner you didn't really do what you were supposed to, but panic not, you're one of those Moon sorts that learn more from life than from any book. That, coupled with a desire to be in charge, will breed a strong ambition, and you're more than likely to do better than a lot of folks who have done very well academically but don't possess your charm.

Although you can achieve great things, you might do best by making sure you have good courtiers around you who can push you when you feel as if sleeping in would do you more good. You can sometimes be that big old lion sleeping under the tree whilst others are going out and finding the prey. But you won't get away with that too often.

Careers that need the force of personality that you have and the ability to switch on people's enthusiasm would suit you well. Sales and marketing, acting, teaching dance and working with disadvantaged young people would be appealing.

Running your own business suits you; it puts you at the centre of your universe, calling the shots, using your creativity and showing your leadership skills. Why do I think you might do well running a hairdresser's? Just a hunch.

Parents and Family

A Leo Moon is a dramatic Moon, and as she represents family, the root of who you are, you may have had a dramatic upbringing. That can of course range from having a theatrical mother right through to dramas that were far from entertaining.

It's likely that you were pushed to be a success at school when all you really wanted to do was create your own interpretation of life rather than learn parrot fashion. This could have meant tension with a parent who was already established as a pillar of the community, or following an older sibling and finding it hard to walk in their shoes.

The family home could have been noisy, and fighting to have your say might not have been easy. It may even have caused you to wonder how you fitted in and whether you really belonged to any of it! Fantasies of far-off lands and castles may have been closer to the truth, or at least a spiritual and past-life truth.

As a teenager, your tantrums could have been legendary – hardly an endearing quality, but sometimes the only way to get attention is to create a drama. Or perhaps it was diverting the attention away from those you thought had had enough of it already?

As a parent, you're likely to be great fun. Your children will love the fact that you can play the same games as them and with the same gusto, throwing yourself into dressing up, using funny voices when you read them stories and generally being their full-on entertainment manager!

Creating a busy home and making sure there is a lot of colour and activity isn't just for the kids. Whether you have children or not, your home is an important part of who you are and you will spend a lot of time letting the world know it. Your mates are likely to find your extravagant tastes amusing, though some might be hurt by the fact that you're proud of your extravagance and you even take things to the extreme now and again to test them.

If you have a family feud, take care not to allow it to go on and on. The longer it does, the more likely it is that ambassadors will be recalled, and it will take a very long time to re-establish connections. Being king sometimes means saying sorry even when it wasn't your fault.

Health

This is a robust and healthy placement for the Moon, but your cardiovascular system is the thing you need to pay particular attention to, so yes, that does mean lots of aerobic workouts, and if you can really feel the burn rather than focus on how great you look in that designer gym outfit, you should stay healthy when your peers are making their way to sick bay.

Life Skills

It's clear you have a Moon sign that won't be messed with, one of great power and influence, and power and influence are probably things you've been used to in past lives. The trick in this life is to use your charm to create the world you want to live in rather than allow others to use your abilities to make what *they* want happen.

Think about what you can organize or get out of other people that nobody else can and why you do it: to help them. Your life skills are to oversee what's going on but also to act when needed. Even though you won't be getting your hand down the toilet anytime soon, you're happy to make sure it's done and could talk a countess into helping out.

Stumbling Blocks

Perhaps the one thing you may be accused of more than anything else is being egotistical, and it's true, you are likely to have an ego bigger than most, but it's that very thing that makes you stand out, so really it's learning how to show that as confidence rather than arrogance that could be the stumbling block.

Often you're displaying it because you're not actually sure what to do next and you think that if you look as if you're sure of yourself nobody will notice. They may not notice your insecurity, but when you try too hard, you overcompensate, so better to admit you need help; humility beats arrogance every single time.

You're the actor of Moon signs and sometimes you will put on a show to impress, to get people to like you or perhaps just to entertain them, but they will take this as your authentic self and you could end up pretending to be what they want you to be forever.

Remember, stumbling blocks are lessons waiting to be learned. Think about changes you can make to let your fabulous true self shine.

Spiritual Lesson

There are all sorts of rulers – there are tyrants and there are benevolent and much-loved monarchs. Which will you be? Your spiritual lesson is to wield your power for the betterment of not only yourself but also those around you. Whilst that might sound grand, why shouldn't it be so? If you're given a gift, it can be given back freely or it can be overpriced and overtly about you and how fabulous you are. Your spiritual lesson is to make that choice.

SUN SIGN, MOON SIGN

So now you know a little more about your Moon sign, but how does that work with your Sun sign?

Sun Aries, Moon Leo

With double Fire energy you're hardly likely to be the quiet sort; in fact if there's a commotion somewhere, you're likely to be at the heart of it. That's not necessarily a bad thing – you can create havoc for sure, but you're an instigator of many a creative idea and can motivate a team like nobody else.

Like all those who stand out from the crowd, you're easily damaged by the dissenters, those who won't applaud no matter how well you perform, and that could cause you to go into full-on tantrum mode, which may not do you any favours. Learning how to channel your amazing energy without assuming everyone will agree could be a challenge in life, but once mastered, the combination of grabbing what life can bring you and letting go of those who don't want to come with you could be very useful indeed.

In love, you're a passionate individual and any partner or would-be partner should be ready to throw themselves into the relationship 100 per cent. You don't do half-measures.

Sun Taurus, Moon Leo

What any Leo Moon needs in their chart is some Earth to bring them into line, so this combination works well and offers all that dramatic, creative and powerful Moon energy somewhere to go and good strong foundations to support the building of great things.

Fiery energy mixed with earthy practicality means you can finish projects instead of leaving them half-done, and professionally you will be very successful, no matter what you choose to do, although working in the performing arts – everything from running a theatre to being on stage – could be particularly good for you. Whatever you choose, never underestimate your ability to lead, inspire and get the job done.

In love, you're the real deal and want the security of a committed relationship. You give loyalty and want it returned. Woe betide any partner who strays even slightly from that path. When met with a half-bull, half-lion creature like you, they'd better know how to handle you or how to run!

Sun Gemini, Moon Leo

Sparkling wit and charm will bring you many things, and amongst them could be trouble if you don't watch out. Watch your mouth, basically, and if you're told to keep something secret, do just that, no matter what the dramatic effect or brownie points if you didn't! Gossip? You? Never.

A natural salesperson, you can convince anyone to go along with whatever it is you're selling. Your enthusiasm and chatter appeal to most people and they get carried away with it all. Get yourself a job on one of those home-shopping channels – you'll find it easy to talk about a fountain pen for half an hour and will shift more than anyone else. Alternatively, do something really useful and head up a charity or school.

In love, you want the ideal relationship and there will be plenty of practice along the way, but when you find 'the one', they are likely to be outgoing, able to keep up with your social flitting around (or maybe that's 'put up with it') and above all a great listener. Chat much? You?!

Sun Cancer, Moon Leo

The introvert Sun and extrovert Moon are a tricky combination. You could want to stay at home, but how are you going to reach your goals if you do, and you will have goals, big ones. Home doesn't have to be a place, and feeling secure needn't be a lock on the door – both can be about people, and it's likely you're home and secure when you're with those you love or you know they are only a phone call away.

One of your greatest challenges could be taking that first step into a world that needs to hear what you have to say or see what you can produce. That may sound a bit haughty, but a desire to show what you can do is far from it. You just know what you're here for and you're going to get on with it, but first you need to know you have a strong base to start from.

In love, you're the nurturing sort, the parent and guardian, and will protect your partner and expect the same in return. Those who don't stand up for you when you need them to won't last long, and you might even test them on it, consciously or not.

Sun Leo, Moon Leo

This is a double-dipped, sequin-covered, spangly, tap-dancing, 'Look at me!' kind of union that will no doubt have you surrounded by many friends and admirers. But are they there to be entertained *by* you or to entertain you? Probably both, but when they get it the wrong way round you could feel as if you're the one making all the effort, and should you find yourself falling out with friends, it's likely to be a massive drama.

The dramatic arts suit you well, but you don't have to have a stage to put on a performance. Sometimes even your closest friends won't know if you're being serious or playing for laughs. Of course you will revel in the fact that you can fool some of the people some of the time, but can you do it all of the time? Those who can see through your act will be rare, very rare. Does that make them a threat or an asset?

In love, anyone can see the real you is an asset. If they are wise, they will step back and let you get on with it, knowing they can't steal your limelight and not particularly wanting to. The worst choice for a partner would be a boyfriend who was prettier than you, or a girlfriend who got on far too well with your mates.

Sun Virgo, Moon Leo

On a good day you're a great guide, helping those who need assistance to reach their goals, and everything from cleaning someone's house when they're ill through to taking on a role as a teacher in the most difficult of circumstances is highly possible. And on a bad day? The finger-wagging 'Don't do it that way, do it this way, oops, told you so!' side might come out.

Usually, thankfully, you're in the middle, so whilst there are frustrations, your main aim is to be of service to others by inspiring them and showing them that a little enthusiasm and attention to detail can go a very long way.

In love, you're affectionate and want intimacy. To be shown how someone feels about you is important. If you're denied this (and it could simply be that your partner is busy), you can go down the martyr route: just listen to the slamming of that washing-machine door as you empty it *again*…! Learn to bring the fun times of Leo out from behind the serious side of Virgo.

Sun Libra, Moon Leo

Who wouldn't want to spend time around you? Witty, funny and full of character, you're the life and soul of any party, but what happens when the balloons are popped and everyone has left the building? Hopefully you turn to your partner and they help you tidy up as you talk about who said what to whom and just how fabulous you look in that designer outfit.

Yes, love, love, lovitty, love, love is what you're all about, and be it with your other half or your best mate, you don't want to be alone, thank you very much. The adoration of others is always very welcome, but those who show you false flattery don't know you very well, and your Leo Moon will leap out and growl at them if they do, causing you to give them one of your famous looks followed by a swift exit stage left.

In a relationship, you want romance. You *demand* romance. A partner who holds your hand in public and brings you another glass of champagne at just the perfect moment would be good too. When choosing a partner, choose wisely: you can fall in love with the idea of love rather than an individual, and that will lead to dramas.

Sun Scorpio, Moon Leo

A direct conversation will always clear the air, but sometimes those conversations can be hurtful, for you or another, but you're able to deal with that. This Sun–Moon mix brings you the ability to tackle tough questions and make critical decisions even if the path ahead is jagged.

You will have a need to stay out of sight and yet a desire to be centre stage – clearly not an easy mix. This is the superstar who wanders around in a crowd in dark glasses, saying, 'Yes, it's me, but don't talk to me.' If you bring these two opposites together, well, you could be that superstar. This combination is one of the most enigmatic there is. People will be drawn to you for inspiration, to follow you and to learn from you.

In love, you're passionate in every sense of the word, and finding a partner who loves you just as intensely is important, but you will shy away from very open and public displays of affection, preferring to keep that sort of thing behind closed doors. Change in your relationship is likely to be a dramatic affair – no quiet transition for you.

Sun Sagittarius, Moon Leo

An ambitious combination that encourages you to see the world and to learn from all it has to offer. When you've learned it, you're likely to want to talk about it and perhaps teach it. Be it philosophy, religion, travel or horse management, you're the expert!

Restraint isn't something you're likely to show very often. When you have money, you will spend it on luxury; when you have time, you will fill it with travel or seeking knowledge through books, attending the theatre or learning about different religions. Everything is likely to be big, including your heart. You are a generous sort, but try to keep something back for yourself now and again.

In a relationship, you will give your all and expect the same in return. To highlight this need for total commitment you will notice little things, like a partner who goes to the fridge for a drink and doesn't ask if you want one, and then make sure that little thing becomes a massive thing.

You love the good things in life and want to share them with a partner, so make sure you pick one who's prepared to travel. Those who like the sofa too much won't work well with you.

Sun Capricorn, Moon Leo

You really do like the finer things in life and will do everything you can to make sure you get them, and you will. Perhaps it will be late in life that you will have your greatest success, but whenever it comes, you're more likely to be your own boss than any other Leo Moon and Sun combination. Running your own empire will take more than just inspiring others, which you can do easily; it will take an understanding of practical matters and business acumen. But you have that too.

With a high regard for old-fashioned values but no fear of mixing them with a modern twist, you're able to play to those who want things to stay as they are as well as those who want to see new and creative ideas. This truly noble placement means you can swish about with the princes, but when it's needed you can wash up with the paupers as well – and then return to your palace!

In love, too, you have high standards, and any partner will have a lot to live up to. But once you settle and trust someone, your playful side comes out and so does your seriously funny sense of humour.

Your family will be everything to you and the inspiration to make the most of your ability to succeed.

Sun Aquarius, Moon Leo

The placement of opposite Sun–Moon signs is confusing. Will you be the monarch or the fool? Don't be misled by the word 'fool' – the fool may have been the only one at court who could truly say what was going on and get away with it. So the question really is whether you are taking a detached, perhaps autocratic route or using your sense of humour to make a very valid point?

Standing up for the little guy is something you could find yourself doing a lot; wherever this sort of injustice shows itself, you could be ready to step in and sort things out. Don't panic – you don't have to wear your pants over your tights and learn to fly. It's not superhuman to stand up for your fellow man or woman; it's how it's meant to be. And if things aren't how they're meant to be, you're going to say so.

In love, you're able to romance your partner or would-be love interest with words and grand gestures. You play the starring role and lead the chase, plan the amazing getaways and happy surprises and don't really expect them in return. Much!

Sun Pisces, Moon Leo

A sense of purpose is only useful if you're prepared to step out and meet it. Perhaps looking more closely at what it is and admitting to it would be a good start? You may be too humble for your own good. Looking at others and comparing yourself to them is a waste of your energy. You are unique and have gifts that are yours and yours alone. Using them rather than denying them could be challenging but hugely helpful.

An artistic individual who can create mental images that can then be transferred to paper, photography and film, you will find that when your Piscean vision sits with your Leo showmanship, transferring emotion onto a palette that can be used to colour your world and that of others is truly your gift. Make something of it.

In love, you're really one of the most romantic combinations, and your ability to look ethereal and alluring should mean you're not short of offers. When you decide on your knight in shining armour, they should have the qualities of a true knight: honour, nobility and dignity. And look great in a T-shirt and jeans.

VIRGO MOON

*'Be regular and orderly in your life, so that you may be
violent and original in your work.'*

FLAUBERT

Archetype

The accountant. The one taking stock of where you are, what
you have and what you want to make of it all, keeping order and
striving to be what you know you can be. You have the ability to
make the most of your organizational skills and to let those around
you know what your goals really are. This Moon is all about auditing
your emotions and using them to best effect: feel them, analyse
them, deal with them.

VIRGO MOON ♍

The Moon isn't at her happiest in this sign, she's fidgety and nervous,
and you might deal with emotions in much the same way – not
sure what to do or say or where to be to make things work out for
the best. Action could be buried under worry about getting things
right; in fact the best thing might be to do nothing at all. It won't
work anyway, so why bother?

Well, that's a great start, isn't it?! Don't panic – there are plenty
of ways to deal with the above, as well as many blessings to your
Moon, and we will get to them, but in order to do that these
tendencies need to be outed. By bringing them out of the closet

you can take a really good look at them and learn to make them work for you. Seem impossible?

What you're really good at is analysing things, and when it comes to analysing yourself, you're especially good at it. Self-help books abound when you're around, and going through those lists of things to do to understand yourself better will go some way to making things easier for you, but you must practise what you learn rather than just having the knowledge and doing nothing with it.

When things get in the way of your goals, you could find yourself nit-picking over who said what to whom and why they were wrong and if you did it this way things would be better, 'but what about *her*, she doesn't do it that way and everyone *loves* her, I do it and nobody thinks anything of it…' Calm down. Take a deep breath, check where you are and where you want to be, and use your amazing organizing skills to get there without worrying about what anyone else is doing.

What other people think of you could rule your decisions, and letting that get out of hand is to be avoided if you can. You bring the need to be of service to others with you – the choice of a Virgo Moon has given you that – but serving is different from allowing the judgements of others to affect you negatively. Learning to let that go could mean letting go of your own judgements. If you don't do it, you will tell your subconscious that other people don't do it, and surprise, surprise, the magic of the universe will mean that other people actually *won't* do it.

Your mates will come to you when they need to have it told how it really is rather than wrapped up in fluffy stuff, and you will be able to give them some sound advice, but watch where you stop, as advice is one thing and interference another. Friends may also come to you when they are ill. You have a natural healing ability and may choose a career in nursing and care working as a consequence. Working as teacher or in a vet's practice would suit you well too.

Your process for problem-solving is likely to be very logical, and as long as you can stay away from the more challenging aspects of this Moon that were mentioned earlier, you can sort things out more quickly than most. Watch your tendency to get bogged down in the details rather than look at the bigger picture, though, and being critical of others in a shared project isn't a bad thing, but if you start to wag your finger and assume nobody can do anything right except you, you could end up with more to do, and that could start a downward spiral into fidgety land.

Writing is something you're likely to enjoy, perhaps even editing other people's work and delighting in debate over just where that comma should go. You might actually be the sort of individual who takes their pen to mistakes in menus or marches into shops and tells the owners where they can stick their apostrophe.

Instead of letting an issue go round and round in your head, gathering mutterings and harrumphs, spit it out. Don't let things fester or eventually they will pop with an almighty splodge that could leave those around you backing off and none too excited about getting involved in any projects with you again. Say things little and often rather than in one big eruption.

Your social conscience is likely to be very well developed, and getting involved in local politics may be something that interests you, but if you do, make sure you follow through on your ideas and don't allow others to take the credit for them. That really won't go down well with you, and neither should it, but will you say so at the time?

When dealing with facts and figures (and you're likely to), you won't assume that what you have been told is right unless you know it to be so. Those who produce reams of graphs and charts will amuse you, and you're likely to do the same, but unless you have produced those figures yourself, you won't trust them. Presentations at work are likely to be thorough and meticulously planned, but watch out for sub-section three, phase two, rules is rules overload. PowerPoint is your friend.

You will love your home. All Earth sign Moons adore being at home. Your home offers you security and comfort, and woe betide anyone who dares arrange the beans with the labels facing the wrong way. Talking of beans, healthy food is your thing too, and an array of organic this, that and the other as well as magnetic mattresses and ionizers may be part of your healthy home set-up.

Financially, your accountancy skills will help you keep things balanced and you're likely to be canny with money. That's not to say you're mean with it at all – in fact you're generous with friends – but any gifts will be well thought-out and funny first. How much they cost is likely to be secondary and not exceeding a tenner. Just saying.

Like your fellow Earth Moon Taurus, you will love your garden, and if you don't have one you will love the great outdoors. Being part of nature will feed your soul and help you process your emotions too. If you find yourself with some tough choices to make, get to the forest, walk in the hills or stick your hands in that plant pot – anything to connect to the power of Mother Earth.

Virgo has a reputation for being a very tidy sign and you might think that's not you at all. Some Virgo Moons *are* untidy, as are some Virgo Suns, but your ability to find order in your own chaos will be extraordinary, and others trying to tidy it up for you could be something you really don't like at all. You will have a system, even if your system looks like chaos to others.

You may not want to be at the forefront at work and would prefer to work behind the scenes whilst some sparkling wit takes all the glory. Richard Branson's PA would be a great job for you: he does all the prancing about, but everyone knows just who runs the show.

In a relationship, things might appear the same way: your partner could be louder than you, but everyone knows who is paying the bills and choosing the pants.

The eternal student, you enjoy learning new things and could have several books on the go at once, as well as several theories on a pet subject. You will come up with your unique take on things once all the facts and figures are in. And when faced with a so-called expert in their field you will grill them on their subject to prove to yourself that they can be trusted. You would make a great research analyst.

Love Life

Your sense of duty will also be expressed in a relationship. That's fine as long as it is reciprocated by your partner; if it isn't, you could find you're basically the maid. You don't mind being in the background making sure things run smoothly, of course, and if your other half is in a high-pressured job (and they often can be), you're happy to play your part. What you won't be happy with is being taken advantage of, and you certainly shouldn't be. Learn to speak up when things are getting a little one-sided. Tell His Royal Highness the staff are having a night off and get dinner booked.

Sex isn't the be-all and end-all for you. That doesn't mean you live like a monk, by the way, it's just that you don't need to be swinging from the chandelier twice nightly with a day off on Sundays. I am resisting the missionary position joke that's associated with Virgo, and so should you, it's no joke if you're a missionary. Perhaps you simply find the whole thing a little too messy and undignified?

When looking for a partner, you're likely to be drawn to someone who has practical skills. They may be older than you, and someone who is slightly more extrovert than you without tipping over into Liberace mode would be preferable. They should have a great sense of humour and make you laugh, but without resorting to bawdy barrack-room ballads. You don't do coarse. Unless it's pâté, and even then it has to be on a refined biscuit.

If things aren't going well with a relationship, let it unfold in its own time rather than worry about who said what and when and end up creating a scenario that eventually will come true because, consciously or not, you have driven it that way. Better to use your critical brain to step back, look at the facts and deal only in those facts without creating those worry-monster visions.

A partner who respects you, who values your opinion and will support you no matter what choices you make isn't impossible to find, and when you stick to what you're looking for rather than compromise, things will come your way and work your way. That's probably not only about your love life, it has to be said – it could go for any part of your Virgo Moon life.

Partnering a Virgo Moon

Your Virgo Moon will need validation that they are playing their part. No doubt they are, but sometimes they will question that and wonder if what they are doing is of value. They value loyalty, give loyalty and expect it in return.

If there are difficulties in a relationship, things need to be addressed straight away. Leaving them to stew will create a mighty big pot of the stuff to sort out later. Sup up.

Best fit Sun signs are Virgo, Capricorn, Taurus and Pisces.

Career

You're good with your hands and anything that requires you to make things would suit you well, from bread to bedsteads and all points in between. You're also very good with money, sorting out other people's money in particular, so you could get paid for looking at what others get paid and what they do with it! Bonus. Some of these roles could also be part-time. Your ability to earn pretty much what you want is based on what time you want to give to the working part of your life.

When working with others, you will see their flaws very quickly. That can be very useful, of course, but how you handle it and indeed *if* you handle it is the question, for that takes diplomacy and you may not be the most diplomatic type.

You work best in the company of people who have something to say for themselves, something more than what they had for their tea and what happened in last night's soaps. You're not interested in trivia, especially not at work, and whilst gossip is something you will listen to, you won't repeat it or get involved in any whispering in corners. Work is work, you're there to get it done, get home and get to enjoying all the things you work for.

Parents and Family

Your mum or perhaps both parents may have been strict – dinner at a certain time, homework done of course, in your jim-jams by seven, bed by eight, and all this at 16 years old! The pressure to be perfect may have been felt early on and holding your achievements up against those of your siblings or classmates may have been a favourite pastime of your parents. Later in life your mother could have become hypercritical of your choices or it could have been very difficult for you to understand hers.

Your father may have been your role model, the one who showed you what worked and what didn't, and his own work ethic is likely to have been something you admired. Whilst your mother was running the home like clockwork, your father would probably have been the one upsetting that routine, and always with a sweetie in his pocket for you, even if it wasn't treat day.

The home is likely to have been well organized and run, without much luxury but without much money wasted either, and it will have been instilled in you that if you can't afford it, you shouldn't have it. Your parents aren't likely to have been big on credit for big ticket items.

With your own children, you may be strict and encourage them to do well at school, overlooking their need to play for the sake of it. Having said that, some Virgo Moons look on their children as the perfect way to express their own need to play and actively encourage them to play as long as they too can let go and have some fun!

You may be very fussy over what's served up at family mealtimes and your children may have a no chocolate rule, at least until the weekend. You will encourage them to work things out for themselves and won't always give them the answers they seek, helping them problem-solve from a very early age.

Wiping your feet before coming into the house or even taking your shoes off is to be advised when visiting a Virgo Moon home, and expect to see at least one furry creature in it, and I am talking about cats and dogs rather than Uncle Bob and his beard.

Health

If you're not well, think about where the dis-ease is coming from. What has upset your nervous system and is now manifesting as an illness? You're likely to suffer from itchy skin, sore tummies and headaches, which are all associated with stress and strain.

To maintain good health, keep eating healthy food, which you tend to do anyway, but also incorporate some exercise into your routine. Yoga or perhaps *tai chi*, something that calms the mind as well as tests the body, would suit you well.

Life Skills

An ability to know intuitively what people are thinking, to figure them out and to have their next step already plotted on your radar is a great skill to have, but allow that next step to manifest before you go planning the next six moves.

You can reorganize people's lives as well as their wardrobes, and using that skill could bring you money and recognition, but can you use it on your own life? With your knicker drawer most definitely, but emotionally you may have to use another skill – your ability to self-analyse – before making any changes.

Stumbling Blocks

Your Moon is emotional, not logical. It won't put things in boxes for you – you have to be the one who does that. This means that if not checked, your Moon could run off with an idea or go to town on a scenario and your emotions could feed off the images you create, getting bigger and bigger and possibly out of control. So, take control, feel the emotion and deal with the emotion.

Self-criticism is a big stumbling block for you. You're too fat, too thin, too old, too stupid, too this, that or the other – but is any of it true? No. You can do whatever you want to do, so perhaps the easiest way to think about it is that the biggest stumbling block is you.

Faith in your abilities will come slowly – and you can deal with slowly, so that's a good thing – but giving up too early is also a Virgo Moon trait. Persevere – you're worth it.

Spiritual Lesson

Perhaps you have had past lives where you have been cloistered, with bells to tell you when to eat and when to pray, or you have had simple lives where things weren't as complicated as they appear to be in this modern world. *Appear to be.* Actually, this life needn't be complicated either. Simplifying your life and removing the fuss and worry could be a spiritual lesson for you and an opportunity to let yourself blossom into the rose you're meant to be.

SUN SIGN, MOON SIGN

So now you know a little more about your Moon sign, but how does that work with your Sun sign?

Sun Aries, Moon Virgo

Do you really know where you're heading or are you rushing to be anywhere other than where you are now? This stop–start line-up needs careful handling if you're to achieve your goals. Using it wisely means having the idea (being first to have the idea usually) and then, without fear or worry about the 100 different things that could go wrong, starting to plan the easiest way to put it into practice.

Having confidence in your ability to succeed is important. That's really having confidence and not just telling everyone that you have. To be the absolute best at what you do, gain as much knowledge as you can and practise, practise, practise. Having that solid grounding will make you unstoppable.

In love, you might desire the roses round the door and two kids, but would that satisfy you? Perhaps mountain bikes in the back garden, a muddy 4x4 on the drive and an adventure weekend with your partner and the kids are more your style?

When looking for romance, seek a partner who is able to join in the adventure but can also calm your worries and be the rock that allows you to climb.

Sun Taurus, Moon Virgo

A sound builder, proceeding steadily, brick by brick, with method and attention to detail, you can achieve anything you set your mind to, but first you might have to leave the sofa. Once you get going, it's impossible to stop you, but first you need the motivation, and that can only come from you. What do you want to achieve?

Working with food, property, animals or in the health industry would suit you well.

You could find yourself going over old ground because you don't quite believe or trust in what you have been told. That's fine, but if you find yourself going over and over stuff you have done yourself, that's a lack of belief in yourself. Writing things down and having copious numbers of lists will help.

In love, all you want is perfection. It's not much to ask. Well, actually it is, and letting your other half off the hook now and again will make things easier. So what if they didn't put the towel back on the rail the correct way? What you want are cuddles, security and to be safe in the knowledge that they adore you. Towels? Not that important. Really.

Sun Gemini, Moon Virgo

If your mind were a cake, it would be one of those with everything in it, like rocky road, full of marshmallows and little nutty bits. Your ability to leap from one subject to another but still maintain an excellent grasp of all is a gift, but it can also be the very thing that drives you to distraction. Making a choice is based on asking questions, isn't it, but questions bring answers and more questions, and so you go on. Make a choice.

Nothing will be good enough for you and you may overdo things, turning what was perfectly fine into something that's hard for others to understand by overloading it with too many facts and figures. However, working in the media suits you well – publishing, newspapers and television, for example.

In love, you're hard work, as emotionally you need to work out the motive behind everything your other half says or does, but once you let go of that and start to live in the moment rather than several moments all at once, you appreciate them more.

When looking for love, you are looking for someone who is very good-looking, as perfect as you can get, but what about their listening skills? Better be good too.

Sun Cancer, Moon Virgo

The mother hen is a role you're happy to take on and your natural nurturing side needs that outlet, but when you find yourself worrying about some of your chicks a little bit too much, perhaps it's time to learn where the boundaries lie. If you become too involved, you could turn 'mother' into 'smother', and those you've been trying to help might just see you as interfering, again. Set boundaries.

You're a refined individual who won't want to listen to what her from next door has been up to at the weekend with the ice-cream van driver and how you can never look a 99 in the face again. Remove yourself from the gossip, or the foul-mouthed den of sailors that some call the staff canteen, and get some air, get some nature and let her nurture your soul with beauty.

In love, you're truly supportive of your other half and happiest when feeding them, in fact feeding the entire family and having them all together. When looking for love, look for an old-fashioned sort. Anyone remotely radical won't really suit you. If you're not in a relationship and don't really want one, get a cat. That love has got to go somewhere!

Sun Leo, Moon Virgo

This combination makes you the really cool maths teacher, the one who can convey a tricky subject whilst making it seem like fun and looking fabulous! In an effort to make sure everything is perfect, you could make a drama out of it all, but when it comes to the performance, nobody will be allowed to notice that bit of it.

You need a stage, somewhere to shine and somewhere for you to get the validation you need to let you know that you're on the right track and everyone values what you do. A need to be of service to others is a good thing, but make sure you don't take it so far that you forget to be of service to your own self and have some fun just for the sake of it.

In a relationship, you are likely to be the ruler of all you survey, and a partner who has a shinier light or better hair than you just won't do. Seek a partner who is fun to be with but knows that when the curtain goes up, you're the star. Plenty will be only too happy to play the supporting role in your life. You inspire adoration and I suspect you won't be short of offers.

Sun Virgo, Moon Virgo

Whilst sitting at your desk with your giant quill pen taking down notes about who said what to whom, what's been spent on the shopping this week and just what is she wearing, you're observing every detail of your life and the lives of those around you. You're not sitting in judgement, though, just observing so that when asked you can step in and help the best you can.

You're generous with your time, but those you are helping had better be ready to listen. To ask for your assistance is to get the whole package, not just a snippet of advice; you will analyse their motivation through to a positive outcome. Perhaps channelling that in a professional role would help. Jobs as business analysts, crisis managers and secret shoppers suit you very well.

In love, you're the sentimental sort. You want to make sure everyone knows you are there for them and that your partner feels you're not only a lover but a best friend and excellent cook too. If you're not appreciated, you might still stay in a relationship, as you believe working hard at it will solve any problems, but where is the limit?

When looking for love, look for someone who is well grounded and has a very nice and very sensible anorak.

Sun Libra, Moon Virgo

As you watch that supermodel walk down the catwalk, are you looking at the clothes and how they are cut or is it the way she walks that intrigues you? Just how does she manage to look so composed when all eyes are on her? You're a watcher and a quick learner, and never more so than where beauty is concerned. You could find yourself working in the arts, and fashion is of course high art.

You only want to see beauty, but there are times when you will have to get the toilet cleaned and make sure Mr Schnookums doesn't leave little presents in the park. That's the dog by the way, not the boyfriend. You get the unpleasant stuff done quickly, leaving room for the nice stuff, and where possible you get someone else to do it for you.

In a relationship, you truly want to help your other half to be all that they can be and are happy to support their ideas as long as they include you in negotiations from the start. You're very big on debating; in fact if anyone thinks they can better you, they might want to think again.

When looking for love, look for someone refined, talkative and happy to wait for an hour or two whilst you get ready to go out. Just saying.

Sun Scorpio, Moon Virgo

Hoocha magoocha! You're fierce and ready to take on the world, and with a mind that's razor sharp and a personality that can force its way into or indeed out of any situation it pleases, you really are a force to be reckoned with. And when you reckon you're onto a good thing, whether at work or in your personal life, your tenacity and well-thought-out plans will make sure you get it.

A strong sense of what's right and what's wrong and a desire to have some big questions answered makes you a great politician, whether that really is in government or in the office. You can see how things are moving and who is making them shake and can make the most of it.

A strong moral code means you won't settle for half-measures and won't entertain those who think it's OK to bend the rules. Happily, you can spot them a mile away. Avoid.

In love, you're a physical individual who needs intimacy in a relationship, but your need to know how much you're valued goes beyond the bedroom and your partner will have to appreciate the things you do to keep order in the home too.

When looking for love, think powerful, attractive and able to rewire a plug properly.

Sun Sagittarius, Moon Virgo

You might want two of those, three of them and you'll take the whole box of those over there, thank you, but then you start to wonder where it is all going to go and how you can make sure it's all put away tidily. Wanting lots of things is OK, but knowing what you're going to do with them when you get them home is another.

A Fire and Earth mix, as you have, works best by employing the passion and drive of Fire to start something and then the methodical approach of Earth to make sure the job is seen through to the end. As you go along, you will learn more about your subject, and education is what you seek, formal or informal. You may even work in education, with travel and religious or spiritual pursuits a close second.

This need for knowledge may not be formalized, and travel could fulfil your need for a greater understanding of the world in which you live. Travelling with a companion will help you bounce ideas and different philosophies around and lead to some interesting conversations and perhaps an opportunity to show off your worldly knowledge.

In love, you will have to form a very strong mental bond with your other half and any desires beyond that will depend on this link. A relationship for you is about the totality of mind and body.

Looking for love? Think Indiana Jones – adventure and intellect.

Sun Capricorn, Moon Virgo

Whilst quoting the regulations, think about whether or not someone has had a bad morning. Are they in the best place to have someone tell them exactly where they are going wrong? Is that any of your concern? Rules are rules. You're not without compassion, but if people know what they have let themselves in for and continue to break the promises they have made, they should know about it.

It's not just with others that you can be so fixed – you are your own worst critic, and any imperfection could see you throw away weeks of work and start again.

Being harsh on yourself can be tempered by surrounding yourself with friends who aren't so fixed on the rules but don't absolutely trash them either. Having fun is important, and letting your extremely dry sense of humour out for an airing away from work will remind those around you of why you're so appealing.

In a relationship, you need to feel totally secure before you really open up, and talking about your emotions may be a challenge. If you share your concerns with a partner, they should help you in a safe and nurturing way.

When looking for love, you might choose partners who share the qualities of one of your parents, particularly your father.

Sun Aquarius, Moon Virgo

With your pragmatic approach and ability to step back and work out rationally what's going on, you won't be caught up very often in the emotions of a situation. Take care that this approach doesn't create an image of superhuman strength when all you actually want is for someone to say 'Sorry, can I help?' or 'I love you.' Or offer a cuddle. Physical intimacy with family and friends may not be how you show you care, but you will be the first to sort out their problems, arrange a spreadsheet and get them to the right authorities to help with their issues.

A need to be slightly – oh alright, overtly – eccentric fights with your inner desire to play strictly by the rules, but when a balance is struck, your mad professor meets your careful accountant and your ideas not only work but work very well indeed. You may be interested in a role as a business analyst, scientist or very fine astrologer.

Your love life might be a real challenge. The convention of marriage may seem like a business partnership to you, and business partners aren't likely to be the sort that book a room at a romantic destination and only pack a toothbrush and a feather duster. Suits you fine.

If you're looking for a partner, think school teacher with too much marking to do to worry about all that messy nonsense.

Sun Pisces, Moon Virgo

Being so heavenly minded that you're no earthly good is something you need to avoid. Having your feet very firmly on the ground is actually the gift of this combination and being born on a full Moon will help you recognize when it's time to let go of dreams that are never going to fly and deal with the practicalities of realizing the ones that will. Order and structure are what's needed – not to drag your idealistic and dreamy side down, but to help those dreams come to fruition.

With this combination, those who work with images – photography, film and television – can successfully transfer their vision into something we can all see. Poetry may also be an interest, along with anything connected to complementary medicine and spiritual health.

You don't like people who are outright rude and usually you will simply avoid them rather than say anything, but if you can't avoid them you're likely to read them their own horoscope in such a way that they can't be offended and often do make some changes, around you at least!

In love, you want perfection – all heaving bosoms and wet riding breeches as Mr Darcy rises from the lake. That bloke from Packing heading towards you with a kebab in one hand and his mobile phone number in the other won't do it. It's a poet, a romantic, a true lover not a fighter you're looking for. Wait, they are out there!

If you're already in a relationship, don't wait for your other half to instigate romance, get to it yourself.

LIBRA MOON

'To love for the sake of being loved is human, but to love for the sake of loving is Angelic.'

Alphonse De Lamartine

Archetype

The angel. So maybe you don't feel that angelic, and often you really feel as if you're the other end of the scale, but to those around you, when you're at your best, your love will shine through and they will see that in you more than anything else. When you ping across to the other side – and you will – perhaps you're still an angel, but more of the avenging sort. Either way, angel it is.

LIBRA MOON ♎

When you tip your halo towards a goal, there's not a lot that will stop you from achieving it. Other people's opinions, lack of cash, the wrong shoes on, all mean nothing – if it's what you want, you're going to flap those wings and smile that smile until you get it.

You're very persuasive and extremely good in a debate. Bringing people around to your way of thinking is a heavenly gift, and the more you use it, the more you hone it. You're not going to step over the line of what's right, but what's right is a judgement you will make, and you can justify yourself in the face of even your most fervent critics. You're very handy to have around if a case must be put that needs persistence and a well-thought-out argument.

Having people around you is important, and be they best friend or partner, you will do better when you have that support. Now that doesn't mean you can't do things on your own, but if you don't have to, you will avoid it.

When friends pop round for a chat, you will enjoy catching up with gossip and are happy to help them if there's anything they need to discuss, but really, two hours? You can get bored of other people's chit-chat if it goes on, and on, and on, so why not talk about yourself for a bit?

When you're travelling, or perhaps away for work, you prefer some quality to your accommodation and to the way you travel. It may not all be first class, but it's going to have to be pretty classy to get you excited. The thought of a five-star holiday with first-class travel would have you over the Moon. This doesn't make you a snob, it makes you appreciative of the good things in life, and when you're talking about your trip, those who may think you're above your station will very quickly realize you're just excited by it all, like a child. An angelic child.

You may have to watch a tendency to be waspish when you're in company that doesn't particularly thrill you, however, especially if you have an Air sign as your Sun. Perhaps the people you are talking to have dirty clothing on, or appear to be wearing cheap jeans, or maybe they haven't noticed how amazing you are? Be careful what you say; better still, try to appreciate that not everyone has your class and pizzazz and appreciate the goodness in them. It will be there, promise.

Fashion might interest you, high end of course, but you will also be drawn to the beauty industry, or anywhere there's glamour. Your ability to charm your clients into spending loads of money on that must-have item will see you soar, and you do very well when you reach the upper ranks in your chosen profession. You're likely to live and breathe what you do.

A Libra Moon can sometimes cause extreme indecision, and as the Moon is an emotional planet, that can mean those around you aren't sure where they stand. For you, it's very simple: they should acknowledge you, remember you're heaven sent and remind you how much you are loved. The occasional gift now and again should do it.

On their part, those around you may not know how you feel because you've been blowing hot and cold and they aren't sure what to do next in case the big old black wings come out and thunderbolts fly. Temper? You? Not very often, but when it comes out, it really comes out.

As a social Moon sign, you will need to make emotional contact with lots of people, and your opposite-sex relationships will be just as close as those of the same sex. That's not a problem for you, but your other half might see it as one, particularly as you won't be able to stop yourself from flirting with anyone you know likes the cut of your cloth. If you're single, make sure any single friends know they are good friends but nothing more is likely to happen. Unless it is. Natch.

You probably enjoy music and will love to be surrounded by beautiful things. Expensive things perhaps, but not necessarily. At home you need peace and quiet, with candles lit and fragrances doing their stuff, and nothing suits you better than a night in with the full display of lights, textures, fragrances and of course chocolate. A sweet tooth could be a legacy of your Libra Moon. Perhaps you're simply unable to let the sweet trolley go past when you're out for a gourmet meal…

A fascination with cars – luxury cars – could be prevalent, and you will change your car often, each time going for something that little bit more fabulous than the last, with as many toys as you can get rammed into it. A girl needs some wheels and you will love showing them off to your mates. Mobile phones get the same treatment, with a new one every year, or more frequently if you can find a way to charm your phone company into it.

When asked for an opinion, your first thought might be to wonder what someone wants to hear rather than what you really think. Your natural diplomatic nature is likely to kick in, but pretty soon, as you listen to their drivel, you won't be able to help yourself, and you can get very animated if you feel they are being less than fair-minded. You're an adjuster – you will naturally want to balance things and won't stand by if someone is one-sided or, worse still, bigoted. Here comes your avenging angel: how dare people think they can talk like that, act like that and treat other human beings that way! You will find a way to sort things out, but perhaps you will then step back and let others take up the cause, which is probably how it should be. Just make sure that cause is based on facts. If you go off at full speed with anything less, you may have to walk back slowly doing a lot of apologizing along the way.

When you've had a hard day angeling, sit down on the sofa with the one you love or your best friend, have a glass of wine, light a few candles, perhaps open a little box of chocolates or two to keep things sweet and then chat away. Heaven.

Love Life

We all need respect in a relationship, but you need to see it daily, just as you need to hear the words 'I love you' on a regular basis, and are likely to say them frequently too. Make sure they don't become so commonplace that your partner answers with a simple 'I know.' That's just not good enough! What you want is 'I love you too', but sometimes overuse produces an automatic response. This doesn't mean they *don't* love you, not in the slightest; what it means is they know you love them and you should know they love you too, so how about trusting in that and getting on with it?

On the other hand, a lover who understands you well enough will indulge your need to hear those three little words because they know that it's important to you. It all depends on moods, attitudes and whether they are halfway through reading an important document and you're just a bit bored. Just saying.

If you're caught in an argument with your other half, you need to be right, even if you know you're not *totally* right, and will carry on until they concede. *If* they concede. Take great care in heated debates in relationships. Arguing over whose turn it is to take out the bins is rarely going to be about bins, it's usually about one partner feeling that they are doing more than the other and could use some help. Why not start at the root of the problem, gently, and use your ability to charm your partner rather than thrash about in the branches trying to get their attention?

Sexually, you can be a great lover, and the intimacy you have on a mental level can be transferred into a fulfilling and deep relationship. Without that link, you may appear too cool, and your other half could interpret that as you not wanting intimacy when actually what you want is to be chatted up and rolled around the front room until it looks as though you've been burgled.

If you're looking for love, you will want that instant love-at-first-sight feeling, but don't discount those who grow on you too. A sudden flash, a connection, is what tells you someone is for you, and if you follow that instinct rather than thinking, 'They look nice in that designer top,' you won't go far wrong.

Look for a Prince or Princess Charming who believes in their principles rather than just wears the costume.

Partnering a Libra Moon

When they say, 'I love you,' say, 'I love you too, baby, more than anything in the whole wide world.' *Don't* say, 'I know and what's for tea?' Woo your Libra Moon no matter how long you have known them and make sure that every day you let them know what they mean to you. Talk to them, find out how their day has gone, engage and be genuinely interested in what's been happening. Then open a box of chocolates and take a tumble round the bedroom. Nice.

Best fit Sun signs are Libra, Aquarius, Gemini and Aries.

Career

With such good taste and an eye for the aesthetically pleasing, you need a role that will help you express your creativity. Fashion, beauty, interior design, high-end chocolatier would be good (provided you don't eat the profits).

Another route you could take is counselling. This could be as a relationship counsellor, psychotherapist, lawyer or even family planning adviser – anywhere you're able to help others see both sides of an argument or to fight for one side over another, to debate and win. In court, for example. Using your skills to relate to others is something that could make you money.

Catering may also appeal to you, though of course that's not catering as in the Wok's Wong, where, although they do fantastic spring rolls, you might have to stir-fry all day, but catering as in host at the Ritz, or maybe working in a PR position in some swanky hotel where all you have to do is entertain, charm and take that booking. You can do that. Easy.

Just stay away from anything that involves dirt or grime. Yuck.

Parents and Family

As the Moon symbolizes mother, home and early childhood experiences, she is an important planet when helping you understand all things family.

With a Libra Moon your relationship with your mother may have been a tense one. Discussions between the two of you could have been hot-tempered, with each of you digging in on the side of right, and that may continue to this day. When you were growing up, your mum could have been so focused on other things that you could have felt left out and even neglected, though you probably always knew she loved you. Maybe now you realize that whilst sending you off to school without any lunch was tough, it was because she was so caught up trying make ends meet that her mind was elsewhere.

The home environment is likely to have been a quiet place full of books – colouring-in ones for you and poetry or cinema ones for Mum. With a full parade of aunts and uncles, friends and family wandering through, it would never have been dull, though, and this may have left you with a need for a quiet and peaceful family home rather than one full of loud music or the sounds of inner-city life.

If you have siblings, here too you might feel there's a lot left unsaid. Perhaps you have tried to bring things up and they will have none of it? Maybe they have let go and you aren't at that stage yet, either unwilling or unable to forgive and forget and move on. You need to know that any injustices have been noted and where possible put right, with an apology perhaps. Sometimes, however, things that are important to one person just aren't that important to another.

You're likely to surround your own children with love, place them in a great big pink bubble of gorgeousness and offer them guidance and a strong idea of what's right and wrong. While encouraging them to stand up for themselves when challenged, you will also no doubt clothe them in some amazing little designer numbers from a very early age.

As for your home, make it a sanctuary, a place of peace, a place where great nights in with friends happen and where you and your partner can get up close and personal surrounded by beauty and the good things in life, fresh flowers and lovely scents. And keep it tidy!

Health

Problems with kidneys, eyes, ears and breathing are areas to watch out for. Maintaining good health around them is important, but remember that being a Libra Moon doesn't indicate you *will* have issues in these areas.

You may also experience health problems through overeating, and getting a balance between what you eat and how you exercise is important. Yes, it is for everyone, but more so for you and that sweet tooth of yours. Be careful of too much alcohol and perhaps smoking, as they are two social activities and you do like to be out and about. Now I sound like your mother!

Life Skills

Even though you have a Moon that likes the company of at least one other person, you are able to run your life on your own. A partner is exactly that, not a provider. You're happy to pay your share and could find that life requires you to be independent as part of your karmic journey. That doesn't necessarily mean living on your own, though you can if required, more that you have a natural ability to look after number one if you have to.

You can be very focused on a cause and if you put that to good use you can raise a lot of money for your favourite charity, or raise the profile of your company, or perhaps help a friend promote their business.

Your greatest skill has to be your ability to charm those you come into contact with, to have them believe in you and what you say you will achieve. Make sure that you can stick to that plan and that even if someone upsets you, you can continue without bearing any grudges.

Stumbling Blocks

Your ability to see both sides of the coin is a positive one, but sometimes you may be tempted to play double agent, to get caught in the middle by taking both sides rather than remaining neutral. If you're caught out, you could be accused of being two-faced, and even though you were trying to help, that might not be how others see it. Best to stay neutral.

Arguing with your inner self can cost you time and perhaps a relationship, job or those amazing shoes you saw in the sales. Is it worth all that time spent going round and around, asking mates, discussing it with your dog, going online and yakking about things for days with your faceless book friends and finally coming to your conclusion, only to discover the love prospect has moved on, the job has gone and your best mate is wearing those shoes? Work on becoming faster at making choices and perhaps rely on logic now and again rather than allowing your inner debate to get out of hand.

Spiritual Lesson

Having chosen a Libra Moon for your birth Moon, you've brought with you a need to relate, to convince others, in a peaceful way, of your ideas and your thoughts, perhaps even beliefs. In past lives you may have been a warrior, focused on getting the job done no matter who or what got in your way. Now it's time to talk, to bring peace from understanding each other's point of view.

SUN SIGN, MOON SIGN

So now you know a little more about your Moon sign, but how does that work with your Sun sign?

Sun Aries, Moon Libra

This is a full Moon position, so your need to get the job done may be at odds with your desire to make sure everyone understands why you're doing it and will still love you when you're done. They will, won't they? They will. Sure?

The need to have that inner debate could be cut short by your impulsive side. You could suddenly get up, shouting, 'Enough is enough!' and rush into things without giving them too much thought. This see-saw effect between action and procrastination is annoying for you, and for those around you, but it's part of your process, so embrace it. In fact, laugh at it and own it.

In love, you're a devoted sort as long as you know your other half is as devoted, but what does it take to convince you? You may test them in a relationship and that will be something they notice very early on. When you're caught out, put your hands up and simply tell them you need to know you're loved. Get things out into the open, and quickly.

If you're looking for love, look for a go-getting, love-making, hot-tempered, passionate type.

Sun Taurus, Moon Libra

Are you in need of a cuddle? Come on, snuggle up and tell your Uncle David all about it. This is no weakness on your part, you're not looking for a 'there, there' sort of cuddle, what you want is to know that you're supported and that someone is listening to you, and you will use it as a way to process your ideas and come up with your next step.

A good listener yourself, and adept at putting others at their ease, you know that when they feel at ease with you they are more likely to listen to your demands as well as offload what it is they need from you – a great thing in business as well as in love.

Talking of which, a relationship is likely to be very important to you – that's to say having good connections with significant people in your life. With a partner, you're at your happiest, and the closeness you have with them is a cornerstone of your life. You will look for a partner who can help you build a secure and beautiful home, but watch out for stubbornness when you don't get your own way. Lean on your Libra Moon and negotiate rather than stand on your Taurean four legs and refuse to budge.

If you're looking for love, look for a gifted artist who happens to be successful. Easy!

Sun Gemini, Moon Libra

Double Air energy makes you talkative. That's kind of like saying, 'Eating 40 pizzas a day makes you gain weight.' It's inevitable, so how can you use it to your best advantage? Put down your mobile phone, step out of your car, leave the internet alone and avoid any conversations until you've really sorted out what you think rather than dashing here, there and everywhere saying what's on your mind that second. Because some people will take it as your opinion, rather than a work in progress.

Use your fast mind to advantage to deal with matters that need swift decisions. Don't allow yourself too much time to think about what has to happen, and avoid creating negative images. Feed positive ones in and you will get positive results out.

This can be a waspish combination, so if you are going to sting, take a step back and think about how it makes you look and whether using your forgiving side would put you in a better light.

In a relationship, you want gorgeous and social partners. When you get one, you might want an even fitter one! Put some work in and you will soon realize that nobody is absolutely perfect and balancing their imperfections with your own is what it's all about.

Sun Cancer, Moon Libra

Your home is your castle and when you're in it you're the ruler, the interior decorator and the chef. Busying yourself at home is one thing, but when the drawbridge goes down you really will have to enter the big wide world with the rest of us...

Here you're a great listener, an observer who could use those skills to commentate on society, or perhaps paint or write music or plays that reflect what you see. A good knowledge of history, perhaps of your own family, and a love of antiques could bring you some interesting people whom you will no doubt love to talk to.

In relationships, it may be a tough road for you. You could have at least a couple of major relationships in your life and deciding whether you're the parent or the child in a relationship could have your other half confused over whether they need to do as they are told or take charge and look after you. Of course you want both. So do most of us, but you may take the fact that you're not getting what you want to Moodyville instead of talking about it.

Sun Leo, Moon Libra

Get you! Just how fabulous can one person be? With an outgoing personality and an inner voice that helps you understand and relate to those around you, you certainly do have the X-factor in abundance. But isn't it hard being the centre of attention all the time? Don't you sometimes want to get away and just soak in a spa? Of course you do, and I am sure you do it as often as you can, but what do you think about in those quieter moments?

It's when you're alone that you can evaluate your performance, think about who is in your life and how best to make the most of those alliances, and all the time it's about making you number one, leader of the pack and ruler of all you survey, and that's not a bad motivation as long as you help those around you be all that they can be too, and you do.

In a relationship, you're an expensive addition to anyone's life, but happily you will chip in your contribution when it's needed and when it's asked for.

In the first flush of a relationship your suitors had better be able to show you a good time – a very, very good time. Your partner should learn very early on that if they flatter you, they get what they want too. A little praise and that new car is theirs!

Sun Virgo, Moon Libra

It's easy, isn't it, to deal with balance sheets and mortgage statements, taxes and rules? It's not quite so easy to deal with people who don't understand what you're trying to sort out, won't play by the rules and can't be bothered doing things the right way. That's not to say you *can't* do it – you can, and do it in a very cool, calm and collected way – but you really would rather not.

You're a good listener and probably use the power of silence when faced with a situation that requires tough choices. If you're silent, you know those you're talking to will fill that void, and when

114

they do, they will tell you things they otherwise might not. You're a very highly gifted communicator.

In a relationship, your 'Elbows off the table!' attitude might not be easy for others to understand. Choosing a partner who isn't the most flamboyant of sorts will help. You want someone who listens, someone who gives you time to think before you respond and someone who is happy to have fish on Friday, steak on Saturday and sex on schedule.

Sun Libra, Moon Libra

How you do you ever get anything done? Do you spend all day wondering if you should? What if you did this, what if you did that and would Bunnykins still wuv you if you did? Start with what *you* love and then think about what inspires you and where you truly want to be. Listen to your intuition and act without the drama and without the hours of debate. When you do, things move on — magically and usually in your favour.

You're good with people, they respond well to you and you to them, but when they get crass, rude or just plain common, you're not so keen. It's not that you're prissy, you just have standards, and really there's no need for that sort of behaviour. You're one of the beautiful people.

Having both your heart and mind in Libra brings you a need for a relationship. It's something that completes you, but it's really more than that: it can be the thing that helps you understand yourself. In a partner you should and usually do see yourself reflected very clearly. Learn from them and they will learn from you. It's emotional and intellectual, but be careful not to lose yourself in it. Keep a sense of your own identity and independence.

Sun Scorpio, Moon Libra

Naughty and nice, or maybe it's nice to be naughty? A dark chocolate-covered treat that's bitter but oddly delicious and keeps people coming back for more… there's something alluring about you that goes beyond physical good looks, something that draws people towards you, but what are you planning on doing with them when they get there?

In business, this gift can convince customers to buy things they didn't know they wanted in the first place; in love, it means those who chase you are under the illusion they are pursuing you, when the opposite is true. You certainly have the ability to see the good in everyone, but can just as easily see when they are far from it, and are a good judge not only of people but also of people's moods.

In love, you're romantic and physical with your other half, asking them to commit to you fully in mind and body. You will do the same, but if you find them lacking in that commitment, you won't be shy of acting that way yourself either. Does that mean you will say something? No. Saying something only comes after you've said nothing. For days.

Sun Sagittarius, Moon Libra

You want the world to know what's right and what's wrong, what you've learned and where you've learned it, which philosophy has brought you great wisdom and just how much chocolate you can eat before you're sick… In your case, there are no limits.

A great sense of humour and the ability to be a good judge of character make you indispensible when there are any negotiations to be done, and your skill for breaking the ice of cool customers could be a bonus for your boss. Roles in PR, sales and marketing and contract negotiations would suit you well. This doesn't make you Even Steven; in fact you can swing into Raging Roger pretty sharpish if you think someone isn't paying attention, or worse still, taking the Michael.

In love, you want to share the experiences that life has to offer, and a fellow traveller is a must, someone who wants to get their backpack on and follow in the footsteps of great historical characters or see some of the most beautiful views and objects of the world out there… and then come home for a lot of affection, a good old natter and help unpacking those artefacts.

Sun Capricorn, Moon Libra

Success is something all Capricorn Sun signs crave. The measure of that success is a personal thing – for some, it's just staying in work and making sure obligations are met; for others, it's about being the boss and showing the world the trappings of being the boss. So which are you? Today. It changes. Depending on whether you feel it's nice to be nice or it's a dog-eat-dog world kind of day.

Using this combination wisely will guarantee success, and having a plan, an idea about just what you want and how you will measure that success, will work wonders. You can do it by being fair. Being nice all the time may not be possible, but if you realize that what you're really after is fairness and not being judged a tyrant, you can settle into being all that you can and all that you want to be.

In a relationship, you must have some shared interests with your other half and be able to join in with them rather than be separate. Not all the time – clearly you need some time away from each other – but you will want a traditional relationship based on sharing and caring, not keeping things to yourself and having a 'What's mine is mine' attitude. Spontaneity will help prevent the relationship from becoming routine.

Sun Aquarius, Moon Libra

Having joined a gym, you don't want to actually talk to any members, but you don't know what's going on and that's annoying, so what do you do? You do talk to people, find out what's happening, declare the removal of the Power Plates outrageous and campaign to have them put back, and when they are put back, never use them. A rebel with a cause, sometimes *any* cause, that's you, but when turned on to a cause you really do believe in, there's no better campaigner.

You're a cool customer who thinks on their feet and is rarely caught out. Even when it looks as if you might be, you manage to wriggle out of it, even if sometimes you extend the truth or perhaps talk yourself up and then realize you might have to let someone down when the time to learn new skills lets *you* down.

You need glamour and variety in your love life, someone who is at home in the bright lights of the city but happy to walk in the country too. Not much to ask, is it? Chances are, you will see what's missing in a relationship very easily. What you do about that is where a real relationship is made. Start with friendship, the rest will follow.

Sun Pisces, Moon Libra

'Romance' is often a word associated solely with relationships. It's easy to see why, but with this Sun–Moon combination, it could be associated with your relationship with life. You see the beauty in everything, perhaps even when nobody else does, and you're able to convey it in conversation, in the way you use images through your work, perhaps in the photography and film industry, and in how you write, be that in the form of novels or journalism.

This idealism will of course meet with those who are less than impressed now and again. As if you care – and that's your true strength. You *do* care about other people, but you believe in what you believe in, and although some may seek to change your mind, with your debating skills it's more likely that you'll change theirs.

In love, you're happier than the happiest fairy in the glen. You love to be in love, but it's got to be sparkly gossamer-winged with fireflies lighting your way kind of romantic love – and why not? Some will say 'the one' isn't out there, but they are. All you need do is shine your light and refuse to settle for pseudo-fairy folk who talk the talk but can't make it fly.

SCORPIO MOON

'I try not to drink too much because when I'm drunk, I bite.'
BETTE MIDLER

Archetype

The vampire. Yes, the creature of the night, feared, alluring and so sexy it's just not fair. Your Moon brings you sex appeal and mystery, but walking in the light sometimes burns you. Exposing the truth of your emotions is a tough thing for you, but once you do, you transform.

SCORPIO MOON ♏

The Moon is in fall in this sign. Simply put, that makes her unhappy and brings out the more challenging side of her influence. And in this sign of course she's operating with Scorpio's dark secrets too… Intriguing, isn't it? You like intrigue, you like to delve deep into a subject to find out what's really going on – not the headline news, the stuff that's truly happening. Be careful your need for the truth or to have some of life's more intense experiences doesn't take you too far down a path that could lead to trouble.

You could have already had some intense experiences anyway. You might have had some near-death experiences, or perhaps been mixed up with what your mother would call the 'wrong crowd' in your youth, or maybe you just took to your room aged 13 and weren't really seen much for three years or so... The comfort of locking yourself away – to think, to process stuff, to eat dark chocolate with peanut butter on it – may still be with you. It could be how you resolve emotional dramas in your life. If it's your way, it's your way, but don't stay hidden too long.

As a fixed Moon sign, change isn't something you want to have too often and you may stay in a job for longer than you should. Learn to see the signs that you've outgrown it and plan to make your exit before things get too difficult for you to stay. If you're truly content, that's fine, but if you're grumbling over a double espresso and a double chocolate muffin with your mates, it may be time to think again.

Even though you might be talking about what's going on with your mates, you will rarely ask for actual assistance from them, preferring to sort things out yourself, which is fine as long as you don't seek extreme measures that could have been avoided if you had asked. Going to a loan shark for money instead of asking your bank manager, or meeting that wayward ex without telling anyone where you're going are to be avoided.

Sometimes people with Scorpio in their chart, be it Sun sign, rising sign or heavy planets in this placement, think they can do anything and come out unscathed, relying perhaps on Scorpio's reputation for being tough and stinging to defend itself. Here's the thing: scorpions aren't hard-shelled, they are soft, and they only sting when really provoked and sometimes sting themselves in the process. You're tenderer than you think, especially with your Moon in Scorpio, and that goes double bubble for your emotions.

Do you find yourself weeping at adverts for sick or homeless puppies, wishing you could take them in (but what would the six cats you already have think about that)? An animal lover, yes, a sentimental sort, definitely, but you hide it so well when faced with people you don't know. On first meeting you could shine back a dark mirror, a complete blank that shows them nothing but themselves, and some people may mistake that as hostility. What you're really doing is protecting yourself, giving nothing away until you get to know someone. When you do, you will let them in slowly but surely. Many of your friends will tell you they weren't sure of you when they first met you – something you quite like, if truth be known.

If, however, you like the look of someone for another reason, a sexual one, you're far from shy. Then your true vampire nature comes out and you're hardly bashful with the signals you send. And if they respond to your magic, they really have no escape…

When you're mid-drama, you can be the full Bridget Jones, complete with torch songs and tubs of ice-cream, curtains drawn and 'Why, why, why?!' When a mate is in the same place, you're more likely to indulge them for an hour then tell them to shut up, get some lippy on and get out and find another one. Let's go!

Watch out for jealousy. It never ends well, so best avoid any dramas.

Emotionally, you could be likened to a volcano – all that stuff sitting underneath for ages and ages, warming up until finally it blows and causes devastation. Better to let things out gently and when you feel them rather than send them into the pits of your emotional volcano to warm up with the heat of resentment, confusion or maybe that infamous jealousy before whooshing up.

You're an amazing judge of character – you possess an almost psychic ability to know what's going on with people and you're likely to be the first to notice when a mate or family member is out of sorts. That's when advice should be offered – as soon as you see it is needed rather than when the other person has retreated and made it difficult to get to them.

You have no fear of the darker things in life, the stuff that some shy away from. You would make a good nurse, pathologist, undertaker and private detective. You take life's mysteries, including death, as a challenge, and like to squeeze a spot or two. You may also study and practise the psychic arts – something you will be very good at, but make sure you keep your intentions pure. No bad fairies, please.

A tenacious individual, you will keep going and going until the job is done. That doesn't mean you hurry things along. You want to do things properly, so time won't be an issue. You have a keen eye for detail and may notice things that nobody else sees, but then again you might miss the glaringly obvious!

Sexually, you're a real player. Sex is an important part of your life and an even more important part of your love life. You may use it as a weapon, holding it back or offering it to get what you want, and you will have few boundaries in the bedroom. Now your mates are looking at you in a whole different light, having read that out loud over a glass of wine and a cheese and pickle fancy!

With people in the office, or the gym, or with your peers, you may find yourself in the Marmite category – they either love you or hate you. The latter may simply misunderstand you, of course, but have you ever bared your teeth at them just for a laugh and to keep the myth alive? You wouldn't do that… would you?

Boring you are not, intriguing you most definitely are, and anyone willing to move beyond the smokescreen you throw up around yourself on first meeting will find a loyal and protective friend. Even if they only see you at night. Oddly enough.

Love Life

In the words of Victoria Wood, 'Melt the buttons on my flame-proof nightie.' You can do it, and you can do it all over again.

Hardly the shy sort on the sexual front, you can be oddly timid when it comes to meeting people, but once you recognize they are interested, your inner vampire is released and your seduction skills put into action.

You're likely to be experimental physically. Just watch you don't put your back out, as you may not be as young as you think, and in a relationship the intensity of your love life is something that binds you to your other half. And to the headboard too, no doubt.

Away from the adult content now as we look at your emotional commitment in a relationship. You have a need to know what your other half is thinking, but you actually do that naturally. You can have an almost psychic link with them, but don't go solely on what you feel, check it out in the real world too, as sometimes you might get it wrong. Mad as that sounds.

It's odd that you care so much about what your partner is feeling and yet you aren't so generous in letting them in on what's going on with you. When you feel yourself getting on the huffy bus, ask what price the fare? Maybe it's better to stay off it, turn around and discuss how you're feeling rather than expect everyone to be as psychic as you.

When single and looking for romance, try to get over your shyness. It can be appealing to some, and you might find that there are those who are attracted to you because you look shy, but when they get to know you, it might be a bit of a surprise! This doesn't mean you have to hand out cards with your telephone number on, but if you like the look of someone, at least smile. Just be careful they don't see your fangs. Then again…

What you really demand above everything else is trust, total trust. If you don't have it, work at it. If it's never going to happen, ask yourself if you're in the right relationship. In order to gain trust you must of course let go, stop wondering why he said that, where she was last night, etc., and concentrate on thinking happy thoughts and realizing trust is earned. On both sides.

Partnering a Scorpio Moon

Invest in shares in a chocolate company and make sure you have copious amounts of ideas to keep your horizontal dancing fuelled with new routines. Scorpio Moons are intense, moody and magnificent, demanding sometimes, but worth the effort. Look them in the eye and tell them how you feel. If you skip around any issues, they will know it and won't be happy until you tell them what's going on.

Best fit Sun signs are Scorpio, Pisces, Cancer and Taurus.

Career

The tougher side of life holds no fear for you; in fact it may draw you in, so roles in police forensics, pathology, nursing and undertaking could appeal – not for the macabre side, but out of a fascination with life's bigger questions. Death is, after all, one of the biggest. On the lighter side of life, you make a very good salesperson, as you have an instinct for knowing what people want and how to fit their needs with your product, and can be very persuasive.

Your Moon may also draw you towards the sea. Its allure could have you working around it or on it, or maybe you're just happy to go and visit it to clear your mind?

Work can become an obsession, and when you get caught in something you love, working long hours won't be a challenge for you. It might, however, be a challenge for those you love. It's likely you have a vocation rather than just a job, and that's fantastic, but just take care that the home–work balance isn't tipped so far towards work that it doesn't do you any favours in the long run.

Psychic disciplines may also attract you and working as an astrological consultant, tarot reader or healer could be a part-time hobby that turns into a full-time career.

Parents and Family

This is a tough one. Your early years may not have been the most comfortable. Many Scorpio Moon children have difficult circumstances around their birth, parents or formative years. You may have wondered if you'd been adopted at some point, as you just didn't think you fitted in. Perhaps you just saw things differently and weren't prepared to compromise, to pretend to fit in. And why should you?

You're a fixed Moon sign and anything your parents or siblings said to you that you found less than acceptable is probably still with you. The memory could still affect those relationships, and the triggers set up in your childhood should be recognizable to you. Work with them to understand them and deactivate them. Chances are that those who helped set them up didn't even realize it.

A deep understanding of the cycles of life and death could have come from being part of a large extended family where there were many births and deaths in your earlier years. Some people don't experience the death of a close relation until they are well into adulthood; for you, that's unlikely to be the case.

Your mum may have been the secretive sort. Hardly a spy… but then again? She may not have shown much affection, but you knew that she cared deeply, even if 'I love you' never passed her lips. She may also have been an intriguing figure and perhaps had contact with the psychic arts, whether discussed or not.

If you're a mum yourself, try not to be over-possessive with your children. Let them make their own mistakes as you stand by to help them rather than constantly protect them. You may be protecting them from important lessons. Express your feelings with your children and let them know they can come to you with anything they need to discuss, especially when they reach their teenage years.

Health

Normally a very robust individual, pay attention to headaches and perhaps migraines. These will usually be brought about by stress and over-worrying about situations you may not actually be able to change much. Blood pressure problems later in life could be prevalent, but good routines with diet and exercise will help. Sexual organs are governed by the Moon, and Scorpio Moon women may experience period pain above the norm.

Life Skills

You're a bright cookie, brighter than you think and not as nutty as some would have you think. Often you can see what other people can't, but do you do anything with that gift? Whilst you're right to exercise caution, you might hold back a little too much. Find the middle ground and above all trust in yourself.

When the going gets tough, the tough get going, and not many are as tough and tenacious as you, so you know what to do: get going! Taking action means that sometimes you have to come out from under your rock when you would rather hide away, but great things can be achieved when you're courageous enough to face your fear and do it anyway.

Stumbling Blocks

Joy and pain, like sunshine and rain… Don't worry, I'm not going to burst into song, and neither are you when you hear what has to be said: you're your own worst enemy. Sometimes you poke the hornets' nest for the sake of it, and when you're attacked for it, you can run away in the opposite direction denying all knowledge. So, think before you poke and prod. Sometimes it's the right thing to do, but when it is, wouldn't it be better to stand your ground rather than run afterwards?

You are a Moon sign of extremes, but you like extremes. Nothing makes you feel more alive than when things are out of their mundane and boring routines or you have a mystery to solve. If you keep your head up, your keen eye on everything and everyone around you and always act from your truth, you will never stumble. Or learn anything?

Spiritual Lesson

Security isn't a set of locks on a door, or a million pounds in the bank, or a partner who tells you they love you 100 times a day. It's something within, it's knowing that whatever happens you can not only deal with it but also rise like the phoenix from the flames. This is your spiritual symbol, a bird that moves from egg to amazing creature because of, rather than in spite of, the heat applied.

SUN SIGN, MOON SIGN

So now you know a little more about your Moon sign, but how does that work with your Sun sign?

Sun Aries, Moon Scorpio

You want things done now! But what if you don't get them, do you give up or do you go into full fester mode, waiting and watching for a mistake you can take advantage of, or perhaps creating change to make sure you get what you want? And you usually do get exactly what you want.

Happily, you're not selfish with your talents, you encourage those around you to keep going and be equally as tenacious in their endeavours, and because of that you could make a great coach, be that sports coach or life coach. Others might think you're a little full-on, perhaps ego-driven, but that's a defence mechanism. You are in fact far more concerned about what people think of you than you let on.

In a relationship you're highly sexed and need intense partners who want the physical, mental, emotional and spiritual connection you're offering. You don't fare well with shy and retiring types, but those who are prepared to argue back get your respect.

If looking for love, look for someone who gives as good as they get then gets up and gives it again.

Sun Taurus, Moon Scorpio

This is a full Moon position, and your Moon in Scorpio brings you a whole new level of intensity, as well as the ability to let go and walk away when things aren't right and never look back, but your Taurus Sun sometimes needs a push. It can be loyal beyond the tolerance of others, but when you go, you really go.

With your feet firmly rooted in the Earth, you have strong foundations to support you and can be whatever you choose to be. You build careers and relationships slowly, but with fierce and direct honesty. You don't suffer those who spin a yarn very well, seeing straight through their overuse of words and lack of action.

A great business individual with an eye for detail and an ability to make even the toughest of deals appealing on a whole new level – 'Great offices, great food and a great feeling of being part of something that's caring and rewarding!' – you make a good boss.

In love, you're very passionate and sensual. It has to be everything for you, the whole experience, and all dipped in chocolate. Be careful of the green-eyed monster – jealousy is never attractive, especially when it's based on a fantasy that never happened. Take it easy, lover.

Sun Gemini, Moon Scorpio

As a Gemini, you can be hard to read, as it can be difficult to know what's going to change next, but with this Moon you're even tougher to get to know, as you hide your true feelings – or do you? Who can be sure what you're thinking, what you're feeling or if what you're saying is really what you mean? This isn't intentionally deceptive on your part, but probably because you talk out what you're feeling deep inside and those around you take that as a decision when in fact it's part of the process.

You're particularly good at finding out what others have been up to, and quick to put two and two together and come up with a need to look a little further whilst you still have the advantage of surprise. Great police work is built on your skills, as is investigative journalism. Nosey, is that what's being said? Not nosey, just inquisitive.

In love, you're a tough one for someone to get to know. Are they waking up next to Casanova or Coco the clown? You need someone who will listen, advise you on all sorts of things and step back when you go in the totally opposite direction, then step back in again when you need their help.

Sun Cancer, Moon Scorpio

A sensitive placement for your Moon, this highlights your emotional needs and asks for stroking, for care when dealing with you, or you might just turn around and bite! Of course that's a last resort. First of all, you will take yourself off for a bit of a think and pretend nothing is wrong. Then you will let them have it! Remember that it's better to deal with things as they come up and avoid baring your teeth.

You could be called upon by your family and friends to help with their emotional dramas, something you do very well. Helping others understand the depths of what they are feeling is something you're likely to be very good at. It may even be something that becomes a career choice – are you a psychiatric nurse, counsellor or social worker?

In love, you're hard to understand but easy to please. If a partner listens and opens their heart as well as their ears, things should go just fine. Provided they don't take your natural nurturing skills for granted, that is. It's good to share the more mundane tasks, and if they do, it shows you they truly do care.

Sun Leo, Moon Scorpio

What a brilliant actor, able to let those emotions show through, to move others to tears and have them rushing to help. Now do that on stage and you could make a career out of it!

You can feel to the depths of your soul, you can remember those feelings and you can recreate them when you need to, but do you need to? Some folks may see you perform and then wonder if that's what you're doing with them. Be clear about who you are, what you want and when to use your greatest gift. There will be times when it is really appropriate, but don't let it become a habit.

You were made to lead the way and there will be no shortage of those who will follow you. A trendsetter in many ways, you are able to spot the next big thing way before lesser mortals.

In love, you're passionate and funny and there's never a dull moment, but some may not appreciate the dramas. Love can blossom with a partner who knows when you've gone a little Whitney on them, steps back until the diva has had her moment and then moves in to listen to what's really going on and offer emotional support. Whatever.

Sun Virgo, Moon Scorpio

A strong and focused individual, that's you, and first choice to get things done with minimum fuss and to maximum effect. But whilst the thought of being punctual, good at what you do and capable is appealing, there's a part of you that wants to be in the control tower with the swivel chair and the white cat, 'Come in, Mr Bond' and all that malarkey. World domination may not really be what you're after, but you certainly have everything you need to dominate your world.

No stranger to flip charts and wall planners, you're clearly organized, but what happens when Agent X doesn't do what they are supposed to? That's when your Scorpio Moon isn't just first to notice something isn't right, she's first to remind you to let them know. They may not like you if you do, though. Make up your mind.

In love, you might show a bit more commitment to your partner by actually putting down your laptop or stopping filling out your tax return when they get amorous. 'Pull my nightie down when you've finished' isn't quite the response they are looking for. Take things slowly, learn to release your Scorpio Moon and things could get very interesting indeed, Mr Bond.

Sun Libra, Moon Scorpio

A sense of justice prevails here. You won't stand idly by while others suffer – unless, of course, you're the one holding the tickling stick. A lightness of touch could be your secret weapon. Certainly your ability to get others to like you, to schmooze the crowd, is a sure-fire way of finding out what you need to know without anyone getting hurt! You will stand up for the underdog and bare your teeth at anyone who threatens them, but only when it's really, really the last resort.

Great detective work is your forte; you're able to find out things others can't, and when you do, you can deliver your findings with that *Watchdog* air of confidence that says, 'Don't mess with me, I have right on my side.' In fact, give *Watchdog* a call – they could use people like you.

In love – and you do like to be in love – you can be demanding of a partner both physically and emotionally, and they of you. The depth you seek in a relationship should be balanced with lots of light touches, Post-It notes with romantic messages and foot massages whilst watching your favourite soap. But for you, the key to longevity in love has to be the one that opens the door to intensity and that deep, deep connection.

Sun Scorpio, Moon Scorpio

Hanging upside down in the rafters can be tiring, but not half as tiring as attempting to get through a day without someone laying their troubles at your door/lid/hatchway. It's odd – you want to be alone, but everyone else wants to find out what you have to say about their relationship, family life or sleek new hairdo. Such is the lesson you have chosen: to help others is to see how you can help yourself. Is that mysterious enough for you?

Likely to wear a lot of black, you want to present an interesting front to people but equally want to alone – a dilemma indeed. No matter what you do, you will always be enigmatic. People will talk about you, and deep down you will love it, even playing up to your 'mistress of the dark' tag every now and again. You could be deeply psychic – another reason people are attracted to you – and could study the psychic arts or work in them.

In love, look out for anyone who eats too much garlic and avoid them – good advice for any sign. You're loyal and take your commitment to your partner very seriously. They will know it and reward you with the same level of commitment. And if they cross you? Like you don't know.

Sun Sagittarius, Moon Scorpio

I am having so much fun with your Moon sign, it offers such scope for innuendo and it's such a great thing to be able to push those limits and frankly take the Mickey. You might know something about that?

A great judge of people, you won't overstep the mark very often, but can sometimes get very close to it. You have the ability to let people share in your wisdom whilst maintaining their interest by letting them think there's more to come, and there usually is. A great depth in you makes you a powerhouse of information, often on some of life's greatest secrets and mysteries.

Your natural optimism can sometimes be dampened by a fear that may not be rooted in any reality. Use your inquisitive mind to find out the facts and put your concerns behind you.

In love, you can be a tough one to keep up with as you dash from adventure to adventure, and you will need a partner who can keep up with you. Seldom wrong, you might find your other half can take umbrage when you *are* in fact wrong. Nothing unusual in that, but most people either let it go or admit their failing. Not you.

Sun Capricorn, Moon Scorpio

A sure-footed goat is always going to be successful, but when you equip it with extraordinary instincts and the ability to inspire others to follow, you know it's going to be more successful than most. If it wants to be. Well, why wouldn't you want to be? Maybe you're thinking of success as monetary, possessions, just stuff, and that doesn't appeal to you? Then your success will be your reputation for being top of your game, or the feeling you get when you help others achieve the impossible.

You're likely to have a great sense of humour, with witty responses your stock in trade. Piercing wit can also be used to get your point across, but make sure you use it when it's appropriate, or not everyone will get the joke.

In love, you're a great provider, excellent parent and what my granny would call a 'good catch'. What Granny doesn't need to know about is just what goes on behind closed doors, and neither does anyone else, which is just as well, as you put in as much effort here as you do in being a success at work. But you're not one for discussing your love life over a coffee with your mates, unlike some signs I could mention. Gemini.

Sun Aquarius, Moon Scorpio

Generally people who appear to be the big 'I am' don't really attract much positive press, but you seem to manage it, and the confidence you exude is clear for everyone to see. In fact it may make you something of an expert in your chosen field, and your manner and bearing will only feed your reputation. Think consultant.

Knowing your stuff is important too, and you will take great care to make sure that is the case. Analytical roles are particularly good for you and once you have a set of facts and figures in your head, you will be able to recall them at will, impressing those who are hanging on your every word.

However, you can sometimes come up against those who won't get you, those who will see ego before professionalism. When you do, it's best to avoid them. Walk away rather than engage in any debates that could bring out your inner vampire. Fierce.

In love, you're either passionate, hot-blooded and likely to be twice nightly or you're as cold as an Eskimo's extremities. This makes it tough for a partner, but as long as they recognize you're in charge, that's fine. And if they don't? Then they are perfect for you, as they teach you that sometimes you might not know as much as you think you do. So there.

Sun Pisces, Moon Scorpio

Double trouble here, as this watery combination brings you emotional overflow and perhaps a lack of mindful communication to explain what's really going on. There's that sucking in of breath as you try to say what you're feeling, but the words can't get out.

You are highly intuitive, and it's the sort of intuition that others might wonder about. Just what do you do at night and why did you want a lock of their hair? Teenage witches are made of this stuff. The magic of the craft and the knowledge of worlds within worlds are intriguing, and you can be just as magically intriguing to those around you. Pointy hats are so last century, though – you can lose those.

To keep yourself grounded, take on roles that require you to use your mind, to organize things and to deal with facts and figures, or jobs that get you out and about into the world of nature. But take the bus – broomsticks draw attention.

In love, you're bewitching – come on, I couldn't miss that one out – and would-be partners are likely to be smitten early on. In a committed relationship, you need romance, love and intimacy, but don't forget you need to pay the gas bill and do the washing-up now and again. Apparently.

SAGITTARIUS MOON

'The teacher who is indeed wise does not bid you to enter the house of his wisdom but rather leads you to the threshold of your mind.'

KAHLIL GIBRAN

Archetype

The sage. Not the type you put in your stuffing at Christmas – think more along the lines of the wise old man sitting by the side of the road as you travel to the temple. As a Sagittarius Moon, people will stop and ask you the way, seeking your advice because they know you have walked this road yourself and have accumulated wisdom that you are happy to share. But you don't just sit there, you too have paths to walk and wisdom to seek. Pack your bags, pick up your books and jog on.

SAGITTARIUS MOON ♐

The difficulty with knowing so much, even at a young age, is that you may feel alone even when you're in the middle of a very large group. It's not that you don't want to be there, or even dislike those you are with, but you wonder whether they are actually seeing things the same way you are. Chances are, they're not.

You will seek to understand things on all levels and look perhaps at even the simplest things in a different way. Why would someone just dump their plate on a side table for someone else to clear up? Why not hand it to a host or take it to the kitchen?

Total disregard for others is something you don't like at all, but is it disregard for others or just people being people? Whatever the case, what drives you is a strong moral sense, a sense of what is right, a judgement made by your higher self.

Reading, writing and even working in publishing could interest you – anywhere you can gather information and knowledge and listen to what people have to say. It all helps you to help others with your accumulated wisdom, which makes you very popular in social gatherings, as you're never short of something to say and chances are you will have something in common with half the room: been there, done that, have the T-shirt!

Travel could be a big part of your life; if not physically, then perhaps through the sort of books you read or television shows you watch. It's all about experiencing the big wide world and fulfilling your need for information. Spiritual or religious journeys may be something you yearn to do or perhaps have done: a visit to Glastonbury, to Machu Picchu, Tibet or Uluru.

With this need for wide open spaces, you may be claustrophobic, though perhaps only in a small way. For a friend of mine who is Sagittarius Moon, it's lifts – he can use them but isn't comfortable in them at all. He wouldn't get in one if it was crammed full, and when in one, full or not, he doesn't speak. That in itself is unusual for a Sagittarius Moon: you do like a natter.

Your Moon is a mutable Moon, which means you change your mind a lot, and that can be frustrating for those around you. You can also go on and on about something you want until you get it, and when you do get it, you don't want it any more. This can be challenging for family and friends, but keeps them on their toes. It's not a petulant, pouty, shouty thing at least – you're more likely to just ignore the brand new sandwich toaster; one sandwich and it's in the garage.

You need time on your own to experience the greatness of the world, to stand on the beach with nobody around, to wander in the forest without seeing anybody, and the thought of travelling on your own doesn't faze you, until you get bored. But even then you can make friends amongst your fellow travellers and are adept at picking the interesting ones rather than those who want to show you their collection of napkins from around the world.

This ability stems from your sensitivity towards people – you can sense who is calm, who is angry and who might be up for a bit of karaoke-dokey by the pool bar. You might come across as shy at first, but nothing could be further from the truth, and once you warm to people, and to the karaoke machine, you're the life and soul of the party. Your laugh, when you really laugh, is likely to be one of those throw your head back, let's see your teeth and gums laughs. Yes, I am saying you laugh like a horse.

You need to keep moving and could choose work that has a lot of different elements to it. A repetitive role won't suit you. You also need to be up and about; sitting at a desk all day is something you would and should avoid. Choose roles in marketing, or PR perhaps, where you have a chance to meet people, impress them with your knowledge and help them make the most of their product.

You're extremely good at bringing out the best in people without appearing overbearing or dominating the process. Instead, you encourage them to have faith in themselves. You may even appear to have a sixth sense as far as others are concerned. Your ability to see what will and won't work may look magical to them, but you know it comes from all the experience you have amassed… and that crystal around your neck given to you by a mystic on the road to Mandalay.

You're a very honest individual and that gains you respect from your peers. Some may find your honesty disarming, too, and that can be a great strength in business. However, you're also very good at dressing things up so that people can accept the information you're giving them, even if it's difficult, and it's rare that anyone would take bad news from you personally, probably because it's very rare that you would be delivering it from a personal point of view.

But you're no saint. When riled, you can deliver wrath better than all the gods of Olympus, firing lightning bolts and thunderous great booming words that would shake even the toughest of your critics in their boots, but you're also very forgiving and can find that once the air is clear and everyone understands each other better, you can all move on and go from strength to strength. Or part company with no ill feeling.

Money is something we all like to have and you're no exception, but it's not usually your main driving force. You can sometimes go from boom to bust and back again, but always seem to manage somehow. Financial success is more likely later in life, when you get a hold of your tendency to buy emotional happiness when things don't go the way you wanted them to. Put those shoes down and step away from the credit card.

At work, you could seem very relaxed, almost too laid-back, but that's probably because you spent the last hour on the way in sorting out what others would take three hours to do and instead of watching soaps on telly last night you were online doing your research and working on a presentation. You work better where it's quieter; distractions are usually other people wanting you to sort out their stuff, a box of doughnuts that means coffee and a gossip, or the temptation to watch everyone in the office wondering what's really going on underneath those neatly arranged pencils and fluorescent-haired gonk. (That's a desk ornament by the way, not the trainee that's just started.)

You could hanker after a home in another country and could have strong links overseas through friends, family and work. Those links could bring some of your happiest times, but before taking the plunge and moving your entire life, make sure you really will be able to settle and your idea of a life abroad doesn't go the way of that sandwich toaster.

To gain wisdom, you must gather information, make mistakes along the way, forgive yourself for them and learn not to repeat them. And to do that you must step into the big wide world and give it a go.

Love Life

Your best chance of a relationship that works is to find a partner who doesn't cling on, one who appreciates your need for freedom and is very welcome to travel with you but knows when you need that little space that's so very precious to you.

They won't be doing you any favours if they nag when you're not home in time for tea. You hate sticking to a schedule or being asked to commit to too much in advance. The saddle has to come off and you have to be left to roam the pastures on your own now and again. You can't be cooped up.

You need to be able to have a very open line of communication with a partner, to be able to talk to them about anything you like, and to do it your way. One who picks at your expressions or the words you use isn't for you. If they misunderstand your humour or fail to be as easy-going as you can be, it could turn into constant bickering, and that's something you really, really don't like in any relationship.

Like us all, you need to feel loved, but you also need a connection that's about good communication. Basically you need a lover, best friend, teacher and student. Not much to ask for, is it?

Imperfections won't worry you – it's where you learn most about yourself as well as your partner – but take care not to take on the role of the fount of all knowledge. That will grate on even the most patient partner and could make you appear bossy.

Your subconscious need to learn in a relationship could lead you to choose a partner from another culture, or one who is older or younger, or from a completely different background.

With a Sagittarius Moon, there's sometimes a tendency to talk about relationship matters with friends rather than your partner. You're probably just venting or trying to come to a better understanding of what's going on, but your partner won't see it that way. Much as you wouldn't if you thought they were doing the same.

You're likely to be very generous with your partner. Lovely as that is, make sure that it doesn't turn into you putting your hand in your pocket more than they do, as it could become expected and lead to some tough talking.

Sexually, you're as adventurous as you are in every other part of your life and are happy to explore your sexuality in a safe and committed relationship. As long as you're the one who gets to wear the bush jacket and fedora and carry the whip.

Partnering a Sagittarius Moon

Make sure you keep them interested with new and exciting things, travel and adventure and don't restrict them in any way. Schedules are good, but spontaneity is better, so have a loose idea of what's happening next week but don't bring out your clipboard and stopwatch if things aren't running like clockwork.

To catch a Sagittarius Moon, bring out your holiday snaps, the interesting ones of all those city breaks to the world's capitals.

Best fit Sun signs are Sagittarius, Leo, Aries and Gemini.

Career

Working in the travel industry would suit you well, as would publishing, working in bookstores and teaching on a subject you're passionate about – and I think we have already established that won't be maths or accountancy. You may teach spirituality, either as a hobby or as your full-time job, and your knowledge of more than one of the world's faith and belief systems is likely to be good regardless.

You will want to work for the best – you don't do well with second best – and as a result have very high standards, which should be appreciated by your boss! You're unlikely to blow your own trumpet at work and even when you are congratulated on your achievements, you will react with great humility and an 'It was nothing' attitude. There are, however, the occasional and rare Sagittarius Moon sign individuals who aren't so humble. Step up, Mr Simon Cowell.

Sometimes you may take on too much at work. Saying 'no' isn't one of your fortes and you may find yourself working harder than you really should. Perhaps the lesson here is to be honest with yourself about some of life's limits, despite your perception of a limitless world. Sometimes structure is a good thing, even for you.

Parents and Family

In your early years, your parents, especially your mum, may not have been the most affectionate of individuals. Some families are cuddly and some aren't. Yours probably wasn't, which doesn't mean to say you weren't loved; it may be your parents were busy working hard or perhaps one of them was away for extended periods of time. It may be that your birth mother was not even present and an aunt or an adopted family took her place.

This lack of direct affection could either be something you're not going to allow to happen with your own children or be something that you do yourself. Remember that knowledge offers an opportunity to change.

Your home is likely to be clean and well ordered, full of things from your travels, and you will probably love to be reminded of those happy times as you wander around the house – that little statue here, the picture there and what is that in the bathroom? Not to everyone's taste, but you love it! You won't shy away from ambitious ideas to restructure your home to better suit your needs, and may even take the hammer to the walls yourself, but get someone with real knowledge if you can. Just saying.

You probably have at least one animal in the home. Cats are likely to be a favourite, perhaps because they reflect your wandering personality? As a child, you may have wanted a pony or even been lucky enough to have had one. Riding may have been a hobby or a much-desired one.

If you have children of your own, you will be very proud of them, in particular any educational achievements they may have, bragging about them over cappuccino with the other yummy mummies at one of those knit and bake things. What am I saying? Knit and bake? Maybe not, but bragging? Oh, yes!

You could be asked to work away from your children and these decisions will be tough to make. This may mirror what happened in your own childhood and it could seem as if you have no choice. Really? You're likely to be loved by your children for your ability to make everything work out, to be the one who can sort out the toughest of their challenges. As they grow up, however, remember that's an advisory role, then an honorary one. Know where the boundaries lie.

Health

Traditionally it's your legs and hips that need more attention, but sometimes blood disorders could also be a problem, perhaps brought about by overeating or eating too much of one type of food rather than having a balanced diet. Take care not to plunge into one of the many complementary treatments around rather than add things to your health regime gently.

The gym will be something you have an on–off love affair with. When you're with it, you're really with it and go every day, and when you're off, you pay your membership and don't bother. Try to find a sport that you love rather than a gym routine that will never work for you.

Your weight could yo-yo. You know why and what to do about it. Ah – knowledge without action. Let's talk about that later.

Life Skills

You have the ability to soak up information like a sponge and at school you were probably an easy student for your teachers. But you don't just pick up information from formal teaching, you pick it up everywhere and from anyone, and that is a real skill.

Your ability to be affable, to fit in with any crowd, means you can put yourself wherever you want to be and look as if you belong, but it takes concentration and sometimes it also takes courage. Using your talents is one of your biggest lessons. Having the confidence to step out sometimes isn't easy, but it always pays off.

Stumbling Blocks

So now can we have that chat about knowledge without action? You might know what to do and when to do it, but do you? Knowing something and doing something with it are two different things, so commit to doing something that scares you every now and again, whether that's telling someone they are wrong or moving yourself out of a damaging relationship.

A tendency to spend money based on an emotional response to things going on in your life needs to be checked, that 'I deserve this' attitude to justify spending money you may not have. There is no doubt that you deserve whatever you want, but the real question is 'Can I afford this?'

A little control will go a very long way. You're a fantastically adventurous and full-on sign, but sometimes you need to put some structure into your life, depending on what else is going on in your natal chart.

Spiritual Lesson

In past lives you may have been overprotective of your knowledge, or perhaps quick to talk your way out of bother by blaming someone else. In this incarnation you're being asked to go public with your beliefs, to show others a path of greater wisdom. No matter if that's on a small scale or a grand one, your message is an optimistic one and you can accept your mistakes and learn from them (and so can I, being a Sagittarius Moon).

SUN SIGN, MOON SIGN

So now you know a little more about your Moon sign, but how does that work with your Sun sign?

Sun Aries, Moon Sagittarius

A quiet individual, shy and retiring with simple tastes. Lives frugally. *Not!* You're the direct opposite of all of those. You like to live life to the maximum and those around you should thrive on your enthusiasm. With a glass half-full philosophy, you are optimistic and willing to give most things a go, and that will ultimately bring you success in life.

You want to make grand plans happen and you're likely to be thinking of some amazing plan whilst others are still trying to get out of bed in the morning, but make sure you finish what you start or there could be a trail of half-completed amazing ideas in your wake. 'Never mind, try this, this will work, I promise' could wear on some who have been through a few ideas that haven't been a success, but they should stick with you, as you're a very lucky individual.

In love, you're easy to get along with. You tell it how it is and you're enthusiastic in the bedroom as well as in the kitchen, front room and occasionally garage. A partner should be prepared to drop everything and join you in your next adventure. Yeeha!

Sun Taurus, Moon Sagittarius

A bull and a horse, what sort of beast are you? Do you want a nice big field to munch your way through or are you ready to leap the fences and run off into the big wide world? Earth and Fire are not the happiest of bedfellows, so you could find that just as you get settled you're longing for adventure and as soon as you're on your way to greatness, you long for a warm fire and a cosy night in.

Fighting either urge is useless, so just give in to it. When you're feeling cuddly, cuddle up; when you want to explore the left bank of the Limpopo, saddle up. But here's the deal: maintain a stable home, but take a job that offers long holidays, like teaching, for example, and make space for all that you are.

This combination makes you good at earning money. You're also great at spending it on luxury goods, but hey, you know how to top up those funds. Later in life you're likely to be comfortably off.

In a relationship, you must have absolute loyalty, and that's what you give too. Your partner should also understand your need for travel and go with you on your journeys whenever possible.

Sun Gemini, Moon Sagittarius

When I was a little boy growing up in Scotland, my favourite word was: 'Why?' My mum says I used to say it all the time: 'Why? Why? Why? Why?' An answer was met with another question, and another. Yes, I am indeed a Gemini with Moon in Sagittarius.

With this full Moon position, no matter whether you're asking questions or getting out and seeing for yourself, you're likely to have an extremely enquiring mind that needs to be kept busy or boredom sets in. So have a role in life that's varied; have a job that offers you the chance to travel and to write, to communicate what you have discovered, and share your beliefs when asked.

In love, you are very generous, perhaps overly so on occasion, and will like a good debate with your other half. Debate is good, but preaching can turn into screeching if you do it too often. You may see what your partner or best friend is doing wrong, but remember that's only from your perspective… and of course from your well-seasoned wisdom.

You will find it pays to learn the art of silence. I am saying nothing. Shhh. Nothing. Absolutely nothing. No Thing. Going now. Bye. See ya. Bye. Silence.

Sun Cancer, Moon Sagittarius

You're likely to be the sort of person others naturally gravitate towards. They are attracted to your wisdom, your great advice and your readiness to offer a lovely flaky pastry and great coffee.

That mothering instinct coupled with that wise Moon could, however, see you tied to family or friends under the mistaken belief that they couldn't survive without you. So, help, nurture and support, but remember to leave room for others to learn and for you to fulfil your need to travel and to have new experiences.

You may be highly intuitive, with a sixth sense that knows what others are thinking, and unlike some signs, you get it right most of the time. Use your gifts to help those you care for. Perhaps some form of spiritual healing could help you take those talents further?

Having extremely high standards when it comes to what you expect from a partner could prove a concern if they don't meet them. Allow them some wiggle room, and if you do feel let down, say something rather than retreat into your shell for a sulk. Just saying.

Sun Leo, Moon Sagittarius

Oh, how we laughed! What at? Probably nothing in particular. And when you repeated the story, it wasn't as funny as being there, was it? But you do know how to laugh and do it often.

Your outgoing nature is very suited to the performing arts. Being the centre of attention is something that you will enjoy and that can take you far in your professional life.

You're an honest individual and even if you do play a role to get that job, girl, boy, diamond watch, you will always come clean quickly and with humility. And get away with it.

In a relationship, you will want to be the golden one, the shiny one, but a partner who is beige won't work for you at all, so look for someone who is shiny too, just not as shiny as you are. And make sure that you share mundane tasks. You may just want to do the pretty stuff, but cleaning the loo now and again is important too.

When you travel, it will be at the top end of the scale and you will work hard to achieve that five-star rating. If possible, make sure it's paid for without the need for plastic. In fact, avoid large credit limits as much as you can.

Sun Virgo, Moon Sagittarius

A grand castle in the distance isn't easily reached, but with planning and hard work you can get there, and you have both the vision and the organizational skills to do it. If you recognize your need to break through barriers, to show just how far you can go, and reconcile it with ordering the pencils, great things could come your way.

You would make a great travel agent, wonderful teacher and inspiring minister. The way you marry your beliefs with your down-to-earth approach is something others will respond to, and they could find you inspirational, but your opinion of yourself is still likely to be 'Not good enough'. Take some time to pat yourself on the back and remind yourself you're doing just fine – in fact better than fine, you're doing great.

In love, your great expectations may be tough for a would-be partner to live up to. Perhaps a little more realism on your part would be good – recognition that now and again your other half could leave dental floss in the kitchen sink. But hey, those supermodels lead a busy life.

To keep love alive, have a busy life, get things ticked off your joint to-do list and find a partner who wants to embrace life as much as you do. Paris, tick. Rome, tick. China, tick. Get a list, get a life.

Sun Libra, Moon Sagittarius

Doing what pleases us is something we all aspire to. Feeding our inner nature and recognizing the beauty of the world as we wander through it, stopping to smell the roses, is just perfect, but is it reality? It is if you recognize that no matter what or where you are in life, if you embrace it as an educational and beautiful thing then it becomes just that.

Self-help gone mad or your true philosophy? The point is that living your beliefs does make life better for you. You can do it better than most and even though some may wag their tongues in your direction, you couldn't care less. Well done, you, can I have a pint of whatever you're on?

The artistic sort, appreciating it or making it, you have a big vision for life and can help others not only see it but achieve it too. You're supportive of those who are positive in life and should learn early on to leave behind those who are not and let them figure it out for themselves.

In love, you're a true romantic, but you do need a partner who gives you the freedom to explore the world you live in – anything from taking a weekend on your own to going on a retreat or having a spa day to refocus your intention and realign your chakras. Om.

Sun Scorpio, Moon Sagittarius

You're a passionate individual ready to come out fighting for your beliefs and armed with enough information to combat any who think they know better! Fools! But then again you can change your mind… A piece of information that needs mulling over will be taken back to your lair and you will investigate it fully, and if you feel it turns things on their head, you will switch, fervently believing in your newfound truth.

It's the taking things to your lair bit that could have others wary of you. Those long silences and withdrawal from friends and family alike are hard to equate with the gregarious, outgoing and larger-than-life character you can also be. People who know you well will get used to both and know when to leave you alone until you come out of your hideaway, be that physically or emotionally.

When travelling, you will need to have a corner seat on the bus, a window seat on the plane and a table with a clear view of the door: you're not good at turning your back on a crowd.

In love, you're a direct individual with a high sex drive. Your partner will be in no doubt about what you want and when you want it. Now. Your other half will get used to your moods early on, and if they are wise, they will leave you to it when you're in thinking mode and be ready to discuss what happened and why when you come out of it.

Sun Sagittarius, Moon Sagittarius

If your nose isn't in a book, it could be in a travel brochure, but shouldn't your mind be on your work? Maybe you could combine both. Working in travel, journalism, publishing and teaching would suit you well. You need information, crave it and want to be able to repeat it when you can to keep others updated and impressed by your knowledge, but in an altruistic way – you simply want to share.

A great sense of humour is something you want to share too. A witty conversationalist, you're probably sought after at parties and could enjoy a wide and varied social life. People fascinate you and listening to their tales is better than any television show. Inspiration to write a book could come through your experiences with others and through your travels.

In love, you could be drawn to someone who is more practical, someone who remembers to water the plants and pay the bills whilst your mind is concerned with the bigger questions, but that doesn't mean to say you should marry a housekeeper either. Your partner should be ready to explore the world with you too, to sit next to a giant Buddha in silence for hours soaking up the atmosphere, safe in the knowledge that they have cancelled the milk and booked the cat sitter.

Sun Capricorn, Moon Sagittarius

At school, when they did that pick a team thing, you'd be the one most people would pick, wouldn't you, whether it was a quiz or a sporting challenge? A powerful sort with the charisma that gets you picked for most things, you're a force to be reckoned with and you know it, but you still don't take anything for granted and have natural humility.

You get things right too – there's no room for half-measures – and have a great sense of integrity. You would turn your back on a project that could make you lots of money if it didn't sit well with your belief system. You can debate those beliefs with anyone; in fact you probably enjoy it and use those conversations to adjust and refine your attitude to some of life's bigger questions.

When the goat combines with the horse, a sure-footed creature that can go the distance is produced, and in publishing, training, teaching and the military, your sense of order will guarantee success, but taking risks now and again is what really pays off for you.

In love, you're very devoted to a partner. Sharing your travels will bring you even closer, and if that involves a tent now and again, you'll be fine with that. You know you're in the right relationship when you can sit in a room together, both reading a book, and as you look up, a smile says it all.

Sun Aquarius, Moon Sagittarius

There's really no messing about with you, is there? Straight to the point and with those arrows of truth from the centaur within, you're sure to let people know where they stand. Most people are OK with that, but what about the less robust, the shy creature in the corner who may be in awe of your knowledge and power? Happily, you'll see them and your humanitarian side will want to nurture and protect the little guy. In fact you could go to extraordinary lengths to protect the little guy.

You can sometimes appear to have more than a touch of the eccentric about you, doing things in a unique way that makes you stand out, for example taking adventure holidays to less popular destinations rather than heading for beach resorts.

A social individual, you will be part of many groups and want to get involved in all sorts of charity events. Taking up a challenge to raise money could be something you get involved in.

In love, you're tough to keep up with. High-flying ideas and exciting projects could have you here, there and everywhere, and your need for freedom may make it hard to build a relationship in the first place. I know someone with this placement who went out shopping on a Saturday and got home the following Monday, forgetting to tell his girlfriend where he was or when he might be home. A little lesson in the needs of others may be required!

Sun Pisces, Moon Sagittarius

A spiritual individual, you will have the desire to explore life's philosophical side and that could take you physically to holy and spiritually revered sites, places where you can connect to the divine. Your ethereal bearing is calming to those around you and they may also seek you out for advice. A role as a counsellor will suit you, perhaps using psychic, spiritual or religious training to do it.

Writing, making movies, telling stories through photographs – any way of connecting people to the magical worlds you can see could be something that attracts you. From an early age you could have been a great fan of the movies, especially those with a very clear message for humanity, such as *Avatar*.

Take care, though, that those whose sorry tale tugs at your heartstrings don't take advantage of your good nature. Have a sense of reality in what can sometimes be a harsh world.

In a relationship, you are likely to be very committed, but do need a Prince or Princess Charming. A refined and romantic relationship suits you best. Your partner needn't be rich or the best-looking, just charming and able to recognize your need to explore your magical world and bring it to those who have less magic in theirs.

CAPRICORN MOON

'I like bossy girls. I don't like girls who just do whatever they think you want them to do and follow you around trying to please you all the time.'

JARVIS COCKER

Archetype

The werewolf. OK, so you're not growing hair on your palms around the full Moon (or maybe you are), but it's not that sort of werewolf. Think the power to transform and the ability to deal with competition, to ally yourself with vampires if you have to and to hide your true nature. You're a negotiator, physically strong and able to change to gain power in a world that sometimes doesn't play by the rules. Good doggy.

CAPRICORN MOON ♑

The Moon is in detriment in this sign, so she is uncomfortable, but sometimes a little restlessness is a good thing – it keeps you on your paws, keeps you alert and ahead of the pack.

Self-respect is important to you and being dependent on another isn't on the agenda. Providing for them may very well be, and you take your responsibilities very seriously, especially when it comes to family commitments. This makes you a finisher. You can see a task through, and anyone who has the brilliant idea of using astrology in the workplace will assign you tasks that need to be finished instead of left hanging about half-done.

I know a very competent Capricorn Moon who is self-employed doing just that. She moves in when others have failed to meet targets or budgets and helps them to make sure the job is done. Sometimes that's uncomfortable, as people don't want to hear they have failed, but she does it with cool efficiency rather than personal finger-pointing and certainly no gossipy tongue-wagging.

You're not prone to short bursts of energy followed by the need for a lie-down in a darkened room. To those with boom and bust energy systems, you appear to be in control and ready to go at any moment, which is exactly what you are.

Autonomy is what you crave, and having others interfere with your work isn't welcome. Whether it's sorting out a spreadsheet or being a homemaker, you're not one for constant supervision. Anyone who knows you well will respect this and allow you to get on with things. Those who don't will learn very quickly.

When you were a cub you could have been the last to volunteer. The runt, some may say, but often the runt is the one that outlasts everyone else or has a growth spurt later in life that pushes them way ahead of the rest of the pack. You learn by watching and imitating those you admire, the more powerful creatures you want to become one day, and it's achievable.

You may be seen as a little old-fashioned by your peers, but the truth is you prefer the classics. You want something that's built to last and, even if it is expensive, is good value for money. That is something you're very keen on – value for money. So next time your friends complain about their Primani falling to bits after a couple of washes, remind them of the benefits of buying quality.

Your strong work ethic isn't just about being the best (although that is a big drive), it's also about making sure you build a nest egg for your retirement. Even at a very young age you will be thinking about your pension. This may lead you into roles that are renowned for providing a pension – teaching, government, the armed forces and emergency services – as well as working for yourself and creating your own empire, of course.

Money may be a constant worry, and that could be why you take care of it so well, but wouldn't it be better to accept that you do money really well and even if there are times when you feel you don't have any, you adapt and use what you do have wisely. Suggesting that you don't worry about money is likely to fall on deaf ears of course, so maybe carry on worrying if you must, but trust in yourself to do what's right when it's right, just as you do with everything else. You tend to be more successful later in life, which could be a reassuring thought.

Emotionally, you could be very stoic. Hiding your true feelings isn't something you do intentionally, it's something you do naturally. You're hard to read, and that can be a bonus in your professional life, but may not pay off when it comes to your personal life.

Those around you will see you as a rock, someone solid in their lives, and even if they do buy you a pipe and slippers for your twenty-first birthday, take that as a compliment: it means you're Steady Eddie. For you, going a little wild now and again could mean getting a little tipsy and forgetting to say thank you when your drink is delivered. Rarely, if ever, would it involve a drag queen, a penguin and a long night sitting under a tarpaulin at the funfair. Don't ask.

A great sense of humour will add to your popularity. Although those who work for you or come up against your inner Alan Sugar won't see it, it's very dry and usually delivered with the same directness Lord Sugar would use when firing a candidate. A reputation for being ruthless with your humour is probably well deserved.

Friends are probably few but very good and loyal, the sort you may not see all the time but when you do you just take up where you left off. Your shared experiences will make your friends feel more like family. Protecting them and helping when they need it are high on your list and you will be prepared to shift even work commitments to make sure you are there for them. Must be important!

Now let's talk about your bossy side. Don't give me that look, the look that says, 'Me, bossy?!' You so know you are, and what's more you love the fact that people see you that way! And of course you're only bossy because everyone else is so incompetent and if you weren't there being bossy things would descend into chaos, so there.

Taking your bossiness with a pinch of salt is a positive way to use it, but if you overdo it, you could lose your flavour very quickly and those you work with could go from admiring and willing followers to whispering deserters. Know your limits, let others put in their ideas and when you're wrong, admit it. Just saying.

You don't do coarseness. That doesn't mean you can't swear like a stoker when you want to; it does mean you don't do it as part of your daily routine and won't warm to those who do. You like a certain refinement in your life. Things must be just so, be it the way the curtains hang, the cushion is plumped or everyone stands up when you enter a room.

Your practical hands-on nature makes you useful to have around. You are good at DIY and excellent at sorting out that untidy garage or scrambling on the roof to waggle a satellite dish or two. However, you are likely to be a physically strong individual, so make sure that whatever you are waggling, you don't waggle it so hard that it falls off.

Some people may think you're boring. I know, silly, isn't it? What you are is traditional, practical and methodical. Boring you most definitely are not. If they only knew what happens around those full Moons.

Love Life

You take everything seriously, including your love life. A partner who is flippant, disrespectful, untidy and dare I say unhygienic won't last long at all. One who is the opposite of all of those you might even consider marrying.

In a relationship, you want a partner who is exactly that: a partner. With equal responsibility. As long as they know you're in charge, of course, and are working towards the same goals as you are.

It's not sounding very romantic, is it? Well, hearts and flowers and roses scattered in the bath aren't your style. The fact that you've regrouted the bathroom or cooked your partner's favourite dinner may be as far as that goes. It's not that you *can't* be romantic – of course you can, it's just that there are things that need to be done. Now.

Whilst a supportive partner is a must for everyone, it may not be easy for you to ask for help from someone else, no matter how capable you know they are, but once you get over that, a true partnership will be born, and even if you hardly ever do ask for help, knowing that you can will make all the difference.

Someone who nurtures you could be a good match – the sort that makes sure your home is run smoothly, your belly is filled with good food and your bills are paid on time. They could also help release the inner nurturer in *you*. Making a safe place for you to express yourself is definitely to be encouraged.

Like a good bottle of wine, you get better with age, and sex improves too as you learn more. You're a good learner and a thorough one, even if it does take you a few goes to get it right! As you get older, your relationship with your partner will strengthen and the understanding that you have in your everyday life will result in more intensity in the bedroom.

A downside of your love choices may be a decision to become involved with challenging individuals. Perhaps they are physically very attractive but need work in other areas, like commitment or basic respect. Whilst the challenge may be appealing, the rows, usually over silly little things, won't work long term. This doesn't mean to say you should choose a really submissive partner;

sometimes you do need to be put in your place too, I suspect. Find the happy mid-point: someone who challenges you but works with you, someone you can take to dinner with your boss and be proud of, someone who is happy to cook tea because you look worn out, someone you can laugh out loud with and someone who is your best friend as well as your lover.

Partnering a Capricorn Moon

There may be certain rules to abide by, but only if you're comfortable with that. Don't be bossed about by your Capricorn Moon or they will add more rules as they go! They are funny, but often that's built on sarcasm. Get that and you're onto a winner. Dependable, secure and loyal, they are keepers, and as long as things are kept equal, the relationship will work out well.

Best fit Sun signs are Capricorn, Taurus, Virgo and Cancer.

Career

A Moon sign of structure, organized, you're a bonus to any employer. Doing things by the rules, not easily being swayed by those who want to bend things even a little, will bring you success in your chosen field. The military (particularly the army), banking, teaching and insurance are areas you work well in; architecture too, which is of course the ultimate in structure and organization!

You're not one for quick decisions and reckless risks, preferring to work at your own pace even if that sees the mavericks at work climbing faster than you. You will see them when they are on the way down, you will outlast them and a slow but steady pace will win in the end.

What you earn and who earns more than you for doing less may be something that really gets your goat, something that becomes a 'thing' at work. Remember your skills and that slow, steady pace, and be confident that you will achieve what you want, be it in or out of the organization you're currently working for.

Therein may lie a problem: you are very loyal at work and could stay with one company for a long time when things may move faster for you elsewhere. You may have to decide between playing the long game where you are now and risking transferring to an institution you're not sure of. The risk to your pension must be considered too, of course.

One thing that's certain with Capricorn Moons is that they are going to be successful, no matter how long it takes!

Parents and Family

Your parents are everything to you. They may not have found parenting easy in their youth, but you will realize the sacrifices they made for you and be there for them whenever they need you. This may cause friction in a relationship, especially when Christmas dinner is *always* at your mum and dad's house rather than alternate years. Just saying.

Sometimes this Moon placement can signify the loss of a parent early on in life, a tragedy that means you have to grow up faster than others of your age. You could even become a carer or perhaps a major breadwinner for the family at a younger age than anyone would choose. If this has been the case for you, you are likely to have borne it well and it could have left you with an even greater sense of responsibility, in contrast to some signs, who might use it to justify the total opposite.

If you're a parent yourself, you may be seen as a strict disciplinarian. Your family is the reason you work so hard, and you want structure in your life to be able to enjoy it. For you, there will be no 'work hard, never around' parenting role — you take both work and parenting very seriously.

There may be some run-ins with your kids when it comes to what their friends are allowed to do and they are not. Every parent gets that one, but you won't be swayed, and the sooner your kids realize that, the better! As they get older, they will come to appreciate why, and they are likely to be well rounded because of it.

At home, things are likely to be traditional, with colours muted and furniture high quality and built to last, or at least to be recovered every three years or so! When making house purchases, you will find older houses appeal more to you than modern homes. Ideally, the one you choose will have a good garden for the children to play in and somewhere for you to relax amongst your flowers and your home-grown veg – what a great way to save money!

House and home for you are Sunday roast – plenty of it, thank you – either at your parental home or, if it's your own, with all of your family around the table that you paid for, eating the food you've bought and cooked. You are happy to show how successful you are and to share that success with those you love.

Health

Traditionally, you should look after your teeth, bones and skin in particular, so make sure you get those dental check-ups regularly and have healthy well-balanced meals that include calcium for strong bones and teeth. If you do have skin issues, seek help immediately and don't discount stress management as a way of relieving any symptoms. You will work hard, and that's fine, but remember to work smart too. Look after yourself. Use your gift for organization to make sure it happens!

Life Skills

You're able to make a list and stick to it, which may not sound like much, but actually so few can. Your ability to make sure things are done extends beyond yourself – you can inspire those around you to do the same, but make sure it's inspiration and not bossy boots time!

Having a plan also makes it easier to monitor success and to keep things heading in the direction you want them to. By taking control of your life, you can achieve your goals.

Often with planets, or luminaries as the Moon is, it's best to think of the creature that represents the sign, so your Moon makes you a goat – able to climb any mountain as long as it takes its time, sure-footed and, if it does occasionally slip, able to get right back on the path. Whilst eating everything in sight.

Stumbling Blocks

When you're not feeling at your best, how would anyone know? You don't appear any different, and if you don't ask for help, you can sit there wondering what to do when a fresh pair of eyes could guide you. Your stoic attitude may need to be rethought sometimes.

Although structure and tradition are important, failure to recognize when change is needed and a modern approach would make things easier may put you back a bit. 'If it ain't broke, don't fix it' could be something you say, but who is to say something new wouldn't improve things? Doing things the same way day in, day out may need to be reviewed.

Being in charge is your natural state of being, but does it always have to be that way? Hand over those passports and tickets to someone else on holiday and relax for once, rather than be the one who has to get everything organized. Go on, give it a go.

Spiritual Lesson

Although you're clearly in control of things, perhaps your spiritual lesson is to learn to let go. Sometimes control comes from knowing when it's right to go with the flow rather than attempt to build a dam or rechannel the flow.

Past lives could have involved riding roughshod over others in order to realize your ambitions. This time round, it's about using your talents with balance and humility. This gifted and powerful Moon needs careful handling. Releasing your inner beast is sometimes necessary, but use it wisely.

SUN SIGN, MOON SIGN

So now you know a little more about your Moon sign, but how does that work with your Sun sign?

Sun Aries, Moon Capricorn

Sharply dressed and ready to state your case, you are prepared for a fight, but always with right on your side and the facts at your disposal. This is the perfect balance of creative initiator and well-thought-out finisher, and success for you is about being first and last: first with the idea and last to leave at the end of the day when you are making it all happen.

A real fighter, you take what others have to say to you on the chin. If you're wrong, you won't throw your rattle out of the pram, you will change what you have to and prove yourself at least half-right, while developing something better in the process.

You are a leader who prefers to lead from the front but can double back and rally the troops when needed and help wash out the pots and pans to gauge the feeling in the camp before proceeding.

When looking for love, you're likely to be as upfront as you are in business. It takes a strong individual to tolerate that sort of energy, so a strong individual it will have to be. Shy away from those who think pink, avoid the fluffy toy and wuv-woo bear brigade and go for someone who tells it like it is and can take it as well as give it.

Sun Taurus, Moon Capricorn

When immovable object meets strong structure, you have the beginnings of something that is strong, well-grounded and highly practical, but may be unable to react quickly or be flexible if needed.

You want to have things organized just so, everything running the way it should, perfection wherever you look, and you want to make sure there's growth – growth at work, rest and play. But to have real growth you must add some Water to all that Earth you have, to nurture and feed those who can help you achieve your goals, so think about the emotional response to your requests.

You have an uncanny ability to judge what others are and indeed are not capable of and allocate tasks accordingly, but once people get to know you they see you're not quite the machine you appear to be. When relaxed, you love music, and probably a truly filthy joke, and above all you are loyal to those who show you the same courtesy.

In love, nothing less than devotion to your other half is good enough, and you expect the same in return. Look for someone who can put up with your more stubborn moments and nurture your emotional needs by coaxing you into talking things out in a safe environment. Basically, find yourself a head teacher with a love of chocolate body paint and Wagner.

Sun Gemini, Moon Capricorn

It's hard to float like a butterfly when your wings are tipped with iron. Getting things off the ground isn't really a problem for you, it's keeping them there when the responsibility you feel for everything you've ever said is weighing you down and trying to do it all to the best of your ability is all-consuming. You smile and smile and smile some more and tell everyone you're fine, but deep inside you're anything but and finding it harder and harder to stay in flight.

Balance is the key: get others to go along with your amazing ideas and then organize things so that they help you. Don't take it all on your own shoulders. Learn to delegate, then all you have to do is flit between the various camps making sure everything is running the way it should.

Learning new things is something that's likely to fire you up and you could sign up for a whole variety of courses to fuel your need to be learning new tricks all the time.

In love, you're a tough one to pin down. Your need for variety may mean you take your time in finding your soul mate and even then they are likely to be the unpredictable sort. That will keep you interested, but then again you would really like to settle down, to be home at six for your tea, be watching the soaps at seven… wouldn't you? You would last a week. Boredom is your enemy, be it in love, work or play.

Sun Cancer, Moon Capricorn

Not only can you bake a decent Victoria sponge, you can manage a department of 100 and have them all more loyal to you than a Labrador is to liver treats.

You're likely to be a very serious individual, ambitious too, but you will have a warmth that encourages people to help you. That's not in any manipulative way; it's honest and humble – people just warm to you and want to see you succeed.

The good thing is you're happy to see them succeed too, unless of course they are going for the same job as you, in which case game on, but if up for best actress, your 'Well done, you' face would be the only one that was telling the truth when your opponent won.

Your family is without a doubt your reason for being. Making sure they are provided for, be it parents or children, is your priority. You're there for them and woe betide anyone who gets in the way of 'the family' (said in an East End accent).

In love, you adore your life partner and make life as comfortable for them as you can. Even though work can sometimes get in the way, you're likely to provide a beautiful home environment. Getting the same guarantee from your partner is important too, but is it always possible?

Sun Leo, Moon Capricorn

As you bound out onto the world stage, you're the image of supreme confidence: 'Look at me, ruler of all I survey!' But inside you could be shaking like a little girl at her first dance performance.

That vulnerability is the very thing that draws people to you. They somehow see that no matter how impressive you are (and you *are*), you still have moments of doubt like the rest of us. Endearing!

This is a real *X-Factor* placement, one that shines on stage, and even if things aren't always perfect, there is a quality about you that brings success, perhaps in the performing arts.

But when you have tap-danced your way across the stage and taken your bow, you may want nothing more than some time on your own to sit and ponder, to think about how you performed and how you can improve. That's all well and good, and improving is good, but beating yourself up for not being good enough is another thing. Don't.

In love, you're a generous individual, gregarious and happy to share your success with your other half, but sometimes you can be difficult if some of your glitter falls on that other half. Sharing the limelight may not be easy for you. Does that mean you pick dowdy partners? Have a word. You want the best-looking, tallest, richest, most fabulous partner of all your peers. Good luck with that.

Sun Virgo, Moon Capricorn

Life, don't talk to me about life… One minute it's a rich tapestry, next it's worn out and in need of some tender loving care. Life…

Cheer up! Perhaps an overload of information may not be a good thing for you. Maybe you could take some time to weigh what you know against the reality of how it's applied, or explore some of life's less analytical subjects. How about considering the simple beauty of a landscape or wandering through an art gallery and losing yourself in the passion and emotion of the exhibits?

Over-thinking is something you need to be wary of, but on the other hand you are a treasure trove of information and what you don't know you can find out. People will come to you to find out how things work and you make a great researcher, teacher or medical practitioner.

If you feel you're not popular at work, it's usually because you're so efficient you put others to shame. Slow down now and again, smell the cappuccino, let them catch up and share a bagel.

In love, you could be cautious when entering a relationship, but once you do, you give 100 per cent. This may sometimes lead you to 'not worthy' territory when you feel you're not performing as you should be. Learn to talk about your feelings with your partner, but most of all get out and about and do lots of things together that bring shared experiences and fun into your life.

Sun Libra, Moon Capricorn

This combination brings together the artistic world and the business world beautifully. It's fashion design success and art dealer heaven. I know of a beauty therapist turned director of a huge beauty product house with this placement, and she walks and talks her role, even telling the waitress at dinner what products would be best for her skin type!

Law is also represented here, and even if you don't do it on a professional level, your sense of right and wrong is something that others will value in you. It seems you have the uncanny knack of being able to pick those with integrity and those it may be best to steer away from. Unless you're in love.

In love, you may make some odd choices, because you're looking for an ideal: the perfect love with the perfect partner. Does it exist? 'Drop your standards' may be something you hear from your mates after a long spell of being single, 'as nobody living can meet them.' But *can* you drop your standards?

Ask yourself this question: are you in love with that millionaire playboy or are you in love with the idea of being in love with him? True love may actually be on offer from the mechanic who adores you, calls you 'princess' and would do anything for you. Being in love with love often equates to putting up with things when you really shouldn't. Just saying.

Sun Scorpio, Moon Capricorn

Like the creature that represents your Sun sign, you do like to hide in the shadows, but the success required and indeed offered by your lunar goat means you have to come out now and again, even if it is at night.

This Sun–Moon combination quite frankly makes you ruthless, able to strike at the perfect moment and to keep your intentions hidden from those who don't need to know what you're up to. That's fine in business, but with friends it could sometimes lead them to think you're keeping things from them. Perhaps you are, but usually it's not intentional, it's just habit. So, do consciously make an effort to keep them up to date with what's going on.

You'd make a great pathologist, lab worker, politician, lawyer or detective – jobs where attention to detail is important, as is the ability to have your say regardless of who gets upset by it. You are, after all, only speaking the truth. Something that's very, very important to you.

In love, you're passionate and highly physical, so an energetic and robust partner would suit you best! You need one who can coax you out of the emotional shadows, provide a safe place for you to talk about your feelings and then cover you in chocolate sauce and get stuck in. Whipped cream with that?

Sun Sagittarius, Moon Capricorn

You're happy to throw dice to decide which route you're going to take and then plan every detail down to the last toilet break, but this combination of the grandeur of Sagittarius and the control of Capricorn should work in your favour. All you need to do is remember to let go when you're feeling restricted and to apply the brakes when you're charging off recklessly with no idea where you're heading. Easy.

A gregarious soul, you will need lots of friend and hobbies, along with a job that allows you time to fit them all in, and if you can work on the side building up your own travel agency or teaching kids to play the trumpet, so much the better.

You may take on too much sometimes, but you're capable of trimming things down when you feel that's the case. One thing you will never do is *not* take on enough!

In love, you're passionate and embrace your relationship with every fibre of your being. A partner who wants to travel and find out what the world has to offer suits you best. Perhaps you're attracted to someone from another country or would like to live overseas. The world is just about big enough to contain your ambitions – *just* – but get out and test it anyway.

Sun Capricorn, Moon Capricorn

I'm surprised to see you here. Is someone else reading this for you as you shrug your shoulders and say you don't believe in all this stuff? Typical Capricorn.

If it's not been approved by at least one governmental body, it can't be right; if it doesn't have a stamp of approval from three of your friends and hasn't been signed off by a lawyer, how can it be it be worthy of your time? Joking aside, you do like to see evidence before you take anyone at their word, and that is a very good thing indeed.

It also makes you incredibly successful, and your cool-headed methods at work, along with your attention to detail and planning, will have you in the director's chair faster than most. No doubt you'll be taking on every role offered to you, but do make sure that you build in some time to rest. You are not a machine. Some would argue with that actually, but between you and me you're as human as the rest of us, so take some time to recharge the battery.

Also like the rest of us, you need love in your life, someone you can turn to for comfort and can try out your next presentation on, but also someone who doesn't need you to be the big 'I am', someone with whom you can be the little kid who just wants to play, to laugh and to make a mess now and again.

Now get back to work.

Sun Aquarius, Moon Capricorn

This is where the mad professor meets the means to earn enough funds to carry out his experiments! Oh, OK you're not as mad as you would have some people believe, but occasionally you can come up with some strange ideas, and it's that entrepreneurial side to you that could bring you unexpected success. Don't discount any flashes of inspiration you may have, do something with them!

You're a real self-starter – there's no need for a boss to be constantly on your case as you get things done, and you are better off getting them done your way. In fact isn't that the only way?

Investigating the latest technology is something you're likely to enjoy and your ability to get things right comes from knowing your stuff.

A sense of self-worth helps you negotiate fair pay for what you do, and what you do could be medical research, teaching, writing or any kind of scientific or engineering work – anything technological that could float that hover-sea-and-space-plane you're inventing.

'Inventive' is a good word for you, but make sure you are using your inquisitive nature in the best way, or it could cause you to poke around where you really shouldn't. But then again, investigative journalism would suit you.

In love, you're loyal and your Capricorn Moon brings a need for your family environment to be perfect – but that's your sort of perfect and it's unlikely to be anyone else's. You are sure to have an eclectic home with radical ideas on love and family.

Emotionally, try to remember your family is important. Sometimes this Sun–Moon combination can be a cool alliance, one that tends to be very rational and not over-emotional. That won't suit all of the people all of the time.

Sun Pisces, Moon Capricorn

Can you change the world all by yourself? Given enough time, probably, but there are many things to take care of other than changing the world, and losing yourself in a cause may have to wait – unless of course you can find a job that means you can fulfil your desire to make a difference as well as your need to furnish your life with the trappings of success.

Careers in photography, the film industry and marketing may appeal, but there will have to be an ethical edge to everything you do.

Making dreams come true is hard work; others with your Pisces Sun know what it's like to dream, but few know how to turn those dreams into reality. But here's the thing – you do. And you can help those with nothing achieve something. You can also inspire them to be more like you. In fact, by being yourself, simply by being yourself, you can change the world.

And then, after a hard day fundraising for the homeless or looking after that sick seal cub, there's nothing nicer than a soak in the hot tub, a glass of cold wine and a slice of chocolate cake.

In love, you're a romantic and are likely to put a lot of hard work into it, but should it be so well planned? Yes! How else is it going to look so seamlessly spontaneous? You want a partner who is just as well prepared and puts in just as much effort, but they must also be prepared for you to forget your own name on occasion. Adorable.

AQUARIUS MOON

*'The degree of one's emotions varies inversely with
one's knowledge of the facts.'*

BERTRAND RUSSELL

Archetype

The inventor. In your lab with your mad hair, doing those experiments to find out just what will happen if you mix this with that, even if you've been told you must never, ever do that. One way to get you to do something is to tell you to never, ever do it. Cantankerous you may be, but your archetype also makes you exciting, inventive and unpredictable, and those who get that get a fiend, sorry, I mean friend, for life.

AQUARIUS MOON ≈

Having an Aquarian Moon can sometimes make you seem cool, not in a hip and trendy way but detached, perhaps even aloof. But of course nothing could be further from the truth – you are friendly and can be outrageous when you're around people you know. I know an Aquarius Moon who for no reason starting break-dancing in a bar. Not too outrageous, you would think, but he was 50 when he did it.

This coolness can sometimes extend to being accused of not displaying your emotions very well, even to being cold when it comes to the L.O.V.E. in your life. It seems to some that you don't really feel the way that others do, but what you're really doing is rationalizing your emotions. You feel them well enough, but very swiftly start to think about how you can process them. Then very often you come up with a solution that puts them back in a box and practicalities take over.

As your archetype would suggest, you're very clever. And whether you have a degree from Cambridge or a degree from the University of Life, you use what you have learned. Many with this Moon find themselves extending their educational journey or working in education. Seeing other people grow is something that could interest you too. Again, that may be formally as a teacher, life coach or business guru, or informally as a mentor to family and friends who recognize your problem-solving abilities.

When you do offer help, others should listen. If they don't, they could find themselves ending up on the outskirts of your life. Nothing says 'bye, bye' faster than someone who won't take your advice and help themselves out of some bother or who constantly bothers you when all they are really after is someone to dump their worries on. You can be brutal in your assessment of their efforts to date and that may seem harsh, but it's been my experience with this Moon placement that all you are doing is telling people the truth. Harsh as it sometimes is.

Eccentricity is something you could display, and as this is your Moon and not your Sun, that can sometimes come across as opinions that are out of synch with those of others, opinions based on those cool analytical tendencies you have. You may not empathize with those who could clearly help themselves if they bothered and this could cause you to stand out from the crowd. Your adventurous solutions, possibly containing risk as well as some whacky ideas, won't sit well with everyone. Hence the label 'eccentric'.

Labels are also something you won't think much of, and people who fall into tribes aren't likely to get your vote. The sporty types, the preppy types, the yummy mummies and dolly dealers aren't displaying what you consider to be the Holy Grail of human existence: individuality. You may even be very vocal when faced with stereotypes, particularly those who dress the same, think the same and do the same at work. You will graduate to the table of misfits at lunch. Sorry, was that 'misfits' or 'free-thinkers'?

When things go wrong in your own life, you're not great at asking for help, preferring to sort things out for yourself, and even when direct assistance is offered you're likely to give a flat 'no'. It's your problem, you can deal with it. But what if you can't? Just saying.

When dramas do occur, you rationalize what's going on and start to deal with things swiftly, but sometimes that's too fast for those around you. They would appreciate some time to think things over, but can find themselves down a road they don't want to be on, but you do, so there! You know that teamwork is important and you can see who plays what role, but sometimes you might want to think about who made you king.

If someone stands up to you, you can take criticism very well, listen to their point of view and take on any changes you think would help the situation, but it does take a brave individual to tackle you. With such a powerful mind, you can remember things that others have forgotten and bring up subjects that illustrate just what changes they need to make, what happened the last time they tried to do this and why you're so great at what you do. Justifying a course of action is really what you do best. Now apply that to business and you can see why you could make a very good consultant.

With your great sense of humour, you get the oddest things, things that others might miss. You can also send very strange birthday gifts to friends to make them laugh, even if it is just for five minutes, and your loyalty to your mates is admirable. Plenty would call you a friend, by the way, but you're likely to have only a few very good friendships.

When you were young, particularly in your teenage years, you could have been rebellious and perhaps had real tantrum and tiara moments. Making sense of the world meant challenging it and testing beliefs and how things worked. That will continue into adult life, but without the tantrums, we hope!

This different perspective that you have could lead you to ponder conspiracy theories, to look beyond what's presented to you by governments and countries and to think about your own role in humanity, what that really means to you. This could bring on an interest in alternative faiths and beliefs, as well as a love of complementary medicine, but you will always be looking for the link between them and the conventional sciences. On the other hand, being the cantankerous sort that you are, you could poo-poo the whole lot of it. If it's not scientifically proven, you're not interested. There will be no middle ground.

If an idea comes into your head, be it changing the wallpaper in the front room or changing the world, you really go for it. It can consume your every waking hour as you make posters, set up PowerPoint and get your banners ready for waving. Balance out this intensity with some fun – something you're very good at having when you let yourself go, but you may not think you have the time. You have.

You can actually be quite flexible with time. Going to the shop for ten minutes could turn into a four-hour trip and lunch, but you could forget to tell those who are waiting for you to return with the milk. You need your independence, and that's fine, but let people know you've changed the schedule.

Keeping things interesting is your greatest gift. You can invent new ways to make old journeys much more fascinating, and when faced with what others could see as a brick wall, you can construct a way around, under or over it.

Love Life

When you're in a relationship, you must maintain that air of individuality. That doesn't mean to say you're not fully committed, it just means less of the 'we did this, we did that' and more wiggle room to be yourself. Find a partner with a strong self-identity to balance yours. When you do, the relationship will be stronger for it.

Look for someone who doesn't fall into the old joke about the first three things in a wedding ceremony: aisle, altar, hymn. What you want is someone who may be thinking about how they can support you, someone who is excited about their own projects and preferably someone who has that spark of the unusual about them. You may choose a partner who is older or younger, from a different ethnic or religious background, or someone with an interesting story.

To work with your sometimes cool Moon – did I mention that? – you do best with someone who offers you attention on the emotional front, someone you feel safe with and can talk to about how you feel, but not someone who makes it their life's work to warm you up. That won't do.

You can be romantic – a bag of crisps and a candle to eat them by is romantic – but it's likely you show your love through the support you give to your partner's interests and in those silent moments when you're both engrossed in a new book or fascinating website.

When it comes to the more physical side of your love life, you can be just as inventive here too, and in fact you should try to be – something that can be fun of course, but make sure the roof joists are strong enough to support that swing and that the whipped cream comes out of your tufted shag easily.

If someone is wooing you, they either need to whisk you off to somewhere very glamorous or write love letters to you from their year helping out with Doctors without Borders. You're a sucker for a stretch limousine or someone who does their bit for charity, but avoid footballers – a WAG you are not.

Now a delicate subject: fidelity. You like a bit of excitement and you like change, and there's no reason why your other half can't provide both, but what if they don't? We all know the answer to that, so choose carefully and remember to work at keeping the variety you need alive and well.

Partnering an Aquarius Moon

Sign up to help out with some charity work, have a passion of your own, make sure you're inventive in the bedroom and don't follow the pack. There you have it, short and sweet.

Just one more thing: if you're a mind reader, it will make it easier to find out what they are feeling.

Best fit Sun signs are Aquarius, Gemini, Libra and Leo.

Career

You need to be able to learn on the job, not just through the work you do but also the inspirational people you meet. Something logical would suit you too. The NHS, banking, IT, education and a scientific environment would all suit you well, but there must be room for elevation, space for you to achieve great things, and of course the personal freedom to do it your way.

Reinventing and improving things is what you do best. Consultancy work can allow your entrepreneurial spirit to fly and keep things from becoming samey as well as satisfy your need for independence. You could also do well anywhere you have to deal with tough choices. Redundancies and budget cuts are something you can tackle without becoming emotionally involved.

Putting something back is also important to you. Heading up a charity or doing some voluntary work on the side will use your talents, and even if you're not being paid for it, it can still count as part of your career plan.

One thing is for sure: with this Moon sign, you're not the stay-at-home type. You will want to be out in the world making your mark.

Parents and Family

As a child, you may have experienced an upbringing that was far from conventional, or felt that your parents treated you differently from those of the other kids. This may have been because of their strict rules or the total opposite, where not many restrictions were put on you and freedom of expression reigned.

Your parents may have been frugal. Not mean, but cautious with money, and when it comes to your own children, and your home too, you can also be canny with the cash. Your home is likely to be unique as well – peaceful, and of course somewhere you can come and go without any questions being asked, sometimes at odd times of the day and night.

Mum may have been the real driving force of the home, controlling money, where you were educated, what you wore and who you were and weren't allowed to play with. This would of course have made your father the one who let you get away with things. He is likely to have been your ally when things didn't go the way your mum would have liked!

Showing affection may not have been high on the list and you will either make a huge show of affection with your own children or also remain quite cool. That doesn't mean to say you don't love them, simply that you prefer to show your love through day-to-day support, funding extra school trips and buying those gadgets they can't be without. Mainly because you want to play with them.

Your children will love your eccentric nature and enjoy the fact that you can be as mad as a fish on a bicycle and play along with their games. In fact you're likely to encourage them to explore their own true nature through as many hobbies and pastimes as they please, and if they change their minds next week, who cares, as long as they are learning?

Honesty is important to you, and never more so than within the family unit. Here you expect to be told the truth when asked and will do the same. Perhaps your kids will be the first to realize the tooth fairy isn't who we think it is and Santa has some undiscovered secrets too. What you won't put up with is blame-shifting. If you have more than one child and they play that game, they are unlikely to do it twice.

A conventional parent you're not – and all the more interesting for it.

Health

Traditionally, your lower legs, calves and ankles are the weaker parts of your body, so take care to stretch before your Zumba class and if your varicose veins start to look like the M25, get them checked out sooner rather than later. Circulation is something worth making sure you look after too. Oxygen getting to the system is of course important to us all, but for you it can sometimes need a little extra push, so add some aerobic work to your gym routine.

Life Skills

You need freedom to be who you want to be, to come and go, be it in your home or in your working environment, and all the time you're doing that, you're learning new skills and keeping yourself interested. You're a real live wire when you're fully engaged with life and one way you know when you need to make some changes is when you feel that light dim.

Travel brings you a wide perspective on many things and using your social skills you can strike up a conversation wherever you are, something that could bring you a wide set of contacts. Throughout your life these contacts will move in and out, helping you as you help them and bringing you opportunities in life. Networking, no matter what the reason, is a real skill you should use as much as you can.

Stumbling Blocks

From a very early age, younger now than ever it seems, we all bow to peer pressure, and though you're more individual than most, you too will try to fit in to keep some people on your side.

Imagine that as throwing a cloth over your true self, a great big, dirty old cloth that hides your vibrant energy. So now do you want to do it? You will fit in where you're meant to fit in; if you don't fit in where you are now, then keep on moving.

The other way of dealing with this is to stand up and wave a banner for the freedom of all, to try to change who or what you see, and that's admirable. But know what you're up against and have a sense of what victory will cost you and those who come with you. The very thing that makes you exciting to be around could be the stumbling block you fall over.

The answer? Be aware of your surroundings and watch the emotional responses of those around you. Know when to hold and when to fold.

Spiritual Lesson

All that you are is amazing; all that you need to learn is, however, the opposite to how you feel. Contrary? That will be an Aquarius Moon! Spiritually, you're learning how to show more compassion, how to let go and just have fun and when to come out of the snowy tower you inhabit and play in the sunny meadows. But never ever lose your sense of uniqueness.

SUN SIGN MOON SIGN

So now you know a little more about your Moon sign, but how does that work with your Sun sign?

Sun Aries, Moon Aquarius

You are a force to be reckoned with, but make sure you show the reckoning part before the forceful bit or you could scare some people off. What they may see is someone fixed on doing things their way with no regard for anyone else's input. To be fair, that might sometimes be the case, but you do actually care about the greater good, you're just not fond of those who dither about.

Getting yourself into any group or organization you fancy won't be difficult. At school you may have been at one with the geeks as well as the sporty types and managed to maintain friendships quite happily where others struggled.

In love, you're hard to read – one minute all arms and legs and 'Let's swing from the chandelier!' and the next off down the pub with your mates wondering if you should go home soon but deciding to stay and why not pop across the Channel for some beers while you're at it? No need to tell your other half, just get stuck into the adventure of it all.

But all is forgiven when you turn on the charm (which you have in abundance), say the right things and bring back some duty-free for all.

Sun Taurus, Moon Aquarius

Having something to hang onto is always going to give you stability, be it gold under the bed or a principle in your head. You need to know where you stand, and that's just admirable. But sometimes you want to jack it all in and embrace the adventure, give it all up and see where life takes you.

It's a tough one, but the combination of sense and seemingly senselessly abandoning all you've worked for is something that could pay off for you. You're nothing if not unpredictable, it's what helps you build strong friendships throughout the world and actually can provide you with a home from home in many homes away from home.

An eclectic mix of objects from your travels could adorn your home and mix with your love of gadgetry to provide you with the perfect lair for a James Bond character, but are you villain or hero? Depends on the weather.

In love, you're cuddly but cool, collected but ready to abandon all your inhibitions for the right person. All you need is the right person! Although you enjoy flirting, unless you can see a future you're not going to be sharing cornershop croissants with some random eager to impress. Been there, done that.

Sun Gemini, Moon Aquarius

Whilst texting on your BlackBerry or playing games on your ibored, you might even manage to have a conversation with someone! What a busy bee, but are you stopping long enough to smell the flowers, never mind gather the honey that could be yours?

You can be in two places at once with all the modern technology at your disposal, but does that mean you should be? Just saying.

Taking time to engage your brain in some puzzle-solving is important. Without exercising it, you're likely to get into mischief, as your natural talent for invention must be shown. This can sometimes manifest as gossip, and if there's nothing to gossip about, that might not stop you. 'Who said what? She didn't, did she? And as for him, he's neither use nor ornament!' That will get you into trouble, beware!

In love, you're a fast talker, and talking someone into sharing a sunrise with you won't be too tough a task, but asking them to leave you alone by teatime might be. That's an awesome power you have there, or are you just pleased to see me?

Partners should be able to hold three conversations at once and remember that no matter what, you're right.

Sun Cancer, Moon Aquarius

Having somewhere out of the limelight to retire to is essential. You need to feel the warmth of the central heating around you, smell the new-baked bread and hear the sound your computer makes as it connects you to the world, all from the comfort of your front room.

Whilst browsing the homeware department of your favourite online store and visualizing just how great those table lamps would look in your house, you're also likely to think about those who have no table to put them on, or house to put them in for that matter. You will have a strong sense of human family as well as strong feelings for those born into yours.

A deeply sensitive soul, it's not easy for you to confront those who have overreached themselves around you, but you do it better than most. In fact what you feel is a weakness may be one of your greatest strengths: you say what's on your mind, but you do it with natural empathy.

In love, you're looking for a free-thinking plumber, a poetic bricklayer or perhaps a doctor of physics with a penchant for cake-making. Good luck with that. Ideally, you need a partner who is sensitive to your moods, with a psychic connection that helps them know how you're feeling without you actually telling them. Or a Labrador.

Sun Leo, Moon Aquarius

This full Moon position brings you an over-the-top sense of occasion, or is that drama? Same thing. One thing is for sure: you're not going to be a boring character, ever, but for some you may seem too much. They aren't any concern of yours, of course, and you're quick to dismiss their application for would-be friend. Well done, you.

Unique of course, you're also someone who can stand out in a crowd, be it with your funky hair or your leopard-print hot pants, and some of the women are just as bad. You intentionally make your presence felt, have the confidence to carry it off and quite frankly would be on speed dial if you were my friend.

Dramas may occur around you, and there's the clue: if they are around you, then you are at the centre of them. They might be your way of problem-solving, especially when those around you are doing nothing about what you see as an injustice.

In love, it takes a fireproof suit and a tin hat to get near you. You radiate heat, but when you let someone in that means they are in for a warm reception. What you will not stand for is someone who isn't as honest as they could be. Any would-be partner will learn very early on not to tell you they went to the pub when in fact they went for a bag of chips.

Fun to be around, yes, but do you ever turn it down? Hope so.

Sun Virgo, Moon Aquarius

Your anorak could be made of tin-foil, but that is, after all, the best way to stop aliens from abducting you. Oh alright, I jest – it won't stop them and you know it, in fact you know everything and what you don't know you can find out in a second and pass off as if you've known it for years.

Analytical work suits you very well. You're happy crunching numbers or rows and rows of computer codes, but please leave that out of the conversation if you're chatting someone up. Unless they too are in a silver anorak.

A tendency to over-think could make you a nervous individual. Perhaps too much theory and not enough practice has you creating scenarios that aren't practical realities? If your mind runs off with you, use its power to remind yourself to live in the here and now, not in the future where robots rule the world.

In love, you're a riot. Oh alright, maybe you could *cause* a riot by insisting your other half is quite simply wrong and section three, sub-section four, proves it. Or you could give in to your hidden desire to swing from the chandelier wearing a cowboy hat and not much else. I vote cowboy hat.

Sun Libra, Moon Aquarius

A glamorous combo, one that offers a decent manicure and some spangly designer wear that gets you noticed and into all the right places. If you feel less than glamorous, take some time to release your inner goddess. It won't take much; she is very close to the surface.

The combination of Venus and Uranus brings you a spontaneity and charm that makes you enchanting and an ability to talk people into your way of thinking that makes you dangerous!

Getting your own way isn't hard for you; in fact it can be easy to take it for granted and you could become complacent. That way danger lies. You could be accused of being emotionally too cool, so make sure you take steps to tell your fluffy bunnykins that you wuv them and show them with a hug now and again.

That leads us neatly onto your love life generally. You love to be in love, you love nothing more than showing off the fact that you're in a relationship and the relationship has to be with Peter Perfect, who is not only good looking but also able to show a girl a very good time indeed. But take the time to look beneath the surface. Perhaps you would be happier with his mate Olly Ordinary, a nice decent chap who treats you like a princess?

Sun Scorpio, Moon Aquarius

'Aloof' may be one of the words associated with you on first meeting. Nothing is further from the truth, but on first contact you can look at folks as if they are aliens: just why are they here, what do they want and why don't they leave you alone?

Once you warm to them – and they have to prove themselves – there is no more loyal friend. You would do whatever was needed to protect and help a mate in their hour of need and they would return the compliment.

Attracting such loyalty is something that works really well for you professionally, but honesty from your peers as well as your superiors is needed. Woe betide anyone who thinks they can keep something from you – your ability to wheedle out even the biggest so-called secret is a thing of legend and you will just 'know' what's happening before anyone else. Perhaps the look that says 'I know what you're thinking' is what does it?

In love, you're a passionate and inventive individual who is happy to let themselves go with the right partner. As with friendships, that could take some time to come to fruition. But when it does, sales of whipped cream and chocolate sauce could go up in your area. Cherry with that?

Sun Sagittarius, Moon Aquarius

So, going anywhere nice for your holidays? Bet you are, bet you're going somewhere really nice, and if you're not, you're thinking about it, planning a trip or reading a book about someone who has been there, done that and got the T-shirt.

An over-the-top response to challenges could be something you need to keep an eye on. Swinging from rational thought to senseless action could jeopardize your plans. Finding the middle ground may sound boring, but it's probably practical now and again. Having said that, your ability to take risks is something that could pay off for you. Just make them well calculated.

Working in the travel industry could fuel your sense of adventure and provide you with perks that mean you won't break the bank following your dreams, something that's easy for you to do. Money doesn't feature big in your world, but unfortunately it does feature pretty big in the real one.

Your entrepreneurial spirit also includes a philanthropic one: you want to make sure everyone gets their share and could work for charity organizations in far-off places.

In a relationship, you need the stability of a partner who stays at home making sure you have somewhere to come home to or picks up their rucksack and joins you. Later in life, settling down could be a problem, but who says you have to? Buy a caravan, but make sure it's one of those big shiny silver jobs.

Sun Capricorn, Moon Aquarius

What's the point of rules if you can't break them now and again? Maybe the thought of breaking a few is too much for you, so how about bending them? Is that better? Part of you wants to be a rebel, to say what you're really thinking, whilst another part of you knows you have to play by the rules. Have to?

You can bide your time, you can see what's coming up next, even if 'next' is months or actually years away, and you can plan accordingly. So, no worries – success is assured, as is getting there ethically.

Yes, things have to be right, above board, fair and equal for you. Your sense of equality sees you standing up for the little guy in the face of those who think they have a right to stand on him. Working as a union lawyer or perhaps an environmental warrior gives you a platform to play by the rules and to challenge them at the same time. You may even enter politics to right what you feel are unacceptable wrongs.

In love, you could be seen as the conventional type, but are you really such a traditionalist? Whilst you're likely to want the home, the car and the 2.5 children, you're also keen on a partner who has that spark of rebellion in them – a nurturer, a provider, yes, but also someone who would put themselves out on a limb for those who need it, just as you would. Wishy-washy types not welcome.

Sun Aquarius, Moon Aquarius

Do I have to write this? Telling you what to do isn't something I would want to do. In fact I suspect that when you were a child your parents found that out early on and suggested you did the direct opposite of what they wanted. Say 'Turn right' and you're likely to turn left. But cantankerous? You? Never.

This spontaneity within you is hard for others to keep pace with. You're likely to change your mind mid-plan and forget to let anyone know, so you're the only one under the station clock at nine o'clock whilst everyone else was there at eight. Not to worry – you're permanently wired into the World Wide Web, so texts, e-mails and anything else you can witter on with will have things corrected quick smart.

Smart is something you certainly are, as bright as a 100-watt lamp, but just like that lamp, you use up some energy. In fact you use up a lot of it. You might even find your white goods fail quicker than most as you zap them on the way past every day. Take care with your energy – replenish it with rest and don't forget to eat!

In love, you're not an easy one to understand. You may feel as if you're being open with your feelings, but your other half is seeing a wall of ice. So, come out of the cold and say 'thawy' now and again. Bad joke. But do make an effort to speak plainly about how you feel and then get on with enjoying the craziness that's life with a double Aquarius – never dull.

Sun Pisces, Moon Aquarius

Is life one long fantasy adventure or are you lost in the mist and not sure if that's a spaceship up ahead or the petrol station you are looking for? Keeping your feet on the ground may not be easy for you and some real effort to ground yourself is required.

Use your Aquarius Moon to offer rational reasoning for what some may see as fantastic dreams or ambitions. Use this combination to be your own seer, the prophet of your own amazing future, but don't leave that future in the realms of fantasy, get to some practical application of what is an incredible talent for seeing what's possible.

Making good use of your vision could see you working in the film industry, sales and marketing, photography or medical research.

You're likely to be very psychic and it may come through flashes of inspiration rather than hours of meditation. Learn to trust these insights, be they for you or those around you.

In love, you're a very romantic individual and would want that in return from any partner, but try to be realistic with your expectations. Your other half may not be able to get a Bedouin tent and five camels at three in the morning in Watford. So let them surprise you in small ways. A Post-It to say 'I love you' on the fridge is just as romantic as camels in Watford.

PISCES MOON

'I believe, though I do not comprehend, and I hold by faith what I cannot grasp with the mind.'

Saint Bernard

Archetype

Saint. Oh alright, you're hardly perfect, but your Moon holds all the information from all the signs behind it. It's the last one – or is it the first in a new wheel? A deeply spiritual Moon, it offers you a rare connection. You see things few notice and without trying you can bring peace to those around you. That's saintly.

You may not feel saintly, least of all when some idiot cuts you up on the motorway. Your language then, both verbal and sign, is hardly likely to be what anyone would call holy. Being holy isn't the point, though; you are generous with your being to family and friends, help those who can't or won't help themselves, and even when the idiot does cut you up and you react to it, two minutes later you're apologizing in your head and chastising yourself for being less than generous.

PISCES MOON ♓

This Moon has many blessings, but sometimes you might feel as if you're not living up to any of them. The feeling that you could do better is what drives you, it pushes you to the self-help section of the bookshop to improve your lot, but here's the really funny thing: all you truly have to do is believe in your own magic.

You will spend a lot of your waking and indeed sleeping hours trying to figure out why you are here, what happens when you die and whether there is an afterlife. And what about angels and does your spirit guide really exist? Of course there are lots of things you can do to answer those questions, or at least give yourself more to think about, but even if you do the course, sign up for that attunement or wiggle your wand at a full Moon, you will always be searching for another experience.

So far you sound as if you will be wrapped in purple (something flowing, I suspect), smelling slightly of incense and patchouli, and maybe going round with flowers in your hair. But in the modern world that's not practical, and neither is it really who you are. You do practical, you do modern and you do your witchcraft at night when nobody is looking.

You are just as conscious of your need to succeed at work as anyone else, and if you can use your amazing imagination, then so much the better. Careers in sales and marketing, conceptual ideas, design, photography and film-making suit you. Be sure to work on toughening yourself up for the competitiveness you will undoubtedly experience in the workplace. If you don't, a harsh comment or criticism of your work could send you spiralling away from reaching a goal when you were so close.

With colleagues as well as family and friends, you're generous with your support and make a good listener. Sometimes you may need to know that listening is enough. You can take things to the extreme and, with your saintly demeanour, open your door to all and sundry, offering comfort, lunch and a bed for the night... or the next six months.

Sometimes people really can't help being in a difficult situation, but sometimes they just help themselves to what's on offer and thrive on the generosity of others without any intention of making changes in their life. Be sure you know what you're getting into when you aim to help, or at least have some bottom lines that mustn't be crossed. If they are, you must follow through on the consequences. Yes, in short, don't let people take advantage of your good nature.

Nobody should be fooled into thinking you would rather hug a panda and play with the fairy folk all day than challenge them, however, because when you do, you really do. You can give as good as you get and your inner moral compass works particularly well with bullies. Be it standing up for yourself or standing up for the little guy, you're fierce.

In fact, you're so sensitive to what others are thinking and feeling, you may jump to defend yourself before they have even said anything. Just remember that even a psychic soul like you can sometimes get it wrong, and physical manifestation of someone's intent is really needed before you take final action.

This natural awareness that you have can see you in a different world from others, at least some of the time. It can help you see what's going on underneath a family situation or in the office, and if you use it wisely, it can prepare you for so-called surprise announcements that you kind of, maybe, sort of, possibly knew about already.

If you are practising any psychic, healing, clairvoyant or mediumistic skills, you're probably best separating them from your working life – unless they *are* your working life, of course – as you will be pestered by everyone from the cleaner to the managing director to do your stuff.

Your mates are your lifeline, you learn from them and they from you, but more importantly good friends won't ask you for favours all the time. Over time you will graduate to people who have their lives sorted, learn from them and improve your own wellbeing by implementing those lessons.

Having a Water sign rule your Moon makes you more emotional than most and even a telly advert could have you reaching for the tissues to wipe away those tears. Water may be something you want to live beside, you could choose swimming as your preferred sport, and on a healthy note, drinking plenty of water will keep you operating better than if you let your reservoir run dry.

When you come home at the end of the day it must be to a peaceful place, even if half the down-and-outs in town are staying there, and you need to know that when you close the door you can be Lord or Lady Bountiful, passing on your wisdom to the kids, the neighbourhood kids and anyone else who needs it. This isn't from a point of ego either, but because it feeds your soul.

You may not be the world's best cook and when you forget you've put the pot on the stove, the smoke alarm could be your best friend. That's irrelevant to most people – what they really want is your company and it doesn't matter if the hearty stew and dumplings you planned turn into extra-large Hawaiian pizza to go.

Romance is important to you, and not only from your other half. You like a happy ending and could choose books that reflect that as well as be the one who sends beautiful cards on birthdays. Woe betide anyone who sends you one with anything rude on it for yours! Been there, done that, won't be doing it again…

Living in a city won't feed your need to have nature around you. How are the fairy folk going to get to you if you're surrounded by concrete? A garden, no matter how small, is essential for your spiritual wellbeing, and your weekends should have at least some time spent amongst Mother Nature's gifts.

Any true saint shows love, compassion, wisdom and understanding, but won't be trodden on by those who seek to dull that light. Just saying.

Love Life

Just as I started to write this, the song 'Sexual Healing' by Marvin Gaye started playing on the radio. How apt! You are the Moon sign that pays more attention to 'signs' in their life than any other, and that song perfectly describes your love life. You need to be totally committed in a relationship to indulge in and enjoy sex, but in that act you find the safe place to totally let go and be your full-on loving and emotional self, and that is quite a power.

You need a partner who wants to know you on the deepest level possible, where those more intimate moments are so intense they are almost unbearably beautiful. If a relationship isn't heading in that direction, you may need to work at it or consider if it's for you, as you really do need the storybook romance.

When you are in a relationship, you are a supportive partner and expect the same in return. You should be willing to share your dreams with your other half and they must be supportive of them and you of theirs, which is a measure of the perfection you're seeking, but is that easy to find? It may *not* be easy; it may even seem impossible, but your faith will make it happen. A clear vision of what it would look and feel like is something you could have from a very young age. Keep that image in your powerful subconscious and it will bring it to you.

Any suitors will be expected to bring on the full candlelit dinners, boat trips, etc., and if it's a picnic, there had better be a red gingham tablecloth to spread on the ground for all those delicious treats. Are you influenced by Hollywood at all? Much?

If things go wrong in your love life, you can descend into full-on Bridget Jones territory, sitting on the sofa playing torch songs with a tub of ice-cream for company. That's a good thing – go on, let it all out, and when you've finished, realize that it wasn't meant to be and rely on your knowledge of how the universe works to start making your way towards something that is.

Heroes, or she-roes, are what you're after – not to rescue you from anything, but to stand beside you as you help others. Admirable.

Partnering a Pisces Moon

If you think grabbing a bunch of flowers from the garage on the way home is going to get you in their good books, think again! A full-on bouquet of white lilies, please, and whilst you're at it, get home early and fill the bedroom with candles. Romance is what they are after; nothing less will do.

Best fit Sun signs are Pisces, Cancer, Scorpio, Virgo.

Career

Your energy can sometimes take large dips for no apparent reason. Sometimes it's simply your sensitivity to what's going on around you in the workplace. Use it as a barometer; if you don't feel right, chances are something isn't quite right. Being the office confessional won't help either – if you're taking on people's stuff it's likely to be draining your energy reserve.

Jobs that suit you are artistic roles in music, painting and dancing as well as anything where you can use your imagination, like working with food, flowers and fashion. Often you're found where an eye for the right line is needed, perfect measurements need to be made or critical systems need to be maintained.

Of course you also make an exceptional tarot card reader, astrologer, healer, medium and clairvoyant – in fact any role that taps into your natural ability to not only read others' auras but link into the universal energy system too.

Avoid the mundane, avoid being locked up in an airless factory and definitely avoid anywhere that stifles your natural creativity. Look for roles where you can travel, too. Experiencing other cultures brings wisdom to you and an edge to what you do. A well-travelled soul has more to offer than one that endures routine and mediocrity.

Parents and Family

With your Moon in Pisces, you may have been the last child born into your family, you may have suffered the loss of your mother early on and adoption is possible. You may well have had an isolated childhood, either by your own choice or the circumstances of your birth, one where you retreated into your own fantasy world full of knights in shining armour or fairies at the bottom of the garden. You may have been accused of being a dreamer by other family members. Nothing wrong with that, I say!

A Piscean Moon friend of mine was sent to a boarding school early in her life. It was residential, so she was absent from the family home, and she remembers going through phases where she could barely recall her parents and would make them up in her head. That was tough when she did eventually go home, as the real ones didn't quite live up to the fantasy. Creating perfect scenarios around your family and home will make reality tough to live up to; better to remind yourself of the real world now and again.

At least one of your parents may have been big on religion, perhaps making you to go to church on a Sunday when you would rather have been playing in the woods.

At school you would have stuck out as someone who wasn't quite like everyone else. There's that 'dreamer' word again, and as kids are kids, that could have led to being picked on by those whose psychic vision was impaired. Yes, even at a young age imaginary friends were very real to you and could have been closer to you than the children around you.

With your own children, you are likely to encourage their imagination, to revel in their childhood years and to help them express their creativity through painting, dancing and performing. Dressing little girls up in princess and fairy outfits and sitting in makeshift tepees with the boys will be part of what you do, and your children won't care if you don't behave like everyone else's parents; in fact they will be the opposite: proud of it.

Your home is probably immaculate. If you're currently laughing at the thought, remember there's always the odd exception to any rule, but generally with a Pisces Moon your need for perfection extends to your home. The look has to be out of a glossy magazine and usually the areas that are seen by the public are treated to the flowers and air freshener treatment first. Keep up those appearances!

Books will feature at home too, lots of them, anything from palm-reading tomes to movie almanacs.

Health

Illness is often described as disease – that's dis-ease – and not being comfortable with yourself or your environment can certainly bring on sickness for you. You should never underestimate the value of keeping yourself away from negativity, whether it is found in people or places.

Conventional astrological wisdom would tell you to look after your feet, and reflexology could be a very useful complementary therapy for you. Talking of which, your highly sensitive nature means drugs and conventional treatments can be very harsh on you. Balance them with complementary treatments where appropriate.

Life Skills

When faced with decisions that must be made and there's a fear of getting it wrong, try relying on your most valuable asset: your link to the energetic worlds. Meditation works very well for you, as does visualization, so sit somewhere comfortable and 'try out' your different scenarios. See yourself as having taken one decision and see what happens as a consequence, repeat it for another choice you could make, then trust in your own intuition to show you the way. Without knowing it, you probably do this anyway, but this is a more formal way of using it.

A dream diary also makes good use of your skills. Write down what you dreamed and then interpret it. As much as there are some excellent dream books out there, try using your own intuition first – after all, those images did come from it in the first place.

Stumbling Blocks

As your energy is so susceptible to your environment and the people around you, it doesn't pay to be overgenerous with it. Setting clear boundaries for yourself is a tough thing for you to do, but without it you will run out of energy completely and be neither use nor ornament.

Your body, too, may be vulnerable to the food you put into it. Anything that makes you bloated or feel less than well when you eat it should clearly be avoided — which won't be easy if it's the stuff you really like to eat. As it usually is… For complete wellbeing it may be better to remove this stumbling block with some good dietary advice.

Finally, if you get involved in the mess of others, your own stuff could get untidy too. That in turn would unsettle you, so clearly putting your own needs first wouldn't go amiss. Just saying.

Spiritual Lesson

In past lives you may have been in a position where you served others, perhaps as a nurse, a religious figure, or even a monarch. You still want to be of service and still can be, but now you must also reach for your own star, your own goals and make your own dreams come true.

SUN SIGN, MOON SIGN

So now you know a little more about your Moon sign, but how does that work with your Sun sign?

Sun Aries, Moon Pisces

Big, bold and brave, everyone's champion, ready to smite those who need smiting, you're a courageous character, but are you wearing unexpected wee-wee pants? Presenting the image of a super-hero is a challenge, but somehow you overcome your fears and that's admirable. Acknowledge that now and again you do feel a little scared by it all, but celebrate your ability to have a go. Know just how gutsy you are.

When the princess is saved from the dragon or when the (k) night is over, all you want to do is get back to your own castle and be at one with your stuff – your hard-earned and pretty stuff.

A creative role in life is essential. You need to see your ideas turned into something tangible, and when they are, you're filled with pride – not false pride, but the justifiable 'I did that' sort born of hard work.

In love, you need to be up close and personal with your other half, and they should be ready to speak their mind, as you will yours, but most of all they should be ready to move on very quickly from an argument. Romance is a given – you need it to make a relationship work – but you need to be surprised in the airing cupboard now and again too. Don't we all!

Sun Taurus, Moon Pisces

Oh, for the love of chocolate you would go to the ends of the Earth and back again. For a Walnut Whip, you'd face the demons and slay their leader. Alright, calm down – it's just chocolate. But the passion you show for all things food, art, music and soft furnishings is what life is all about for you – the good things worth fighting for.

Of course you have to pay for it all, and that means getting a job. Annoying, I know, but most folks do it, so what will suit an artistically bent creature like yourself? The art world? Not rocket science, is it, and that's something you might want to avoid actually – it needs too many maths skills and you're more the touchy-feely sort.

Are you a great singer, a wonderful chef or an amazing home designer? Whatever gets your juices going can become a great business if you take things slowly. Just don't allow your Pisces Moon to sidetrack you into dreaming about things and not making them manifest. If you strike a balance between the practicality of Taurus and the vision of Pisces, you can leave all your truffles behind and be rich in every sense of the word.

In love you're touchy-feely, emotionally needy at times, but isn't that what it's supposed to be about? You have to have someone who can go with your floaty moments and bring you back to Earth, but then, when you've become stuck in a rut, encourage you to fly.

Sun Gemini, Moon Pisces

You could have done better – should have said this, could have done that, might have thought about… what? It's all too easy to beat yourself up about what might have happened, but surely the point is dealing with what is happening in the here and now? Your mind is likely to create a whole variety of scenarios of how things could have gone. Learn to dismiss them and concentrate on what you can do going forward.

That mind of yours is mighty powerful, by the way, and if you can harness it, you can change your world. Having a vision of where you want to be fixed in your mind, a photograph of success, will drive your Pisces Moon towards helping you to project the image into your life. Use visualization as a tool, fire up your imagination and have the courage to keep it moving forward, no matter how many stumbles you make along the way.

With your great writing ability, be it expressed via book or screenplay, you can inspire others and cause them to question things that they would otherwise have taken for granted. You can expose secrets and destroy lies – a skill that could see you successful as a detective, undercover journalist or very good friend to have on anyone's side.

In love, you would be on the Olympic talking squad if there were one, but your partner will soon get used to it and learn to tune into *Gardener's Question Time*, nod now and again, say, 'Yes dear,' and hold your hand adoringly. Adoration, romance and the occasional nod – these things are what love is made of.

Sun Cancer, Moon Pisces

Having a double dose of Water in your chart isn't easy. It brings waves of emotion and great rivers of tears whenever a puppy develops a cough or that old tune your granny used to play comes on the radio. A rom-com, a chick-flick and a tub of ice-cream on a wet Saturday morning cuddled up with Bob the Builder and you're fixed for the day.

You're a traditionalist, someone who wants things to be just as they should be. 'Should be' by whose values? Hopefully yours, but sometimes you may do or say things to please others when they are not necessarily what you're thinking or feeling. Speaking up even if you do hurt those you love is important. Having your say may be challenging, but unless you do, you will only internalize the frustration and that will come out in a great big moody.

Careers in catering, nursing, hospitality and music would suit you well. The nurturing side is evident in the first three, but the latter works too because you can show your emotions through your music. Debbie Harry has this Sun–Moon combination.

In love, your need for tradition shines through. Someone who plays by the rules of engagement, wines and dines you, wants to meet your parents and doesn't mind that you have the bridal magazines out three days after meeting would be ideal.

You might have to learn to hold back on that last one. Scaring people off by getting in too deep too fast could be something to look at. But once you're over that, the only question is 'Three bridesmaids or four?'

Sun Leo, Moon Pisces

Stage fright is a terrible thing. It can incapacitate some people to the point where they can't move. No matter which stage you're on, it can be something that's hard for you to overcome. On the one hand you want to perform and on the other you're not sure you can.

More often than not you pull through, you get on with it and do it well and then run for the sanctity of your home, where everything must be dramatically beautiful, a scene set with flowers and candles, ready for the diva to calm down. Or you have to move the kids' toys, then remind the kids themselves that you're having one of your heads and need a lie-down before dinner.

On the subject of children, you're hugely protective of your cubs.

On the subject of life, it's not easy being fabulous, but somehow you will make it work.

When friends need wisdom, they know where to find you. They can expect some humour. They can also expect to be told in no uncertain manner what will happen if they proceed with the course of action they are currently set on. And they can expect to be told those shoes do not match that bag. A flair for fashion coupled with a Gok Wan delivery makes you a popular individual.

In a relationship, you're a dreamer, desiring the perfect romance with the perfect suitor – or two. One just wouldn't be dramatic enough.

When you do make your choice, the cream is the only thing suitable for this cat.

Just try to remember that every performance needs the scenery painters, lighting engineers and cleaners. The boring details need taking care of too.

Sun Virgo, Moon Pisces

After a night sleeping in silken sheets surrounded by rose petals and a box of caramels, it's time to get up and empty the cat box. Oh no. But you're not bothered – you have a good balance of romance and practicality and know that if routines aren't kept, you won't have time for all the finer things in life.

This is a full Moon position, making it easy for you to say your piece when those who think you're going to be a walkover pull on their boots. They are in for a very big surprise and you're not afraid to show your emotional side as well as deal with any functional issues they might have. Usually you end up as the one walking all over them.

Teaching is something you do well. You can inspire your students in the study of even the dullest of subjects. Medical roles could call you too – doctor, nurse, specialist in neurology – and with attention to detail your stock in trade, by-the-book methods will suit you well.

In a relationship, it's sex on a Saturday and fish for tea on a Friday, and what you do for the rest of the week is pretty much up to you! I jest – the rest of the week will be as planned as those two days, but sometimes you surprise everyone and forget what day it is altogether, throwing caution to the wind and having no plan at all. Imagine!

Your partner should love your organized side, but let them take you by surprise and occasionally wear their shirt with the button undone.

Sun Libra, Moon Pisces

Nice. Don't you think that word is something and nothing? He's nice. She's nice. That's nice. How do I look? Nice. Just not enough really, is it? But you *are* nice – you're easy on the eye, easy to get on with and easy-going. Nice.

But when friends give you some encouragement, 'nice' turns into 'exceptional', it turns into 'inspirational', and you can do just about anything you set your mind to when you have that sort of encouragement.

Your ability to get the best out of people and to get their secrets out of them too could serve you well as a solicitor, counsellor or perhaps in the beauty industry, where gossip stays between you and your client. The art world will attract you too, as will esoteric roles such as Reiki therapist and angel expert.

Having love in your life is of course part of the experience for any Libra Sun, but when coupled with your Pisces Moon it makes it something magical for you. A fairytale is what you're after and you may have planned your wedding ever since you were very young.

Don't be put off by those who belittle your great ideas and high ideals – pursue them even in the face of those who call you 'nice'.

Sun Scorpio, Moon Pisces

Are you the pirate king? Surely something exotic with an edge of danger, a swashbuckling romantic heritage, must be yours, or at the very least you could dress to stand out from the crowd.

That's an odd thing really – drawing attention to yourself when actually all you want to do is hide away. Perhaps your inner world is more exciting than the mundane trip on the 159 to work every day? It probably is, but still, going to work is what pays for those hooped earrings. Striking a balance is important. Indulge your wonderful imagination through writing, acting or developing a movie script, but apply your eye for detail in the real world by inspecting tax forms or becoming food hygiene officer or even pathologist.

You're not afraid to talk about the bigger questions of sex, death and the mysteries of life – in fact, the more mysterious, the better. This deeply psychic line-up could have opened you up to some odd experiences as a child, but it may have been a few years into adulthood before you decided to explore them further. It could also lead to work as a tarot reader or medium, but no tea leaves, thank you – you prefer strong espresso.

In love, you're passionate but extraordinarily sensitive – perhaps too sensitive on occasion. You may take to your bed with one of your heads, but if what you actually need is some time alone to think things through, why not say so? Still, you are complex, fascinating, alluring and worth the effort!

Sun Sagittarius, Moon Pisces

As you sit filling in another spreadsheet with numbers that mean very little to you, in your head you're on a beach with the sun beating down, a good book and the prospect of flirting with Manuel as the karaoke gets underway later tonight. Then your boss asks you for a print-out, and you're back in the room.

You can live for your two weeks in the summer, or you can recognize that you were meant to be out in the big wide world, stuff the spreadsheets and retrain in the travel industry or take some time out for a great adventure of your own – say, a year travelling around the globe. Adventure and risk aren't things that worry you – what worries you is a life without them.

But luxury and fine things don't come cheap, so that fine line between yet another trip and those spreadsheets needs to be walked. Perhaps something a little more entrepreneurial at work would help? Great big ideas are something you have aplenty. Doing something with them could be all you have to overcome!

In love, you're likely to rush in and then discover the other person keeps pigeons and can't possibly be separated from them for longer than a day or two. That's not going to work. The well-travelled appeal to you, the well-read, those who can hold a conversation (and your attention) for longer than ten minutes.

Sun Capricorn, Moon Pisces

There's an old joke about someone who doesn't believe in astrology, with the punchline being 'Typical Capricorn'. That sums up the dilemma you have: on the one hand practical and well grounded, and on the other happy to consider the hand of fate in your life, that indefinable something…

When you're operating as Little Miss Efficiency, you're a sight to behold, a wonder of organizational skills and business management diplomas, but then from nowhere comes a 'Well, it wasn't meant to be' or perhaps 'Let go and let God', which might confuse the CEO. Good! It makes you much more interesting.

You can put on a great show of being in control, of knowing what happens next and who does what and when, but when you get home it's likely you're as confused as the rest of us, though nobody would ever know. Then a little meditation helps you refocus.

Visionary business ideas are your stock in trade and you could work for yourself if you chose. You might worry about a regular income, but really you shouldn't. You're one of life's success stories, so maybe you should follow those dreams?

In love, it's tough for a partner to know whether you need a cuddle or a contract. Giving off mixed signals is usual for most of us, to be fair, but you may show such extremes a partner will tread carefully until they are sure which side they are dealing with. Offer them a clue now and again.

Sun Aquarius, Moon Pisces

So, what are we going to be today? The mad professor or the mysterious stranger with magical powers that nobody can quite figure out? You're a seeker of truth, someone who wants to know the secrets of the universe, whether you express it through a fascination with astrology or astronomy, science or belief.

Knowing where you fit into the great scheme of things is important to you and if you can figure that out, you can pass that information and know-how on to those who can use it for themselves. If you can find the secret to eternal youth along the way, so much the better. In your mind, nothing is impossible – a healthy outlook, I say!

You may want to heal the world, to sort out its ills, and not be bothered about taking all the credit. That's what really makes you interesting. Align yourself with charity work, be it full-time or something you do to feed your soul after a long day in the laboratory.

In love, you can be a cool customer, but underneath all you want is a cuddle and understanding, so why not thaw out a bit and let your Pisces Moon take over? It knows what to do. Show your emotions, they won't bite. Much.

Sun Pisces, Moon Pisces

A new Moon position and of course one that means you have a double whammy of Piscean energy. How's that working for you? Here's a little test: what day of the week is it? Oh alright, maybe you're not that bad. Then again? Forgetfulness is just one of those things, but it isn't really about forgetting, is it, Pisces? What's really going on is that you are spending part of every waking hour in your own little world, because it's lovely there.

Who can blame you? Certainly not me, but it becomes difficult when someone asks you a question and you haven't a clue what they are talking about because you have been too busy visualizing that bloke on Reception dressed as Archangel Michael.

You can be shy when introduced to people and can take your time getting to know them, but if you like them you can become a great friend, a loyal friend in fact, even if now and again you do forget you were meeting for coffee.

Try to overcome some of your shyness if you find it's impairing you in some way. Fear is a motivator if used properly, so make your motto 'Feel the fear and do it anyway.' Use it to move you forward, not back.

Working in the spiritual arts is something that could appeal to you and you do especially well with healing.

When you're in love, you shine. You can light up half of London when it's the right person, and they will be adored as long as they tell you the truth. A practical and well-grounded partner would suit you best – a nice Virgo perhaps, someone who remembers to put the bins out then comes back in and slips that Archangel costume back on.

MOON ON MOON

So now you know your Moon sign, how does it rack up with the Moon sign of that bloke you fancy, or even your current partner? It's not the toughest thing to find out their Moon sign. You don't even need to tell them you know, just smile when that Taurus Moon suggests another bag of doughnuts at the funfair or gaze lovingly as your Pisces Moon suggests they read you poetry and remind yourself that they're probably warming you up for some hot and heavy.

Remember the Moon, and your Sun for that matter, are only a small part of your chart, and relationship astrology is more complex than just Moon on Moon, but it's a good starting-point, especially considering the emotional qualities of the Moon. So don't phone – it's just for fun!

Aries Moon with:

Aries Moon: A passionate affair with lots of heat. Just make sure you cool down now and again to actually finish what you've started.

Taurus Moon: A nurturing relationship where cuddles are required and offered happily. Buy chocolate.

Gemini Moon: '…and another thing: she said I should, so I did, and then he said it was great and it was.' Bothered?

Cancer Moon: The roses round the door will need watering now and again, but will blossom with true emotional sharing.

Leo Moon: Drama queens, the pair of you. Just remember the one that shouts the loudest isn't always the winner. Oh! OK, they are.

Virgo Moon: Whilst the Aries is busy being chaotic, the Virgo is busy putting things in order. See any problems?

Libra Moon: Lovey, dovey, smurfy, fluffy, wuffy — until a decision has to be made and then it's all-out war.

Scorpio Moon: Leather becomes you. In fact rubber would suit you too. Talcum powder needed to get in and out of this one.

Sagittarius Moon: Never at home, so it's time to travel and look for cheap last-minute deals. That's hotels, not boyfriends.

Capricorn Moon: Your marching orders have been issued: it's off into a military-style relationship with strict rules of engagement.

Aquarius Moon: Who is right and who is wrong? Hey, it's not a competition. Really? Are you sure about that?

Pisces Moon: Hard to meditate when someone is banging a drum… Pisces wants peace; Aries wants attention. Hmmm…

Taurus Moon with:

Taurus Moon: Wrap each other up in chocolate and dip yourselves in cream — what a perfect way to spend a Sunday!

Gemini Moon: Laughter is an aphrodisiac, so expect to be worn out by the end of the week. Happy memories.

Cancer Moon: Stability, a lovely set of sitting-room curtains and dinner on the table — bliss.

Leo Moon: Watch the wallet, as this combination likes luxury and plenty of it. Nice jewellery, by the way.

Virgo Moon: Building an empire needs strong foundations and a plan. Build away. What about a cuddle, Virgo? Is it in the schedule?

Libra Moon: Venus rocks this one – she rules both signs and puts the Moon in a happy mood. Heaven on Earth.

Scorpio Moon: Opposites attract and can challenge each other, but isn't that what makes it work? Hot.

Sagittarius Moon: See you on Friday! Time apart could be part of the routine. Get some shared interests and fresh air.

Capricorn Moon: Chief cook and bottle washer – which one is which? Define roles for a stable future. Nice.

Aquarius Moon: Telling the truth is all that's required, but what about a cuddle now and again? Cool to moderate.

Pisces Moon: Dream-time, with fairy folk at the bottom of the garden and plastic unicorns on the sideboard. Magic.

Gemini Moon with:

Gemini Moon: Talk is cheap, so spend as much as you can as often as you can. Expensive phone bills, however.

Cancer Moon: Ice forms when cool air meets water. There'll be a frosty reception here if things aren't warmed up now and again.

Leo Moon: Laughter is good, but rolling about whilst there are better things to do could get tiresome. Dramas.

Virgo Moon: Worry is fed by over-analysing a situation, so learn to support each other without feeding it.

Libra Moon: Is there an off-button or is it always noisy around here? Chatter on the airwaves. Friendly.

Scorpio Moon: Nothing cuts like words. Better stay away from sharp objects like verbs then. Sarcastic.

Sagittarius Moon: Opposites attract and sit beside each other on long flights. Have plenty of them for pleasure. Pack your bags.

Capricorn Moon: Hang on – wasting time rushing off without a plan is not allowed. A stabilizing relationship.

Aquarius Moon: Oh my goodness! Really? Are you sure? Earplugs all round, I think. Sorry, did you say something?

Pisces Moon: Settling down isn't easy and focusing on one goal not practical, so learn to be flexible. Distracting.

Cancer Moon with:

Cancer Moon: Hopefully moods will fall into synch, so you're both in the same emotional place at the same time. Ebb and Flo!

Leo Moon: Knowing which buttons to push can be a good thing or it can be very tricky. Avoid the big red one.

Virgo Moon: Your mother will be pleased with this steady and nice pairing. Why not knit matching bobble hats?

Libra Moon: Bubbly and can be fun, but clashes are likely over what colour the duvet cover should be. Interior design nightmare.

Scorpio Moon: A race to see which one reaches for the ice-cream and sofa first after a tough day. Emotional.

Sagittarius Moon: Stay in or go out, read a book or cook tea, it's all going on. Or not. Frustrating.

Capricorn Moon: One teaches the other to open up emotionally and the favour is returned with security and stability.

Aquarius Moon: Time together may be something that only works with time apart. A balancing act.

Pisces Moon: What lies beneath will eventually bubble up to the top, so best dig it out regularly. Deep.

Leo Moon with:

Leo Moon: As playful as two little kittens until the claws come out. Copious amounts of fun with the occasional drama.

Virgo Moon: Picking up their pants from the floor is fine if you threw them there. Just saying.

Libra Moon: How much can you love one person? Tell me, then show me, then tell me again. A rom-com.

Scorpio Moon: A lion and a scorpion – both powerful, but in different ways. Claws and stinging tails.

Sagittarius Moon: Indiana Jones couldn't keep up with you. Slap on some sun cream. Hot, hot, hot.

Capricorn Moon: Pomp and circumstance – a right royal affair or one too many show-offs?

Aquarius Moon: Some people get away with saying anything to each other. Most of the time.

Pisces Moon: Crashing in on sensitive issues may cause some problems. Learn to walk gently with each other.

Virgo Moon with:

Virgo Moon: If it conforms to standard 345 of the European relationship code, it's fine by you. Get a clipboard.

Libra Moon: This one could take a while to get off the ground. Lots of talk and not much action.

Scorpio Moon: Picky on details, able to spot a fault from outer space – which is where one of you might be better off being.

Sagittarius Moon: Studious. You have books in common. A solitary thing, a book. Learn to share information.

Capricorn Moon: This one is built to last, but can get stuck in a rut sometimes. Wear your pants on your head for fun.

Aquarius Moon: Technically a tough one, but can work if you don't live in each other's pockets.

Pisces Moon: Understanding and compassionate, mindful of each other's needs and well balanced.

Libra Moon with:

Libra Moon: 'Do you like it? I like it if you like it. Do you like it? If you do, then so do I.' Sweet and sugary.

Scorpio Moon: Different perspectives can work, but mutual respect is an absolute must. Dark and light.

Sagittarius Moon: Boundaries are important, and what's important is there aren't any. Saddle up.

Capricorn Moon: Straight to the point Capricorn may not appreciate indecisive Libra. Wishy-washy.

Aquarius Moon: Shiny, happy people... Have fun – but someone has to get serious. Says who?

Pisces Moon: An elegant and stylish couple with fine taste in food, wine and single-estate chocolate.

Scorpio Moon with:

Scorpio Moon: Make sure you decide whose turn it is to sit in the dark, brooding. Don't both do it at the same time. Sexy.

Sagittarius Moon: Time for dressing up and having an adventure until someone gets huffy. You know who you are.

Capricorn Moon: Why not use the finer things in life to show the world what a successful couple you are? (Are they paid for?)

Aquarius Moon: Vivacious until someone says the wrong thing, then fizzy.

Pisces Moon: Still waters run deep. Take some time to find out what's going on underneath. Dive.

Sagittarius Moon with:

Sagittarius Moon: Throw your rucksack on your back and get out there and explore the world together.

Capricorn Moon: A balance of foolhardy rushing in and sensible reasoning could work.

Aquarius Moon: A knowledgeable union, but who knows more and who is right? Challengingly interesting.

Pisces Moon: Make each other's fantasies come true. I was thinking travel and adventure; if you're thinking maid and chauffeur, that's OK.

Capricorn Moon with:

Capricorn Moon: Running a relationship like a business could work if you want a business, not a relationship. Break a few rules.

Aquarius Moon: Too restrictive to be easy, this is a challenge and will only work if control issues don't take over.

Pisces Moon: Protective and nurturing. Well-defined roles will make this highly productive. On schedule.

Aquarius Moon with:

Aquarius Moon: See much of each other? Doing your own thing oddly makes it work well. See ya!

Pisces Moon: Not sure which one is magical and which one is eccentric? You're as barking as each other. Freaks.

Pisces Moon with:

Pisces Moon: A dreamy, floaty experience that to others may seem more than a little wafty, but you both know that's what's called romance. Fairytale.

MOON TABLES

The times shown here are GMT. If you were born outside the UK, please readjust your time of birth to GMT. Alternatively, you can find your moon sign at www.davidwells.co.uk

Jan 1920 – Jun 1920

Jan 1920	Feb 1920	Mar 1920	Apr 1920	May 1920	Jun 1920
02 22:12 Gem	01 07:54 Can	01 17:22 Leo	02 09:59 Lib	02 01:37 Sco	03 08:04 Cap
04 22:19 Can	03 09:06 Leo	03 20:40 Vir	04 18:33 Sco	04 12:58 Sag	05 20:37 Aqu
06 22:30 Leo	05 11:18 Vir	06 01:52 Lib	07 05:41 Sag	07 01:39 Cap	08 07:42 Pis
09 00:45 Vir	07 16:19 Lib	08 10:09 Sco	09 18:24 Cap	09 14:08 Aqu	10 15:56 Ari
11 06:47 Lib	10 01:13 Sco	10 21:34 Sag	12 06:31 Aqu	12 00:31 Pis	12 20:35 Tau
13 16:56 Sco	12 13:20 Sag	13 10:24 Cap	14 15:49 Pis	14 07:23 Ari	14 21:57 Gem
16 05:43 Sag	15 02:13 Cap	15 21:57 Aqu	16 21:29 Ari	16 10:35 Tau	16 21:26 Can
18 18:33 Cap	17 13:19 Aqu	18 06:24 Pis	19 00:07 Tau	18 11:13 Gem	18 21:01 Leo
21 05:39 Aqu	19 21:38 Pis	20 11:43 Ari	21 01:14 Gem	20 11:01 Can	20 22:44 Vir
23 14:34 Pis	22 03:36 Ari	22 14:58 Tau	23 02:22 Can	22 11:49 Leo	23 04:05 Lib
25 21:32 Ari	24 08:05 Tau	24 17:25 Gem	25 04:48 Leo	24 15:10 Vir	25 13:18 Sco
28 02:43 Tau	26 11:41 Gem	26 20:01 Can	27 09:21 Vir	26 21:49 Lib	28 01:14 Sag
30 06:05 Gem	28 14:40 Can	28 23:20 Leo	29 16:18 Lib	29 07:32 Sco	30 14:05 Cap
		31 03:47 Vir		31 19:20 Sag	

Jul 1920 – Dec 1920

Jul 1920	Aug 1920	Sep 1920	Oct 1920	Nov 1920	Dec 1920
03 02:30 Aqu	01 19:17 Pis	02 16:19 Tau	02 02:32 Gem	02 13:37 Leo	01 22:44 Vir
05 13:36 Pis	04 04:09 Ari	04 20:57 Gem	04 05:28 Can	04 17:03 Vir	04 03:49 Lib
07 22:38 Ari	06 10:55 Tau	07 00:03 Can	06 08:13 Leo	06 22:22 Lib	06 11:50 Sco
10 04:45 Tau	08 15:14 Gem	09 02:02 Leo	08 11:23 Vir	09 05:49 Sco	08 22:09 Sag
12 07:40 Gem	10 17:11 Can	11 03:54 Vir	10 15:44 Lib	11 15:26 Sag	11 09:58 Cap
14 08:03 Can	12 17:41 Leo	13 07:10 Lib	12 22:13 Sco	14 03:02 Cap	13 22:38 Aqu
16 07:32 Leo	14 18:27 Vir	15 13:18 Sco	15 07:29 Sag	16 15:43 Aqu	16 11:02 Pis
18 08:12 Vir	16 21:27 Lib	17 22:57 Sag	17 19:15 Cap	19 03:39 Pis	18 21:29 Ari
20 12:02 Lib	19 04:11 Sco	20 11:08 Cap	20 07:51 Aqu	21 12:44 Ari	21 04:21 Tau
22 20:02 Sco	21 14:44 Sag	22 23:32 Aqu	22 18:56 Pis	23 18:01 Tau	23 07:15 Gem
25 07:30 Sag	24 03:21 Cap	25 09:57 Pis	25 02:52 Ari	25 20:00 Gem	25 07:13 Can
27 20:21 Cap	26 15:35 Aqu	27 17:34 Ari	27 07:33 Tau	27 20:12 Can	27 06:16 Leo
30 08:36 Aqu	29 01:54 Pis	29 22:49 Tau	29 09:59 Gem	29 20:32 Leo	29 06:37 Vir
	31 10:02 Ari		31 11:34 Can		31 10:06 Lib

Jan 1921 – Jun 1921

Jan 1921	Feb 1921	Mar 1921	Apr 1921	May 1921	Jun 1921
02 17:26 Sco	01 10:02 Sag	03 05:02 Cap	02 01:21 Aqu	01 21:46 Pis	03 01:03 Tau
05 03:57 Sag	03 22:13 Cap	05 17:45 Aqu	04 13:27 Pis	04 08:13 Ari	05 05:17 Gem
07 16:09 Cap	06 10:58 Aqu	08 05:43 Pis	06 23:30 Ari	06 15:31 Tau	07 06:47 Can
10 04:49 Aqu	08 23:03 Pis	10 15:57 Ari	09 06:59 Tau	08 19:51 Gem	09 07:18 Leo
12 17:10 Pis	11 09:50 Ari	13 00:14 Tau	11 12:15 Gem	10 22:18 Can	11 08:40 Vir
15 04:14 Ari	13 18:44 Tau	15 06:28 Gem	13 15:58 Can	13 00:16 Leo	13 12:09 Lib
17 12:39 Tau	16 00:54 Gem	17 10:36 Can	15 18:47 Leo	15 02:51 Vir	15 18:10 Sco
19 17:23 Gem	18 03:57 Can	19 12:52 Leo	17 21:21 Vir	17 06:46 Lib	18 02:27 Sag
21 18:35 Can	20 04:34 Leo	21 14:08 Vir	20 00:24 Lib	19 12:21 Sco	20 12:38 Cap
23 17:46 Leo	22 04:20 Vir	23 15:49 Lib	22 04:53 Sco	21 19:52 Sag	23 00:23 Aqu
25 17:04 Vir	24 05:20 Lib	25 19:33 Sco	24 11:44 Sag	24 05:34 Cap	25 13:03 Pis
27 18:46 Lib	26 09:27 Sco	28 02:33 Sag	26 21:27 Cap	26 17:16 Aqu	28 01:02 Ari
30 00:24 Sco	28 17:35 Sag	30 12:57 Cap	29 09:25 Aqu	29 05:50 Pis	30 10:13 Tau
				31 17:04 Ari	

Jul 1921	Aug 1921	Sep 1921	Oct 1921	Nov 1921	Dec 1921
02 15:22 Gem	01 03:18 Can	01 13:07 Vir	03 01:36 Sco	01 16:08 Sag	01 08:32 Cap
04 16:56 Can	03 03:11 Leo	03 13:05 Lib	05 06:21 Sag	03 23:37 Cap	03 18:40 Aqu
06 16:34 Leo	05 02:18 Vir	05 15:23 Sco	07 14:44 Cap	06 10:16 Aqu	06 07:02 Pis
08 16:26 Vir	07 02:51 Lib	07 21:20 Sag	10 02:12 Aqu	08 22:50 Pis	08 19:36 Ari
10 18:27 Lib	09 06:32 Sco	10 06:57 Cap	12 14:50 Pis	11 10:51 Ari	11 05:45 Tau
12 23:42 Sco	11 13:58 Sag	12 19:00 Aqu	15 02:33 Ari	13 20:19 Tau	13 12:07 Gem
15 08:04 Sag	14 00:29 Cap	15 07:38 Pis	17 12:08 Tau	16 02:40 Gem	15 15:12 Can
17 18:42 Cap	16 12:41 Aqu	17 19:28 Ari	19 19:20 Gem	18 06:40 Can	17 16:35 Leo
20 06:43 Aqu	19 01:20 Pis	20 05:40 Tau	22 00:31 Can	20 09:32 Leo	19 18:02 Vir
22 19:23 Pis	21 13:29 Ari	22 13:41 Gem	24 04:08 Leo	22 12:16 Vir	21 20:51 Lib
25 07:41 Ari	24 00:06 Tau	24 19:05 Can	26 06:40 Vir	24 15:31 Lib	24 01:32 Sco
27 17:57 Tau	26 07:57 Gem	26 21:57 Leo	28 08:48 Lib	26 19:37 Sco	26 08:01 Sag
30 00:36 Gem	28 12:17 Can	28 23:01 Vir	30 11:33 Sco	29 01:02 Sag	28 16:16 Cap
	30 13:31 Leo	30 23:40 Lib			31 02:31 Aqu

Jan 1922	Feb 1922	Mar 1922	Apr 1922	May 1922	Jun 1922
02 14:43 Pis	01 10:34 Ari	03 04:51 Tau	01 20:28 Gem	01 09:11 Can	01 22:47 Vir
05 03:41 Ari	03 22:40 Tau	05 14:48 Gem	04 03:46 Can	03 14:05 Leo	04 01:43 Lib
07 14:57 Tau	06 07:41 Gem	07 21:18 Can	06 08:12 Leo	05 17:19 Vir	06 04:42 Sco
09 22:26 Gem	08 12:29 Can	10 00:09 Leo	08 10:09 Vir	07 19:21 Lib	08 08:18 Sag
12 01:47 Can	10 13:40 Leo	12 00:22 Vir	10 10:36 Lib	09 21:00 Sco	10 13:30 Cap
14 02:20 Leo	12 12:59 Vir	13 23:43 Lib	12 11:07 Sco	11 23:32 Sag	12 21:25 Aqu
16 02:12 Vir	14 12:35 Lib	16 00:12 Sco	14 13:25 Sag	14 04:25 Cap	15 08:24 Pis
18 03:20 Lib	16 14:22 Sco	18 03:33 Sag	16 19:01 Cap	16 12:45 Aqu	17 21:11 Ari
20 07:01 Sco	18 19:31 Sag	20 10:40 Cap	19 04:27 Aqu	19 00:20 Pis	20 09:08 Tau
22 13:32 Sag	21 04:04 Cap	22 21:17 Aqu	21 16:42 Pis	21 13:11 Ari	22 18:01 Gem
24 22:28 Cap	23 15:11 Aqu	25 09:55 Pis	24 05:37 Ari	24 00:45 Tau	24 23:27 Can
27 09:16 Aqu	26 03:44 Pis	27 22:49 Ari	26 17:07 Tau	26 09:28 Gem	27 02:28 Leo
29 21:33 Pis	28 16:40 Ari	30 10:37 Tau	29 02:19 Gem	28 15:26 Can	29 04:36 Vir
				30 19:33 Leo	

Jul 1922	Aug 1922	Sep 1922	Oct 1922	Nov 1922	Dec 1922
01 07:04 Lib	01 20:34 Sag	02 18:11 Aqu	02 11:39 Pis	01 07:03 Ari	01 02:59 Tau
03 10:29 Sco	04 03:21 Cap	05 05:41 Pis	05 00:35 Ari	03 19:39 Tau	03 13:33 Gem
05 15:05 Sag	06 12:18 Aqu	07 18:28 Ari	07 13:19 Tau	06 06:33 Gem	05 21:33 Can
07 21:12 Cap	08 23:22 Pis	10 07:23 Tau	10 00:44 Gem	08 15:22 Can	08 03:32 Leo
10 05:27 Aqu	11 12:04 Ari	12 18:49 Gem	12 09:51 Can	10 22:05 Leo	10 08:08 Vir
12 16:15 Pis	14 00:57 Tau	15 03:12 Can	14 16:01 Leo	13 02:36 Vir	12 11:39 Lib
15 04:58 Ari	16 11:41 Gem	17 07:47 Leo	16 19:04 Vir	15 05:00 Lib	14 14:14 Sco
17 17:27 Tau	18 18:39 Can	19 09:08 Vir	18 19:43 Lib	17 05:59 Sco	16 16:28 Sag
20 03:09 Gem	20 21:45 Leo	21 08:44 Lib	20 19:26 Sco	19 06:53 Sag	18 19:34 Cap
22 08:56 Can	22 22:15 Vir	23 08:27 Sco	22 20:05 Sag	21 09:31 Cap	21 01:08 Aqu
24 11:26 Leo	24 22:05 Lib	25 10:10 Sag	24 23:33 Cap	23 15:35 Aqu	23 10:13 Pis
26 12:21 Vir	26 23:01 Sco	27 15:15 Cap	27 06:59 Aqu	26 01:39 Pis	25 22:22 Ari
28 13:26 Lib	29 02:26 Sag	30 00:02 Aqu	29 18:06 Pis	28 14:19 Ari	28 11:12 Tau
30 15:58 Sco	31 08:53 Cap				30 22:02 Gem

Jan 1923	Feb 1923	Mar 1923	Apr 1923	May 1923	Jun 1923
02 05:39 Can	02 22:11 Vir	02 08:41 Vir	02 19:26 Sco	02 05:59 Sag	02 21:03 Aqu
04 10:34 Leo	04 23:38 Lib	04 09:01 Lib	04 19:33 Sag	04 07:14 Cap	05 04:42 Pis
06 13:59 Vir	07 01:37 Sco	06 09:16 Sco	06 22:19 Cap	06 12:04 Aqu	07 16:01 Ari
08 16:58 Lib	09 04:58 Sag	08 11:05 Sag	09 04:47 Aqu	08 21:05 Pis	10 04:56 Tau
10 20:04 Sco	11 10:07 Cap	10 15:33 Cap	11 14:50 Pis	11 09:11 Ari	12 17:02 Gem
12 23:33 Sag	13 17:18 Aqu	12 23:01 Aqu	14 03:08 Ari	13 22:14 Tau	15 03:09 Can
15 03:56 Cap	16 02:43 Pis	15 09:07 Pis	16 16:06 Tau	16 10:26 Gem	17 11:11 Leo
17 10:05 Aqu	18 14:19 Ari	17 21:05 Ari	19 04:32 Gem	18 21:02 Can	19 17:22 Vir
19 18:57 Pis	21 03:14 Tau	20 09:59 Tau	21 15:27 Can	21 05:40 Leo	21 21:44 Lib
22 06:36 Ari	23 15:30 Gem	22 22:32 Gem	23 23:50 Leo	23 11:53 Vir	24 00:20 Sco
24 19:33 Tau	26 00:57 Can	25 09:04 Can	26 04:56 Vir	25 15:25 Lib	26 01:46 Sag
27 07:07 Gem	28 06:30 Leo	27 16:13 Leo	28 06:48 Lib	27 16:35 Sco	28 03:19 Cap
29 15:18 Can		29 19:36 Vir	30 06:33 Sco	29 16:38 Sag	30 06:43 Aqu
31 19:57 Leo		31 20:06 Lib		31 17:27 Cap	

Jul 1923	Aug 1923	Sep 1923	Oct 1923	Nov 1923	Dec 1923
02 13:27 Pis	01 08:10 Ari	02 16:49 Gem	02 11:59 Can	01 04:59 Leo	03 00:24 Lib
04 23:50 Ari	03 20:21 Tau	05 03:58 Can	04 21:14 Leo	03 12:06 Vir	05 02:14 Sco
07 12:24 Tau	06 08:46 Gem	07 11:53 Leo	07 02:40 Vir	05 15:23 Lib	07 01:57 Sag
10 00:36 Gem	08 19:07 Can	09 16:16 Vir	09 04:35 Lib	07 15:38 Sco	09 01:31 Cap
12 10:33 Can	11 02:19 Leo	11 18:03 Lib	11 04:25 Sco	09 14:38 Sag	11 03:09 Aqu
14 17:53 Leo	13 06:43 Vir	13 18:47 Sco	13 04:08 Sag	11 14:37 Cap	13 08:34 Pis
16 23:09 Vir	15 09:27 Lib	15 20:05 Sag	15 05:42 Cap	13 17:39 Aqu	15 18:07 Ari
19 03:05 Lib	17 11:38 Sco	17 23:13 Cap	17 10:28 Aqu	16 00:46 Pis	18 06:20 Tau
21 06:08 Sco	19 14:12 Sag	20 04:52 Aqu	19 18:42 Pis	18 11:24 Ari	20 19:02 Gem
23 08:43 Sag	21 17:49 Cap	22 13:02 Pis	22 05:32 Ari	20 23:52 Tau	23 06:39 Can
25 11:32 Cap	23 23:02 Aqu	24 23:23 Ari	24 17:47 Tau	23 12:31 Gem	25 16:39 Leo
27 15:42 Aqu	26 06:24 Pis	27 11:22 Tau	27 06:28 Gem	26 00:27 Can	28 00:50 Vir
29 22:22 Pis	28 16:14 Ari	30 00:05 Gem	29 18:38 Can	28 11:01 Leo	30 06:51 Lib
	31 04:11 Tau			30 19:18 Vir	

Jan 1924	Feb 1924	Mar 1924	Apr 1924	May 1924	Jun 1924
01 10:22 Sco	01 21:03 Cap	02 07:11 Aqu	03 03:45 Ari	02 20:36 Tau	01 14:47 Gem
03 11:48 Sag	03 23:43 Aqu	04 12:44 Pis	05 14:11 Tau	05 08:47 Gem	04 03:26 Can
05 12:22 Cap	06 04:12 Pis	06 20:25 Ari	08 02:12 Gem	07 21:30 Can	06 15:28 Leo
07 13:54 Aqu	08 11:36 Ari	09 06:35 Tau	10 14:51 Can	10 09:29 Leo	09 01:40 Vir
09 18:13 Pis	10 22:08 Tau	11 18:43 Gem	13 02:14 Leo	12 18:56 Vir	11 08:40 Lib
12 02:22 Ari	13 10:33 Gem	14 07:07 Can	15 10:20 Vir	15 00:28 Lib	13 11:57 Sco
14 13:47 Tau	15 22:33 Can	16 17:30 Leo	17 14:26 Lib	17 02:10 Sco	15 12:17 Sag
17 02:27 Gem	18 08:08 Leo	19 00:26 Vir	19 15:24 Sco	19 01:33 Sag	17 11:29 Cap
19 14:05 Can	20 14:45 Vir	21 04:00 Lib	21 15:05 Sag	21 00:48 Cap	19 11:42 Aqu
21 23:33 Leo	22 18:57 Lib	23 05:27 Sco	23 15:33 Cap	23 02:04 Aqu	21 14:51 Pis
24 06:48 Vir	24 21:46 Sco	25 06:29 Sag	25 18:29 Aqu	25 06:49 Pis	23 21:55 Ari
26 12:14 Lib	27 00:15 Sag	27 08:36 Cap	28 00:38 Pis	27 15:15 Ari	26 08:26 Tau
28 16:08 Sco	29 03:12 Cap	29 12:46 Aqu	30 09:38 Ari	30 02:22 Tau	28 20:50 Gem
30 18:52 Sag		31 19:12 Pis			

Jul 1924	Aug 1924	Sep 1924	Oct 1924	Nov 1924	Dec 1924
01 09:27 Can	02 13:05 Vir	01 02:37 Lib	02 15:54 Sag	01 00:38 Cap	02 13:38 Pis
03 21:10 Leo	04 20:19 Lib	03 06:54 Sco	04 18:02 Cap	03 02:52 Aqu	04 20:10 Ari
06 07:15 Vir	07 01:23 Sco	05 10:00 Sag	06 21:19 Aqu	05 07:34 Pis	07 05:33 Tau
08 14:54 Lib	09 04:31 Sag	07 12:40 Cap	09 02:06 Pis	07 14:39 Ari	09 16:52 Gem
10 19:36 Sco	11 06:20 Cap	09 15:33 Aqu	11 08:30 Ari	09 23:43 Tau	12 05:20 Can
12 21:31 Sag	13 07:52 Aqu	11 19:16 Pis	13 16:49 Tau	12 10:34 Gem	14 18:12 Leo
14 21:48 Cap	15 10:28 Pis	14 00:41 Ari	16 03:22 Gem	14 22:56 Can	17 06:06 Vir
16 22:11 Aqu	17 15:32 Ari	16 08:38 Tau	18 15:47 Can	19 23:10 Vir	19 15:14 Lib
19 00:30 Pis	19 23:54 Tau	18 19:23 Gem	21 04:21 Leo	22 06:51 Lib	21 20:25 Sco
21 06:11 Ari	22 11:13 Gem	21 07:53 Can	23 14:32 Vir	24 10:17 Sco	23 21:55 Sag
23 15:35 Tau	24 23:48 Can	23 19:51 Leo	25 20:48 Lib	26 10:38 Sag	25 21:18 Cap
26 03:36 Gem	27 11:18 Leo	26 05:06 Vir	27 23:26 Sco	28 09:58 Cap	27 20:41 Aqu
28 16:11 Can	29 20:18 Vir	28 10:53 Lib	30 00:03 Sag	30 10:25 Aqu	29 22:05 Pis
31 03:37 Leo		30 14:00 Sco			

Jan 1925	Feb 1925	Mar 1925	Apr 1925	May 1925	Jun 1925
01 02:56 Ari	02 05:32 Gem	01 13:25 Gem	02 22:31 Leo	02 18:37 Vir	01 12:29 Lib
03 11:30 Tau	04 18:10 Can	04 01:37 Can	05 09:54 Vir	05 03:26 Lib	03 18:21 Sco
05 22:52 Gem	07 06:49 Leo	06 14:21 Leo	07 18:04 Lib	07 08:21 Sco	05 20:33 Sag
08 11:32 Can	09 18:00 Vir	09 01:24 Vir	09 23:03 Sco	09 10:28 Sag	07 20:45 Cap
11 00:13 Leo	12 03:06 Lib	11 09:43 Lib	12 02:05 Sag	11 11:30 Cap	09 20:54 Aqu
13 11:54 Vir	14 09:54 Sco	13 15:37 Sco	14 04:32 Cap	13 13:08 Aqu	11 22:39 Pis
15 21:32 Lib	16 14:27 Sag	15 19:51 Sag	16 07:22 Aqu	15 16:23 Pis	14 03:02 Ari
18 04:11 Sco	18 17:02 Cap	17 23:06 Cap	18 11:02 Pis	17 21:34 Ari	16 10:15 Tau
20 07:33 Sag	20 18:21 Aqu	20 01:50 Aqu	20 15:44 Ari	20 04:41 Tau	18 19:56 Gem
22 08:23 Cap	22 19:36 Pis	22 04:33 Pis	22 21:59 Tau	22 13:50 Gem	21 07:36 Can
24 08:09 Aqu	24 22:21 Ari	24 08:04 Ari	25 06:32 Gem	25 01:07 Can	23 20:30 Leo
26 08:45 Pis	27 04:03 Tau	26 13:34 Tau	27 17:44 Can	27 13:58 Leo	26 09:21 Vir
28 11:59 Ari		28 22:07 Gem	30 06:36 Leo	30 02:34 Vir	28 20:14 Lib
30 18:57 Tau		31 09:41 Can			

Jul 1925	Aug 1925	Sep 1925	Oct 1925	Nov 1925	Dec 1925
01 03:32 Sco	01 17:46 Cap	02 04:02 Pis	01 15:06 Ari	02 09:43 Gem	02 03:18 Can
03 06:54 Sag	03 17:41 Aqu	04 05:02 Ari	03 18:20 Tau	04 19:05 Can	04 15:12 Leo
05 07:24 Cap	05 17:23 Pis	06 08:27 Tau	06 00:34 Gem	07 07:15 Leo	07 04:13 Vir
07 06:49 Aqu	07 18:46 Ari	08 15:38 Gem	08 10:32 Can	09 20:06 Vir	09 15:51 Lib
09 07:06 Pis	09 23:24 Tau	11 02:34 Can	10 23:08 Leo	12 06:51 Lib	12 00:03 Sco
11 09:52 Ari	12 07:56 Gem	13 15:29 Leo	13 11:42 Vir	14 14:05 Sco	14 04:23 Sag
13 16:04 Tau	14 19:38 Can	16 03:56 Vir	15 21:57 Lib	16 18:12 Sag	16 05:59 Cap
16 01:37 Gem	17 08:40 Leo	18 14:17 Lib	18 05:12 Sco	18 20:38 Cap	18 06:35 Aqu
18 13:32 Can	19 21:12 Vir	20 22:17 Sco	20 10:11 Sag	20 22:47 Aqu	20 07:51 Pis
21 02:31 Leo	22 08:05 Lib	23 04:17 Sag	22 13:57 Cap	23 01:37 Pis	22 10:57 Ari
23 15:16 Vir	24 16:44 Sco	25 08:36 Cap	24 17:12 Aqu	25 05:31 Ari	24 16:24 Tau
26 02:29 Lib	26 22:49 Sag	27 11:29 Aqu	26 20:14 Pis	27 10:46 Tau	27 00:18 Gem
28 10:55 Sco	29 02:19 Cap	29 13:19 Pis	28 23:34 Ari	29 17:50 Gem	29 10:26 Can
30 15:55 Sag	31 03:41 Aqu		31 03:29 Tau		31 22:26 Leo

Jan 1926	Feb 1926	Mar 1926	Apr 1926	May 1926	Jun 1926
03 11:25 Vir	02 06:10 Lib	01 12:03 Lib	02 12:07 Sag	01 23:32 Cap	02 11:53 Pis
05 23:43 Lib	04 16:38 Sco	03 22:27 Sco	04 18:04 Cap	04 03:31 Aqu	04 14:45 Ari
08 09:18 Sco	07 00:01 Sag	06 06:39 Sag	06 22:00 Aqu	06 06:31 Pis	06 18:28 Tau
10 15:01 Sag	09 03:49 Cap	08 12:06 Cap	09 00:03 Pis	08 08:55 Ari	08 23:42 Gem
12 17:09 Cap	11 04:37 Aqu	10 14:40 Aqu	11 01:02 Ari	10 11:33 Tau	11 07:14 Can
14 17:07 Aqu	13 03:57 Pis	12 15:04 Pis	13 02:30 Tau	12 15:46 Gem	13 17:28 Leo
16 16:48 Pis	15 03:47 Ari	14 14:52 Ari	15 06:20 Gem	14 22:52 Can	16 05:48 Vir
18 18:03 Ari	17 06:08 Tau	16 16:06 Tau	17 13:54 Can	17 09:19 Leo	18 18:18 Lib
20 22:15 Tau	19 12:21 Gem	18 20:41 Gem	20 01:07 Leo	19 21:53 Vir	21 04:39 Sco
23 05:54 Gem	21 22:27 Can	21 05:29 Can	22 13:58 Vir	22 10:03 Lib	23 11:34 Sag
25 16:29 Can	24 10:59 Leo	23 17:34 Leo	25 01:52 Lib	24 19:41 Sco	25 15:18 Cap
28 04:51 Leo	26 23:59 Vir	26 06:36 Vir	27 11:18 Sco	27 02:13 Sag	27 17:01 Aqu
30 17:48 Vir		28 18:26 Lib	29 18:18 Sag	29 06:24 Cap	29 18:13 Pis
		31 04:16 Sco		31 09:18 Aqu	

Jul 1926	Aug 1926	Sep 1926	Oct 1926	Nov 1926	Dec 1926
01 20:14 Ari	02 11:24 Gem	01 01:48 Can	03 07:48 Vir	02 03:22 Lib	01 22:39 Sco
03 23:58 Tau	04 20:07 Can	03 13:00 Leo	05 20:28 Lib	04 14:37 Sco	04 07:32 Sag
06 05:56 Gem	07 07:12 Leo	06 01:40 Vir	08 07:58 Sco	06 23:51 Sag	06 13:52 Cap
08 14:16 Can	09 19:38 Vir	08 14:22 Lib	10 17:53 Sag	09 07:10 Cap	08 18:21 Aqu
11 00:50 Leo	12 08:26 Lib	11 02:15 Sco	13 01:46 Cap	11 12:41 Aqu	10 21:43 Pis
13 13:07 Vir	14 20:17 Sco	13 12:21 Sag	15 07:02 Aqu	13 16:22 Pis	13 00:32 Ari
16 01:51 Lib	17 05:39 Sag	15 19:36 Cap	17 09:29 Pis	15 18:28 Ari	15 03:23 Tau
18 13:07 Sco	19 11:23 Cap	17 23:22 Aqu	19 09:56 Ari	17 19:54 Tau	17 06:59 Gem
20 21:10 Sag	21 13:31 Aqu	20 00:06 Pis	21 10:01 Tau	19 22:10 Gem	19 12:19 Can
23 01:28 Cap	23 13:15 Pis	21 23:20 Ari	23 11:50 Gem	22 02:54 Can	21 20:16 Leo
25 02:48 Aqu	25 12:30 Ari	23 23:12 Tau	25 17:07 Can	24 11:09 Leo	24 07:01 Vir
27 02:46 Pis	27 13:24 Tau	26 01:50 Gem	28 02:30 Leo	26 22:35 Vir	26 19:30 Lib
29 03:13 Ari	29 17:38 Gem	28 08:34 Can	30 14:42 Vir	29 11:13 Lib	29 07:28 Sco
31 05:46 Tau		30 19:09 Leo			31 16:49 Sag

Jan 1927	Feb 1927	Mar 1927	Apr 1927	May 1927	Jun 1927
02 22:51 Cap	01 12:22 Aqu	03 00:05 Pis	01 10:31 Ari	02 20:52 Gem	01 09:50 Can
05 02:10 Aqu	03 13:07 Pis	04 23:18 Ari	03 09:36 Tau	04 23:51 Can	03 15:37 Leo
07 04:05 Pis	05 13:20 Ari	06 23:07 Tau	05 10:25 Gem	07 06:38 Leo	06 00:55 Vir
09 05:59 Ari	07 14:50 Tau	09 01:29 Gem	07 14:41 Can	09 17:02 Vir	08 12:48 Lib
11 08:55 Tau	09 18:54 Gem	11 07:29 Can	09 22:59 Leo	12 05:26 Lib	11 01:15 Sco
13 13:30 Gem	12 01:50 Can	13 16:51 Leo	12 10:18 Vir	14 17:51 Sco	13 12:15 Sag
15 19:58 Can	14 11:10 Leo	16 04:22 Vir	14 22:53 Lib	17 04:57 Sag	15 20:51 Cap
18 04:31 Leo	16 22:15 Vir	18 16:48 Lib	17 11:19 Sco	j19 14:10 Cap	18 03:04 Aqu
20 15:09 Vir	19 10:30 Lib	21 05:20 Sco	19 22:48 Sag	21 21:15 Aqu	20 07:25 Pis
23 03:26 Lib	21 23:08 Sco	23 17:05 Sag	22 08:34 Cap	24 02:01 Pis	22 10:29 Ari
25 15:53 Sco	24 10:33 Sag	26 02:38 Cap	24 15:42 Aqu	26 04:37 Ari	24 12:54 Tau
28 02:20 Sag	26 18:55 Cap	28 08:38 Aqu	26 19:37 Pis	28 05:50 Tau	26 15:26 Gem
30 09:11 Cap	28 23:13 Aqu	30 10:53 Pis	28 20:43 Ari	30 07:02 Gem	28 19:03 Can
			30 20:29 Tau		

Jul 1927	Aug 1927	Sep 1927	Oct 1927	Nov 1927	Dec 1927
01 00:48 Leo	02 04:43 Lib	01 00:35 Sco	03 07:12 Cap	01 22:26 Aqu	01 10:36 Pis
03 09:26 Vir	04 17:15 Sco	03 13:09 Sag	05 15:06 Aqu	04 03:55 Pis	03 14:20 Ari
05 20:47 Lib	07 05:13 Sag	05 23:28 Cap	07 18:50 Pis	06 05:53 Ari	05 15:47 Tau
08 09:16 Sco	09 14:22 Cap	08 05:49 Aqu	09 19:15 Ari	08 05:37 Tau	07 16:11 Gem
10 20:36 Sag	11 19:45 Aqu	10 08:16 Pis	11 18:18 Tau	10 05:03 Gem	09 17:11 Can
13 05:06 Cap	13 22:04 Pis	12 08:18 Ari	13 18:12 Gem	12 06:15 Can	11 20:31 Leo
15 10:31 Aqu	15 22:57 Ari	14 08:03 Tau	15 20:49 Can	14 10:47 Leo	14 03:24 Vir
17 13:43 Pis	18 00:12 Tau	16 09:28 Gem	18 03:06 Leo	16 19:13 Vir	16 13:54 Lib
19 15:58 Ari	20 03:08 Gem	18 13:48 Can	20 12:42 Vir	19 06:40 Lib	19 02:31 Sco
21 18:23 Tau	22 08:18 Can	20 21:12 Leo	23 00:27 Lib	21 19:25 Sco	21 14:58 Sag
23 21:46 Gem	24 15:38 Leo	23 07:01 Vir	25 13:07 Sco	24 07:53 Sag	24 01:37 Cap
26 02:30 Can	27 00:55 Vir	25 18:29 Lib	28 01:47 Sag	26 19:00 Cap	26 09:54 Aqu
28 09:00 Leo	29 12:02 Lib	28 07:05 Sco	30 13:21 Cap	29 04:06 Aqu	28 16:00 Pis
30 17:41 Vir		30 19:53 Sag			30 20:18 Ari

Jan 1928	Feb 1928	Mar 1928	Apr 1928	May 1928	Jun 1928
01 23:14 Tau	02 11:21 Can	02 22:38 Leo	01 11:53 Vir	01 03:35 Lib	02 10:37 Sag
04 01:20 Gem	04 15:53 Leo	05 05:51 Vir	03 21:46 Lib	03 15:37 Sco	04 22:59 Cap
06 03:27 Can	06 22:09 Vir	07 15:04 Lib	06 09:27 Sco	06 04:32 Sag	07 09:40 Aqu
08 06:52 Leo	09 07:03 Lib	10 02:30 Sco	08 22:19 Sag	08 17:08 Cap	09 17:53 Pis
10 12:53 Vir	11 18:40 Sco	12 15:23 Sag	11 10:55 Cap	11 03:57 Aqu	11 23:13 Ari
12 22:17 Lib	14 07:31 Sag	15 03:33 Cap	13 21:06 Aqu	13 11:34 Pis	14 01:45 Tau
15 10:25 Sco	16 18:53 Cap	17 12:30 Aqu	16 03:19 Pis	15 15:30 Ari	16 02:24 Gem
17 23:06 Sag	19 02:46 Aqu	19 17:20 Pis	18 05:40 Ari	17 16:26 Tau	18 02:34 Can
20 09:48 Cap	21 07:05 Pis	21 18:54 Ari	20 05:36 Tau	19 15:57 Gem	20 04:02 Leo
22 17:27 Aqu	23 09:09 Ari	23 19:06 Tau	22 05:09 Gem	21 15:57 Can	22 08:26 Vir
24 22:24 Pis	25 10:42 Tau	25 19:53 Gem	24 06:13 Can	23 18:16 Leo	24 16:42 Lib
27 01:47 Ari	27 13:07 Gem	27 22:41 Can	26 10:11 Leo	26 00:06 Vir	27 04:16 Sco
29 04:42 Tau	29 17:04 Can	30 04:04 Leo	28 17:27 Vir	28 09:35 Lib	29 17:12 Sag
31 07:46 Gem				30 21:39 Sco	

Jul 1928	Aug 1928	Sep 1928	Oct 1928	Nov 1928	Dec 1928
02 05:23 Cap	03 05:34 Pis	01 17:26 Ari	01 03:59 Tau	01 14:40 Can	01 01:28 Leo
04 15:32 Aqu	05 10:33 Ari	03 20:07 Tau	03 05:09 Gem	03 17:14 Leo	03 05:16 Vir
06 23:22 Pis	07 14:18 Tau	05 22:42 Gem	05 07:21 Can	05 22:41 Vir	05 12:51 Lib
09 05:03 Ari	09 17:22 Gem	08 01:51 Can	07 11:17 Leo	08 07:04 Lib	07 23:45 Sco
11 08:49 Tau	11 20:03 Can	10 05:49 Leo	09 17:13 Vir	10 17:52 Sco	10 12:28 Sag
13 10:59 Gem	13 22:57 Leo	12 11:01 Vir	12 01:14 Lib	13 06:20 Sag	13 01:29 Cap
15 12:20 Can	16 03:07 Vir	14 18:12 Lib	14 11:28 Sco	15 19:24 Cap	15 13:35 Aqu
17 14:06 Leo	18 09:52 Lib	17 04:04 Sco	16 23:44 Sag	18 07:39 Aqu	17 23:49 Pis
19 17:52 Vir	20 19:56 Sco	19 16:22 Sag	19 12:49 Cap	20 17:18 Pis	20 07:15 Ari
22 01:01 Lib	23 08:28 Sag	22 05:15 Cap	22 00:33 Aqu	22 23:14 Ari	22 11:25 Tau
24 11:46 Sco	25 20:58 Cap	24 16:00 Aqu	24 08:49 Pis	25 01:30 Tau	24 12:40 Gem
27 00:34 Sag	28 06:56 Aqu	26 23:01 Pis	26 13:04 Ari	27 01:23 Gem	26 12:17 Can
29 12:46 Cap	30 13:30 Pis	29 02:31 Ari	28 14:16 Tau	29 00:43 Can	28 12:07 Leo
31 22:33 Aqu			30 14:11 Gem		30 14:12 Vir

Jan 1929	Feb 1929	Mar 1929	Apr 1929	May 1929	Jun 1929
01 20:07 Lib	03 01:58 Sag	02 10:02 Sag	01 07:02 Cap	01 03:18 Aqu	02 05:57 Ari
04 06:09 Sco	05 14:59 Cap	04 22:54 Cap	03 19:17 Aqu	03 13:50 Pis	04 10:34 Tau
06 18:49 Sag	08 02:34 Aqu	07 10:43 Aqu	06 04:51 Pis	05 20:50 Ari	06 11:57 Gem
09 07:50 Cap	10 11:42 Pis	09 19:43 Pis	08 10:57 Ari	08 00:17 Tau	08 11:36 Can
11 19:32 Aqu	12 18:40 Ari	12 01:51 Ari	10 14:17 Tau	10 01:22 Gem	10 11:25 Leo
14 05:21 Pis	15 00:01 Tau	14 06:04 Tau	12 16:13 Gem	12 01:44 Can	12 13:19 Vir
16 13:06 Ari	17 04:01 Gem	16 09:23 Gem	14 18:04 Can	14 03:02 Leo	14 18:38 Lib
18 18:36 Tau	19 06:45 Can	18 12:23 Can	16 20:50 Leo	16 06:33 Vir	17 03:32 Sco
20 21:43 Gem	21 08:41 Leo	20 15:27 Leo	19 01:05 Vir	18 12:52 Lib	19 15:02 Sag
22 22:52 Can	23 10:58 Vir	22 19:05 Vir	21 07:13 Lib	20 21:53 Sco	22 03:44 Cap
24 23:16 Leo	25 15:15 Lib	25 00:11 Lib	23 15:34 Sco	23 09:03 Sag	24 16:23 Aqu
27 00:47 Vir	27 22:53 Sco	27 07:49 Sco	26 02:15 Sag	25 21:34 Cap	27 03:58 Pis
29 05:18 Lib		29 18:25 Sag	28 14:42 Cap	28 10:16 Aqu	29 13:21 Ari
31 13:56 Sco				30 21:37 Pis	

Jul 1929	Aug 1929	Sep 1929	Oct 1929	Nov 1929	Dec 1929
01 19:31 Tau	02 08:15 Can	02 18:27 Vir	02 06:09 Lib	03 04:46 Sag	02 23:25 Cap
03 22:13 Gem	04 08:11 Leo	04 20:51 Lib	04 11:39 Sco	05 15:56 Cap	05 11:57 Aqu
05 22:20 Can	06 08:23 Vir	07 02:20 Sco	06 20:18 Sag	08 04:32 Aqu	08 00:27 Pis
07 21:37 Leo	08 10:55 Lib	09 11:37 Sag	09 07:48 Cap	10 16:29 Pis	10 10:56 Ari
09 22:09 Vir	10 17:21 Sco	11 23:44 Cap	11 20:24 Aqu	13 01:42 Ari	12 17:49 Tau
12 01:53 Lib	13 03:44 Sag	14 12:16 Aqu	14 07:39 Pis	15 07:18 Tau	14 20:48 Gem
14 09:43 Sco	15 16:20 Cap	16 23:06 Pis	16 16:02 Ari	17 09:53 Gem	16 21:05 Can
16 20:59 Sag	18 04:49 Aqu	19 07:30 Ari	18 21:29 Tau	19 10:53 Can	18 20:34 Leo
19 09:47 Cap	20 15:45 Pis	21 13:45 Tau	21 00:54 Gem	21 11:58 Leo	20 21:21 Vir
21 22:19 Aqu	23 00:46 Ari	23 18:24 Gem	23 03:24 Can	23 14:31 Vir	23 01:02 Lib
24 09:38 Pis	25 07:54 Tau	25 21:52 Can	25 05:55 Leo	25 19:22 Lib	25 08:11 Sco
26 19:12 Ari	27 13:02 Gem	28 00:27 Leo	27 09:08 Vir	28 02:39 Sco	27 18:11 Sag
29 02:24 Tau	29 16:03 Can	30 02:51 Vir	29 13:39 Lib	30 12:07 Sag	30 05:55 Cap
31 06:42 Gem	31 17:27 Leo		31 20:01 Sco		

Jan 1930	Feb 1930	Mar 1930	Apr 1930	May 1930	Jun 1930
01 18:29 Aqu	03 00:22 Ari	02 06:08 Ari	03 03:42 Gem	02 13:54 Can	03 00:36 Vir
04 07:04 Pis	05 09:48 Tau	04 15:18 Tau	05 08:11 Can	04 16:32 Leo	05 04:03 Lib
06 18:26 Ari	07 16:07 Gem	06 22:15 Gem	07 11:09 Leo	06 19:10 Vir	07 09:29 Sco
09 02:58 Tau	09 18:55 Can	09 02:34 Can	09 13:11 Vir	08 22:30 Lib	09 16:55 Sag
11 07:34 Gem	11 19:01 Leo	11 04:25 Leo	11 15:17 Lib	11 03:06 Sco	12 02:20 Cap
13 08:35 Can	13 18:14 Vir	13 04:54 Vir	13 18:44 Sco	13 09:38 Sag	14 13:38 Aqu
15 07:38 Leo	15 18:50 Lib	15 05:43 Lib	16 00:49 Sag	15 18:39 Cap	17 02:11 Pis
17 06:57 Vir	17 22:44 Sco	17 08:46 Sco	18 10:06 Cap	18 06:03 Aqu	19 14:14 Ari
19 08:44 Lib	20 06:48 Sag	19 15:23 Sag	20 21:58 Aqu	20 18:33 Pis	21 23:35 Tau
21 14:24 Sco	22 18:12 Cap	22 01:39 Cap	23 10:22 Pis	23 05:55 Ari	24 05:00 Gem
23 23:56 Sag	25 06:56 Aqu	24 14:04 Aqu	25 21:09 Ari	25 14:15 Tau	26 06:57 Can
26 11:52 Cap	27 19:12 Pis	27 02:23 Pis	28 05:08 Tau	27 19:07 Gem	28 07:06 Leo
29 00:35 Aqu		29 12:59 Ari	30 10:26 Gem	29 21:25 Can	30 07:28 Vir
31 12:58 Pis		31 21:23 Tau		31 22:45 Leo	

Jul 1930	Aug 1930	Sep 1930	Oct 1930	Nov 1930	Dec 1930
02 09:47 Lib	03 04:24 Sag	01 20:34 Cap	01 15:08 Aqu	02 23:34 Ari	02 18:31 Tau
04 14:55 Sco	05 14:34 Cap	04 08:27 Aqu	04 03:47 Pis	05 09:37 Tau	05 01:32 Gem
06 22:49 Sag	08 02:26 Aqu	06 21:06 Pis	06 15:51 Ari	07 16:58 Gem	07 05:31 Can
09 08:49 Cap	10 15:02 Pis	09 09:20 Ari	09 02:14 Tau	09 22:05 Can	09 07:53 Leo
11 20:22 Aqu	13 03:31 Ari	11 20:17 Tau	11 10:29 Gem	12 01:45 Leo	11 10:04 Vir
14 08:56 Pis	15 14:37 Tau	14 05:00 Gem	13 16:29 Can	14 04:41 Vir	13 13:05 Lib
16 21:25 Ari	17 22:45 Gem	16 10:42 Can	15 20:19 Leo	16 07:27 Lib	15 17:19 Sco
19 07:53 Tau	20 03:02 Can	18 13:18 Leo	17 22:25 Vir	18 10:36 Sco	17 22:54 Sag
21 14:38 Gem	22 03:58 Leo	20 13:46 Vir	19 23:43 Lib	20 15:00 Sag	20 06:11 Cap
23 17:22 Can	24 03:13 Vir	22 13:44 Lib	22 01:32 Sco	22 21:41 Cap	22 15:43 Aqu
25 17:19 Leo	26 02:58 Lib	24 15:07 Sco	24 05:23 Sag	25 07:22 Aqu	25 03:35 Pis
27 16:35 Vir	28 05:10 Sco	26 19:34 Sag	26 12:26 Cap	27 19:32 Pis	27 16:28 Ari
29 17:18 Lib	30 11:04 Sag	29 03:48 Cap	28 22:53 Aqu	30 08:05 Ari	30 03:51 Tau
31 21:04 Sco			31 11:22 Pis		

Jan 1931	Feb 1931	Mar 1931	Apr 1931	May 1931	Jun 1931
01 11:34 Gem	02 03:24 Leo	01 14:25 Leo	02 00:49 Lib	01 11:26 Sco	02 03:07 Cap
03 15:21 Can	04 02:56 Vir	03 14:21 Vir	04 00:50 Sco	03 13:14 Sag	04 10:22 Aqu
05 16:32 Leo	06 02:54 Lib	05 13:33 Lib	06 02:51 Sag	05 17:35 Cap	06 21:00 Pis
07 17:06 Vir	08 05:04 Sco	07 14:03 Sco	08 08:20 Cap	08 01:36 Aqu	09 09:43 Ari
09 18:48 Lib	10 10:20 Sag	09 17:29 Sag	10 17:39 Aqu	10 13:01 Pis	11 21:54 Tau
11 22:40 Sco	12 18:38 Cap	12 00:38 Cap	13 05:48 Pis	13 01:56 Ari	14 07:21 Gem
14 04:50 Sag	15 05:14 Aqu	14 11:02 Aqu	15 18:47 Ari	15 13:53 Tau	16 13:38 Can
16 13:01 Cap	17 17:22 Pis	16 23:26 Pis	18 06:50 Tau	17 23:26 Gem	18 17:36 Leo
18 23:03 Aqu	20 06:20 Ari	19 12:23 Ari	20 16:55 Gem	20 06:25 Can	20 20:32 Vir
21 10:54 Pis	22 18:53 Tau	22 00:44 Tau	23 00:42 Can	22 11:27 Leo	22 23:22 Lib
23 23:54 Ari	25 05:12 Gem	24 11:18 Gem	25 06:03 Leo	24 15:07 Vir	25 02:34 Sco
26 12:09 Tau	27 11:46 Can	26 19:04 Can	27 09:09 Vir	26 17:51 Lib	27 06:26 Sag
28 21:18 Gem		28 23:28 Leo	29 10:35 Lib	28 20:07 Sco	29 11:35 Cap
31 02:09 Can		31 00:57 Vir		30 22:47 Sag	

Jul 1931	Aug 1931	Sep 1931	Oct 1931	Nov 1931	Dec 1931
01 18:56 Aqu	03 01:09 Ari	01 20:58 Tau	01 15:03 Gem	02 13:39 Leo	02 00:16 Vir
04 05:09 Pis	05 14:04 Tau	04 08:42 Gem	04 00:37 Can	04 18:07 Vir	04 03:44 Lib
06 17:39 Ari	08 01:01 Gem	06 17:14 Can	06 06:49 Leo	06 20:03 Lib	06 05:43 Sco
09 06:13 Tau	10 08:10 Can	08 21:47 Leo	08 09:34 Vir	08 20:21 Sco	08 07:04 Sag
11 16:13 Gem	12 11:31 Leo	10 23:03 Vir	10 09:50 Lib	10 20:39 Sag	10 09:17 Cap
13 22:30 Can	14 12:25 Vir	12 22:43 Lib	12 09:17 Sco	12 22:52 Cap	12 14:09 Aqu
16 01:41 Leo	16 12:45 Lib	14 22:40 Sco	14 09:51 Sag	15 04:39 Aqu	14 22:50 Pis
18 03:21 Vir	18 14:10 Sco	17 00:39 Sag	16 13:18 Cap	17 14:31 Pis	17 10:48 Ari
20 05:06 Lib	20 17:46 Sag	19 05:47 Cap	18 20:38 Aqu	20 03:08 Ari	19 23:45 Tau
22 07:56 Sco	22 23:58 Cap	21 14:17 Aqu	21 07:31 Pis	22 15:59 Tau	22 10:59 Gem
24 12:18 Sag	25 08:37 Aqu	24 01:28 Pis	23 20:20 Ari	25 03:11 Gem	24 19:21 Can
26 18:22 Cap	27 19:27 Pis	26 14:08 Ari	26 09:11 Tau	27 12:09 Can	27 01:16 Leo
29 02:24 Aqu	30 07:56 Ari	29 03:06 Tau	28 20:47 Gem	29 19:05 Leo	29 05:40 Vir
31 12:45 Pis			31 06:26 Can		31 09:17 Lib

Jan 1932	Feb 1932	Mar 1932	Apr 1932	May 1932	Jun 1932
02 12:23 Sco	03 01:38 Cap	01 07:06 Cap	02 05:04 Pis	01 22:46 Ari	03 06:32 Gem
04 15:15 Sag	05 07:48 Aqu	03 13:59 Aqu	04 16:52 Ari	04 11:45 Tau	05 17:20 Can
06 18:37 Cap	07 16:14 Pis	05 23:15 Pis	07 05:43 Tau	07 00:19 Gem	08 02:14 Leo
08 23:43 Aqu	10 03:17 Ari	08 10:34 Ari	09 18:26 Gem	09 11:34 Can	10 09:06 Vir
11 07:48 Pis	12 16:04 Tau	10 23:19 Tau	12 05:46 Can	11 20:46 Leo	12 13:41 Lib
13 19:06 Ari	15 04:27 Gem	13 12:02 Gem	14 14:21 Leo	14 03:13 Vir	14 16:00 Sco
16 08:01 Tau	17 14:02 Can	15 22:45 Can	16 19:21 Vir	16 06:32 Lib	16 16:46 Sag
18 19:46 Gem	19 19:48 Leo	18 05:55 Leo	18 21:00 Lib	18 07:15 Sco	18 17:31 Cap
21 04:22 Can	21 22:24 Vir	20 09:18 Vir	20 20:33 Sco	20 06:48 Sag	20 20:11 Aqu
23 09:39 Leo	23 23:22 Lib	22 09:57 Lib	22 19:57 Sag	22 07:12 Cap	23 02:25 Pis
25 12:47 Vir	26 00:19 Sco	24 09:35 Sco	24 21:14 Cap	24 10:30 Aqu	25 12:33 Ari
27 15:07 Lib	28 02:38 Sag	26 10:07 Sag	27 02:04 Aqu	26 17:56 Pis	28 01:07 Tau
29 17:43 Sco		28 13:07 Cap	29 10:54 Pis	29 05:08 Ari	30 13:34 Gem
31 21:06 Sag		30 19:29 Aqu		31 18:04 Tau	

Jul 1932	Aug 1932	Sep 1932	Oct 1932	Nov 1932	Dec 1932
03 00:06 Can	01 15:56 Leo	02 08:32 Lib	01 18:44 Sco	02 04:54 Cap	01 16:46 Aqu
05 08:18 Leo	03 21:15 Vir	04 10:06 Sco	03 19:02 Sag	04 08:05 Aqu	03 22:07 Pis
07 14:32 Vir	06 00:55 Lib	06 11:59 Sag	05 21:00 Cap	06 15:05 Pis	06 07:34 Ari
09 19:12 Lib	08 03:49 Sco	08 15:11 Cap	08 01:43 Aqu	09 01:24 Ari	08 19:40 Tau
11 22:27 Sco	10 06:31 Sag	10 20:15 Aqu	10 09:26 Pis	11 13:33 Tau	11 08:25 Gem
14 00:37 Sag	12 09:38 Cap	13 03:30 Pis	12 19:35 Ari	14 02:13 Gem	13 20:27 Can
16 02:35 Cap	14 13:53 Aqu	15 13:00 Ari	15 07:23 Tau	16 14:31 Can	16 07:12 Leo
18 05:44 Aqu	16 20:13 Pis	18 00:33 Tau	17 20:02 Gem	19 01:35 Leo	18 16:08 Vir
20 11:34 Pis	19 05:17 Ari	20 13:13 Gem	20 08:25 Can	21 10:07 Vir	20 22:31 Lib
22 20:51 Ari	21 16:55 Tau	23 01:13 Can	22 18:56 Leo	23 15:07 Lib	23 01:52 Sco
25 08:53 Tau	24 05:33 Gem	25 10:31 Leo	25 02:02 Vir	25 16:38 Sco	25 02:42 Sag
27 21:25 Gem	26 16:49 Can	27 16:06 Vir	27 05:15 Lib	27 15:59 Sag	27 02:31 Cap
30 08:07 Can	29 01:02 Leo	29 18:22 Lib	29 05:31 Sco	29 15:17 Cap	29 03:22 Aqu
	31 05:58 Vir		31 04:40 Sag		31 07:15 Pis

Jan 1933	Feb 1933	Mar 1933	Apr 1933	May 1933	Jun 1933
02 15:12 Ari	01 10:39 Tau	03 07:17 Gem	02 03:49 Can	01 23:06 Leo	02 23:14 Lib
05 02:36 Tau	03 23:04 Gem	05 19:42 Can	04 15:15 Leo	04 08:40 Vir	05 02:24 Sco
07 15:18 Gem	06 11:12 Can	08 06:17 Leo	06 23:32 Vir	06 14:17 Lib	07 02:32 Sag
10 03:16 Can	08 21:16 Leo	10 13:41 Vir	09 04:00 Lib	08 16:07 Sco	09 01:32 Cap
12 13:26 Leo	11 04:43 Vir	12 18:03 Lib	11 05:32 Sco	10 15:43 Sag	11 01:40 Aqu
14 21:41 Vir	13 09:59 Lib	14 20:27 Sco	13 05:52 Sag	12 15:15 Cap	13 04:49 Pis
17 04:02 Lib	15 13:46 Sco	16 22:18 Sag	15 06:53 Cap	14 16:45 Aqu	15 11:49 Ari
19 08:24 Sco	17 16:42 Sag	19 00:46 Cap	17 10:02 Aqu	16 21:33 Pis	17 22:11 Tau
21 10:54 Sag	19 19:22 Cap	21 04:38 Aqu	19 15:53 Pis	19 05:44 Ari	20 10:25 Gem
23 12:18 Cap	21 22:28 Aqu	23 10:15 Pis	22 00:14 Ari	21 16:26 Tau	22 23:06 Can
25 13:57 Aqu	24 02:56 Pis	25 17:49 Ari	24 10:30 Tau	24 04:31 Gem	25 11:16 Leo
27 17:31 Pis	26 09:42 Ari	28 03:31 Tau	26 22:17 Gem	26 17:11 Can	27 22:00 Vir
30 00:20 Ari	28 19:19 Tau	30 15:12 Gem	29 10:57 Can	29 05:32 Leo	30 06:10 Lib
				31 16:05 Vir	

Jul 1933	Aug 1933	Sep 1933	Oct 1933	Nov 1933	Dec 1933
02 10:56 Sco	02 21:40 Cap	01 06:59 Aqu	02 22:51 Ari	01 13:52 Tau	01 06:44 Gem
04 12:32 Sag	04 22:21 Aqu	03 09:44 Pis	05 06:17 Tau	04 00:01 Gem	03 18:52 Can
06 12:16 Cap	07 00:10 Pis	05 14:14 Ari	07 16:17 Gem	06 12:04 Can	06 07:48 Leo
08 12:05 Aqu	09 04:40 Ari	07 21:34 Tau	10 04:28 Can	09 00:57 Leo	08 19:59 Vir
10 14:01 Pis	11 12:44 Tau	10 08:00 Gem	12 17:01 Leo	11 12:23 Vir	11 05:18 Lib
12 19:30 Ari	13 23:57 Gem	12 20:24 Can	15 03:24 Vir	13 20:12 Lib	13 10:26 Sco
15 04:48 Tau	16 12:31 Can	15 08:30 Leo	17 10:07 Lib	15 23:51 Sco	15 11:49 Sag
17 16:43 Gem	19 00:22 Leo	17 18:13 Vir	19 13:28 Sco	18 00:34 Sag	17 11:09 Cap
20 05:24 Can	21 10:07 Vir	20 00:51 Lib	21 14:54 Sag	20 00:23 Cap	19 10:37 Aqu
22 17:18 Leo	23 17:29 Lib	22 05:00 Sco	23 16:13 Cap	22 01:20 Aqu	21 12:15 Pis
25 03:35 Vir	25 22:44 Sco	24 07:48 Sag	25 18:48 Aqu	24 04:49 Pis	23 17:15 Ari
27 11:43 Lib	28 02:21 Sag	26 10:23 Cap	27 23:17 Pis	26 11:12 Ari	26 01:42 Tau
29 17:21 Sco	30 04:51 Cap	28 13:26 Aqu	30 05:40 Ari	28 20:02 Tau	28 12:42 Gem
31 20:26 Sag		30 17:26 Pis			31 01:06 Can

Jan 1934	Feb 1934	Mar 1934	Apr 1934	May 1934	Jun 1934
02 13:55 Leo	01 08:00 Vir	03 00:01 Lib	01 13:35 Sco	01 01:01 Sag	01 11:55 Aqu
05 02:08 Vir	03 17:59 Lib	05 06:59 Sco	03 17:37 Sag	03 02:53 Cap	03 14:06 Pis
07 12:19 Lib	06 01:31 Sco	07 11:58 Sag	05 20:45 Cap	05 05:05 Aqu	05 18:31 Ari
09 19:10 Sco	08 06:14 Sag	09 15:21 Cap	07 23:42 Aqu	07 08:26 Pis	08 01:16 Tau
11 22:17 Sag	10 08:23 Cap	11 17:36 Aqu	10 02:52 Pis	09 13:08 Ari	10 10:13 Gem
13 22:37 Cap	12 08:57 Aqu	13 19:25 Pis	12 06:40 Ari	11 19:23 Tau	12 21:13 Can
15 21:56 Aqu	14 09:27 Pis	15 22:00 Ari	14 11:55 Tau	14 03:37 Gem	15 09:52 Leo
17 22:17 Pis	16 11:39 Ari	18 02:45 Tau	16 19:41 Gem	16 14:16 Can	17 22:51 Vir
20 01:27 Ari	18 17:03 Tau	20 10:50 Gem	19 06:26 Can	19 02:54 Leo	20 09:58 Lib
22 08:25 Tau	21 02:16 Gem	22 22:12 Can	21 19:09 Leo	21 15:34 Vir	22 17:24 Sco
24 18:53 Gem	23 14:21 Can	25 11:02 Leo	24 07:19 Vir	24 01:43 Lib	24 20:49 Sag
27 07:23 Can	26 03:13 Leo	27 22:44 Vir	26 16:31 Lib	26 07:51 Sco	26 21:24 Cap
29 20:11 Leo	28 14:45 Vir	30 07:36 Lib	28 22:07 Sco	28 10:29 Sag	28 21:02 Aqu
				30 11:12 Cap	30 21:37 Pis

Jul 1934	Aug 1934	Sep 1934	Oct 1934	Nov 1934	Dec 1934
03 00:38 Ari	01 13:24 Tau	02 15:39 Can	02 11:43 Leo	01 08:35 Vir	01 04:38 Lib
05 06:47 Tau	03 21:48 Gem	05 04:31 Leo	05 00:30 Vir	03 19:40 Lib	03 13:05 Sco
07 15:54 Gem	06 09:12 Can	07 17:15 Vir	07 11:20 Lib	06 03:32 Sco	05 17:52 Sag
10 03:20 Can	08 22:07 Leo	10 04:22 Lib	09 19:31 Sco	08 08:33 Sag	07 20:09 Cap
12 16:06 Leo	11 10:58 Vir	12 13:19 Sco	12 01:32 Sag	10 11:56 Cap	09 21:33 Aqu
15 05:06 Vir	13 22:32 Lib	14 20:03 Sag	14 06:04 Cap	12 14:51 Aqu	11 23:30 Pis
17 16:46 Lib	16 07:50 Sco	17 00:35 Cap	16 09:32 Aqu	14 17:56 Pis	14 02:51 Ari
20 01:30 Sco	18 14:11 Sag	19 03:06 Aqu	18 12:09 Pis	16 21:26 Ari	16 07:56 Tau
22 06:27 Sag	20 17:27 Cap	21 04:14 Pis	20 14:28 Ari	19 01:46 Tau	18 14:58 Gem
24 08:03 Cap	22 18:18 Aqu	23 05:13 Ari	22 17:34 Tau	21 07:47 Gem	21 00:10 Can
26 07:44 Aqu	24 18:08 Pis	25 07:46 Tau	24 22:57 Gem	23 16:24 Can	23 11:37 Leo
28 07:20 Pis	26 18:44 Ari	27 13:32 Gem	27 07:45 Can	26 03:53 Leo	26 00:32 Vir
30 08:45 Ari	28 21:54 Tau	29 23:14 Can	29 19:41 Leo	28 16:51 Vir	28 12:58 Lib
	31 04:54 Gem				30 22:41 Sco

Jan 1935	Feb 1935	Mar 1935	Apr 1935	May 1935	Jun 1935
02 04:26 Sag	02 18:26 Aqu	02 05:16 Aqu	02 15:32 Ari	02 02:09 Tau	02 20:43 Can
04 06:44 Cap	04 17:47 Pis	04 05:13 Pis	04 16:18 Tau	04 05:26 Gem	05 06:19 Leo
06 07:04 Aqu	06 17:49 Ari	06 04:40 Ari	06 19:35 Gem	06 11:49 Can	07 18:25 Vir
08 07:17 Pis	08 20:22 Tau	08 05:43 Tau	09 02:48 Can	08 21:54 Leo	10 06:59 Lib
10 09:02 Ari	11 02:35 Gem	10 10:10 Gem	11 13:51 Leo	11 10:25 Vir	12 17:34 Sco
12 13:24 Tau	13 12:23 Can	12 18:51 Can	14 02:46 Vir	13 22:47 Lib	15 00:56 Sag
14 20:42 Gem	16 00:35 Leo	15 06:47 Leo	16 15:00 Lib	16 08:54 Sco	17 05:21 Cap
17 06:37 Can	18 13:32 Vir	17 19:51 Vir	19 01:09 Sco	18 16:12 Sag	19 07:56 Aqu
19 18:26 Leo	21 02:02 Lib	20 08:07 Lib	21 09:06 Sag	20 21:20 Cap	21 09:55 Pis
22 07:19 Vir	23 13:03 Sco	22 18:44 Sco	23 15:13 Cap	23 01:08 Aqu	23 12:21 Ari
24 19:58 Lib	25 21:39 Sag	25 03:23 Sag	25 19:43 Aqu	25 04:13 Pis	25 15:54 Tau
27 06:45 Sco	28 03:04 Cap	27 09:48 Cap	27 22:39 Pis	27 06:58 Ari	27 21:06 Gem
29 14:10 Sag		29 13:41 Aqu	30 00:26 Ari	29 09:59 Tau	30 04:26 Can
31 17:47 Cap		31 15:15 Pis		31 14:11 Gem	

Jul 1935	Aug 1935	Sep 1935	Oct 1935	Nov 1935	Dec 1935
02 14:12 Leo	01 09:06 Vir	02 16:21 Sco	02 08:40 Sag	03 04:38 Aqu	02 14:02 Pis
05 02:08 Vir	03 21:54 Lib	05 02:48 Sag	04 17:02 Cap	05 08:20 Pis	04 16:53 Ari
07 14:51 Lib	06 09:56 Sco	07 10:07 Cap	06 22:20 Aqu	07 09:54 Ari	06 19:03 Tau
10 02:14 Sco	08 19:24 Sag	09 13:44 Aqu	09 00:26 Pis	09 10:29 Tau	08 21:36 Gem
12 10:27 Sag	11 01:09 Cap	11 14:15 Pis	11 00:20 Ari	11 11:52 Gem	11 01:53 Can
14 15:03 Cap	13 03:21 Aqu	13 13:21 Ari	12 23:53 Tau	13 15:56 Can	13 09:06 Leo
16 16:53 Aqu	15 03:19 Pis	15 13:10 Tau	15 01:17 Gem	15 23:50 Leo	15 19:32 Vir
18 17:31 Pis	17 02:55 Ari	17 15:47 Gem	17 06:20 Can	18 11:09 Vir	18 07:57 Lib
20 18:32 Ari	19 04:07 Tau	19 22:26 Can	19 15:34 Leo	20 23:52 Lib	20 20:02 Sco
22 21:20 Tau	21 08:25 Gem	22 08:49 Leo	22 03:43 Vir	23 11:35 Sco	23 05:44 Sag
25 02:41 Gem	23 16:16 Can	24 21:18 Vir	24 16:31 Lib	25 21:08 Sag	25 12:27 Cap
27 10:42 Can	26 03:00 Leo	27 10:05 Lib	27 04:14 Sco	28 04:28 Cap	27 16:46 Aqu
29 21:03 Leo	28 15:20 Vir	29 22:05 Sco	29 14:17 Sag	30 09:59 Aqu	29 19:42 Pis
	31 04:07 Lib		31 22:30 Cap		31 22:15 Ari

Jan 1936	Feb 1936	Mar 1936	Apr 1936	May 1936	Jun 1936
03 01:10 Tau	01 10:38 Gem	01 22:25 Can	03 00:07 Vir	02 18:42 Lib	01 14:10 Sco
05 05:03 Gem	03 16:57 Can	04 07:20 Leo	05 12:30 Lib	05 07:16 Sco	04 01:37 Sag
07 10:28 Can	06 01:25 Leo	06 18:17 Vir	08 01:05 Sco	07 18:53 Sag	06 11:02 Cap
09 18:01 Leo	08 11:47 Vir	09 06:25 Lib	10 13:02 Sag	10 04:56 Cap	08 18:17 Aqu
12 04:04 Vir	10 23:45 Lib	11 19:03 Sco	12 23:22 Cap	12 12:46 Aqu	10 23:27 Pis
14 16:09 Lib	13 12:23 Sco	14 07:05 Sag	15 06:48 Aqu	14 17:52 Pis	13 02:46 Ari
17 04:38 Sco	15 23:56 Sag	16 16:50 Cap	17 10:37 Pis	16 20:13 Ari	15 04:48 Tau
19 15:10 Sag	18 08:20 Cap	18 22:51 Aqu	19 11:21 Ari	18 20:47 Tau	17 06:29 Gem
21 22:18 Cap	20 12:46 Aqu	21 00:59 Pis	21 10:38 Tau	20 21:12 Gem	19 09:08 Can
24 02:02 Aqu	22 13:56 Pis	23 00:31 Ari	23 10:37 Gem	22 23:19 Can	21 14:05 Leo
26 03:34 Pis	24 13:35 Ari	24 23:37 Tau	25 13:22 Can	25 04:41 Leo	23 22:15 Vir
28 04:36 Ari	26 13:51 Tau	27 00:31 Gem	27 20:02 Leo	27 13:47 Vir	26 09:22 Lib
30 06:37 Tau	28 16:29 Gem	29 04:51 Can	30 06:21 Vir	30 01:38 Lib	28 21:52 Sco
		31 13:03 Leo			

Jul 1936	Aug 1936	Sep 1936	Oct 1936	Nov 1936	Dec 1936
01 09:26 Sag	02 09:25 Aqu	02 22:43 Ari	02 08:25 Tau	02 20:00 Can	02 09:43 Leo
03 18:33 Cap	04 12:36 Pis	04 23:04 Tau	04 08:37 Gem	05 00:36 Leo	04 16:30 Vir
06 00:56 Aqu	06 14:21 Ari	07 00:54 Gem	06 11:28 Can	07 08:59 Vir	07 02:55 Lib
08 05:10 Pis	08 16:11 Tau	09 05:15 Can	08 17:44 Leo	09 20:14 Lib	09 15:27 Sco
10 08:10 Ari	10 19:11 Gem	11 12:12 Leo	11 03:01 Vir	12 08:51 Sco	12 04:06 Sag
12 10:45 Tau	12 23:51 Can	13 21:19 Vir	13 14:18 Lib	14 21:33 Sag	14 15:25 Cap
14 13:38 Gem	15 06:19 Leo	16 08:12 Lib	16 02:46 Sco	17 09:20 Cap	17 00:42 Aqu
16 17:27 Can	17 14:44 Vir	18 20:31 Sco	18 15:37 Sag	19 19:10 Aqu	19 07:43 Pis
18 22:57 Leo	20 01:16 Lib	21 09:23 Sag	21 03:37 Cap	22 02:04 Pis	21 12:26 Ari
21 06:53 Vir	22 13:35 Sco	23 20:52 Cap	23 12:59 Aqu	24 05:36 Ari	23 15:05 Tau
23 17:30 Lib	25 02:09 Sag	26 04:52 Aqu	25 18:27 Pis	26 06:29 Tau	25 16:24 Gem
26 05:53 Sco	27 12:34 Cap	28 08:39 Pis	27 20:09 Ari	28 06:12 Gem	27 17:36 Can
28 17:55 Sag	29 19:12 Aqu	30 09:10 Ari	29 19:34 Tau	30 06:40 Can	29 20:14 Leo
31 03:23 Cap	31 22:05 Pis		31 18:49 Gem		

Jan 1937	Feb 1937	Mar 1937	Apr 1937	May 1937	Jun 1937
01 01:45 Vir	02 07:09 Sco	01 15:22 Sco	03 00:16 Cap	02 18:07 Aqu	01 08:57 Pis
03 10:54 Lib	04 19:58 Sag	04 04:07 Sag	05 10:38 Aqu	05 01:56 Pis	03 14:21 Ari
05 22:57 Sco	07 07:33 Cap	06 16:22 Cap	07 16:59 Pis	07 05:47 Ari	05 16:36 Tau
08 11:42 Sag	09 16:00 Aqu	09 01:35 Aqu	09 19:28 Ari	09 06:32 Tau	07 16:46 Gem
10 22:53 Cap	11 21:09 Pis	11 06:50 Pis	11 19:39 Tau	11 05:56 Gem	09 16:32 Can
13 07:24 Aqu	14 00:11 Ari	13 09:00 Ari	13 19:34 Gem	13 06:00 Can	11 17:44 Leo
15 13:28 Pis	16 02:34 Tau	15 09:54 Tau	15 21:02 Can	15 08:27 Leo	13 22:00 Vir
17 17:48 Ari	18 05:22 Gem	17 11:18 Gem	18 01:11 Leo	17 14:18 Vir	16 06:07 Lib
19 21:06 Tau	20 09:03 Can	19 14:25 Can	20 08:15 Vir	19 23:34 Lib	18 17:30 Sco
21 23:53 Gem	22 13:50 Leo	21 19:35 Leo	22 17:50 Lib	22 11:17 Sco	21 06:25 Sag
24 02:38 Can	24 20:04 Vir	24 02:43 Vir	25 05:20 Sco	25 00:10 Sag	23 18:57 Cap
26 06:07 Leo	27 04:26 Lib	26 11:46 Lib	27 18:04 Sag	27 12:52 Cap	26 05:53 Aqu
28 11:30 Vir		28 22:50 Sco	30 06:56 Cap	30 00:13 Aqu	28 14:36 Pis
30 19:48 Lib		31 11:31 Sag			30 20:50 Ari

Jul 1937	Aug 1937	Sep 1937	Oct 1937	Nov 1937	Dec 1937
03 00:34 Tau	01 09:29 Gem	01 21:21 Leo	01 08:28 Vir	02 07:48 Sco	02 02:05 Sag
05 02:15 Gem	03 11:34 Can	04 01:34 Vir	03 15:31 Lib	04 19:45 Sag	04 15:07 Cap
07 02:53 Can	05 13:35 Leo	06 07:48 Lib	06 00:54 Sco	07 08:49 Cap	07 03:39 Aqu
09 03:59 Leo	07 16:54 Vir	08 16:58 Sco	08 12:43 Sag	09 21:18 Aqu	09 14:20 Pis
11 07:15 Vir	09 22:58 Lib	11 04:58 Sag	11 01:46 Cap	12 07:06 Pis	11 21:54 Ari
13 14:03 Lib	12 08:36 Sco	13 17:50 Cap	13 13:36 Aqu	14 12:59 Ari	14 01:49 Tau
16 00:35 Sco	14 20:58 Sag	16 04:50 Aqu	15 22:03 Pis	16 15:12 Tau	16 02:42 Gem
18 13:19 Sag	17 09:36 Cap	18 12:19 Pis	18 02:32 Ari	18 15:10 Gem	18 02:02 Can
21 01:50 Cap	19 20:04 Aqu	20 16:31 Ari	20 04:09 Tau	20 14:47 Can	20 01:48 Leo
23 12:19 Aqu	22 03:28 Pis	22 18:49 Tau	22 04:40 Gem	22 15:55 Leo	22 03:56 Vir
25 20:20 Pis	24 08:23 Ari	24 20:46 Gem	24 05:46 Can	24 19:55 Vir	24 09:52 Lib
28 02:15 Ari	26 11:56 Tau	26 23:24 Can	26 08:42 Leo	27 03:21 Lib	26 19:44 Sco
30 06:31 Tau	28 15:01 Gem	29 03:13 Leo	28 14:01 Vir	29 13:45 Sco	29 08:11 Sag
	30 18:03 Can		30 21:46 Lib		31 21:16 Cap

Jan 1938	Feb 1938	Mar 1938	Apr 1938	May 1938	Jun 1938
03 09:30 Aqu	02 01:58 Pis	01 09:13 Pis	02 04:42 Tau	01 15:45 Gem	02 02:08 Leo
05 20:06 Pis	04 09:54 Ari	03 16:16 Ari	04 07:33 Gem	03 16:51 Can	04 04:21 Vir
08 04:28 Ari	06 15:58 Tau	05 21:29 Tau	06 10:07 Can	05 18:42 Leo	06 09:35 Lib
10 10:05 Tau	08 20:07 Gem	08 01:33 Gem	08 13:04 Leo	07 22:16 Vir	08 18:00 Sco
12 12:50 Gem	10 22:25 Can	10 04:45 Can	10 16:51 Vir	10 04:05 Lib	11 04:56 Sag
14 13:22 Can	12 23:33 Leo	12 07:23 Leo	12 22:01 Lib	12 12:15 Sco	13 17:20 Cap
16 13:10 Leo	15 00:57 Vir	14 10:05 Vir	15 05:21 Sco	14 22:40 Sag	16 06:07 Aqu
18 14:13 Vir	17 04:27 Lib	16 14:08 Lib	17 15:18 Sag	17 10:50 Cap	18 18:02 Pis
20 18:26 Lib	19 11:36 Sco	18 20:53 Sco	20 03:30 Cap	19 23:37 Aqu	21 03:39 Ari
23 02:54 Sco	21 22:33 Sag	21 07:00 Sag	22 16:09 Aqu	22 11:07 Pis	23 09:49 Tau
25 14:50 Sag	24 11:27 Cap	23 19:31 Cap	25 02:53 Pis	24 19:35 Ari	25 12:25 Gem
28 03:57 Cap	26 23:35 Aqu	26 07:55 Aqu	27 10:08 Ari	27 00:16 Tau	27 12:28 Can
30 15:59 Aqu		28 17:51 Pis	29 14:01 Tau	29 01:52 Gem	29 11:46 Leo
		31 00:33 Ari		31 01:52 Can	

Jul 1938	Aug 1938	Sep 1938	Oct 1938	Nov 1938	Dec 1938
01 12:24 Vir	02 06:49 Sco	01 00:27 Sag	03 08:57 Aqu	02 05:08 Pis	02 00:02 Ari
03 16:08 Lib	04 17:01 Sag	03 12:29 Cap	05 20:26 Pis	04 14:34 Ari	04 07:00 Tau
05 23:48 Sco	07 05:32 Cap	06 01:10 Aqu	08 05:22 Ari	06 20:40 Tau	06 10:18 Gem
08 10:44 Sag	09 18:14 Aqu	08 12:28 Pis	10 11:42 Tau	09 00:03 Gem	08 11:08 Can
10 23:21 Cap	12 05:44 Pis	10 21:40 Ari	12 16:10 Gem	11 01:59 Can	10 11:17 Leo
13 12:05 Aqu	14 15:34 Ari	13 04:53 Tau	14 19:30 Can	13 03:49 Leo	12 12:37 Vir
15 23:55 Pis	16 23:25 Tau	15 10:22 Gem	16 22:19 Leo	15 06:37 Vir	14 16:27 Lib
18 10:02 Ari	19 04:50 Gem	17 14:09 Can	19 01:08 Vir	17 11:03 Lib	16 23:12 Sco
20 17:30 Tau	21 07:39 Can	19 16:26 Leo	21 04:43 Lib	19 17:25 Sco	19 08:30 Sag
22 21:42 Gem	23 08:27 Leo	21 18:01 Vir	23 10:00 Sco	22 01:56 Sag	21 19:38 Cap
24 22:54 Can	25 08:43 Vir	23 20:19 Lib	25 17:53 Sag	24 12:37 Cap	24 07:58 Aqu
26 22:25 Leo	27 10:26 Lib	26 00:56 Sco	28 04:38 Cap	27 00:58 Aqu	26 20:40 Pis
28 22:16 Vir	29 15:25 Sco	28 09:01 Sag	30 17:07 Aqu	29 13:29 Pis	29 08:13 Ari
31 00:34 Lib		30 20:19 Cap			31 16:47 Tau

Jan 1939	Feb 1939	Mar 1939	Apr 1939	May 1939	Jun 1939
02 21:19 Gem	01 09:22 Can	02 19:30 Leo	01 04:39 Vir	02 17:36 Sco	01 07:15 Sag
04 22:20 Can	03 09:06 Leo	04 19:17 Vir	03 05:48 Lib	04 23:10 Sag	03 15:49 Cap
06 21:32 Leo	05 08:03 Vir	06 19:26 Lib	05 08:21 Sco	07 07:33 Cap	06 02:40 Aqu
08 21:08 Vir	07 08:29 Lib	08 21:59 Sco	07 13:47 Sag	09 18:40 Aqu	08 15:03 Pis
10 23:10 Lib	09 12:21 Sco	11 04:22 Sag	09 22:46 Cap	12 07:08 Pis	11 03:09 Ari
13 04:53 Sco	11 20:23 Sag	13 14:34 Cap	12 10:32 Aqu	14 18:40 Ari	13 12:42 Tau
15 14:09 Sag	14 07:40 Cap	16 03:01 Aqu	14 23:04 Pis	17 03:28 Tau	15 18:32 Gem
18 01:43 Cap	16 20:21 Aqu	18 15:31 Pis	17 10:12 Ari	19 09:06 Gem	17 21:06 Can
20 14:14 Aqu	19 08:51 Pis	21 02:40 Ari	19 18:56 Tau	21 12:23 Can	19 21:58 Leo
23 02:50 Pis	21 20:23 Ari	23 11:58 Tau	22 01:16 Gem	23 14:33 Leo	21 22:56 Vir
25 14:41 Ari	24 06:18 Tau	25 19:14 Gem	24 05:43 Can	25 16:50 Vir	24 01:30 Lib
28 00:28 Tau	26 13:46 Gem	28 00:19 Can	26 08:54 Leo	27 20:05 Lib	26 06:24 Sco
30 06:49 Gem	28 18:06 Can	30 03:14 Leo	28 11:26 Vir	30 00:47 Sco	28 13:38 Sag
			30 14:02 Lib		30 22:53 Cap

Jul 1939	Aug 1939	Sep 1939	Oct 1939	Nov 1939	Dec 1939
03 09:53 Aqu	02 04:41 Pis	03 10:46 Tau	03 01:37 Gem	01 13:41 Can	03 02:22 Vir
05 22:17 Pis	04 17:21 Ari	05 20:01 Gem	05 08:16 Can	03 18:01 Leo	05 05:22 Lib
08 10:49 Ari	07 04:46 Tau	08 01:51 Can	07 12:10 Leo	05 20:56 Vir	07 08:57 Sco
10 21:26 Tau	09 13:05 Gem	10 04:11 Leo	09 13:46 Vir	07 23:03 Lib	09 13:32 Sag
13 04:20 Gem	11 17:21 Can	12 04:09 Vir	11 14:16 Lib	10 01:13 Sco	11 19:51 Cap
15 07:16 Can	13 18:09 Leo	14 03:38 Lib	13 15:18 Sco	12 04:41 Sag	14 04:42 Aqu
17 07:31 Leo	15 17:20 Vir	16 04:43 Sco	15 18:36 Sag	14 10:41 Cap	16 16:13 Pis
19 07:07 Vir	17 17:04 Lib	18 09:01 Sag	18 01:21 Cap	16 19:59 Aqu	19 05:02 Ari
21 08:10 Lib	19 19:19 Sco	20 17:10 Cap	20 11:39 Aqu	19 07:59 Pis	21 16:31 Tau
23 12:03 Sco	22 01:13 Sag	23 04:23 Aqu	23 00:05 Pis	21 20:35 Ari	24 00:37 Gem
25 19:09 Sag	24 10:33 Cap	25 16:59 Pis	25 12:27 Ari	24 07:22 Tau	26 05:03 Can
28 04:50 Cap	26 22:08 Aqu	28 05:21 Ari	27 23:08 Tau	26 15:09 Gem	28 07:05 Leo
30 16:14 Aqu	29 10:42 Pis	30 16:28 Tau	30 07:31 Gem	28 20:11 Can	30 08:29 Vir
	31 23:14 Ari			30 23:33 Leo	

Jan 1940	Feb 1940	Mar 1940	Apr 1940	May 1940	Jun 1940
01 10:43 Lib	02 01:35 Sag	02 15:02 Cap	01 07:12 Aqu	01 01:55 Pis	02 10:43 Tau
03 14:35 Sco	04 09:26 Cap	05 01:07 Aqu	03 19:10 Pis	03 14:51 Ari	04 20:49 Gem
05 20:12 Sag	06 19:21 Aqu	07 13:06 Pis	06 08:09 Ari	06 03:12 Tau	07 04:02 Can
08 03:29 Cap	09 06:58 Pis	10 02:00 Ari	08 20:38 Tau	08 13:33 Gem	09 09:00 Leo
10 12:41 Aqu	11 19:48 Ari	12 14:43 Tau	11 07:31 Gem	10 21:33 Can	11 12:40 Vir
13 00:03 Pis	14 08:35 Tau	15 01:52 Gem	13 16:03 Can	13 03:22 Leo	13 15:43 Lib
15 12:54 Ari	16 19:09 Gem	17 09:56 Can	15 21:43 Leo	15 07:17 Vir	15 18:31 Sco
18 01:15 Tau	19 01:46 Can	19 14:15 Leo	18 00:34 Vir	17 09:40 Lib	17 21:34 Sag
20 10:31 Gem	21 04:19 Leo	21 15:21 Vir	20 01:23 Lib	19 11:12 Sco	20 01:44 Cap
22 15:35 Can	23 04:11 Vir	23 14:48 Lib	22 01:32 Sco	21 13:00 Sag	22 08:14 Aqu
24 17:11 Leo	25 03:28 Lib	25 14:33 Sco	24 02:48 Sag	23 16:34 Cap	24 17:55 Pis
26 17:12 Vir	27 04:13 Sco	27 16:31 Sag	26 06:49 Cap	25 23:18 Aqu	27 06:12 Ari
28 17:43 Lib	29 07:54 Sag	29 21:59 Cap	28 14:38 Aqu	28 09:38 Pis	29 18:51 Tau
30 20:17 Sco				30 22:18 Ari	

Jul 1940	Aug 1940	Sep 1940	Oct 1940	Nov 1940	Dec 1940
02 05:15 Gem	03 01:20 Leo	01 12:57 Vir	02 23:12 Sco	01 10:21 Sag	03 03:12 Aqu
04 12:10 Can	05 02:50 Vir	03 12:54 Lib	04 23:53 Sag	03 12:22 Cap	05 11:34 Pis
06 16:12 Leo	07 03:49 Lib	05 13:16 Sco	07 03:28 Cap	05 18:02 Aqu	07 23:26 Ari
08 18:44 Vir	09 05:45 Sco	07 15:36 Sag	09 10:43 Aqu	08 03:45 Pis	10 12:26 Tau
10 21:06 Lib	11 09:28 Sag	09 20:45 Cap	11 21:17 Pis	10 16:12 Ari	13 00:07 Gem
13 00:06 Sco	13 15:14 Cap	12 04:51 Aqu	14 09:49 Ari	13 05:12 Tau	15 09:19 Can
15 04:04 Sag	15 23:07 Aqu	14 15:24 Pis	16 22:49 Tau	15 17:00 Gem	17 16:16 Leo
17 09:17 Cap	18 09:09 Pis	17 03:42 Ari	19 10:59 Gem	18 02:52 Can	19 21:34 Vir
19 16:21 Aqu	20 21:13 Ari	19 16:45 Tau	21 21:17 Can	20 10:38 Leo	22 01:36 Lib
22 01:58 Pis	23 10:16 Tau	22 05:04 Gem	24 04:50 Leo	22 16:10 Vir	24 04:29 Sco
24 14:00 Ari	25 22:12 Gem	24 14:56 Can	26 09:09 Vir	24 19:24 Lib	26 06:36 Sag
27 02:55 Tau	28 06:53 Can	26 21:08 Leo	28 10:37 Lib	26 20:44 Sco	28 08:58 Cap
29 14:03 Gem	30 11:31 Leo	28 23:41 Vir	30 10:25 Sco	28 21:18 Sag	30 13:08 Aqu
31 21:32 Can		30 23:46 Lib		30 22:50 Cap	

Jan 1941	Feb 1941	Mar 1941	Apr 1941	May 1941	Jun 1941
01 20:34 Pis	03 04:40 Tau	02 12:22 Tau	01 08:06 Gem	01 01:55 Can	02 00:38 Vir
04 07:33 Ari	05 17:08 Gem	05 01:11 Gem	03 19:43 Can	03 11:33 Leo	04 05:17 Lib
06 20:27 Tau	08 02:57 Can	07 12:03 Can	06 04:25 Leo	05 18:05 Vir	06 07:13 Sco
09 08:26 Gem	10 09:07 Leo	09 19:18 Leo	08 09:21 Vir	07 21:11 Lib	08 07:24 Sag
11 17:33 Can	12 12:21 Vir	11 22:51 Vir	10 10:54 Lib	09 21:33 Sco	10 07:32 Cap
13 23:39 Leo	14 14:07 Lib	13 23:51 Lib	12 10:32 Sco	11 20:50 Sag	12 09:41 Aqu
16 03:45 Vir	16 15:52 Sco	16 00:02 Sco	14 10:08 Sag	13 21:03 Cap	14 15:32 Pis
18 06:59 Lib	18 18:36 Sag	18 01:07 Sag	16 11:38 Cap	16 00:14 Aqu	17 01:30 Ari
20 10:03 Sco	20 22:53 Cap	20 04:24 Cap	18 16:30 Aqu	18 07:33 Pis	19 14:02 Tau
22 13:16 Sag	23 05:01 Aqu	22 10:33 Aqu	21 01:06 Pis	20 18:33 Ari	22 02:44 Gem
24 17:01 Cap	25 13:18 Pis	24 19:29 Pis	23 12:33 Ari	23 07:25 Tau	24 13:51 Can
26 22:05 Aqu	27 23:54 Ari	27 06:39 Ari	26 01:22 Tau	25 20:09 Gem	26 22:54 Leo
29 05:34 Pis		29 19:13 Tau	28 14:10 Gem	28 07:36 Cam	29 06:02 Vir
31 16:01 Ari				30 17:14 Leo	

Jul 1941	Aug 1941	Sep 1941	Oct 1941	Nov 1941	Dec 1941
01 11:16 Lib	01 22:49 Sag	02 11:38 Aqu	02 00:17 Pis	03 03:18 Tau	02 21:59 Gem
03 14:33 Sco	04 01:16 Cap	04 17:51 Pis	04 09:36 Ari	05 15:51 Gem	05 10:21 Can
05 16:13 Sag	06 04:32 Aqu	07 02:28 Ari	06 20:51 Tau	08 04:25 Can	07 21:42 Leo
07 17:21 Cap	08 09:50 Pis	09 13:31 Tau	09 09:22 Gem	10 15:48 Leo	10 07:12 Vir
09 19:36 Aqu	10 18:12 Ari	12 02:05 Gem	11 21:52 Can	13 00:28 Vir	12 13:45 Lib
12 00:41 Pis	13 05:31 Tau	14 14:08 Can	14 08:28 Leo	15 05:21 Lib	14 16:51 Sco
14 09:34 Ari	15 18:08 Gem	16 23:35 Leo	16 15:35 Vir	17 06:40 Sco	16 17:10 Sag
16 21:29 Tau	18 05:37 Can	19 05:28 Vir	18 18:54 Lib	19 05:53 Sag	18 16:27 Cap
19 10:09 Gem	20 14:15 Leo	21 08:17 Lib	20 19:26 Sco	21 05:11 Cap	20 16:53 Aqu
21 21:14 Can	22 19:52 Vir	23 09:24 Sco	22 19:01 Sag	23 06:46 Aqu	22 20:32 Pis
24 05:47 Leo	24 23:21 Lib	25 10:24 Sag	24 19:40 Cap	25 12:08 Pis	25 04:23 Ari
26 12:03 Vir	27 01:48 Sco	27 12:44 Cap	26 23:02 Aqu	27 21:26 Ari	27 15:42 Tau
28 16:40 Lib	29 04:12 Sag	29 17:16 Aqu	29 05:50 Pis	30 09:17 Tau	30 04:26 Gem
30 20:08 Sco	31 07:17 Cap		31 15:37 Ari		

Jan 1942	Feb 1942	Mar 1942	Apr 1942	May 1942	Jun 1942
01 16:41 Can	02 18:57 Vir	02 03:05 Vir	02 19:54 Sco	02 06:03 Sag	02 15:59 Aqu
04 03:32 Leo	05 01:17 Lib	04 08:23 Lib	04 21:04 Sag	04 06:04 Cap	04 19:13 Pis
06 12:41 Vir	07 05:55 Sco	06 11:50 Sco	06 22:41 Cap	06 07:55 Aqu	07 02:10 Ari
08 19:48 Lib	09 09:06 Sag	08 14:28 Sag	09 01:56 Aqu	08 12:43 Pis	09 12:15 Tau
11 00:24 Sco	11 11:19 Cap	10 17:08 Cap	11 07:19 Pis	10 20:31 Ari	12 00:11 Gem
13 02:31 Sag	13 13:28 Aqu	12 20:30 Aqu	13 14:48 Ari	13 06:36 Tau	14 12:49 Can
15 03:07 Cap	15 16:50 Pis	15 01:08 Pis	16 00:17 Tau	15 18:14 Gem	17 01:19 Leo
17 03:52 Aqu	17 22:46 Ari	17 07:40 Ari	18 11:36 Gem	18 06:48 Can	19 12:32 Vir
19 06:43 Pis	20 07:57 Tau	19 16:38 Tau	21 00:09 Can	20 19:20 Leo	21 21:03 Lib
21 13:07 Ari	22 19:46 Gem	22 03:59 Gem	23 12:20 Leo	23 06:06 Vir	24 01:50 Sco
23 23:18 Tau	25 08:15 Can	24 16:32 Can	25 22:02 Vir	25 13:21 Lib	26 03:08 Sag
26 11:43 Gem	27 19:05 Leo	27 04:03 Leo	28 03:49 Lib	27 16:32 Sco	28 02:29 Cap
29 00:03 Can		29 12:36 Vir	30 05:59 Sco	29 16:39 Sag	30 02:00 Aqu
31 10:36 Leo		31 17:36 Lib		31 15:44 Cap	

Jul 1942	Aug 1942	Sep 1942	Oct 1942	Nov 1942	Dec 1942
02 03:45 Pis	03 01:47 Tau	01 20:39 Gem	01 17:02 Can	03 01:18 Vir	02 18:54 Lib
04 09:10 Ari	05 12:53 Gem	04 08:59 Can	04 05:34 Leo	05 09:21 Lib	05 00:06 Sco
06 18:22 Tau	08 01:30 Can	06 21:15 Leo	06 16:13 Vir	07 13:27 Sco	07 01:34 Sag
09 06:09 Gem	10 13:39 Leo	09 07:30 Vir	08 23:32 Lib	09 14:47 Sag	09 01:06 Cap
11 18:51 Can	13 00:08 Vir	11 15:04 Lib	11 03:46 Sco	11 15:18 Cap	11 00:56 Aqu
14 07:07 Leo	15 08:30 Lib	13 20:18 Sco	13 06:10 Sag	13 16:48 Aqu	13 02:55 Pis
16 18:08 Vir	17 14:37 Sco	15 23:57 Sag	15 08:13 Cap	15 20:27 Pis	15 08:03 Ari
19 03:01 Lib	19 18:34 Sag	18 02:48 Cap	17 11:01 Aqu	18 02:30 Ari	17 16:16 Tau
21 09:01 Sco	21 20:46 Cap	20 05:27 Aqu	19 15:05 Pis	20 10:37 Tau	20 02:45 Gem
23 11:58 Sag	23 22:07 Aqu	22 08:33 Pis	21 20:36 Ari	22 20:34 Gem	22 14:45 Can
25 12:38 Cap	25 23:55 Pis	24 12:57 Ari	24 03:52 Tau	25 08:16 Can	25 03:35 Leo
27 12:37 Aqu	28 03:38 Ari	26 19:34 Tau	26 13:18 Gem	27 21:09 Leo	27 16:09 Vir
29 13:49 Pis	30 10:28 Tau	29 05:04 Gem	29 00:59 Can	30 09:28 Vir	30 02:44 Lib
31 17:55 Ari			31 13:47 Leo		

Jan 1943	Feb 1943	Mar 1943	Apr 1943	May 1943	Jun 1943
01 09:39 Sco	01 23:15 Cap	01 07:18 Cap	01 18:27 Pis	01 04:39 Ari	02 00:29 Gem
03 12:34 Sag	03 23:10 Aqu	03 08:56 Aqu	03 21:17 Ari	03 09:57 Tau	04 10:45 Can
05 12:35 Cap	05 23:07 Pis	05 09:54 Pis	06 01:37 Tau	05 17:15 Gem	06 23:02 Leo
07 11:42 Aqu	08 01:00 Ari	07 11:41 Ari	08 08:41 Gem	08 03:16 Can	09 12:02 Vir
09 12:03 Pis	10 06:16 Tau	09 15:53 Tau	10 19:02 Can	10 15:37 Leo	11 23:21 Lib
11 15:20 Ari	12 15:24 Gem	11 23:38 Gem	13 07:38 Leo	13 04:21 Vir	14 06:58 Sco
13 22:21 Tau	15 03:24 Can	14 10:49 Can	15 19:58 Vir	15 14:43 Lib	16 10:36 Sag
16 08:38 Gem	17 16:18 Leo	16 23:40 Leo	18 05:40 Lib	17 21:19 Sco	18 11:30 Cap
18 20:53 Can	20 04:19 Vir	19 11:42 Vir	20 12:03 Sco	20 00:32 Sag	20 11:34 Aqu
21 09:43 Leo	22 14:29 Lib	21 21:20 Lib	22 15:56 Sag	22 01:59 Cap	22 12:36 Pis
23 22:02 Vir	24 22:24 Sco	24 04:22 Sco	24 18:39 Cap	24 03:23 Aqu	24 15:52 Ari
26 08:46 Lib	27 03:59 Sag	26 09:23 Sag	26 21:21 Aqu	26 05:57 Pis	26 21:51 Tau
28 16:50 Sco		28 13:04 Cap	29 00:35 Pis	28 10:16 Ari	29 06:26 Gem
30 21:33 Sag		30 15:57 Aqu		30 16:24 Tau	

Jul 1943	Aug 1943	Sep 1943	Oct 1943	Nov 1943	Dec 1943
01 17:12 Can	03 00:45 Vir	01 18:33 Lib	01 10:04 Sco	02 03:36 Cap	01 13:01 Aqu
04 05:39 Leo	05 12:50 Lib	04 04:20 Sco	03 17:02 Sag	04 07:09 Aqu	03 15:35 Pis
06 18:44 Vir	07 22:39 Sco	06 11:38 Sag	05 22:10 Cap	06 10:15 Pis	05 18:59 Ari
09 06:43 Lib	10 05:08 Sag	08 16:13 Cap	08 01:39 Aqu	08 13:10 Ari	07 23:30 Tau
11 15:40 Sco	12 08:09 Cap	10 18:18 Aqu	10 03:44 Pis	10 16:32 Tau	10 05:32 Gem
13 20:36 Sag	14 08:37 Aqu	12 18:46 Pis	12 05:12 Ari	12 21:31 Gem	12 13:46 Can
15 22:06 Cap	16 08:07 Pis	14 19:09 Ari	14 07:26 Tau	15 05:22 Can	15 00:36 Leo
17 21:45 Aqu	18 08:32 Ari	16 21:14 Tau	16 12:06 Gem	17 16:26 Leo	17 13:21 Vir
19 21:30 Pis	20 11:39 Tau	19 02:41 Gem	18 20:27 Can	20 05:21 Vir	20 01:54 Lib
21 23:08 Ari	22 18:33 Gem	21 12:09 Can	21 08:11 Leo	22 17:18 Lib	22 11:45 Sco
24 03:52 Tau	25 05:06 Can	24 00:33 Leo	23 21:09 Vir	25 02:09 Sco	24 17:43 Sag
26 12:03 Gem	27 17:48 Leo	26 13:29 Vir	26 08:37 Lib	27 07:35 Sag	26 20:24 Cap
28 23:03 Can	30 06:46 Vir	29 00:56 Lib	28 17:14 Sco	29 10:43 Cap	28 21:21 Aqu
31 11:42 Leo			30 23:14 Sag		30 22:17 Pis

Jan 1944	Feb 1944	Mar 1944	Apr 1944	May 1944	Jun 1944
02 00:33 Ari	02 17:16 Gem	01 00:05 Gem	02 02:53 Leo	01 23:04 Vir	03 06:31 Sco
04 04:58 Tau	05 02:39 Can	03 08:37 Can	04 15:48 Vir	04 11:39 Lib	05 14:27 Sag
06 11:44 Gem	07 14:19 Leo	05 20:19 Leo	07 04:21 Lib	06 22:17 Sco	07 19:41 Cap
08 20:47 Can	10 03:07 Vir	08 09:17 Vir	09 15:11 Sco	09 06:26 Sag	09 23:12 Aqu
11 07:57 Leo	12 15:54 Lib	10 21:54 Lib	12 00:02 Sag	11 12:33 Cap	12 01:58 Pis
13 20:38 Vir	15 03:23 Sco	13 09:11 Sco	14 06:55 Cap	13 17:09 Aqu	14 04:40 Ari
16 09:28 Lib	17 12:14 Sag	15 18:30 Sag	16 11:45 Aqu	15 20:35 Pis	16 07:51 Tau
18 20:27 Sco	19 17:32 Cap	18 01:13 Cap	18 14:28 Pis	17 23:03 Ari	18 12:11 Gem
21 03:53 Sag	21 19:27 Aqu	20 04:55 Aqu	20 15:36 Ari	20 01:15 Tau	20 18:28 Can
23 07:26 Cap	23 19:09 Pis	22 05:59 Pis	22 16:29 Tau	22 04:26 Gem	23 03:25 Leo
25 08:10 Aqu	25 18:31 Ari	24 05:42 Ari	24 18:58 Gem	24 10:03 Can	25 14:57 Vir
27 07:48 Pis	27 19:36 Tau	26 06:01 Tau	27 00:48 Can	26 19:04 Leo	28 03:39 Lib
29 08:14 Ari		28 08:58 Gem	29 10:35 Leo	29 06:58 Vir	30 15:09 Sco
31 11:06 Tau		30 15:58 Can		31 19:37 Lib	

Jul 1944	Aug 1944	Sep 1944	Oct 1944	Nov 1944	Dec 1944
02 23:38 Sag	01 14:42 Cap	02 04:14 Pis	01 14:30 Ari	02 01:28 Gem	01 15:16 Can
05 04:41 Cap	03 17:10 Aqu	04 03:27 Ari	03 13:46 Tau	04 05:04 Can	03 21:52 Leo
07 07:14 Aqu	05 17:35 Pis	06 03:28 Tau	05 14:59 Gem	06 12:43 Leo	06 08:03 Vir
09 08:39 Pis	07 17:43 Ari	08 06:13 Gem	07 19:55 Can	08 23:58 Vir	08 20:28 Lib
11 10:18 Ari	09 19:19 Tau	10 12:46 Can	10 05:02 Leo	11 12:44 Lib	11 08:41 Sco
13 13:16 Tau	11 23:38 Gem	12 22:50 Leo	12 17:03 Vir	14 00:47 Sco	13 18:50 Sag
15 18:11 Gem	14 07:03 Can	15 11:00 Vir	15 05:54 Lib	16 11:01 Sag	16 02:21 Cap
18 01:21 Can	16 17:07 Leo	17 23:47 Lib	17 18:03 Sco	18 19:19 Cap	18 07:44 Aqu
20 10:50 Leo	19 05:00 Vir	20 12:10 Sco	20 04:49 Sag	21 01:46 Aqu	20 11:39 Pis
22 22:24 Vir	21 17:44 Lib	22 23:16 Sag	22 13:48 Cap	23 06:18 Pis	22 14:42 Ari
25 11:07 Lib	24 06:12 Sco	25 07:55 Cap	24 20:18 Aqu	25 08:57 Ari	24 17:24 Tau
27 23:16 Sco	26 16:51 Sag	27 13:09 Aqu	26 23:53 Pis	27 10:22 Tau	26 20:26 Gem
30 08:49 Sag	29 00:12 Cap	29 14:58 Pis	29 00:53 Ari	29 11:55 Gem	29 00:43 Can
	31 03:44 Aqu		31 00:45 Tau		31 07:19 Leo

Jan 1945	Feb 1945	Mar 1945	Apr 1945	May 1945	Jun 1945
02 16:48 Vir	01 12:45 Lib	03 08:32 Sco	02 03:07 Sag	01 19:39 Cap	02 15:25 Pis
05 04:43 Lib	04 01:22 Sco	05 20:44 Sag	04 13:50 Cap	04 04:05 Aqu	04 18:50 Ari
07 17:12 Sco	06 12:56 Sag	08 06:37 Cap	06 21:27 Aqu	06 09:20 Pis	06 20:23 Tau
10 03:55 Sag	08 21:29 Cap	10 12:39 Aqu	09 01:10 Pis	08 11:25 Ari	08 21:15 Gem
12 11:27 Cap	11 02:12 Aqu	12 14:50 Pis	11 01:37 Ari	10 11:25 Tau	10 23:01 Can
14 15:57 Aqu	13 03:52 Pis	14 14:33 Ari	13 00:39 Tau	12 11:12 Gem	13 03:19 Leo
16 18:27 Pis	15 04:12 Ari	16 13:55 Tau	15 00:31 Gem	14 12:51 Can	15 11:07 Vir
18 20:20 Ari	17 05:04 Tau	18 15:04 Gem	17 03:13 Can	16 17:56 Leo	17 22:06 Lib
20 22:47 Tau	19 08:00 Gem	20 19:31 Can	19 09:51 Leo	19 02:55 Vir	20 10:35 Sco
23 02:34 Gem	21 13:42 Can	23 03:31 Leo	21 20:02 Vir	21 14:42 Lib	22 22:26 Sag
25 08:04 Can	23 21:58 Leo	25 14:10 Vir	24 08:14 Lib	24 03:20 Sco	25 08:14 Cap
27 15:32 Leo	26 08:13 Vir	28 02:14 Lib	26 20:52 Sco	26 15:10 Sag	27 15:36 Aqu
30 01:08 Vir	28 19:56 Lib	30 14:49 Sco	29 08:55 Sag	29 01:24 Cap	29 20:51 Pis
				31 09:34 Aqu	

Jul 1945	Aug 1945	Sep 1945	Oct 1945	Nov 1945	Dec 1945
02 00:29 Ari	02 11:23 Gem	03 03:19 Leo	02 17:33 Vir	01 10:07 Lib	01 04:42 Sco
04 03:04 Tau	04 15:22 Can	05 11:36 Vir	05 04:16 Lib	03 22:29 Sco	03 17:29 Sag
06 05:19 Gem	06 20:52 Leo	07 21:48 Lib	07 16:23 Sco	06 11:17 Sag	06 05:23 Cap
08 08:10 Can	09 04:23 Vir	10 09:47 Sco	10 05:17 Sag	08 23:35 Cap	08 15:33 Aqu
10 12:43 Leo	11 14:20 Lib	12 22:37 Sag	12 17:32 Cap	11 09:58 Aqu	10 23:20 Pis
12 19:57 Vir	14 02:24 Sco	15 10:10 Cap	15 03:06 Aqu	13 17:04 Pis	13 04:15 Ari
15 06:12 Lib	16 14:55 Sag	17 18:19 Aqu	17 08:33 Pis	15 20:24 Ari	15 06:30 Tau
17 18:28 Sco	19 01:30 Cap	19 22:18 Pis	19 10:09 Ari	17 20:48 Tau	17 07:03 Gem
20 06:35 Sag	21 08:32 Aqu	21 23:10 Ari	21 09:31 Tau	19 20:03 Gem	19 07:27 Can
22 16:28 Cap	23 12:05 Pis	23 22:53 Tau	23 08:50 Gem	21 20:14 Can	21 09:30 Leo
24 23:16 Aqu	25 13:30 Ari	25 23:31 Gem	25 10:10 Can	23 23:11 Leo	23 14:43 Vir
27 03:26 Pis	27 14:34 Tau	28 02:38 Can	27 14:54 Leo	26 05:58 Vir	25 23:44 Lib
29 06:07 Ari	29 16:46 Gem	30 08:46 Leo	29 23:11 Vir	28 16:17 Lib	28 11:42 Sco
31 08:28 Tau	31 20:59 Can				31 00:32 Sag

Jan 1946	Feb 1946	Mar 1946	Apr 1946	May 1946	Jun 1946
02 12:10 Cap	01 05:23 Aqu	02 20:25 Pis	01 09:16 Ari	02 20:03 Gem	01 06:29 Can
04 21:37 Aqu	03 11:32 Pis	04 23:23 Ari	03 09:57 Tau	04 20:22 Can	03 07:39 Leo
07 04:46 Pis	05 15:38 Ari	07 01:08 Tau	05 10:25 Gem	06 23:04 Leo	05 11:56 Vir
09 09:55 Ari	07 18:46 Tau	09 03:11 Gem	07 12:20 Can	09 04:56 Vir	07 19:56 Lib
11 13:25 Tau	09 21:45 Gem	11 06:28 Can	09 16:37 Leo	11 13:53 Lib	10 07:04 Sco
13 15:42 Gem	12 00:58 Can	13 11:14 Leo	11 23:20 Vir	14 01:08 Sco	12 19:50 Sag
15 17:32 Can	14 04:50 Leo	15 17:32 Vir	14 08:13 Lib	16 13:45 Sag	15 08:39 Cap
17 20:03 Leo	16 10:03 Vir	18 01:40 Lib	16 19:03 Sco	19 02:41 Cap	17 20:15 Aqu
20 00:40 Vir	18 17:35 Lib	20 12:04 Sco	19 07:29 Sag	21 14:30 Aqu	20 05:42 Pis
22 08:31 Lib	21 04:04 Sco	23 00:30 Sag	21 20:27 Cap	23 23:38 Pis	22 12:19 Ari
24 19:39 Sco	23 16:40 Sag	25 13:16 Cap	24 07:55 Aqu	26 05:04 Ari	24 15:55 Tau
27 08:26 Sag	26 05:01 Cap	27 23:50 Aqu	26 15:53 Pis	28 07:03 Tau	26 17:07 Gem
29 20:17 Cap	28 14:34 Aqu	30 06:26 Pis	28 19:45 Ari	30 06:55 Gem	28 17:11 Can
			30 20:31 Tau		30 17:47 Leo

Jul 1946	Aug 1946	Sep 1946	Oct 1946	Nov 1946	Dec 1946
02 20:44 Vir	01 12:04 Lib	02 17:30 Sag	02 14:28 Cap	01 10:35 Aqu	01 04:29 Pis
05 03:20 Lib	03 21:22 Sco	05 06:23 Cap	05 02:26 Aqu	03 20:31 Pis	03 12:04 Ari
07 13:40 Sco	06 09:35 Sag	07 17:40 Aqu	07 11:08 Pis	06 02:28 Ari	05 15:48 Tau
10 02:20 Sag	08 22:23 Cap	10 01:45 Pis	09 16:05 Ari	08 04:49 Tau	07 16:30 Gem
12 15:05 Cap	11 09:23 Aqu	12 06:49 Ari	11 18:20 Tau	10 05:07 Gem	09 15:50 Can
15 02:16 Aqu	13 17:40 Pis	14 10:03 Tau	13 19:36 Gem	12 05:15 Can	11 15:47 Leo
17 11:15 Pis	15 23:37 Ari	16 12:45 Gem	15 21:23 Can	14 06:52 Leo	13 18:08 Vir
19 17:58 Ari	18 03:59 Tau	18 15:41 Can	18 00:35 Leo	16 11:04 Vir	16 00:07 Lib
21 22:35 Tau	20 07:22 Gem	20 19:12 Leo	20 05:35 Vir	18 18:12 Lib	18 09:42 Sco
24 01:18 Gem	22 10:06 Can	22 23:38 Vir	22 12:33 Lib	21 03:57 Sco	20 21:48 Sag
26 02:43 Can	24 12:38 Leo	25 05:40 Lib	24 21:40 Sco	23 15:43 Sag	23 10:49 Cap
28 03:57 Leo	26 15:54 Vir	27 14:11 Sco	27 09:02 Sag	26 04:39 Cap	25 23:29 Aqu
30 06:32 Vir	28 21:15 Lib	30 01:32 Sag	29 21:59 Cap	28 17:29 Aqu	28 10:43 Pis
	31 05:49 Sco				30 19:30 Ari

Jan 1947	Feb 1947	Mar 1947	Apr 1947	May 1947	Jun 1947
02 01:05 Tau	02 13:38 Can	01 20:58 Can	02 08:30 Vir	01 19:23 Lib	02 18:53 Sag
04 03:26 Gem	04 14:02 Leo	03 22:59 Leo	04 12:39 Lib	04 02:35 Sco	05 06:51 Cap
06 03:28 Can	06 14:42 Vir	06 00:46 Vir	06 18:56 Sco	06 12:08 Sag	07 19:37 Aqu
08 02:53 Leo	08 17:39 Lib	08 03:50 Lib	09 04:12 Sag	08 23:54 Cap	10 07:46 Pis
10 03:44 Vir	11 00:28 Sco	10 09:50 Sco	11 16:07 Cap	11 12:40 Aqu	12 17:33 Ari
12 07:53 Lib	13 11:14 Sag	12 19:33 Sag	14 04:50 Aqu	14 00:20 Pis	14 23:45 Tau
14 16:14 Sco	16 00:11 Cap	15 07:59 Cap	16 15:46 Pis	16 08:56 Ari	17 02:21 Gem
17 04:02 Sag	18 12:38 Aqu	17 20:34 Aqu	18 23:25 Ari	18 13:51 Tau	19 02:32 Can
19 17:09 Cap	20 22:57 Pis	20 06:57 Pis	21 03:55 Tau	20 15:51 Gem	21 02:06 Leo
22 05:36 Aqu	23 06:57 Ari	22 14:22 Ari	23 06:27 Gem	22 16:27 Can	23 03:01 Vir
24 16:22 Pis	25 13:07 Tau	24 19:29 Tau	25 08:22 Can	24 17:18 Leo	25 06:50 Lib
27 01:10 Ari	27 17:46 Gem	26 23:15 Gem	27 10:44 Leo	26 19:49 Vir	27 14:16 Sco
29 07:45 Tau		29 02:25 Can	29 14:15 Vir	29 00:53 Lib	30 00:45 Sag
31 11:51 Gem		31 05:22 Leo		31 08:41 Sco	

Jul 1947	Aug 1947	Sep 1947	Oct 1947	Nov 1947	Dec 1947
02 13:02 Cap	01 07:49 Aqu	02 12:02 Ari	02 02:15 Tau	02 17:32 Can	02 02:30 Leo
05 01:49 Aqu	03 19:48 Pis	04 20:10 Tau	04 07:43 Gem	04 20:03 Leo	04 04:23 Vir
07 14:02 Pis	06 06:19 Ari	07 02:18 Gem	06 11:46 Can	06 22:54 Vir	06 08:13 Lib
10 00:34 Ari	08 14:42 Tau	09 06:12 Can	08 14:41 Leo	09 02:42 Lib	08 14:24 Sco
12 08:11 Tau	10 20:17 Gem	11 08:03 Leo	10 16:57 Vir	11 08:02 Sco	10 22:49 Sag
14 12:16 Gem	12 22:49 Can	13 08:51 Vir	12 19:31 Lib	13 15:33 Sag	13 09:13 Cap
16 13:15 Can	14 23:06 Leo	15 10:16 Lib	14 23:45 Sco	16 01:36 Cap	15 21:15 Aqu
18 12:35 Leo	16 22:48 Vir	17 14:10 Sco	17 06:52 Sag	18 13:44 Aqu	18 09:58 Pis
20 12:19 Vir	19 00:03 Lib	19 21:49 Sag	19 17:13 Cap	21 02:15 Pis	20 21:36 Ari
22 14:33 Lib	21 04:44 Sco	22 08:56 Cap	22 05:38 Aqu	23 12:52 Ari	23 06:10 Tau
24 20:40 Sco	23 13:33 Sag	24 21:37 Aqu	24 17:45 Pis	25 20:05 Tau	25 10:47 Gem
27 06:39 Sag	26 01:30 Cap	27 09:24 Pis	27 03:30 Ari	27 23:55 Gem	27 12:03 Can
29 19:01 Cap	28 14:17 Aqu	29 18:58 Ari	29 10:16 Tau	30 01:31 Can	29 11:42 Leo
	31 02:03 Pis		31 14:36 Gem		31 11:47 Vir

Jan 1948	Feb 1948	Mar 1948	Apr 1948	May 1948	Jun 1948
02 14:09 Lib	01 02:27 Sco	01 17:40 Sag	02 23:18 Aqu	02 19:43 Pis	01 15:54 Ari
04 19:50 Sco	03 10:25 Sag	04 03:50 Cap	05 11:55 Pis	05 07:27 Ari	04 01:43 Tau
07 04:40 Sag	05 21:29 Cap	06 16:13 Aqu	07 23:28 Ari	07 16:47 Tau	06 08:06 Gem
09 15:40 Cap	08 09:58 Aqu	09 04:52 Pis	10 08:58 Tau	09 23:19 Gem	08 11:28 Can
12 03:53 Aqu	10 22:36 Pis	11 16:32 Ari	12 16:19 Gem	12 03:38 Can	10 13:12 Leo
14 16:34 Pis	13 10:37 Ari	14 02:40 Tau	14 21:41 Can	14 06:39 Leo	12 14:48 Vir
17 04:43 Ari	15 21:07 Tau	16 10:44 Gem	17 01:16 Leo	16 09:14 Vir	14 17:33 Lib
19 14:41 Tau	18 04:55 Gem	18 16:13 Can	19 03:30 Vir	18 12:07 Lib	16 22:03 Sco
21 21:01 Gem	20 09:08 Can	20 18:58 Leo	21 05:16 Lib	20 15:55 Sco	19 04:28 Sag
23 23:23 Can	22 10:07 Leo	22 19:42 Vir	23 07:49 Sco	22 21:21 Sag	21 12:50 Cap
25 22:59 Leo	24 09:23 Vir	24 20:02 Lib	25 12:31 Sag	25 05:07 Cap	23 23:15 Aqu
27 21:56 Vir	26 09:05 Lib	26 21:49 Sco	27 20:21 Cap	27 15:30 Aqu	26 11:22 Pis
29 22:29 Lib	28 11:23 Sco	29 02:46 Sag	30 07:15 Aqu	30 03:45 Pis	28 23:55 Ari
		31 11:33 Cap			

Jul 1948	Aug 1948	Sep 1948	Oct 1948	Nov 1948	Dec 1948
01 10:39 Tau	02 07:20 Can	02 18:21 Vir	02 04:30 Lib	02 18:10 Sag	02 09:16 Cap
03 17:47 Gem	04 08:14 Leo	04 17:36 Lib	04 04:58 Sco	04 23:39 Cap	04 17:31 Aqu
05 21:06 Can	06 07:33 Vir	06 18:34 Sco	06 07:54 Sag	07 08:40 Aqu	07 04:45 Pis
07 21:53 Leo	08 07:29 Lib	08 22:51 Sag	08 14:30 Cap	09 20:33 Pis	09 17:29 Ari
09 22:03 Vir	10 09:56 Sco	11 06:56 Cap	11 00:42 Aqu	12 09:11 Ari	12 05:08 Tau
11 23:30 Lib	12 15:48 Sag	13 17:58 Aqu	13 13:02 Pis	14 20:23 Tau	14 13:44 Gem
14 03:27 Sco	15 00:51 Cap	16 06:26 Pis	16 01:36 Ari	17 05:01 Gem	16 19:01 Can
16 10:10 Sag	17 12:02 Aqu	18 19:01 Ari	18 12:53 Tau	19 11:11 Can	18 22:03 Leo
18 19:13 Cap	20 00:23 Pis	21 06:45 Tau	20 22:14 Gem	21 15:32 Leo	21 00:18 Vir
21 06:02 Aqu	22 13:05 Ari	23 16:39 Gem	23 05:21 Can	23 18:48 Vir	23 02:59 Lib
23 18:12 Pis	25 01:03 Tau	25 23:45 Can	25 10:09 Leo	25 21:32 Lib	25 06:38 Sco
26 06:56 Ari	27 10:39 Gem	28 03:34 Leo	27 12:53 Vir	28 00:18 Sco	27 11:28 Sag
28 18:33 Tau	29 16:33 Can	30 04:40 Vir	29 14:16 Lib	30 03:51 Sag	29 17:46 Cap
31 03:01 Gem	31 18:41 Leo		31 15:31 Sco		

Jan 1949	Feb 1949	Mar 1949	Apr 1949	May 1949	Jun 1949
01 02:07 Aqu	02 09:03 Ari	01 15:35 Ari	02 22:02 Gem	02 12:42 Can	01 00:35 Leo
03 12:57 Pis	04 21:56 Tau	04 04:32 Tau	05 07:09 Can	04 19:11 Leo	03 04:53 Vir
06 01:40 Ari	07 08:39 Gem	06 16:04 Gem	07 12:59 Leo	06 23:11 Vir	05 07:57 Lib
08 14:02 Tau	09 15:22 Can	09 00:21 Can	09 15:31 Vir	09 01:06 Lib	07 10:13 Sco
10 23:30 Gem	11 18:01 Leo	11 04:33 Leo	11 15:48 Lib	11 01:53 Sco	09 12:24 Sag
13 04:56 Can	13 18:06 Vir	13 05:24 Vir	13 15:28 Sco	13 02:57 Sag	11 15:40 Cap
15 07:08 Leo	15 17:44 Lib	15 04:40 Lib	15 16:23 Sag	15 05:57 Cap	13 21:26 Aqu
17 07:52 Vir	17 18:53 Sco	17 04:25 Sco	17 20:15 Cap	17 12:18 Aqu	16 06:38 Pis
19 09:03 Lib	19 22:49 Sag	19 06:30 Sag	20 03:58 Aqu	19 22:25 Pis	18 18:44 Ari
21 11:59 Sco	22 05:49 Cap	21 12:04 Cap	22 15:07 Pis	22 11:01 Ari	21 07:29 Tau
23 17:08 Sag	24 15:25 Aqu	23 21:09 Aqu	25 04:00 Ari	24 23:41 Tau	23 18:19 Gem
26 00:21 Cap	27 02:53 Pis	26 08:49 Pis	27 16:40 Tau	27 10:26 Gem	26 02:01 Can
28 09:26 Aqu		28 21:41 Ari	30 03:47 Gem	29 18:38 Can	28 07:00 Leo
30 20:25 Pis		31 10:28 Tau			30 10:26 Vir

Jul 1949	Aug 1949	Sep 1949	Oct 1949	Nov 1949	Dec 1949
02 13:22 Lib	03 01:24 Sag	01 12:04 Cap	01 01:13 Aqu	02 05:34 Ari	02 01:21 Tau
04 16:21 Sco	05 06:36 Cap	03 19:36 Aqu	03 11:19 Pis	04 18:36 Tau	04 13:28 Gem
06 19:45 Sag	07 13:33 Aqu	06 05:25 Pis	05 23:27 Ari	07 06:54 Gem	06 23:31 Can
09 00:02 Cap	09 22:45 Pis	08 17:12 Ari	08 12:26 Tau	09 17:34 Can	09 07:27 Leo
11 06:08 Aqu	12 10:19 Ari	11 06:11 Tau	11 01:02 Gem	12 02:00 Leo	11 13:30 Vir
13 15:01 Pis	14 23:17 Tau	13 18:46 Gem	13 11:50 Can	14 07:42 Vir	13 17:44 Lib
16 02:42 Ari	17 11:21 Gem	16 04:51 Can	15 19:34 Leo	16 10:35 Lib	15 20:13 Sco
18 15:35 Tau	19 20:14 Can	18 11:04 Leo	17 23:42 Vir	18 11:19 Sco	17 21:32 Sag
21 02:56 Gem	22 01:07 Leo	20 13:34 Vir	20 00:47 Lib	20 11:16 Sag	19 22:59 Cap
23 10:51 Can	24 02:55 Vir	22 13:42 Lib	22 00:18 Sco	22 12:19 Cap	22 02:24 Aqu
25 15:19 Leo	26 03:24 Lib	24 13:21 Sco	24 00:07 Sag	24 16:24 Aqu	24 09:19 Pis
27 17:36 Vir	28 04:19 Sco	26 14:21 Sag	26 02:10 Cap	27 00:35 Pis	26 20:04 Ari
29 19:20 Lib	30 07:00 Sag	28 18:06 Cap	28 07:49 Aqu	29 12:17 Ari	29 08:57 Tau
31 21:43 Sco			30 17:20 Pis		31 21:12 Gem

Jan 1950	Feb 1950	Mar 1950	Apr 1950	May 1950	Jun 1950
03 06:56 Can	01 22:33 Leo	01 08:30 Leo	02 00:40 Lib	01 11:38 Sco	01 21:27 Cap
05 13:58 Leo	04 02:36 Vir	03 12:24 Vir	04 00:35 Sco	03 10:51 Sag	03 23:17 Aqu
07 19:05 Vir	06 05:19 Lib	05 14:00 Lib	06 00:36 Sag	05 11:08 Cap	06 04:56 Pis
09 23:08 Lib	08 07:50 Sco	07 14:55 Sco	08 02:29 Cap	07 14:21 Aqu	08 14:43 Ari
12 02:27 Sco	10 10:51 Sag	09 16:37 Sag	10 07:24 Aqu	09 21:33 Pis	11 03:11 Tau
14 05:16 Sag	12 14:44 Cap	11 20:06 Cap	12 15:37 Pis	12 08:17 Ari	13 16:04 Gem
16 08:06 Cap	14 19:57 Aqu	14 01:52 Aqu	15 02:31 Ari	14 20:58 Tau	16 03:44 Can
18 12:07 Aqu	17 03:10 Pis	16 09:59 Pis	17 14:59 Tau	17 09:52 Gem	18 13:37 Leo
20 18:41 Pis	19 13:00 Ari	18 20:20 Ari	20 03:53 Gem	19 21:50 Can	20 21:31 Vir
23 04:37 Ari	22 01:11 Tau	21 08:31 Tau	22 16:01 Can	22 08:05 Leo	23 03:09 Lib
25 17:07 Tau	24 14:02 Gem	23 21:27 Gem	25 01:57 Leo	24 15:50 Vir	25 06:18 Sco
28 05:42 Gem	27 01:02 Can	26 09:16 Can	27 08:29 Vir	26 20:25 Lib	27 07:26 Sag
30 15:49 Can		28 18:04 Leo	29 11:25 Lib	28 22:01 Sco	29 07:48 Cap
		30 23:00 Vir		30 21:43 Sag	

Jul 1950	Aug 1950	Sep 1950	Oct 1950	Nov 1950	Dec 1950
01 09:19 Aqu	02 07:02 Ari	01 02:18 Tau	03 10:58 Can	02 05:37 Leo	01 21:53 Vir
03 13:51 Pis	04 18:05 Tau	03 14:44 Gem	05 21:39 Leo	04 14:20 Vir	04 04:28 Lib
05 22:24 Ari	07 06:43 Gem	06 02:53 Can	08 04:53 Vir	06 19:10 Lib	06 07:19 Sco
08 10:12 Tau	09 18:26 Can	08 12:33 Leo	10 08:29 Lib	08 20:28 Sco	08 07:17 Sag
10 23:01 Gem	12 03:36 Leo	10 18:54 Vir	12 09:31 Sco	10 19:51 Sag	10 06:16 Cap
13 10:33 Can	14 10:03 Vir	12 22:27 Lib	14 09:44 Sag	12 19:25 Cap	12 06:34 Aqu
15 19:52 Leo	16 14:30 Lib	15 00:26 Sco	16 10:55 Cap	14 21:14 Aqu	14 10:10 Pis
18 03:05 Vir	18 17:49 Sco	17 02:12 Sag	18 14:26 Aqu	17 02:38 Pis	16 17:57 Ari
20 08:33 Lib	20 20:35 Sag	19 04:48 Cap	20 20:52 Pis	19 11:38 Ari	19 05:09 Tau
22 12:26 Sco	22 23:22 Cap	21 08:59 Aqu	23 05:58 Ari	21 23:07 Tau	21 17:49 Gem
24 14:55 Sag	25 02:52 Aqu	23 15:09 Pis	25 17:02 Tau	24 11:38 Gem	24 06:17 Can
26 16:39 Cap	27 08:01 Pis	25 23:31 Ari	28 05:22 Gem	27 00:13 Can	26 17:44 Leo
28 18:55 Aqu	29 15:44 Ari	28 10:07 Tau	30 18:02 Can	29 12:01 Leo	29 03:40 Vir
30 23:18 Pis		30 22:26 Gem			31 11:19 Lib

Jan 1951	Feb 1951	Mar 1951	Apr 1951	May 1951	Jun 1951
02 15:57 Sco	01 01:16 Sag	02 09:29 Cap	02 22:44 Pis	02 11:25 Ari	01 02:33 Tau
04 17:38 Sag	03 02:52 Cap	04 12:10 Aqu	05 05:15 Ari	04 20:46 Tau	03 14:02 Gem
06 17:32 Cap	05 04:03 Aqu	06 15:45 Pis	07 13:51 Tau	07 07:50 Gem	06 02:31 Can
08 17:36 Aqu	07 06:28 Pis	08 21:16 Ari	10 00:40 Gem	09 20:12 Can	08 15:11 Leo
10 19:55 Pis	09 11:42 Ari	11 05:32 Tau	12 13:03 Can	12 08:48 Leo	11 02:46 Vir
13 02:04 Ari	11 20:32 Tau	13 16:35 Gem	15 01:17 Leo	14 19:43 Vir	13 11:30 Lib
15 12:09 Tau	14 08:17 Gem	16 05:05 Can	17 11:06 Vir	17 03:04 Lib	15 16:16 Sco
18 00:35 Gem	16 20:50 Can	18 16:43 Leo	19 17:13 Lib	19 06:23 Sco	17 17:26 Sag
20 13:05 Can	19 08:00 Leo	21 01:38 Vir	21 19:55 Sco	21 06:44 Sag	19 16:38 Cap
23 00:11 Leo	21 16:42 Vir	23 07:21 Lib	23 20:40 Sag	23 06:07 Cap	21 16:04 Aqu
25 09:25 Vir	23 23:01 Lib	25 10:36 Sco	25 21:19 Cap	25 06:41 Aqu	23 17:49 Pis
27 16:45 Lib	26 03:31 Sco	27 12:40 Sag	27 23:32 Aqu	27 10:04 Pis	25 23:13 Ari
29 22:03 Sco	28 06:49 Sag	29 14:51 Cap	30 04:12 Pis	29 16:52 Ari	28 08:16 Tau
		31 18:02 Aqu			30 19:50 Gem

Jul 1951	Aug 1951	Sep 1951	Oct 1951	Nov 1951	Dec 1951
03 08:27 Can	02 03:07 Leo	03 05:31 Lib	02 18:23 Sco	01 05:20 Sag	02 15:45 Aqu
05 21:00 Leo	04 14:17 Vir	05 11:48 Sco	04 21:48 Sag	03 06:40 Cap	04 18:07 Pis
08 08:35 Vir	06 23:34 Lib	07 16:11 Sag	07 00:29 Cap	05 08:42 Aqu	06 23:17 Ari
10 18:03 Lib	09 06:23 Sco	09 19:06 Cap	09 03:18 Aqu	07 12:22 Pis	09 07:04 Tau
13 00:18 Sco	11 10:31 Sag	11 21:11 Aqu	11 06:46 Pis	09 17:52 Ari	11 16:53 Gem
15 03:03 Sag	13 12:18 Cap	13 23:21 Pis	13 11:19 Ari	12 01:07 Tau	14 04:22 Can
17 03:14 Cap	15 12:53 Aqu	16 02:47 Ari	15 17:37 Tau	14 10:15 Gem	16 17:04 Leo
19 02:41 Aqu	17 13:52 Pis	18 08:41 Tau	18 02:21 Gem	16 21:27 Can	19 05:51 Vir
21 03:28 Pis	19 16:58 Ari	20 17:46 Gem	20 13:41 Can	19 10:11 Leo	21 16:39 Lib
23 07:21 Ari	21 23:26 Tau	23 05:33 Can	23 02:24 Leo	21 22:35 Vir	23 23:38 Sco
25 15:06 Tau	24 09:26 Gem	25 18:07 Leo	25 14:00 Vir	24 08:08 Lib	26 02:27 Sag
28 02:07 Gem	26 21:43 Can	28 05:05 Vir	27 22:25 Lib	26 13:32 Sco	28 02:24 Cap
30 14:41 Can	29 10:09 Leo	30 13:08 Lib	30 03:09 Sco	28 15:20 Sag	30 01:35 Aqu
	31 20:59 Vir			30 15:23 Cap	

Jan 1952	Feb 1952	Mar 1952	Apr 1952	May 1952	Jun 1952
01 02:10 Pis	01 19:50 Tau	02 12:35 Gem	01 07:38 Can	01 04:11 Leo	02 12:25 Lib
03 05:41 Ari	04 04:54 Gem	04 23:40 Can	03 20:09 Leo	03 16:56 Vir	04 20:19 Sco
05 12:42 Tau	06 16:43 Can	07 12:29 Leo	06 08:39 Vir	06 03:38 Lib	07 00:20 Sag
07 22:42 Gem	09 05:35 Leo	10 00:51 Vir	08 18:55 Lib	08 10:49 Sco	09 01:46 Cap
10 10:33 Can	11 18:01 Vir	12 11:16 Lib	11 02:13 Sco	10 14:50 Sag	11 02:26 Aqu
12 23:19 Leo	14 04:59 Lib	14 19:20 Sco	13 07:08 Sag	12 17:09 Cap	13 04:00 Pis
15 11:59 Vir	16 13:44 Sco	17 01:15 Sag	15 10:41 Cap	14 19:14 Aqu	15 07:28 Ari
17 23:19 Lib	18 19:42 Sag	19 05:19 Cap	17 13:43 Aqu	16 22:05 Pis	17 13:10 Tau
20 07:43 Sco	20 22:49 Cap	21 07:54 Aqu	19 16:40 Pis	19 02:06 Ari	19 21:03 Gem
22 12:22 Sag	22 23:48 Aqu	23 09:39 Pis	21 19:56 Ari	21 07:29 Tau	22 07:03 Can
24 13:39 Cap	25 00:00 Pis	25 11:34 Ari	24 00:14 Tau	23 14:37 Gem	24 19:02 Leo
26 13:07 Aqu	27 01:11 Ari	27 15:05 Tau	26 06:40 Gem	26 00:05 Can	27 08:05 Vir
28 12:46 Pis	29 05:01 Tau	29 21:35 Gem	28 16:05 Can	28 11:58 Leo	29 20:17 Lib
30 14:32 Ari				31 00:56 Vir	

Jul 1952	Aug 1952	Sep 1952	Oct 1952	Nov 1952	Dec 1952
02 05:25 Sco	02 22:27 Cap	01 09:03 Aqu	02 19:34 Ari	01 06:58 Tau	03 03:08 Can
04 10:26 Sag	04 22:41 Aqu	03 09:00 Pis	04 21:05 Tau	03 11:02 Gem	05 13:22 Leo
06 12:03 Cap	06 22:04 Pis	05 08:57 Ari	07 01:14 Gem	05 18:12 Can	08 01:57 Vir
08 11:55 Aqu	08 22:33 Ari	07 10:47 Tau	09 09:15 Can	08 04:55 Leo	10 14:34 Lib
10 11:59 Pis	11 01:45 Tau	09 16:05 Gem	11 20:49 Leo	10 17:46 Vir	13 00:38 Sco
12 13:56 Ari	13 08:35 Gem	12 01:23 Can	14 09:50 Vir	13 05:56 Lib	15 06:59 Sag
14 18:44 Tau	15 18:51 Can	14 13:37 Leo	16 21:44 Lib	15 15:18 Sco	17 10:17 Cap
17 02:37 Gem	18 07:18 Leo	17 02:41 Vir	19 07:09 Sco	17 21:33 Sag	19 12:02 Aqu
19 13:04 Can	20 20:22 Vir	19 14:41 Lib	21 14:12 Sag	20 01:40 Cap	21 13:45 Pis
22 01:20 Leo	23 08:41 Lib	22 00:43 Sco	23 19:28 Cap	22 04:51 Aqu	23 16:29 Ari
24 14:24 Vir	25 19:09 Sco	24 08:32 Sag	25 23:27 Aqu	24 07:54 Pis	25 20:45 Tau
27 02:53 Lib	28 02:53 Sag	26 14:05 Cap	28 02:22 Pis	26 11:09 Ari	28 02:47 Gem
29 13:03 Sco	30 07:23 Cap	28 17:24 Aqu	30 04:34 Ari	28 14:54 Tau	30 10:53 Can
31 19:37 Sag		30 18:52 Pis		30 19:53 Gem	

Jan 1953	Feb 1953	Mar 1953	Apr 1953	May 1953	Jun 1953
01 21:16 Leo	03 05:31 Lib	02 11:40 Lib	01 05:19 Sco	03 03:54 Cap	01 14:45 Aqu
04 09:40 Vir	05 17:20 Sco	04 23:30 Sco	03 14:58 Sag	05 09:12 Aqu	03 18:11 Pis
06 22:36 Lib	08 02:19 Sag	07 09:19 Sag	05 22:28 Cap	07 12:46 Pis	05 21:01 Ari
09 09:43 Sco	10 07:31 Cap	09 16:09 Cap	08 03:27 Aqu	09 14:49 Ari	07 23:41 Tau
11 17:13 Sag	12 09:17 Aqu	11 19:37 Aqu	10 05:49 Pis	11 16:12 Tau	10 03:02 Gem
13 20:55 Cap	14 08:58 Pis	13 20:17 Pis	12 06:19 Ari	13 18:27 Gem	12 08:17 Can
15 21:57 Aqu	16 08:31 Ari	15 19:39 Ari	14 06:31 Tau	15 23:16 Can	14 16:26 Leo
17 22:07 Pis	18 09:50 Tau	17 19:44 Tau	16 08:26 Gem	18 07:46 Leo	17 03:36 Vir
19 23:08 Ari	20 14:26 Gem	19 22:34 Gem	18 13:52 Can	20 19:30 Vir	19 16:15 Lib
22 02:20 Tau	22 22:47 Can	22 05:28 Can	20 23:26 Leo	23 08:15 Lib	22 03:57 Sco
24 08:20 Gem	25 10:04 Leo	24 16:13 Leo	23 11:51 Vir	25 19:32 Sco	24 12:47 Sag
26 17:06 Can	27 22:50 Vir	27 05:03 Vir	26 00:40 Lib	28 04:08 Sag	26 18:28 Cap
29 04:05 Leo		29 17:51 Lib	28 11:51 Sco	30 10:16 Cap	28 21:51 Aqu
31 16:34 Vir			30 20:52 Sag		

Jul 1953	Aug 1953	Sep 1953	Oct 1953	Nov 1953	Dec 1953
01 00:08 Pis	01 10:56 Tau	02 03:29 Can	01 18:52 Leo	03 01:50 Lib	02 21:30 Sco
03 02:23 Ari	03 15:10 Gem	04 13:04 Leo	04 06:39 Vir	05 14:11 Sco	05 08:08 Sag
05 05:23 Tau	05 21:59 Can	07 00:47 Vir	06 19:27 Lib	08 01:06 Sag	07 16:32 Cap
07 09:42 Gem	08 07:15 Leo	09 13:27 Lib	09 07:55 Sco	10 10:18 Cap	09 22:59 Aqu
09 15:54 Can	10 18:32 Vir	12 02:05 Sco	11 19:19 Sag	12 17:30 Aqu	12 03:46 Pis
12 00:27 Leo	13 07:07 Lib	14 13:31 Sag	14 04:51 Cap	14 22:17 Pis	14 07:06 Ari
14 11:27 Vir	15 19:43 Sco	16 22:20 Cap	16 11:33 Aqu	17 00:35 Ari	16 09:22 Tau
17 00:03 Lib	18 06:29 Sag	19 03:29 Aqu	18 14:55 Pis	19 01:15 Tau	18 11:27 Gem
19 12:16 Sco	20 13:52 Cap	21 05:06 Pis	20 15:27 Ari	21 01:54 Gem	20 14:40 Can
21 21:58 Sag	22 17:28 Aqu	23 04:30 Ari	22 14:47 Tau	23 04:31 Can	22 20:22 Leo
24 04:06 Cap	24 18:12 Pis	25 03:45 Tau	24 15:04 Gem	25 10:40 Leo	25 05:23 Vir
26 07:03 Aqu	26 17:46 Ari	27 05:00 Gem	26 18:23 Can	27 20:40 Vir	27 17:10 Lib
28 08:07 Pis	28 18:10 Tau	29 09:55 Can	29 01:54 Leo	30 09:05 Lib	30 05:42 Sco
30 08:55 Ari	30 21:06 Gem		31 13:03 Vir		

Jan 1954	Feb 1954	Mar 1954	Apr 1954	May 1954	Jun 1954
01 16:39 Sag	02 15:38 Aqu	0 02 02:06 Aqu	02 15:40 Ari	02 01:42 Tau	02 12:46 Can
04 00:45 Cap	04 18:03 Pis	04 04:32 Pis	04 14:43 Tau	04 01:06 Gem	04 16:34 Leo
06 06:09 Aqu	06 19:14 Ari	06 04:40 Ari	06 14:40 Gem	06 02:29 Can	07 00:06 Vir
08 09:43 Pis	08 20:47 Tau	08 04:32 Tau	08 17:28 Can	08 07:28 Leo	09 10:58 Lib
10 12:27 Ari	10 23:54 Gem	10 06:06 Gem	11 00:05 Leo	10 16:22 Vir	11 23:29 Sco
12 15:09 Tau	13 05:09 Can	12 10:37 Can	13 10:02 Vir	13 04:03 Lib	14 11:36 Sag
14 18:29 Gem	15 12:35 Leo	14 18:16 Leo	15 21:57 Lib	15 16:41 Sco	16 22:04 Cap
16 23:00 Can	17 22:00 Vir	17 04:20 Vir	18 10:31 Sco	18 04:53 Sag	19 06:25 Aqu
19 05:24 Leo	20 09:13 Lib	19 15:57 Lib	20 22:54 Sag	20 15:48 Cap	21 12:36 Pis
21 14:13 Vir	22 21:43 Sco	22 04:25 Sco	23 10:10 Cap	23 00:48 Aqu	23 16:43 Ari
24 01:29 Lib	25 09:59 Sag	24 16:55 Sag	25 19:01 Aqu	25 07:08 Pis	25 19:09 Tau
26 14:02 Sco	27 19:57 Cap	27 03:54 Cap	28 00:21 Pis	27 10:31 Ari	27 20:41 Gem
29 01:42 Sag		29 11:36 Aqu	30 02:08 Ari	29 11:34 Tau	29 22:35 Can
31 10:26 Cap		31 15:16 Pis		31 11:41 Gem	

Jul 1954	Aug 1954	Sep 1954	Oct 1954	Nov 1954	Dec 1954
02 02:16 Leo	03 03:13 Lib	01 22:48 Sco	01 18:40 Sag	03 00:21 Aqu	02 14:37 Pis
04 08:55 Vir	05 15:02 Sco	04 11:31 Sag	04 07:03 Cap	05 07:34 Pis	04 19:34 Ari
06 18:52 Lib	08 03:32 Sag	06 23:09 Cap	06 16:44 Aqu	07 10:42 Ari	06 21:22 Tau
09 07:03 Sco	10 14:19 Cap	09 07:30 Aqu	08 22:16 Pis	09 10:49 Tau	08 21:16 Gem
11 19:18 Sag	12 21:54 Aqu	11 11:55 Pis	10 23:58 Ari	11 09:51 Gem	10 21:06 Can
14 05:39 Cap	15 02:16 Pis	13 13:22 Ari	12 23:31 Tau	13 09:59 Can	12 22:48 Leo
16 13:19 Aqu	17 04:37 Ari	15 13:44 Tau	14 23:09 Gem	15 13:02 Leo	15 03:53 Vir
18 18:32 Pis	19 06:26 Tau	17 14:54 Gem	17 00:49 Can	17 19:51 Vir	17 12:50 Lib
20 22:07 Ari	21 08:56 Gem	19 18:12 Can	19 05:40 Leo	20 06:01 Lib	20 00:43 Sco
23 00:52 Tau	23 12:49 Can	22 00:03 Leo	21 13:44 Vir	22 18:12 Sco	22 13:34 Sag
25 03:30 Gem	25 18:22 Leo	24 08:10 Vir	24 00:11 Lib	25 07:01 Sag	25 01:40 Cap
27 06:41 Can	28 01:43 Vir	26 18:10 Lib	26 12:10 Sco	27 19:23 Cap	27 12:00 Aqu
29 11:10 Leo	30 11:11 Lib	29 05:51 Sco	29 00:58 Sag	30 06:18 Aqu	29 20:09 Pis
31 17:49 Vir			31 13:35 Cap		

Jan 1955	Feb 1955	Mar 1955	Apr 1955	May 1955	Jun 1955
01 01:55 Ari	01 14:02 Gem	02 22:39 Can	01 08:20 Leo	03 04:25 Lib	01 20:53 Sco
03 05:24 Tau	03 16:36 Can	05 02:48 Leo	03 14:30 Vir	05 15:03 Sco	04 09:23 Sag
05 07:04 Gem	05 19:28 Leo	07 08:08 Vir	05 22:33 Lib	08 03:18 Sag	06 22:20 Cap
07 08:00 Can	07 23:42 Vir	09 15:19 Lib	08 08:37 Sco	10 16:18 Cap	09 10:29 Aqu
09 09:41 Leo	10 06:33 Lib	12 01:04 Sco	10 20:41 Sag	13 04:28 Aqu	11 20:31 Pis
11 13:42 Vir	12 16:37 Sco	14 13:12 Sag	13 09:39 Cap	15 13:52 Pis	14 03:23 Ari
13 21:14 Lib	15 05:06 Sag	17 02:01 Cap	15 21:19 Aqu	17 19:20 Ari	16 06:50 Tau
16 08:14 Sco	17 17:33 Cap	19 12:46 Aqu	18 05:28 Pis	19 21:11 Tau	18 07:37 Gem
18 21:00 Sag	20 03:32 Aqu	21 19:44 Pis	20 09:29 Ari	21 20:56 Gem	20 07:15 Can
21 09:08 Cap	22 10:09 Pis	23 23:09 Ari	22 10:30 Tau	23 20:33 Can	22 07:36 Leo
23 18:58 Aqu	24 14:06 Ari	26 00:31 Tau	24 10:24 Gem	25 21:52 Leo	24 10:25 Vir
26 02:10 Pis	26 16:46 Tau	28 01:41 Gem	26 11:09 Can	28 02:15 Vir	26 16:54 Lib
28 07:19 Ari	28 19:24 Gem	30 04:05 Can	28 14:08 Leo	30 10:07 Lib	29 03:04 Sco
30 11:06 Tau			30 19:57 Vir		

Jul 1955	Aug 1955	Sep 1955	Oct 1955	Nov 1955	Dec 1955
01 15:33 Sag	02 22:51 Aqu	01 15:22 Pis	01 05:46 Ari	01 19:23 Gem	01 05:46 Can
04 04:29 Cap	05 08:04 Pis	03 21:23 Ari	03 08:52 Tau	03 20:11 Can	03 06:07 Leo
06 16:17 Aqu	07 14:59 Ari	06 01:36 Tau	05 10:59 Gem	05 22:19 Leo	05 08:49 Vir
09 02:08 Pis	09 20:02 Tau	08 04:58 Gem	07 13:22 Can	08 02:36 Vir	07 14:47 Lib
11 09:32 Ari	11 23:33 Gem	10 08:00 Can	09 16:41 Leo	10 09:15 Lib	09 23:59 Sco
13 14:20 Tau	14 01:50 Can	12 11:02 Leo	11 21:11 Vir	12 18:11 Sco	12 11:33 Sag
15 16:43 Gem	16 03:34 Leo	14 14:33 Vir	14 03:13 Lib	15 05:16 Sag	15 00:23 Cap
17 17:30 Can	18 05:57 Vir	16 19:35 Lib	16 11:23 Sco	17 17:58 Cap	17 13:18 Aqu
19 18:03 Leo	20 10:33 Lib	19 03:18 Sco	18 22:07 Sag	20 06:58 Aqu	20 01:01 Pis
21 20:06 Vir	22 18:36 Sco	21 14:10 Sag	21 10:50 Cap	22 18:09 Pis	22 10:05 Ari
24 01:15 Lib	25 06:02 Sag	24 03:00 Cap	23 23:32 Aqu	25 01:47 Ari	24 15:32 Tau
26 10:18 Sco	27 18:56 Cap	26 15:06 Aqu	26 09:36 Pis	27 05:27 Tau	26 17:33 Gem
28 22:23 Sag	30 06:34 Aqu	29 00:12 Pis	28 15:46 Ari	29 06:11 Gem	28 17:18 Can
31 11:18 Cap			30 18:30 Tau		30 16:36 Leo

Jan 1956	Feb 1956	Mar 1956	Apr 1956	May 1956	Jun 1956
01 17:31 Vir	02 13:32 Sco	03 08:08 Sag	02 04:37 Cap	02 01:27 Aqu	03 07:04 Ari
03 21:43 Lib	05 00:12 Sag	05 20:31 Cap	04 17:23 Aqu	04 13:14 Pis	05 13:21 Tau
06 05:59 Sco	07 13:07 Cap	08 09:18 Aqu	07 04:36 Pis	06 22:05 Ari	07 16:09 Gem
08 17:32 Sag	10 01:51 Aqu	10 20:11 Pis	09 12:46 Ari	09 03:24 Tau	09 16:42 Can
11 06:33 Cap	12 12:51 Pis	13 04:26 Ari	11 18:03 Tau	11 06:00 Gem	11 16:45 Leo
13 19:19 Aqu	14 21:48 Ari	15 10:32 Tau	13 21:30 Gem	13 07:21 Can	13 18:03 Vir
16 06:47 Pis	17 04:48 Tau	17 15:11 Gem	16 00:14 Can	15 08:52 Leo	15 21:58 Lib
18 16:16 Ari	19 09:50 Gem	19 18:47 Can	18 03:00 Leo	17 11:39 Vir	18 05:02 Sco
20 23:11 Tau	21 12:49 Can	21 21:30 Leo	20 06:16 Vir	19 16:25 Lib	20 14:54 Sag
23 03:05 Gem	23 14:11 Leo	23 23:52 Vir	22 10:36 Lib	21 23:26 Sco	23 02:42 Cap
25 04:20 Can	25 15:05 Vir	26 02:59 Lib	24 16:44 Sco	24 08:46 Sag	25 15:25 Aqu
27 04:06 Leo	27 17:20 Lib	28 08:18 Sco	27 01:25 Sag	26 20:10 Cap	28 03:54 Pis
29 04:17 Vir	29 22:44 Sco	30 16:55 Sag	29 12:43 Cap	29 08:51 Aqu	30 14:42 Ari
31 06:55 Lib				31 21:09 Pis	

Jul 1956	Aug 1956	Sep 1956	Oct 1956	Nov 1956	Dec 1956
02 22:25 Tau	01 11:15 Gem	01 23:14 Leo	01 08:24 Vir	01 22:24 Sco	01 12:58 Sag
05 02:25 Gem	03 13:32 Can	03 23:20 Vir	03 10:01 Lib	04 04:56 Sag	03 22:35 Cap
07 03:20 Can	05 13:27 Leo	06 00:04 Lib	05 13:19 Sco	06 14:23 Cap	06 10:15 Aqu
09 02:42 Leo	07 12:50 Vir	08 03:26 Sco	07 19:45 Sag	09 02:19 Aqu	08 22:56 Pis
11 02:34 Vir	09 13:50 Lib	10 10:45 Sag	10 05:47 Cap	11 14:50 Pis	11 10:36 Ari
13 04:54 Lib	11 18:19 Sco	12 21:45 Cap	12 18:08 Aqu	14 01:36 Ari	13 19:15 Tau
15 10:55 Sco	14 02:59 Sag	15 10:27 Aqu	15 06:24 Pis	16 09:12 Tau	16 00:06 Gem
17 20:37 Sag	16 14:46 Cap	17 22:33 Pis	17 16:35 Ari	18 13:45 Gem	18 01:51 Can
20 08:40 Cap	19 03:37 Aqu	20 08:47 Ari	20 00:07 Tau	20 16:18 Can	20 02:11 Leo
22 21:28 Aqu	21 15:46 Pis	22 17:00 Tau	22 05:28 Gem	22 18:10 Leo	22 02:55 Vir
25 09:49 Pis	24 02:29 Ari	24 23:24 Gem	24 09:23 Can	24 20:31 Vir	24 05:38 Lib
27 20:53 Ari	26 11:23 Tau	27 03:59 Can	26 12:27 Leo	27 00:10 Lib	26 11:08 Sco
30 05:39 Tau	28 17:59 Gem	29 06:48 Leo	28 15:09 Vir	29 05:34 Sco	28 19:19 Sag
	30 21:51 Can		30 18:10 Lib		31 05:36 Cap

Jan 1957	Feb 1957	Mar 1957	Apr 1957	May 1957	Jun 1957
02 17:24 Aqu	01 12:20 Pis	03 06:30 Ari	01 23:10 Tau	01 13:46 Gem	02 04:45 Leo
05 06:04 Pis	04 00:41 Ari	05 17:20 Tau	04 07:29 Gem	03 19:08 Can	04 06:59 Vir
07 18:22 Ari	06 11:36 Tau	08 02:03 Gem	06 13:37 Can	05 22:53 Leo	06 09:45 Lib
10 04:26 Tau	08 19:34 Gem	10 07:44 Can	08 17:24 Leo	08 01:36 Vir	08 13:40 Sco
12 10:43 Gem	10 23:38 Can	12 10:12 Leo	10 19:13 Vir	10 03:57 Lib	10 19:09 Sag
14 13:06 Can	13 00:18 Leo	14 10:20 Vir	12 20:08 Lib	12 06:48 Sco	13 02:36 Cap
16 12:51 Leo	14 23:16 Vir	16 09:59 Lib	14 21:45 Sco	14 11:13 Sag	15 12:22 Aqu
18 12:04 Vir	16 22:49 Lib	18 11:14 Sco	17 01:42 Sag	16 18:13 Cap	18 00:14 Pis
20 12:55 Lib	19 01:05 Sco	20 15:53 Sag	19 09:07 Cap	19 04:11 Aqu	20 12:44 Ari
22 17:02 Sco	21 07:22 Sag	23 00:33 Cap	21 19:53 Aqu	21 16:19 Pis	22 23:38 Tau
25 00:51 Sag	23 17:26 Cap	25 12:16 Aqu	24 08:22 Pis	24 04:33 Ari	25 07:06 Gem
27 11:31 Cap	26 05:42 Aqu	28 00:59 Pis	26 20:21 Ari	26 14:42 Tau	27 11:01 Can
29 23:41 Aqu	28 18:24 Pis	30 12:54 Ari	29 06:17 Tau	28 21:46 Gem	29 12:31 Leo
				31 02:05 Can	

Jul 1957	Aug 1957	Sep 1957	Oct 1957	Nov 1957	Dec 1957
01 13:24 Vir	02 01:00 Sco	02 21:05 Cap	02 14:03 Aqu	01 09:17 Pis	01 05:55 Ari
03 15:16 Lib	04 06:46 Sag	05 07:49 Aqu	05 02:17 Pis	03 21:59 Ari	03 17:47 Tau
05 19:09 Sco	06 15:22 Cap	07 20:03 Pis	07 14:56 Ari	06 09:37 Tau	06 03:00 Gem
08 01:20 Sag	09 02:01 Aqu	10 08:44 Ari	10 02:47 Tau	08 19:08 Gem	08 09:16 Can
10 09:34 Cap	11 14:01 Pis	12 20:56 Tau	12 13:00 Gem	11 02:23 Can	10 13:23 Leo
12 19:42 Aqu	14 02:45 Ari	15 07:25 Gem	14 20:54 Can	13 07:36 Leo	12 16:28 Vir
15 07:31 Pis	16 14:59 Tau	17 14:49 Can	17 01:59 Leo	15 11:07 Vir	14 19:22 Lib
17 20:13 Ari	19 00:51 Gem	19 18:30 Leo	19 04:23 Vir	17 13:25 Lib	16 22:35 Sco
20 07:57 Tau	21 06:48 Can	21 19:11 Vir	21 05:03 Lib	19 15:17 Sco	19 02:30 Sag
22 16:33 Gem	23 08:51 Leo	23 18:33 Lib	23 05:31 Sco	21 17:51 Sag	21 07:46 Cap
24 21:05 Can	25 08:26 Vir	25 18:40 Sco	25 07:33 Sag	23 22:29 Cap	23 15:18 Aqu
26 22:16 Leo	27 07:41 Lib	27 21:27 Sag	27 12:40 Cap	26 06:15 Aqu	26 01:40 Pis
28 21:59 Vir	29 08:45 Sco	30 03:58 Cap	29 21:31 Aqu	28 17:15 Pis	28 14:11 Ari
30 22:20 Lib	31 13:06 Sag				31 02:36 Tau

Jan 1958	Feb 1958	Mar 1958	Apr 1958	May 1958	Jun 1958
02 12:21 Gem	01 04:40 Can	02 18:26 Leo	01 06:01 Vir	02 16:14 Sco	01 02:53 Sag
04 18:21 Can	03 07:38 Leo	04 19:15 Vir	03 05:54 Lib	04 16:43 Sag	03 05:22 Cap
06 21:21 Leo	05 08:11 Vir	06 18:36 Lib	05 05:16 Sco	06 19:20 Cap	05 10:33 Aqu
08 22:58 Vir	07 08:23 Lib	08 18:34 Sco	07 06:06 Sag	09 01:29 Aqu	07 19:23 Pis
11 00:51 Lib	09 10:03 Sco	10 20:56 Sag	09 10:00 Cap	11 11:26 Pis	10 07:19 Ari
13 04:01 Sco	11 14:11 Sag	13 02:36 Cap	11 17:40 Aqu	13 23:57 Ari	12 20:11 Tau
15 08:49 Sag	13 20:55 Cap	15 11:27 Aqu	14 04:38 Pis	16 12:49 Tau	15 07:30 Gem
17 15:12 Cap	16 05:51 Aqu	17 22:41 Pis	16 17:22 Ari	19 00:13 Gem	17 16:03 Can
19 23:22 Aqu	18 16:39 Pis	20 11:16 Ari	19 06:16 Tau	21 09:22 Can	19 22:03 Leo
22 09:41 Pis	21 05:01 Ari	23 00:15 Tau	21 18:02 Gem	23 16:14 Leo	22 02:22 Vir
24 22:02 Ari	23 18:04 Tau	25 12:19 Gem	24 03:46 Can	25 20:59 Vir	24 05:42 Lib
27 10:55 Tau	26 05:51 Gem	27 21:52 Can	26 10:43 Leo	27 23:55 Lib	26 08:30 Sco
29 21:46 Gem	28 14:16 Can	30 03:45 Leo	28 14:40 Vir	30 01:33 Sco	28 11:11 Sag
			30 16:06 Lib		30 14:32 Cap

Jul 1958	Aug 1958	Sep 1958	Oct 1958	Nov 1958	Dec 1958
02 19:44 Aqu	01 12:11 Pis	02 19:23 Tau	02 14:49 Gem	01 08:08 Can	03 05:17 Vir
05 03:56 Pis	03 23:14 Ari	05 08:06 Gem	05 01:59 Can	03 17:02 Leo	05 09:30 Lib
07 15:17 Ari	06 12:03 Tau	07 18:21 Can	07 09:50 Leo	05 22:45 Vir	07 11:28 Sco
10 04:08 Tau	09 00:16 Gem	10 00:41 Leo	09 13:49 Vir	08 01:16 Lib	09 12:02 Sag
12 15:46 Gem	11 09:24 Can	12 03:19 Vir	11 14:44 Lib	10 01:29 Sco	11 12:46 Cap
15 00:15 Can	13 14:43 Leo	14 03:44 Lib	13 14:12 Sco	12 01:03 Sag	13 15:37 Aqu
17 05:31 Leo	15 17:07 Vir	16 03:49 Sco	15 14:09 Sag	14 01:54 Cap	15 22:11 Pis
19 08:42 Vir	17 18:17 Lib	18 05:16 Sag	17 16:22 Cap	16 05:52 Aqu	18 08:44 Ari
21 11:11 Lib	19 19:49 Sco	20 09:12 Cap	19 22:03 Aqu	18 13:55 Pis	20 21:37 Tau
23 13:57 Sco	21 22:47 Sag	22 16:02 Aqu	22 07:19 Pis	21 01:28 Ari	23 10:08 Gem
25 17:25 Sag	24 03:38 Cap	25 01:33 Pis	24 19:10 Ari	23 14:29 Tau	25 20:32 Can
27 21:52 Cap	26 10:27 Aqu	27 13:07 Ari	27 08:07 Tau	26 03:00 Gem	28 04:33 Leo
30 03:52 Aqu	28 19:24 Pis	30 01:57 Tau	29 20:49 Gem	28 13:50 Can	30 10:40 Vir
	31 06:34 Ari			30 22:40 Leo	

Jan 1959	Feb 1959	Mar 1959	Apr 1959	May 1959	Jun 1959
01 15:20 Lib	02 03:10 Sag	01 08:32 Sag	01 22:41 Aqu	01 11:57 Pis	02 16:36 Tau
03 18:41 Sco	04 06:28 Cap	03 12:05 Cap	04 06:22 Pis	03 22:18 Ari	05 05:35 Gem
05 20:55 Sag	06 10:40 Aqu	05 17:16 Aqu	06 16:32 Ari	06 10:38 Tau	07 17:43 Can
07 22:49 Cap	08 16:50 Pis	08 00:25 Pis	09 04:31 Tau	08 23:34 Gem	10 04:18 Leo
10 01:51 Aqu	11 01:54 Ari	10 09:53 Ari	11 17:24 Gem	11 11:56 Can	12 12:49 Vir
12 07:39 Pis	13 13:46 Tau	12 21:36 Tau	14 05:47 Can	13 22:40 Leo	14 18:41 Lib
14 17:08 Ari	16 02:39 Gem	15 10:29 Gem	16 15:54 Leo	16 06:37 Vir	16 21:38 Sco
17 05:32 Tau	18 13:50 Can	17 22:27 Can	18 22:27 Vir	18 11:06 Lib	18 22:14 Sag
19 18:15 Gem	20 21:37 Leo	20 07:22 Leo	21 01:18 Lib	20 12:24 Sco	20 22:01 Cap
22 04:46 Can	23 02:05 Vir	22 12:27 Vir	23 01:33 Sco	22 11:51 Sag	22 23:00 Aqu
24 12:13 Leo	25 04:28 Lib	24 14:27 Lib	25 00:58 Sag	24 11:24 Cap	25 03:08 Pis
26 17:13 Vir	27 06:14 Sco	26 14:54 Sco	27 01:32 Cap	26 13:09 Aqu	27 11:26 Ari
28 20:54 Lib		28 15:31 Sag	29 04:55 Aqu	28 18:41 Pis	29 23:10 Tau
31 00:05 Sco		30 17:48 Cap		31 04:17 Ari	

Jul 1959	Aug 1959	Sep 1959	Oct 1959	Nov 1959	Dec 1959
02 12:04 Gem	01 07:23 Can	02 08:30 Vir	01 22:08 Lib	02 10:02 Sag	01 20:11 Cap
05 00:03 Can	03 17:08 Leo	04 12:56 Lib	03 23:53 Sco	04 10:05 Cap	03 20:35 Aqu
07 10:07 Leo	06 00:29 Vir	06 15:53 Sco	06 00:54 Sag	06 12:13 Aqu	06 00:16 Pis
09 18:15 Vir	08 05:56 Lib	08 18:20 Sag	08 02:38 Cap	08 17:35 Pis	08 07:58 Ari
12 00:26 Lib	10 09:59 Sco	10 21:04 Cap	10 06:12 Aqu	11 02:09 Ari	10 18:55 Tau
14 04:33 Sco	12 12:58 Sag	13 00:43 Aqu	12 12:05 Pis	13 13:03 Tau	13 07:23 Gem
16 06:42 Sag	14 15:18 Cap	15 05:54 Pis	14 20:19 Ari	16 01:16 Gem	15 20:00 Can
18 07:42 Cap	16 17:53 Aqu	17 13:15 Ari	17 06:39 Tau	18 13:56 Can	18 07:57 Leo
20 09:05 Aqu	18 21:59 Pis	19 23:12 Tau	19 18:39 Gem	21 02:03 Leo	20 18:29 Vir
22 12:40 Pis	21 04:51 Ari	22 11:15 Gem	22 07:21 Can	23 12:07 Vir	23 02:28 Lib
24 19:53 Ari	23 14:57 Tau	24 23:49 Can	24 19:02 Leo	25 18:40 Lib	25 07:00 Sco
27 06:42 Tau	26 03:18 Gem	27 10:35 Leo	27 03:48 Vir	27 21:21 Sco	27 08:16 Sag
29 19:22 Gem	28 15:32 Can	29 18:03 Vir	29 08:41 Lib	29 21:12 Sag	29 07:38 Cap
	31 01:33 Leo		31 10:14 Sco		31 07:15 Aqu

Jan 1960	Feb 1960	Mar 1960	Apr 1960	May 1960	Jun 1960
02 09:18 Pis	01 00:38 Ari	01 18:18 Tau	03 01:45 Can	02 21:58 Leo	01 16:37 Vir
04 15:20 Ari	03 09:15 Tau	04 05:07 Gem	05 14:00 Leo	05 08:58 Vir	04 01:31 Lib
07 01:22 Tau	05 20:58 Gem	06 17:36 Can	08 00:01 Vir	07 16:29 Lib	06 06:19 Sco
09 13:44 Gem	08 09:36 Can	09 05:24 Leo	10 06:35 Lib	09 20:06 Sco	08 07:31 Sag
12 02:23 Can	10 21:07 Leo	11 14:47 Vir	12 10:01 Sco	11 20:55 Sag	10 06:48 Cap
14 13:58 Leo	13 06:34 Vir	13 21:19 Lib	14 11:38 Sag	13 20:50 Cap	12 06:23 Aqu
17 00:03 Vir	15 13:55 Lib	16 01:37 Sco	16 13:01 Cap	15 21:51 Aqu	14 08:17 Pis
19 08:13 Lib	17 19:23 Sco	18 04:37 Sag	18 15:31 Aqu	18 01:23 Pis	16 13:41 Ari
21 13:58 Sco	19 23:11 Sag	20 07:14 Cap	20 19:55 Pis	20 07:54 Ari	18 22:33 Tau
23 17:02 Sag	22 01:39 Cap	22 10:10 Aqu	23 02:22 Ari	22 16:59 Tau	21 09:45 Gem
25 18:00 Cap	24 03:32 Aqu	24 14:02 Pis	25 10:50 Tau	25 03:54 Gem	23 22:09 Can
27 18:19 Aqu	26 06:03 Pis	26 19:29 Ari	27 21:16 Gem	27 16:06 Can	26 10:51 Leo
29 19:56 Pis	28 10:37 Ari	29 03:13 Tau	30 09:22 Can	30 04:50 Leo	28 22:52 Vir
		31 13:31 Gem			

Jul 1960	Aug 1960	Sep 1960	Oct 1960	Nov 1960	Dec 1960
01 08:45 Lib	02 02:04 Sag	02 12:35 Aqu	01 22:14 Pis	02 15:27 Tau	02 07:00 Gem
03 15:08 Sco	04 03:25 Cap	04 13:51 Pis	04 01:46 Ari	04 23:44 Gem	04 17:51 Can
05 17:42 Sag	06 03:20 Aqu	06 16:26 Ari	06 07:08 Tau	07 10:25 Can	07 06:20 Leo
07 17:35 Cap	08 03:42 Pis	08 21:44 Tau	08 15:16 Gem	09 22:59 Leo	09 19:12 Vir
09 16:43 Aqu	10 06:21 Ari	11 06:30 Gem	11 02:17 Can	12 11:23 Vir	12 06:09 Lib
11 17:19 Pis	12 12:35 Tau	13 18:09 Can	03 14:54 Leo	14 21:07 Lib	14 13:12 Sco
13 21:06 Ari	14 22:29 Gem	16 06:46 Leo	16 02:39 Vir	17 02:53 Sco	16 16:07 Sag
16 04:47 Tau	17 10:42 Can	18 18:06 Vir	18 11:32 Lib	19 05:17 Sag	18 16:17 Cap
18 15:39 Gem	19 23:17 Leo	21 02:58 Lib	20 17:06 Sco	21 06:02 Cap	20 15:49 Aqu
21 04:08 Can	22 10:41 Vir	23 09:17 Sco	22 20:16 Sag	23 07:04 Aqu	22 16:47 Pis
23 16:45 Leo	24 20:09 Lib	25 13:41 Sag	24 22:28 Cap	25 09:49 Pis	24 20:34 Ari
26 04:31 Vir	27 03:23 Sco	27 16:54 Cap	27 00:57 Aqu	27 14:50 Ari	27 03:29 Tau
28 14:32 Lib	29 08:19 Sag	29 19:32 Aqu	29 04:26 Pis	29 21:59 Tau	29 13:01 Gem
30 21:54 Sco	31 11:08 Cap		31 09:11 Ari		

Jan 1961	Feb 1961	Mar 1961	Apr 1961	May 1961	Jun 1961
01 00:21 Can	02 07:47 Vir	01 14:11 Vir	02 16:36 Sco	02 05:25 Sag	02 17:45 Aqu
03 12:53 Leo	04 19:26 Lib	04 01:20 Lib	04 22:33 Sag	04 08:39 Cap	04 19:50 Pis
06 01:47 Vir	07 04:50 Sco	06 10:23 Sco	07 02:51 Cap	06 11:24 Aqu	06 23:23 Ari
08 13:30 Lib	09 11:00 Sag	08 17:03 Sag	09 06:02 Aqu	08 14:22 Pis	09 04:37 Tau
10 22:08 Sco	11 13:50 Cap	10 21:18 Cap	11 08:31 Pis	10 17:55 Ari	11 11:40 Gem
13 02:40 Sag	13 14:15 Aqu	12 23:28 Aqu	13 10:55 Ari	12 22:25 Tau	13 20:49 Can
15 03:41 Cap	15 13:53 Pis	15 00:26 Pis	15 14:16 Tau	15 04:34 Gem	16 08:15 Leo
17 02:55 Aqu	17 14:41 Ari	17 01:32 Ari	17 19:54 Gem	17 13:16 Can	18 21:11 Vir
19 02:32 Pis	19 18:21 Tau	19 04:25 Tau	20 04:49 Can	20 00:44 Leo	21 09:31 Lib
21 04:26 Ari	22 01:51 Gem	21 10:31 Gem	22 16:42 Leo	22 13:37 Vir	23 18:50 Sco
23 09:50 Tau	24 12:48 Can	23 20:21 Can	25 05:30 Vir	25 01:17 Lib	26 00:05 Sag
25 18:49 Gem	27 01:34 Leo	26 08:47 Leo	27 16:34 Lib	27 09:34 Sco	28 01:59 Cap
28 06:21 Can		28 21:29 Vir	30 00:26 Sco	29 14:11 Sag	30 02:17 Aqu
30 19:04 Leo		31 08:20 Lib		31 16:20 Cap	

Jul 1961	Aug 1961	Sep 1961	Oct 1961	Nov 1961	Dec 1961
02 02:52 Pis	02 16:18 Tau	01 05:52 Gem	03 09:42 Leo	02 06:17 Vir	02 03:07 Lib
04 05:11 Ari	04 23:03 Gem	03 14:59 Can	05 22:45 Vir	04 18:41 Lib	04 13:29 Sco
06 10:01 Tau	07 08:56 Can	06 03:00 Leo	08 11:03 Lib	07 04:40 Sco	06 20:24 Sag
08 17:26 Gem	09 20:58 Leo	08 16:04 Vir	10 21:18 Sco	09 11:50 Sag	09 00:30 Cap
11 03:12 Can	12 09:59 Vir	11 04:33 Lib	13 05:20 Sag	11 16:59 Cap	11 03:11 Aqu
13 14:56 Leo	14 22:43 Lib	13 15:22 Sco	15 11:23 Cap	13 20:59 Aqu	13 05:41 Pis
16 03:54 Vir	17 09:43 Sco	15 23:54 Sag	17 15:36 Aqu	16 00:18 Pis	15 08:44 Ari
18 16:37 Lib	19 17:43 Sag	18 05:41 Cap	19 18:09 Pis	18 03:10 Ari	17 12:38 Tau
21 03:04 Sco	21 22:07 Cap	20 08:43 Aqu	21 19:35 Ari	20 06:03 Tau	19 17:47 Gem
23 09:41 Sag	23 23:25 Aqu	22 09:36 Pis	23 21:07 Tau	22 09:59 Gem	22 00:49 Can
25 12:29 Cap	25 23:02 Pis	24 09:40 Ari	26 00:24 Gem	24 16:20 Can	24 10:25 Leo
27 12:42 Aqu	27 22:48 Ari	26 10:42 Tau	28 07:02 Can	27 02:01 Leo	26 22:29 Vir
29 12:13 Pis	30 00:36 Tau	28 14:31 Gem	30 17:28 Leo	29 14:24 Vir	29 11:25 Lib
31 12:55 Ari		30 22:18 Can			31 22:41 Sco

Jan 1962	Feb 1962	Mar 1962	Apr 1962	May 1962	Jun 1962
03 06:23 Sag	01 21:09 Cap	01 06:37 Cap	01 20:42 Pis	01 06:12 Ari	01 17:40 Gem
05 10:24 Cap	03 22:56 Aqu	03 09:51 Aqu	03 20:41 Ari	03 06:49 Tau	03 21:56 Can
07 12:00 Aqu	05 22:52 Pis	05 10:17 Pis	05 20:25 Tau	05 08:16 Gem	06 05:22 Leo
09 12:53 Pis	07 22:50 Ari	07 09:32 Ari	07 21:59 Gem	07 12:27 Can	08 16:11 Vir
11 14:33 Ari	10 00:34 Tau	09 09:40 Tau	10 03:11 Can	09 20:35 Leo	11 04:50 Lib
13 18:01 Tau	12 05:17 Gem	11 12:34 Gem	12 12:35 Leo	12 08:10 Vir	13 16:44 Sco
15 23:41 Gem	14 13:19 Can	13 19:25 Can	15 00:56 Vir	14 21:02 Lib	16 02:03 Sag
18 07:39 Can	17 00:03 Leo	16 05:55 Leo	17 13:53 Lib	17 08:42 Sco	18 08:29 Cap
20 17:49 Leo	19 12:26 Vir	18 18:32 Vir	20 01:36 Sco	19 18:02 Sag	20 12:49 Aqu
23 05:53 Vir	22 01:21 Lib	21 07:28 Lib	22 11:26 Sag	22 01:08 Cap	22 15:58 Pis
25 18:51 Lib	24 13:35 Sco	23 19:28 Sco	24 19:19 Cap	24 06:30 Aqu	24 18:43 Ari
28 06:53 Sco	26 23:46 Sag	26 05:48 Sag	27 01:07 Aqu	26 10:29 Pis	26 21:34 Tau
30 15:58 Sag		28 13:45 Cap	29 04:39 Pis	28 13:15 Ari	29 01:09 Gem
		30 18:43 Aqu		30 15:17 Tau	

Jul 1962	Aug 1962	Sep 1962	Oct 1962	Nov 1962	Dec 1962
01 06:18 Can	02 07:57 Vir	01 03:00 Lib	03 09:39 Sag	02 01:17 Cap	01 14:25 Aqu
03 13:55 Leo	04 20:17 Lib	03 15:45 Sco	05 19:34 Cap	04 09:01 Aqu	03 19:53 Pis
06 00:21 Vir	07 08:55 Sco	06 03:25 Sag	08 02:21 Aqu	06 13:52 Pis	05 23:17 Ari
08 12:46 Lib	09 19:47 Sag	08 12:19 Cap	10 05:28 Pis	08 15:45 Ari	08 00:59 Tau
11 01:05 Sco	12 03:17 Cap	10 17:26 Aqu	12 05:41 Ari	10 15:44 Tau	10 02:07 Gem
13 10:59 Sag	14 07:07 Aqu	12 19:02 Pis	14 04:43 Tau	12 15:44 Gem	12 04:21 Can
15 17:31 Cap	16 08:17 Pis	14 18:33 Ari	16 04:50 Gem	14 17:48 Can	14 09:20 Leo
17 21:07 Aqu	18 08:25 Ari	16 18:01 Tau	18 08:04 Can	16 23:39 Leo	16 17:58 Vir
19 23:00 Pis	20 09:20 Tau	18 19:28 Gem	20 15:29 Leo	19 09:32 Vir	19 05:40 Lib
22 00:33 Ari	22 12:27 Gem	21 00:25 Can	23 02:30 Vir	21 21:57 Lib	21 18:17 Sco
24 02:56 Tau	24 18:33 Can	23 09:06 Leo	25 15:13 Lib	24 10:32 Sco	24 05:32 Sag
26 06:56 Gem	27 03:29 Leo	25 20:30 Vir	28 03:48 Sco	26 21:43 Sag	26 14:18 Cap
28 13:00 Can	29 14:35 Vir	28 09:07 Lib	30 15:19 Sag	29 07:00 Cap	28 20:42 Aqu
30 21:20 Leo		30 21:48 Sco			31 01:20 Pis

Jan 1963	Feb 1963	Mar 1963	Apr 1963	May 1963	Jun 1963
02 04:47 Ari	02 16:02 Gem	01 21:38 Gem	02 14:44 Leo	02 06:12 Vir	01 00:08 Lib
04 07:33 Tau	04 20:40 Can	04 02:07 Can	05 00:20 Vir	04 17:41 Lib	03 12:38 Sco
06 10:14 Gem	07 03:05 Leo	06 09:14 Leo	07 11:49 Lib	07 06:15 Sco	06 01:00 Sag
08 13:41 Can	09 11:35 Vir	08 18:33 Vir	10 00:13 Sco	09 18:42 Sag	08 12:06 Cap
10 19:00 Leo	11 22:17 Lib	11 05:34 Lib	12 12:47 Sag	12 06:13 Cap	10 21:21 Aqu
13 03:06 Vir	14 10:37 Sco	13 17:51 Sco	15 00:26 Cap	14 15:50 Aqu	13 04:20 Pis
15 14:04 Lib	16 22:56 Sag	16 06:26 Sag	17 09:33 Aqu	16 22:31 Pis	15 08:46 Ari
18 02:35 Sco	19 08:59 Cap	18 17:33 Cap	19 14:53 Pis	19 01:47 Ari	17 10:54 Tau
20 14:19 Sag	21 15:23 Aqu	21 01:21 Aqu	21 16:30 Ari	21 02:21 Tau	19 11:44 Gem
22 23:23 Cap	23 18:17 Pis	23 05:04 Pis	23 15:51 Tau	23 01:53 Gem	21 12:46 Can
25 05:13 Aqu	25 19:05 Ari	25 05:38 Ari	25 15:06 Gem	25 02:28 Can	23 15:44 Leo
27 08:35 Pis	27 19:38 Tau	27 04:57 Tau	27 16:27 Can	27 05:58 Leo	25 21:56 Vir
29 10:44 Ari		29 05:13 Gem	29 21:24 Leo	29 13:20 Vir	28 07:40 Lib
31 12:54 Tau		31 08:13 Can			30 19:47 Sco

Jul 1963	Aug 1963	Sep 1963	Oct 1963	Nov 1963	Dec 1963
03 08:10 Sag	02 03:12 Cap	03 01:37 Pis	02 13:48 Ari	01 00:42 Tau	02 10:45 Can
05 19:02 Cap	04 11:25 Aqu	05 03:52 Ari	04 13:50 Tau	02 23:48 Gem	04 12:19 Leo
08 03:36 Aqu	06 16:45 Pis	07 05:02 Tau	06 13:58 Gem	05 00:08 Can	06 17:25 Vir
10 09:52 Pis	08 20:06 Ari	09 06:45 Gem	08 16:00 Can	07 03:23 Leo	09 02:21 Lib
12 14:16 Ari	10 22:37 Tau	11 10:07 Can	10 20:53 Leo	09 10:13 Vir	11 14:03 Sco
14 17:15 Tau	13 01:15 Gem	13 15:29 Leo	13 04:33 Vir	11 20:07 Lib	14 02:53 Sag
16 19:27 Gem	15 04:39 Can	15 22:47 Vir	15 14:23 Lib	14 07:56 Sco	16 15:20 Cap
18 21:44 Can	17 09:16 Leo	18 07:59 Lib	18 01:52 Sco	16 20:39 Sag	19 02:28 Aqu
21 01:14 Leo	19 15:40 Vir	20 19:10 Sco	20 14:31 Sag	19 09:22 Cap	21 11:28 Pis
23 07:06 Vir	22 00:25 Lib	23 07:49 Sag	23 03:20 Cap	21 20:51 Aqu	23 17:40 Ari
25 16:01 Lib	24 11:38 Sco	25 20:14 Cap	25 14:19 Aqu	24 05:31 Pis	25 20:57 Tau
28 03:38 Sco	27 00:15 Sag	28 06:02 Aqu	27 21:35 Pis	26 10:25 Ari	27 21:58 Gem
30 16:07 Sag	29 11:56 Cap	30 11:46 Pis	30 00:39 Ari	28 11:49 Tau	29 22:07 Can
	31 20:36 Aqu			30 11:15 Gem	31 23:08 Leo

Jan 1964	Feb 1964	Mar 1964	Apr 1964	May 1964	Jun 1964
03 02:47 Vir	01 19:25 Lib	02 13:53 Sco	01 09:40 Sag	01 05:42 Cap	02 11:00 Pis
05 10:09 Lib	04 05:12 Sco	05 01:46 Sag	03 22:35 Cap	03 18:05 Aqu	04 18:02 Ari
07 21:03 Sco	06 17:34 Sag	07 14:34 Cap	06 10:23 Aqu	06 03:42 Pis	06 21:19 Tau
10 09:48 Sag	09 06:10 Cap	10 01:35 Aqu	08 18:46 Pis	08 09:15 Ari	08 21:50 Gem
12 22:13 Cap	11 16:39 Aqu	12 09:05 Pis	10 23:08 Ari	10 11:09 Tau	10 21:16 Can
15 08:47 Aqu	14 00:08 Pis	14 13:15 Ari	13 00:36 Tau	12 11:02 Gem	12 21:35 Leo
17 17:03 Pis	16 05:09 Ari	16 15:30 Tau	15 01:05 Gem	14 10:53 Can	15 00:27 Vir
19 23:10 Ari	18 08:45 Tau	18 17:26 Gem	17 02:23 Can	16 12:31 Leo	17 06:53 Lib
22 03:23 Tau	20 11:48 Gem	20 20:11 Can	19 05:39 Leo	18 17:02 Vir	19 16:48 Sco
24 06:04 Gem	22 14:49 Can	23 00:14 Leo	21 11:17 Vir	21 00:41 Lib	22 05:02 Sag
26 07:51 Can	24 18:11 Leo	25 05:41 Vir	23 19:07 Lib	23 10:57 Sco	24 18:01 Cap
28 09:45 Leo	26 22:29 Vir	27 12:47 Lib	26 05:00 Sco	25 23:02 Sag	27 06:21 Aqu
30 13:09 Vir	29 04:46 Lib	29 22:03 Sco	28 16:45 Sag	28 11:59 Cap	29 16:55 Pis
				31 00:32 Aqu	

Jul 1964	Aug 1964	Sep 1964	Oct 1964	Nov 1964	Dec 1964
02 00:52 Ari	02 15:28 Gem	01 00:13 Can	02 12:42 Vir	01 00:24 Lib	03 01:23 Sag
04 05:42 Tau	04 17:13 Can	03 02:36 Leo	04 17:44 Lib	03 08:24 Sco	05 13:52 Cap
06 07:43 Gem	06 18:11 Leo	05 05:12 Vir	07 00:56 Sco	05 18:43 Sag	08 02:57 Aqu
08 07:57 Can	08 19:50 Vir	07 09:19 Lib	09 11:01 Sag	08 07:05 Cap	10 14:59 Pis
10 08:01 Leo	10 23:51 Lib	09 16:19 Sco	11 23:31 Cap	10 20:07 Aqu	13 00:12 Ari
12 09:44 Vir	13 07:30 Sco	12 02:47 Sag	14 12:14 Aqu	13 07:27 Pis	15 05:32 Tau
14 14:40 Lib	15 18:43 Sag	14 15:29 Cap	16 22:32 Pis	15 15:10 Ari	17 07:21 Gem
16 23:32 Sco	18 07:37 Cap	17 03:47 Aqu	19 05:04 Ari	17 18:56 Tau	19 07:03 Can
19 11:27 Sag	20 19:38 Aqu	19 13:22 Pis	21 08:24 Tau	19 19:58 Gem	21 06:31 Leo
22 00:26 Cap	23 05:13 Pis	21 19:43 Ari	23 10:03 Gem	21 20:04 Can	23 07:41 Vir
24 12:30 Aqu	25 12:15 Ari	23 23:46 Tau	25 11:37 Can	23 20:58 Leo	25 12:04 Lib
26 22:35 Pis	27 17:23 Tau	26 02:46 Gem	27 14:13 Leo	26 00:02 Vir	27 20:10 Sco
29 06:25 Ari	29 21:15 Gem	28 05:39 Can	29 18:25 Vir	28 05:53 Lib	30 07:20 Sag
31 12:00 Tau		30 08:52 Leo		30 14:30 Sco	

Jan 1965	Feb 1965	Mar 1965	Apr 1965	May 1965	Jun 1965
01 20:06 Cap	03 02:55 Pis	02 09:38 Pis	01 02:18 Ari	02 20:26 Gem	01 07:05 Can
04 09:03 Aqu	05 12:43 Ari	04 18:44 Ari	03 08:28 Tau	04 22:38 Can	03 07:46 Leo
06 21:05 Pis	07 20:23 Tau	07 01:49 Tau	05 12:54 Gem	07 00:49 Leo	05 09:33 Vir
09 07:07 Ari	10 01:36 Gem	09 07:13 Gem	07 16:24 Can	09 03:47 Vir	07 13:29 Lib
11 14:10 Tau	12 04:13 Can	11 11:02 Can	09 19:23 Leo	11 08:04 Lib	09 20:03 Sco
13 17:48 Gem	14 04:54 Leo	13 13:23 Leo	11 22:14 Vir	13 14:09 Sco	12 05:09 Sag
15 18:35 Can	16 05:05 Vir	15 14:56 Vir	14 01:38 Lib	15 22:31 Sag	14 16:20 Cap
17 17:58 Leo	18 06:45 Lib	17 17:04 Lib	16 06:41 Sco	18 09:19 Cap	17 04:51 Aqu
19 17:55 Vir	20 11:45 Sco	19 21:31 Sco	18 14:31 Sag	20 21:50 Aqu	19 17:28 Pis
21 20:27 Lib	22 20:56 Sag	22 05:36 Sag	21 01:23 Cap	23 10:13 Pis	22 04:28 Ari
24 03:00 Sco	25 09:16 Cap	24 17:06 Cap	23 14:03 Aqu	25 20:18 Ari	24 12:15 Tau
26 13:31 Sag	27 22:14 Aqu	27 05:58 Aqu	26 02:01 Pis	28 02:48 Tau	26 16:18 Gem
29 02:21 Cap		29 17:31 Pis	28 11:11 Ari	30 05:58 Gem	28 17:20 Can
31 15:17 Aqu			30 17:03 Tau		30 16:59 Leo

Jul 1965	Aug 1965	Sep 1965	Oct 1965	Nov 1965	Dec 1965
02 17:11 Vir	01 03:54 Lib	01 23:59 Sag	01 18:28 Cap	03 03:22 Pis	02 23:22 Ari
04 19:42 Lib	03 08:19 Sco	04 10:50 Cap	04 06:47 Aqu	05 14:21 Ari	05 08:10 Tau
07 01:37 Sco	05 16:48 Sag	06 23:33 Aqu	06 19:13 Pis	07 22:29 Tau	07 13:27 Gem
09 10:52 Sag	08 04:22 Cap	09 11:56 Pis	09 05:53 Ari	10 03:54 Gem	09 15:57 Can
11 22:28 Cap	10 17:08 Aqu	11 22:49 Ari	11 14:16 Tau	12 07:29 Can	11 17:08 Leo
14 11:07 Aqu	13 05:37 Pis	14 07:55 Tau	13 20:39 Gem	14 10:13 Leo	13 18:35 Vir
16 23:44 Pis	15 16:56 Ari	16 15:05 Gem	16 01:26 Can	16 12:54 Vir	15 21:33 Lib
19 11:12 Ari	18 02:27 Tau	18 20:00 Can	18 04:51 Leo	18 16:10 Lib	18 02:40 Sco
21 20:13 Tau	20 09:20 Gem	20 22:35 Leo	20 07:13 Vir	20 20:36 Sco	20 10:00 Sag
24 01:47 Gem	22 13:04 Can	22 23:29 Vir	22 09:21 Lib	23 02:56 Sag	22 19:26 Cap
26 03:53 Can	24 14:01 Leo	25 00:15 Lib	24 12:31 Sco	25 11:45 Cap	25 06:43 Aqu
28 03:37 Leo	26 13:37 Vir	27 02:46 Sco	26 18:08 Sag	27 23:03 Aqu	27 19:17 Pis
30 02:54 Vir	28 13:52 Lib	29 08:41 Sag	29 03:04 Cap	30 11:39 Pis	30 07:39 Ari
	30 16:53 Sco		31 14:48 Aqu		

Jan 1966	Feb 1966	Mar 1966	Apr 1966	May 1966	Jun 1966
01 17:45 Tau	02 13:41 Can	01 22:47 Can	02 10:31 Vir	01 19:31 Lib	02 09:38 Sag
04 00:06 Gem	04 14:14 Leo	04 00:56 Leo	04 10:40 Lib	03 21:23 Sco	04 16:10 Cap
06 02:40 Can	06 13:12 Vir	06 00:36 Vir	06 11:30 Sco	06 00:52 Sag	07 01:20 Aqu
08 02:49 Leo	08 12:50 Lib	07 23:48 Lib	08 14:53 Sag	08 07:12 Cap	09 12:56 Pis
10 02:34 Vir	10 15:14 Sco	10 00:46 Sco	10 22:01 Cap	10 16:51 Aqu	12 01:26 Ari
12 03:52 Lib	12 21:32 Sag	12 05:17 Sag	13 08:41 Aqu	13 04:54 Pis	14 12:29 Tau
14 08:08 Sco	15 07:25 Cap	14 13:54 Cap	15 21:13 Pis	15 17:14 Ari	16 20:25 Gem
16 15:39 Sag	17 19:25 Aqu	17 01:34 Aqu	18 09:26 Ari	18 03:48 Tau	19 01:04 Can
19 01:44 Cap	20 08:04 Pis	19 14:18 Pis	20 20:00 Tau	20 11:39 Gem	21 03:29 Leo
21 13:25 Aqu	22 20:29 Ari	22 02:33 Ari	23 04:26 Gem	22 17:00 Can	23 05:08 Vir
24 01:58 Pis	25 07:52 Tau	24 13:31 Tau	25 10:47 Cam	24 20:37 Leo	25 07:22 Lib
26 14:32 Ari	27 17:02 Gem	26 22:41 Gem	27 15:09 Leo	26 23:21 Vir	27 11:03 Sco
29 01:42 Tau		29 05:23 Can	29 17:49 Vir	29 01:59 Lib	29 16:31 Sag
31 09:43 Gem		31 09:12 Leo		31 05:11 Sco	

Jul 1966	Aug 1966	Sep 1966	Oct 1966	Nov 1966	Dec 1966
01 23:51 Cap	03 03:35 Pis	01 22:27 Ari	01 16:46 Tau	02 17:42 Can	02 05:01 Leo
04 09:14 Aqu	05 16:14 Ari	04 10:58 Tau	04 03:43 Gem	04 23:35 Leo	04 08:48 Vir
06 20:39 Pis	08 04:37 Tau	06 21:52 Gem	06 12:12 Can	07 03:09 Vir	06 11:43 Lib
09 09:15 Ari	10 14:37 Gem	09 05:26 Can	08 17:24 Leo	09 04:54 Lib	08 14:17 Sco
11 21:03 Tau	12 20:41 Can	11 09:01 Leo	10 19:27 Vir	11 05:53 Sco	10 17:13 Sag
14 05:51 Gem	14 22:50 Leo	13 09:26 Vir	12 19:29 Lib	13 07:36 Sag	12 21:30 Cap
16 10:44 Can	16 22:35 Vir	15 08:33 Lib	14 19:21 Sco	15 11:36 Cap	15 04:18 Aqu
18 12:28 Leo	18 22:05 Lib	17 08:34 Sco	16 20:59 Sag	17 19:02 Aqu	17 14:16 Pis
20 12:47 Vir	20 23:23 Sco	19 11:21 Sag	19 01:55 Cap	20 05:52 Pis	20 02:39 Ari
22 13:38 Lib	23 03:50 Sag	21 17:52 Cap	21 10:40 Aqu	22 18:30 Ari	22 15:06 Tau
24 16:31 Sco	25 11:36 Cap	24 03:47 Aqu	23 22:20 Pis	25 06:36 Tau	25 01:13 Gem
26 22:04 Sag	27 21:55 Aqu	26 15:48 Pis	26 11:02 Ari	27 16:30 Gem	27 07:58 Can
29 06:04 Cap	30 09:47 Pis	29 04:29 Ari	28 23:05 Tau	29 23:49 Can	29 11:57 Leo
31 16:01 Aqu			31 09:27 Gem		31 14:33 Vir

Jan 1967	Feb 1967	Mar 1967	Apr 1967	May 1967	Jun 1967
02 17:03 Lib	01 01:43 Sco	02 11:52 Sag	01 00:10 Cap	03 00:46 Pis	01 20:06 Ari
04 20:16 Sco	03 05:55 Sag	04 17:34 Cap	03 07:48 Aqu	05 13:09 Ari	04 09:03 Tau
07 00:27 Sag	05 12:09 Cap	07 02:03 Aqu	05 18:28 Pis	08 02:09 Tau	06 20:51 Gem
09 05:53 Cap	07 20:16 Aqu	09 12:40 Pis	08 06:56 Ari	10 14:07 Gem	09 06:17 Can
11 13:05 Aqu	10 06:18 Pis	12 00:52 Ari	10 19:55 Tau	13 00:10 Can	11 13:18 Leo
13 22:44 Pis	12 18:16 Ari	14 13:53 Tau	13 08:14 Gem	15 07:48 Leo	13 18:23 Vir
16 10:47 Ari	15 07:18 Tau	17 02:18 Gem	15 18:36 Can	17 12:51 Vir	15 21:58 Lib
18 23:39 Tau	17 19:14 Gem	19 12:09 Can	18 01:54 Leo	19 15:31 Lib	18 00:25 Sco
21 10:37 Gem	20 03:47 Can	21 18:03 Leo	20 05:42 Vir	21 16:30 Sco	20 02:19 Sag
23 17:50 Can	22 08:04 Leo	23 20:08 Vir	22 06:41 Lib	23 17:06 Sag	22 04:46 Cap
25 21:20 Leo	24 09:04 Vir	25 19:50 Lib	24 06:19 Sco	25 18:58 Cap	24 09:10 Aqu
27 22:36 Vir	26 08:45 Lib	27 19:11 Sco	26 06:27 Sag	27 23:43 Aqu	26 16:49 Pis
29 23:32 Lib	28 09:09 Sco	29 20:08 Sag	28 08:53 Cap	30 08:17 Pis	29 03:52 Ari
			30 14:56 Aqu		

Jul 1967	Aug 1967	Sep 1967	Oct 1967	Nov 1967	Dec 1967
01 16:42 Tau	02 22:31 Can	01 14:08 Leo	01 03:38 Vir	01 15:26 Sco	01 02:10 Sag
04 04:38 Gem	05 04:26 Leo	03 17:07 Vir	03 04:34 Lib	03 14:51 Sag	03 02:24 Cap
06 13:47 Can	07 07:36 Vir	05 18:03 Lib	05 04:14 Sco	05 15:44 Cap	05 04:56 Aqu
08 19:58 Leo	09 09:34 Lib	07 18:44 Sco	07 04:32 Sag	07 19:45 Aqu	07 11:18 Pis
11 00:07 Vir	11 11:44 Sco	09 20:39 Sag	09 07:03 Cap	10 03:42 Pis	09 21:42 Ari
13 03:19 Lib	13 14:52 Sag	12 00:42 Cap	11 12:44 Aqu	12 14:57 Ari	12 10:31 Tau
15 06:17 Sco	15 19:17 Cap	14 07:08 Aqu	13 21:37 Pis	15 03:52 Tau	14 23:17 Gem
17 09:22 Sag	18 01:16 Aqu	16 15:52 Pis	16 08:57 Ari	17 16:39 Gem	17 10:22 Can
19 12:59 Cap	20 09:17 Pis	19 02:46 Ari	18 21:40 Tau	20 04:12 Can	19 19:20 Leo
21 17:59 Aqu	22 19:47 Ari	21 15:20 Tau	21 10:37 Gem	22 13:46 Leo	22 02:20 Vir
24 01:27 Pis	25 08:20 Tau	24 04:20 Gem	23 22:26 Can	24 20:45 Vir	24 07:26 Lib
26 11:59 Ari	27 21:07 Gem	26 15:44 Can	26 07:39 Leo	27 00:48 Lib	26 10:36 Sco
29 00:40 Tau	30 07:34 Can	28 23:41 Leo	28 13:19 Vir	29 02:13 Sco	28 12:09 Sag
31 12:59 Gem			30 15:31 Lib		30 13:11 Cap

Jan 1968	Feb 1968	Mar 1968	Apr 1968	May 1968	Jun 1968
01 15:24 Aqu	02 14:39 Ari	03 10:27 Tau	02 06:39 Gem	02 01:49 Can	03 03:51 Vir
03 20:35 Pis	05 02:14 Tau	05 23:16 Gem	04 19:12 Can	04 12:53 Leo	05 09:48 Lib
06 05:44 Ari	07 15:08 Gem	08 11:20 Can	07 05:28 Leo	06 20:57 Vir	07 12:30 Sco
08 18:01 Tau	10 02:33 Can	10 20:26 Leo	09 12:03 Vir	09 01:20 Lib	09 12:43 Sag
11 06:53 Gem	12 10:49 Leo	13 01:51 Vir	11 15:01 Lib	11 02:29 Sco	11 12:06 Cap
13 17:53 Can	14 16:02 Vir	15 04:23 Lib	13 15:32 Sco	13 01:53 Sag	13 12:46 Aqu
16 02:09 Leo	16 19:21 Lib	17 05:33 Sco	15 15:23 Sag	15 01:30 Cap	15 16:41 Pis
18 08:11 Vir	18 21:59 Sco	19 06:53 Sag	17 16:22 Cap	17 03:21 Aqu	18 00:49 Ari
20 12:47 Lib	21 00:47 Sag	21 09:34 Cap	19 19:56 Aqu	19 08:52 Pis	20 12:24 Tau
22 16:27 Sco	23 04:11 Cap	23 14:16 Aqu	22 02:45 Pis	21 18:13 Ari	23 01:21 Gem
24 19:23 Sag	25 08:36 Aqu	25 21:14 Pis	24 12:31 Ari	24 06:15 Tau	25 13:42 Can
26 21:56 Cap	27 14:42 Pis	28 06:31 Ari	27 00:21 Tau	26 19:11 Gem	28 00:30 Leo
29 01:05 Aqu	29 23:14 Ari	30 17:54 Tau	29 13:10 Gem	29 07:42 Can	30 09:25 Vir
31 06:15 Pis				31 18:53 Leo	

Jul 1968	Aug 1968	Sep 1968	Oct 1968	Nov 1968	Dec 1968
02 16:09 Lib	01 02:11 Sco	01 13:21 Cap	03 03:20 Pis	01 16:50 Ari	01 08:57 Tau
04 20:20 Sco	03 05:10 Sag	03 16:19 Aqu	05 10:35 Ari	04 03:01 Tau	03 21:05 Gem
06 22:04 Sag	05 06:57 Cap	05 20:27 Pis	07 20:06 Tau	06 14:47 Gem	06 09:43 Can
08 22:23 Cap	07 08:37 Aqu	08 02:48 Ari	10 07:43 Gem	09 03:26 Can	08 22:02 Leo
10 23:03 Aqu	09 11:45 Pis	10 12:05 Tau	12 20:22 Can	11 15:44 Leo	11 08:58 Vir
13 02:02 Pis	11 17:52 Ari	12 23:54 Gem	15 08:07 Leo	14 01:54 Vir	13 17:08 Lib
05 08:51 Ari	14 03:35 Tau	15 12:27 Can	17 16:58 Vir	16 08:26 Lib	15 21:31 Sco
17 19:29 Tau	16 15:50 Gem	17 23:25 Leo	19 22:05 Lib	18 11:06 Sco	17 22:27 Sag
20 08:12 Gem	19 04:15 Can	20 07:15 Vir	22 00:05 Sco	20 11:04 Sag	19 21:32 Cap
22 20:30 Can	21 14:39 Leo	22 12:00 Lib	24 00:32 Sag	22 10:20 Cap	21 20:59 Aqu
25 06:54 Leo	23 22:20 Vir	24 14:39 Sco	26 01:13 Cap	24 11:02 Aqu	23 23:00 Pis
27 15:09 Vir	26 03:44 Lib	26 16:30 Sag	28 03:42 Aqu	26 14:52 Pis	26 05:01 Ari
29 21:32 Lib	28 07:38 Sco	28 18:44 Cap	30 08:53 Pis	28 22:25 Ari	28 14:56 Tau
	30 10:40 Sag	30 22:10 Aqu			31 03:10 Gem

Jan 1969	Feb 1969	Mar 1969	Apr 1969	May 1969	Jun 1969
02 15:52 Can	01 10:28 Leo	03 04:06 Vir	01 20:03 Lib	01 09:49 Sco	01 21:07 Cap
05 03:54 Leo	03 20:40 Vir	05 11:33 Lib	04 00:22 Sco	03 11:19 Sag	03 21:03 Aqu
07 14:41 Vir	06 05:00 Lib	07 16:56 Sco	06 02:57 Sag	05 11:57 Cap	05 23:13 Pis
09 23:32 Lib	08 11:17 Sco	09 20:47 Sag	08 05:04 Cap	07 13:27 Aqu	08 04:36 Ari
12 05:31 Sco	10 15:23 Sag	11 23:40 Cap	10 07:45 Aqu	09 17:03 Pis	10 13:05 Tau
14 08:19 Sag	12 17:28 Cap	14 02:09 Aqu	12 11:40 Pis	11 23:08 Ari	12 23:48 Gem
16 08:39 Cap	14 18:31 Aqu	16 05:03 Pis	14 17:13 Ari	14 07:28 Tau	15 11:51 Can
18 08:17 Aqu	16 20:03 Pis	18 09:26 Ari	17 00:42 Tau	16 17:41 Gem	18 00:35 Leo
20 09:20 Pis	18 23:48 Ari	20 16:20 Tau	19 10:28 Gem	19 05:30 Can	20 12:52 Vir
22 13:43 Ari	21 07:01 Tau	23 02:12 Gem	21 22:16 Can	21 18:11 Leo	22 23:03 Lib
24 22:12 Tau	23 17:40 Gem	25 14:17 Can	24 10:50 Leo	24 06:06 Vir	25 05:30 Sco
27 09:52 Gem	26 06:10 Can	28 02:36 Leo	26 21:56 Vir	26 15:06 Lib	27 08:00 Sag
29 22:36 Can	28 18:11 Leo	30 12:53 Vir	29 05:43 Lib	28 20:04 Sco	29 07:45 Cap
				30 21:30 Sag	

Jul 1969	Aug 1969	Sep 1969	Oct 1969	Nov 1969	Dec 1969
01 06:49 Aqu	01 19:54 Ari	02 19:23 Gem	02 14:51 Can	01 11:33 Leo	01 08:13 Vir
03 07:26 Pis	04 02:01 Tau	05 06:56 Can	05 03:24 Leo	04 00:00 Vir	03 19:16 Lib
05 11:16 Ari	06 11:48 Gem	07 19:35 Leo	07 15:20 Vir	06 09:58 Lib	06 02:30 Sco
07 18:52 Tau	08 23:57 Can	10 07:20 Vir	10 00:48 Lib	08 16:17 Sco	08 05:42 Sag
10 05:30 Gem	11 12:37 Leo	12 17:01 Lib	12 07:18 Sco	10 19:30 Sag	10 06:20 Cap
12 17:46 Can	14 00:32 Vir	15 00:24 Sco	14 11:33 Sag	12 21:08 Cap	12 06:27 Aqu
15 06:28 Leo	16 10:50 Lib	17 05:42 Sag	16 14:35 Cap	14 22:52 Aqu	14 07:56 Pis
17 18:41 Vir	18 18:53 Sco	19 09:13 Cap	18 17:21 Aqu	17 01:51 Pis	16 11:55 Ari
20 05:19 Lib	21 00:11 Sag	21 11:31 Aqu	20 20:25 Pis	19 06:31 Ari	18 18:34 Tau
22 13:03 Sco	23 02:48 Cap	23 13:22 Pis	23 00:17 Ari	21 12:52 Tau	21 03:27 Gem
24 17:10 Sag	25 03:35 Aqu	25 15:55 Ari	25 05:32 Tau	23 20:58 Gem	23 14:08 Can
26 18:09 Cap	27 04:03 Pis	27 20:28 Tau	27 13:00 Gem	26 07:10 Can	26 02:20 Leo
28 17:35 Aqu	29 05:57 Ari	30 04:05 Gem	29 23:12 Can	28 19:21 Leo	28 15:19 Vir
30 17:31 Pis	31 10:49 Tau				31 03:17 Lib

Jan 1970	Feb 1970	Mar 1970	Apr 1970	May 1970	Jun 1970
02 12:02 Sco	01 01:49 Sag	02 12:54 Cap	03 00:00 Pis	02 09:32 Ari	03 02:09 Gem
04 16:33 Sag	03 04:21 Cap	04 14:34 Aqu	05 01:31 Ari	04 13:05 Tau	05 10:25 Can
06 17:30 Cap	05 04:19 Aqu	06 14:49 Pis	07 04:02 Tau	06 18:17 Gem	07 21:16 Leo
08 16:48 Aqu	07 03:37 Pis	08 15:16 Ari	09 09:01 Gem	09 02:16 Can	10 10:01 Vir
10 16:37 Pis	09 04:17 Ari	10 17:43 Tau	11 17:32 Can	11 13:21 Leo	12 22:27 Lib
12 18:47 Ari	11 07:58 Tau	12 23:36 Gem	14 05:15 Leo	14 02:10 Vir	15 08:01 Sco
15 00:20 Tau	13 15:28 Gem	15 09:17 Can	16 18:06 Vir	16 14:01 Lib	17 13:39 Sag
17 09:06 Gem	16 02:16 Can	17 21:39 Leo	19 05:34 Lib	18 22:49 Sco	19 16:05 Cap
19 20:13 Can	18 14:52 Leo	20 10:29 Vir	21 14:15 Sco	21 04:11 Sag	21 17:01 Aqu
22 08:39 Leo	21 03:41 Vir	22 21:56 Lib	23 20:14 Sag	23 07:13 Cap	23 18:11 Pis
24 21:32 Vir	23 15:29 Lib	25 07:09 Sco	26 00:26 Cap	25 09:25 Aqu	25 20:51 Ari
27 09:41 Lib	26 01:23 Sco	27 14:06 Sag	28 03:43 Aqu	27 11:58 Pis	28 01:34 Tau
29 19:33 Sco	28 08:37 Sag	29 19:00 Cap	30 06:37 Pis	29 15:26 Ari	30 08:23 Gem
		31 22:08 Aqu		31 20:03 Tau	

Jul 1970	Aug 1970	Sep 1970	Oct 1970	Nov 1970	Dec 1970
02 17:20 Can	01 10:43 Leo	02 18:25 Lib	02 11:35 Sco	01 02:24 Sag	02 18:44 Aqu
05 04:25 Leo	03 23:34 Vir	05 05:54 Sco	04 20:31 Sag	03 08:32 Cap	04 21:55 Pis
07 17:10 Vir	06 12:32 Lib	07 14:57 Sag	07 03:10 Cap	05 13:10 Aqu	07 01:03 Ari
10 06:02 Lib	08 23:56 Sco	09 20:51 Cap	09 07:25 Aqu	07 16:32 Pis	09 04:24 Tau
12 16:40 Sco	11 08:06 Sag	11 23:33 Aqu	11 09:30 Pis	09 18:51 Ari	11 08:33 Gem
14 23:25 Sag	13 12:24 Cap	13 23:56 Pis	13 10:12 Ari	11 20:50 Tau	13 14:32 Can
17 02:19 Cap	15 13:31 Aqu	15 23:34 Ari	15 11:00 Tau	16 05:22 Can	15 23:21 Leo
19 02:44 Aqu	17 13:01 Pis	18 00:20 Tau	17 13:43 Gem	18 14:35 Leo	18 11:03 Vir
21 02:36 Pis	19 12:50 Ari	20 04:01 Gem	19 19:58 Can	21 02:49 Vir	21 00:01 Lib
23 03:42 Ari	21 14:45 Tau	22 11:40 Can	22 06:11 Leo	23 15:38 Lib	23 11:26 Sco
25 07:17 Tau	23 20:03 Gem	24 22:54 Leo	24 18:56 Vir	26 02:24 Sco	25 19:27 Sag
27 13:52 Gem	26 04:57 Can	27 11:52 Vir	27 07:36 Lib	28 10:02 Sag	28 00:01 Cap
29 23:13 Can	28 16:37 Leo	30 00:33 Lib	29 18:14 Sco	30 15:05 Cap	30 02:23 Aqu
	31 05:35 Vir				

Jan 1971	Feb 1971	Mar 1971	Apr 1971	May 1971	Jun 1971
01 04:07 Pis	01 15:48 Tau	03 03:01 Gem	01 16:50 Can	01 09:33 Leo	02 17:25 Lib
03 06:26 Ari	03 20:34 Gem	05 09:46 Can	04 02:05 Leo	03 21:02 Vir	05 05:35 Sco
05 10:00 Tau	06 04:06 Can	07 19:54 Leo	06 14:15 Vir	06 09:58 Lib	07 15:27 Sag
07 15:08 Gem	08 14:05 Leo	10 08:10 Vir	09 03:16 Lib	08 22:03 Sco	09 22:44 Cap
09 22:08 Can	11 01:57 Vir	12 21:05 Lib	11 15:27 Sco	11 08:07 Sag	12 04:02 Aqu
12 07:23 Leo	13 14:49 Lib	15 09:30 Sco	14 02:02 Sag	13 16:08 Cap	14 08:01 Pis
14 18:57 Vir	16 03:21 Sco	17 20:23 Sag	16 10:37 Cap	15 22:19 Aqu	16 11:05 Ari
17 07:52 Lib	18 13:44 Sag	20 04:37 Cap	18 16:45 Aqu	18 02:39 Pis	18 13:38 Tau
19 20:03 Sco	20 20:36 Cap	22 09:28 Aqu	20 20:07 Pis	20 05:11 Ari	20 16:24 Gem
22 05:15 Sag	22 23:42 Aqu	24 11:07 Pis	22 21:08 Ari	22 06:31 Tau	22 20:30 Can
24 10:32 Cap	25 00:05 Pis	26 10:46 Ari	24 21:06 Tau	24 08:01 Gem	25 03:11 Leo
26 12:36 Aqu	26 23:29 Ari	28 10:16 Tau	26 21:58 Gem	26 11:26 Can	27 13:05 Vir
28 13:02 Pis	28 23:53 Tau	30 11:43 Gem	29 01:43 Can	28 18:15 Leo	30 01:22 Lib
30 13:36 Ari				31 04:47 Vir	

Jul 1971	Aug 1971	Sep 1971	Oct 1971	Nov 1971	Dec 1971
02 13:45 Sco	01 08:49 Sag	02 07:03 Aqu	01 19:36 Pis	02 05:55 Tau	01 16:25 Gem
04 23:58 Sag	03 16:31 Cap	04 08:51 Pis	03 19:41 Ari	04 05:27 Gem	03 17:51 Can
07 07:03 Cap	05 20:46 Aqu	06 08:43 Ari	05 18:42 Tau	06 07:14 Can	05 22:16 Leo
09 11:26 Aqu	07 22:34 Pis	08 08:37 Tau	07 18:53 Gem	08 12:55 Leo	08 06:40 Vir
11 14:14 Pis	09 23:26 Ari	10 10:24 Gem	09 22:10 Can	10 22:43 Vir	10 18:18 Lib
13 16:32 Ari	12 00:55 Tau	12 15:20 Can	12 05:29 Leo	13 11:04 Lib	13 07:01 Sco
15 19:10 Tau	14 04:10 Gem	14 23:37 Leo	14 16:15 Vir	15 23:49 Sco	15 18:37 Sag
17 22:46 Gem	16 09:49 Can	17 10:28 Vir	17 04:47 Lib	18 11:29 Sag	18 04:07 Cap
20 03:56 Can	18 17:57 Leo	19 22:46 Lib	19 17:30 Sco	20 21:36 Cap	20 11:32 Aqu
22 11:16 Leo	21 04:18 Vir	22 11:32 Sco	22 05:31 Sag	23 05:51 Aqu	22 17:09 Pis
24 21:09 Vir	23 16:22 Lib	24 23:43 Sag	24 16:04 Cap	25 11:47 Pis	24 21:09 Ari
27 09:11 Lib	26 05:08 Sco	27 09:52 Cap	27 00:11 Aqu	27 15:03 Ari	26 23:45 Tau
29 21:49 Sco	28 16:55 Sag	29 16:38 Aqu	29 04:56 Pis	29 16:08 Tau	29 01:38 Gem
	31 01:54 Cap		31 06:26 Ari		31 04:01 Can

Jan 1972	Feb 1972	Mar 1972	Apr 1972	May 1972	Jun 1972
02 08:21 Leo	01 00:55 Vir	01 18:59 Lib	03 02:26 Sag	02 20:28 Cap	01 12:14 Aqu
04 15:49 Vir	03 11:06 Lib	04 06:59 Sco	05 14:19 Cap	05 06:34 Aqu	03 19:51 Pis
07 02:32 Lib	05 23:17 Sco	06 19:36 Sag	07 23:37 Aqu	07 13:27 Pis	06 00:27 Ari
09 15:02 Sco	08 11:37 Sag	09 06:49 Cap	10 04:57 Pis	09 16:35 Ari	08 02:14 Tau
12 02:57 Sag	10 21:49 Cap	11 14:42 Aqu	12 06:32 Ari	11 16:48 Tau	10 02:24 Gem
14 12:25 Cap	13 04:36 Aqu	13 18:39 Pis	14 05:55 Tau	13 15:58 Gem	12 02:44 Can
16 19:03 Aqu	15 08:11 Pis	15 19:37 Ari	16 05:16 Gem	15 16:16 Can	14 05:09 Leo
18 23:27 Pis	17 09:51 Ari	17 19:28 Tau	18 06:45 Can	17 19:37 Leo	16 11:02 Vir
21 02:35 Ari	19 11:11 Tau	19 20:12 Gem	20 11:46 Leo	20 02:55 Vir	18 20:38 Lib
23 05:17 Tau	21 13:35 Gem	21 23:26 Can	22 20:23 Vir	22 13:35 Lib	21 08:42 Sco
25 08:13 Gem	23 17:51 Can	24 05:45 Leo	25 07:34 Lib	25 02:00 Sco	23 21:14 Sag
27 12:01 Can	26 00:14 Leo	26 14:47 Vir	27 19:55 Sco	27 14:32 Sag	26 08:36 Cap
29 17:21 Leo	28 08:39 Vir	29 01:41 Lib	30 08:30 Sag	30 02:12 Cap	28 18:02 Aqu
		31 13:48 Sco			

Jul 1972	Aug 1972	Sep 1972	Oct 1972	Nov 1972	Dec 1972
01 01:18 Pis	01 14:57 Tau	02 02:11 Can	01 12:24 Leo	02 10:26 Lib	02 03:42 Sco
03 06:21 Ari	03 17:33 Gem	04 06:53 Leo	03 19:30 Vir	04 21:46 Sco	04 16:22 Sag
05 09:24 Tau	05 20:17 Can	06 13:15 Vir	06 04:34 Lib	07 10:16 Sag	07 05:06 Cap
07 11:05 Gem	07 23:55 Leo	08 21:36 Lib	08 15:26 Sco	09 23:10 Cap	09 16:53 Aqu
09 12:29 Can	10 05:22 Vir	11 08:15 Sco	11 03:52 Sag	12 11:01 Aqu	12 02:32 Pis
11 15:05 Leo	12 13:27 Lib	13 20:41 Sag	13 16:43 Cap	14 19:55 Pis	14 08:59 Ari
13 20:15 Vir	15 00:19 Sco	16 09:06 Cap	16 03:50 Aqu	17 00:43 Ari	16 11:59 Tau
16 04:48 Lib	17 12:48 Sag	18 19:04 Aqu	18 11:12 Pis	19 01:52 Tau	18 12:25 Gem
18 16:14 Sco	20 00:37 Cap	21 01:09 Pis	20 14:22 Ari	21 01:04 Gem	20 11:57 Can
21 04:45 Sag	22 09:42 Aqu	23 03:44 Ari	22 14:38 Tau	23 00:30 Can	22 12:34 Leo
23 16:09 Cap	24 15:28 Pis	25 04:27 Tau	24 14:02 Gem	25 02:11 Leo	24 16:02 Vir
26 01:06 Aqu	26 18:40 Ari	27 05:14 Gem	26 14:44 Can	27 07:23 Vir	26 23:21 Lib
28 07:28 Pis	28 20:43 Tau	29 07:38 Can	28 18:14 Leo	29 16:14 Lib	29 10:09 Sco
30 11:50 Ari	30 22:55 Gem		31 00:59 Vir		31 22:51 Sag

Jan 1973	Feb 1973	Mar 1973	Apr 1973	May 1973	Jun 1973
03 11:29 Cap	02 05:55 Aqu	01 14:21 Aqu	02 12:48 Ari	02 01:01 Tau	02 11:21 Can
05 22:46 Aqu	04 14:22 Pis	03 22:30 Pis	04 14:58 Tau	04 01:15 Gem	04 11:49 Leo
08 08:02 Pis	06 20:28 Ari	06 03:37 Ari	06 16:12 Gem	06 01:34 Can	06 14:51 Vir
10 14:57 Ari	09 00:53 Tau	08 06:50 Tau	08 18:04 Can	08 03:36 Leo	08 21:15 Lib
12 19:24 Tau	11 04:09 Gem	10 09:30 Gem	10 21:31 Leo	10 08:12 Vir	11 06:51 Sco
14 21:40 Gem	13 06:44 Can	12 12:28 Can	13 02:46 Vir	12 15:30 Lib	13 18:42 Sag
16 22:38 Can	15 09:12 Leo	14 16:07 Leo	15 09:49 Lib	15 01:09 Sco	16 07:36 Cap
18 23:40 Leo	17 12:31 Vir	16 20:42 Vir	17 18:50 Sco	17 12:41 Sag	18 20:18 Aqu
21 02:23 Vir	19 17:58 Lib	19 02:47 Lib	20 06:01 Sag	20 01:29 Cap	21 07:28 Pis
23 08:15 Lib	22 02:34 Sco	21 11:15 Sco	22 18:48 Cap	22 14:16 Aqu	23 15:47 Ari
25 17:51 Sco	24 14:13 Sag	23 22:25 Sag	25 07:20 Aqu	25 01:05 Pis	25 20:37 Tau
28 06:09 Sag	27 03:03 Cap	26 11:14 Cap	27 17:09 Pis	27 08:14 Ari	27 22:17 Gem
30 18:53 Cap		28 23:12 Aqu	29 22:53 Ari	29 11:28 Tau	29 22:08 Can
		31 07:54 Pis		31 11:53 Gem	

Jul 1973	Aug 1973	Sep 1973	Oct 1973	Nov 1973	Dec 1973
01 21:55 Leo	02 13:12 Lib	01 05:17 Sco	03 12:01 Cap	02 08:57 Aqu	02 04:31 Pis
03 23:30 Vir	04 20:35 Sco	03 15:23 Sag	06 00:48 Aqu	04 20:25 Pis	04 13:49 Ari
06 04:23 Lib	07 07:36 Sag	06 04:00 Cap	08 11:22 Pis	07 04:19 Ari	06 19:08 Tau
08 13:04 Sco	09 20:29 Cap	08 16:29 Aqu	10 18:28 Ari	09 08:25 Tau	08 20:58 Gem
11 00:47 Sag	12 08:51 Aqu	11 02:40 Pis	12 22:35 Tau	11 10:00 Gem	10 20:52 Can
13 13:44 Cap	14 19:13 Pis	13 09:56 Ari	15 01:08 Gem	13 10:46 Can	12 20:44 Leo
16 02:14 Aqu	17 03:15 Ari	15 14:59 Tau	17 03:28 Can	15 12:19 Leo	14 22:20 Vir
18 13:07 Pis	19 09:13 Tau	17 18:47 Gem	19 06:24 Leo	17 15:40 Vir	17 02:53 Lib
20 21:43 Ari	21 13:26 Gem	19 22:00 Can	21 10:18 Vir	19 21:15 Lib	19 10:43 Sco
23 03:40 Tau	23 16:07 Can	22 00:56 Leo	23 15:28 Lib	22 05:06 Sco	21 21:19 Sag
25 06:58 Gem	25 17:49 Leo	24 03:58 Vir	25 22:27 Sco	24 15:10 Sag	24 09:40 Cap
27 08:10 Can	27 19:33 Vir	26 08:00 Lib	28 07:57 Sag	27 03:12 Cap	26 22:42 Aqu
29 08:29 Leo	29 22:52 Lib	28 14:17 Sco	30 19:56 Cap	29 16:16 Aqu	29 11:09 Pis
31 09:34 Vir		30 23:47 Sag			31 21:33 Ari

Jan 1974	Feb 1974	Mar 1974	Apr 1974	May 1974	Jun 1974
03 04:37 Tau	01 16:53 Gem	03 02:59 Can	01 11:40 Leo	02 23:38 Lib	01 11:10 Sco
05 07:59 Gem	03 19:05 Can	05 04:48 Leo	03 13:56 Vir	05 04:43 Sco	03 19:21 Sag
07 08:28 Can	05 19:12 Leo	07 05:33 Vir	05 16:23 Lib	07 12:05 Sag	06 05:48 Cap
09 07:42 Leo	07 18:52 Vir	09 06:52 Lib	07 20:24 Sco	09 22:14 Cap	08 18:01 Aqu
11 07:41 Vir	09 20:10 Lib	11 10:39 Sco	10 03:26 Sag	12 10:33 Aqu	11 06:42 Pis
13 10:21 Lib	12 00:57 Sco	13 18:19 Sag	12 13:55 Cap	14 23:02 Pis	13 17:51 Ari
15 16:53 Sco	14 10:00 Sag	16 05:40 Cap	15 02:33 Aqu	17 09:19 Ari	16 01:46 Tau
18 03:11 Sag	16 22:15 Cap	18 18:37 Aqu	17 14:43 Pis	19 16:10 Tau	18 05:58 Gem
20 15:46 Cap	19 11:20 Aqu	21 06:33 Pis	20 00:20 Ari	21 19:54 Gem	20 07:21 Can
23 04:49 Aqu	21 23:15 Pis	23 16:02 Ari	22 06:53 Tau	23 21:45 Can	22 07:30 Leo
25 17:00 Pis	24 09:12 Ari	25 23:09 Tau	24 11:11 Gem	25 23:11 Leo	24 08:11 Vir
28 03:31 Ari	26 17:11 Tau	28 04:32 Gem	26 14:17 Can	28 01:25 Vir	26 10:57 Lib
30 11:41 Tau	28 23:10 Gem	30 08:39 Can	28 17:03 Leo	30 05:15 Lib	28 16:39 Sco
			30 20:00 Vir		

Jul 1974	Aug 1974	Sep 1974	Oct 1974	Nov 1974	Dec 1974
01 01:20 Sag	02 06:45 Aqu	01 01:28 Pis	03 04:39 Tau	01 18:22 Gem	01 06:22 Can
03 12:18 Cap	04 19:26 Pis	03 12:57 Ari	05 12:00 Gem	03 23:00 Can	03 08:31 Leo
06 00:41 Aqu	07 07:14 Ari	05 22:50 Tau	07 17:29 Can	06 02:29 Leo	05 10:40 Vir
08 13:25 Pis	09 17:12 Tau	08 06:35 Gem	09 21:02 Leo	08 05:18 Vir	07 13:42 Lib
11 01:10 Ari	12 00:14 Gem	10 11:39 Can	11 22:55 Vir	10 07:58 Lib	09 18:13 Sco
13 10:20 Tau	14 03:48 Can	12 13:54 Leo	14 00:10 Lib	12 11:23 Sco	12 00:34 Sag
15 15:53 Gem	16 04:26 Leo	14 14:12 Vir	16 02:23 Sco	14 16:38 Sag	14 09:03 Cap
17 17:56 Can	18 03:42 Vir	16 14:17 Lib	18 07:14 Sag	17 00:41 Cap	16 19:47 Aqu
19 17:43 Leo	20 03:44 Lib	18 16:14 Sco	20 15:43 Cap	19 11:38 Aqu	19 08:11 Pis
21 17:10 Vir	22 06:36 Sco	20 21:46 Sag	23 03:19 Aqu	22 00:11 Pis	21 20:34 Ari
23 18:19 Lib	24 13:33 Sag	23 07:21 Cap	25 15:56 Pis	24 11:58 Ari	24 06:44 Tau
25 22:45 Sco	27 00:14 Cap	25 19:37 Aqu	28 03:13 Ari	26 21:04 Tau	26 13:15 Gem
28 06:59 Sag	29 12:52 Aqu	28 08:14 Pis	30 11:59 Tau	29 02:57 Gem	28 16:15 Can
30 18:10 Cap		30 19:25 Ari			30 17:05 Leo

Jan 1975	Feb 1975	Mar 1975	Apr 1975	May 1975	Jun 1975
01 17:33 Vir	02 05:52 Sco	01 14:33 Sco	02 11:07 Cap	02 05:33 Aqu	01 01:31 Pis
03 19:21 Lib	04 12:09 Sag	03 19:05 Sag	04 21:44 Aqu	04 17:33 Pis	03 14:00 Ari
05 23:38 Sco	06 21:41 Cap	06 03:39 Cap	07 10:16 Pis	07 06:02 Ari	06 01:18 Tau
08 06:38 Sag	09 09:16 Aqu	08 15:09 Aqu	09 22:43 Ari	09 17:03 Tau	08 09:49 Gem
10 15:57 Cap	11 21:45 Pis	11 03:48 Pis	12 09:53 Tau	12 01:44 Gem	10 15:21 Can
13 03:02 Aqu	14 10:21 Ari	13 16:18 Ari	14 19:14 Gem	14 08:07 Can	12 18:45 Leo
15 15:22 Pis	16 22:08 Tau	16 03:52 Tau	17 02:26 Can	16 12:38 Leo	14 21:10 Vir
18 04:03 Ari	19 07:34 Gem	18 13:42 Gem	19 07:14 Leo	18 15:45 Vir	16 23:40 Lib
20 15:20 Tau	21 13:18 Can	20 20:48 Can	21 09:42 Vir	20 18:05 Lib	19 02:58 Sco
22 23:22 Gem	23 15:13 Leo	23 00:31 Leo	23 10:42 Lib	22 20:25 Sco	21 07:34 Sag
25 03:20 Can	25 14:38 Vir	25 01:20 Vir	25 11:40 Sco	24 23:51 Sag	23 13:55 Cap
27 04:00 Leo	27 13:39 Lib	27 00:51 Lib	27 14:19 Sag	27 05:30 Cap	25 22:32 Aqu
29 03:13 Vir		29 01:07 Sco	29 20:08 Cap	29 14:08 Aqu	28 09:32 Pis
31 03:13 Lib		31 04:09 Sag			30 22:01 Ari

Jul 1975	Aug 1975	Sep 1975	Oct 1975	Nov 1975	Dec 1975
03 09:53 Tau	02 04:01 Gem	02 23:07 Leo	02 10:03 Vir	02 20:08 Sco	02 07:33 Sag
05 18:58 Gem	04 10:16 Can	04 23:29 Vir	04 09:39 Lib	04 21:10 Sag	04 10:58 Cap
08 00:23 Can	06 12:44 Leo	06 22:37 Lib	06 09:09 Sco	07 00:45 Cap	06 17:11 Aqu
10 02:50 Leo	08 12:54 Vir	08 22:45 Sco	08 10:35 Sag	09 07:58 Aqu	09 02:51 Pis
12 03:55 Vir	10 12:51 Lib	11 01:40 Sag	10 15:28 Cap	11 18:41 Pis	11 15:05 Ari
14 05:21 Lib	12 14:30 Sco	13 08:10 Cap	13 00:09 Aqu	14 07:16 Ari	14 03:38 Tau
16 08:22 Sco	14 18:59 Sag	15 17:50 Aqu	15 11:39 Pis	16 19:37 Tau	16 14:11 Gem
18 13:31 Sag	17 02:24 Cap	18 05:31 Pis	18 00:20 Ari	19 06:13 Gem	18 21:48 Can
20 20:45 Cap	19 12:08 Aqu	20 18:06 Ari	20 12:42 Tau	21 14:36 Can	21 02:53 Leo
23 05:55 Aqu	21 23:32 Pis	23 06:42 Tau	22 23:51 Gem	23 20:47 Leo	23 06:27 Vir
25 16:58 Pis	24 12:02 Ari	25 18:12 Gem	25 08:56 Can	26 01:04 Vir	25 09:27 Lib
28 05:26 Ari	27 00:44 Tau	28 03:06 Can	27 15:19 Leo	28 03:47 Lib	27 12:27 Sco
30 17:52 Tau	29 11:52 Gem	30 08:20 Leo	29 18:46 Vir	30 05:36 Sco	29 15:52 Sag
	31 19:34 Can		31 19:55 Lib		31 20:16 Cap

Jan 1976	Feb 1976	Mar 1976	Apr 1976	May 1976	Jun 1976
03 02:32 Aqu	01 19:46 Pis	02 14:21 Ari	01 09:33 Tau	01 04:04 Gem	02 04:37 Leo
05 11:34 Pis	04 07:16 Ari	05 03:17 Tau	03 22:15 Gem	03 14:52 Can	04 10:20 Vir
07 23:20 Ari	06 20:12 Tau	07 15:55 Gem	06 09:05 Can	05 23:09 Leo	06 13:59 Lib
10 12:08 Tau	09 08:15 Gem	10 01:58 Can	08 16:36 Leo	08 04:20 Vir	08 15:58 Sco
12 23:19 Gem	11 16:58 Can	12 07:55 Leo	10 20:15 Vir	10 06:39 Lib	10 17:07 Sag
15 07:00 Can	13 21:32 Leo	14 09:59 Vir	12 20:54 Lib	12 07:03 Sco	12 18:45 Cap
17 11:15 Leo	15 22:58 Vir	16 09:45 Lib	14 20:14 Sco	14 07:04 Sag	14 22:31 Aqu
19 13:25 Vir	17 23:13 Lib	18 09:18 Sco	16 20:15 Sag	16 08:31 Cap	17 05:43 Pis
21 15:10 Lib	20 00:13 Sco	20 10:33 Sag	18 22:43 Cap	18 13:02 Aqu	19 16:31 Ari
23 17:47 Sco	22 03:18 Sag	22 14:47 Cap	21 04:47 Aqu	20 21:26 Pis	22 05:21 Tau
25 21:51 Sag	24 08:53 Cap	24 22:19 Aqu	23 14:27 Pis	23 09:06 Ari	24 17:36 Gem
28 03:23 Cap	26 16:48 Aqu	27 08:33 Pis	26 02:36 Ari	25 22:06 Tau	27 03:28 Can
30 10:33 Aqu	29 02:41 Pis	29 20:36 Ari	28 15:37 Tau	28 10:21 Gem	29 10:39 Leo
				30 20:38 Can	

Jul 1976	Aug 1976	Sep 1976	Oct 1976	Nov 1976	Dec 1976
01 15:46 Vir	02 03:55 Sco	02 16:28 Cap	02 03:49 Aqu	03 04:45 Ari	02 23:41 Tau
03 19:34 Lib	04 07:03 Sag	04 22:19 Aqu	04 12:09 Pis	05 17:22 Tau	05 12:37 Gem
05 22:33 Sco	06 10:54 Cap	07 06:11 Pis	06 22:49 Ari	08 06:20 Gem	08 00:20 Can
08 01:05 Sag	08 15:57 Aqu	09 16:17 Ari	09 11:10 Tau	10 18:27 Can	10 10:11 Leo
10 03:49 Cap	10 23:00 Pis	12 04:29 Tau	12 00:14 Gem	13 04:35 Leo	12 17:54 Vir
12 07:53 Aqu	13 08:48 Ari	14 17:31 Gem	14 12:23 Can	15 11:45 Vir	14 23:13 Lib
14 14:35 Pis	15 21:04 Tau	17 05:06 Can	16 21:49 Leo	17 15:33 Lib	17 02:01 Sco
17 00:39 Ari	18 09:53 Gem	19 13:10 Leo	19 03:24 Vir	19 16:32 Sco	19 02:54 Sag
19 13:10 Tau	20 20:33 Can	21 17:16 Vir	21 05:26 Lib	21 16:04 Sag	21 03:11 Cap
22 01:40 Gem	23 03:30 Leo	23 18:28 Lib	23 05:17 Sco	23 16:04 Cap	23 04:48 Aqu
24 11:39 Can	25 07:03 Vir	25 18:34 Sco	25 04:48 Sag	25 18:29 Aqu	25 09:35 Pis
26 18:18 Leo	27 08:42 Lib	27 19:21 Sag	27 05:55 Cap	28 00:47 Pis	27 18:31 Ari
28 22:23 Vir	29 10:05 Sco	29 22:13 Cap	29 10:05 Aqu	30 11:00 Ari	30 06:42 Tau
31 01:13 Lib	31 12:28 Sag		31 17:52 Pis		

Jan 1977	Feb 1977	Mar 1977	Apr 1977	May 1977	Jun 1977
01 19:42 Gem	03 00:11 Leo	02 09:24 Leo	01 01:24 Vir	02 16:24 Sco	01 02:54 Sag
04 07:12 Can	05 06:17 Vir	04 15:18 Vir	03 04:39 Lib	04 15:59 Sag	03 02:07 Cap
06 16:20 Leo	07 10:36 Lib	06 18:34 Lib	05 05:40 Sco	06 15:54 Cap	05 02:43 Aqu
08 23:23 Vir	09 14:04 Sco	08 20:37 Sco	07 06:08 Sag	08 17:59 Aqu	07 06:35 Pis
11 04:47 Lib	11 17:11 Sag	10 22:41 Sag	09 07:40 Cap	10 23:28 Pis	09 14:33 Ari
13 08:44 Sco	13 20:13 Cap	13 01:39 Cap	11 11:23 Aqu	13 08:29 Ari	12 01:56 Tau
15 11:18 Sag	15 23:44 Aqu	15 05:59 Aqu	13 17:49 Pis	15 20:03 Tau	14 14:49 Gem
17 13:02 Cap	18 04:44 Pis	17 12:05 Pis	16 02:51 Ari	18 08:50 Gem	17 03:28 Can
19 15:12 Aqu	20 12:22 Ari	19 20:22 Ari	18 14:02 Tau	20 21:35 Can	19 14:53 Leo
21 19:30 Pis	22 23:05 Tau	22 07:05 Tau	21 02:37 Gem	23 09:12 Leo	22 00:28 Vir
24 03:19 Ari	25 11:49 Gem	24 19:38 Gem	23 15:24 Can	25 18:30 Vir	24 07:35 Lib
26 14:40 Tau	28 00:02 Can	27 08:15 Can	26 02:42 Leo	28 00:28 Lib	26 11:41 Sco
29 03:36 Gem		29 18:39 Leo	28 10:51 Vir	30 02:56 Sco	28 13:02 Sag
31 15:19 Can			30 15:12 Lib		30 12:49 Cap

Jul 1977	Aug 1977	Sep 1977	Oct 1977	Nov 1977	Dec 1977
02 12:56 Aqu	01 01:23 Pis	02 00:51 Tau	01 20:33 Gem	03 05:02 Leo	02 23:05 Vir
04 15:31 Pis	03 06:54 Ari	04 12:26 Gem	04 09:08 Can	05 15:16 Vir	05 07:17 Lib
06 22:02 Ari	05 16:17 Tau	07 01:02 Can	06 20:57 Leo	07 21:50 Lib	07 11:33 Sco
09 08:32 Tau	08 04:29 Gem	09 12:13 Leo	09 05:58 Vir	10 00:41 Sco	09 12:22 Sag
11 21:14 Gem	10 17:03 Can	11 20:34 Vir	11 11:29 Lib	12 01:03 Sag	11 11:26 Cap
14 09:49 Can	13 03:56 Leo	14 02:07 Lib	13 14:11 Sco	14 00:50 Cap	13 11:00 Aqu
16 20:51 Leo	15 12:25 Vir	16 05:45 Sco	15 15:27 Sag	16 01:59 Aqu	15 13:09 Pis
19 05:58 Vir	17 18:48 Lib	18 08:28 Sag	17 16:51 Cap	18 05:58 Pis	17 19:10 Ari
21 13:09 Lib	19 23:35 Sco	20 11:04 Cap	19 19:35 Aqu	20 13:12 Ari	20 04:53 Tau
23 18:13 Sco	22 03:02 Sag	22 14:12 Aqu	22 00:26 Pis	22 23:09 Tau	22 16:50 Gem
25 21:04 Sag	24 05:30 Cap	24 18:29 Pis	24 07:33 Ari	25 10:48 Gem	25 05:29 Can
27 22:14 Cap	26 07:41 Aqu	27 00:40 Ari	26 16:52 Tau	27 23:19 Can	27 17:51 Leo
29 23:04 Aqu	28 10:46 Pis	29 09:21 Tau	29 04:07 Gem	30 11:52 Leo	30 05:13 Vir
	30 16:11 Ari		31 16:39 Can		

Jan 1978	Feb 1978	Mar 1978	Apr 1978	May 1978	Jun 1978
01 14:30 Lib	02 07:13 Sag	01 13:01 Sag	02 00:04 Aqu	01 08:59 Pis	02 03:49 Tau
03 20:34 Sco	04 08:50 Cap	03 15:58 Cap	04 03:20 Pis	03 14:26 Ari	04 13:53 Gem
05 23:03 Sag	06 09:05 Aqu	05 17:50 Aqu	06 07:50 Ari	05 21:52 Tau	07 01:29 Can
07 22:54 Cap	08 09:48 Pis	07 19:45 Pis	08 14:21 Tau	08 07:18 Gem	09 14:06 Leo
09 22:05 Aqu	10 12:56 Ari	09 23:08 Ari	10 23:27 Gem	10 18:41 Can	12 02:34 Vir
11 22:50 Pis	12 19:50 Tau	12 05:17 Tau	13 10:58 Can	13 07:16 Leo	14 12:54 Lib
14 03:04 Ari	15 06:23 Gem	14 14:47 Gem	15 23:30 Leo	15 19:14 Vir	16 19:28 Sco
16 11:29 Tau	17 18:55 Can	17 02:48 Can	18 10:43 Vir	18 04:24 Lib	18 22:01 Sag
18 23:06 Gem	20 07:09 Leo	19 15:11 Leo	20 18:52 Lib	20 09:38 Sco	20 21:52 Cap
21 11:50 Can	22 17:39 Vir	22 01:49 Vir	22 23:38 Sco	22 11:31 Sag	22 21:07 Aqu
24 00:02 Leo	25 02:03 Lib	24 09:41 Lib	25 02:00 Sag	24 11:42 Cap	24 21:56 Pis
26 10:55 Vir	27 08:27 Sco	26 15:01 Sco	27 03:27 Cap	26 12:10 Aqu	27 01:52 Ari
28 20:07 Lib		28 18:37 Sag	29 05:27 Aqu	28 14:36 Pis	29 09:20 Tau
31 03:03 Sco		30 21:23 Cap		30 19:52 Ari	

Jul 1978	Aug 1978	Sep 1978	Oct 1978	Nov 1978	Dec 1978
01 19:37 Gem	03 02:10 Leo	01 20:46 Vir	01 14:16 Lib	02 10:03 Sag	01 20:44 Cap
04 07:33 Can	05 14:28 Vir	04 07:15 Lib	03 21:47 Sco	04 12:40 Cap	03 21:35 Aqu
06 20:12 Leo	08 01:29 Lib	06 15:37 Sco	06 03:06 Sag	06 15:03 Aqu	05 23:36 Pis
09 08:44 Vir	10 10:10 Sco	08 21:39 Sag	08 06:52 Cap	08 18:05 Pis	08 03:39 Ari
11 19:47 Lib	12 15:42 Sag	11 01:19 Cap	10 09:42 Aqu	10 22:11 Ari	10 09:50 Tau
14 03:46 Sco	14 18:03 Cap	13 03:08 Aqu	12 12:12 Pis	13 03:34 Tau	12 17:54 Gem
16 07:49 Sag	16 18:15 Aqu	15 04:09 Pis	14 15:06 Ari	15 10:44 Gem	15 03:49 Can
18 08:33 Cap	18 18:05 Pis	17 05:50 Ari	16 19:22 Tau	17 20:15 Can	17 15:37 Leo
20 07:42 Aqu	20 19:29 Ari	19 09:42 Tau	19 02:05 Gem	20 08:08 Leo	20 04:33 Vir
22 07:26 Pis	23 00:05 Tau	21 16:55 Gem	21 11:51 Can	22 20:56 Vir	22 16:39 Lib
24 09:45 Ari	25 08:30 Gem	24 03:30 Can	24 00:03 Leo	25 08:06 Lib	25 01:32 Sco
26 15:49 Tau	27 19:58 Can	26 16:00 Leo	26 12:31 Vir	27 15:38 Sco	27 06:07 Sag
29 01:30 Gem	30 08:39 Leo	29 04:10 Vir	28 22:50 Lib	29 19:23 Sag	29 07:16 Cap
31 13:27 Can			31 05:52 Sco		31 06:53 Aqu

Jan 1979	Feb 1979	Mar 1979	Apr 1979	May 1979	Jun 1979
02 07:08 Pis	02 22:02 Tau	02 07:09 Tau	03 06:23 Can	03 01:56 Leo	01 22:40 Vir
04 09:41 Ari	05 05:32 Gem	04 12:57 Gem	05 17:57 Leo	05 14:40 Vir	04 11:10 Lib
06 15:17 Tau	07 16:05 Can	06 22:33 Can	08 06:51 Vir	08 02:47 Lib	06 21:04 Sco
8 23:42 Gem	10 04:25 Leo	09 10:46 Leo	10 18:44 Lib	10 12:09 Sco	09 03:14 Sag
11 10:14 Can	12 17:17 Vir	11 23:42 Vir	13 04:15 Sco	12 18:24 Sag	11 06:23 Cap
13 22:16 Leo	15 05:36 Lib	14 11:41 Lib	15 11:18 Sag	14 22:25 Cap	13 08:06 Aqu
16 11:09 Vir	17 16:11 Sco	16 21:48 Sco	17 16:22 Cap	17 01:25 Aqu	15 09:56 Pis
18 23:40 Lib	19 23:50 Sag	19 05:37 Sag	19 20:02 Aqu	19 04:18 Pis	17 12:52 Ari
21 09:50 Sco	22 04:00 Cap	21 10:56 Cap	21 22:41 Pis	21 07:30 Ari	19 17:18 Tau
23 16:07 Sag	24 05:12 Aqu	23 13:52 Aqu	24 00:51 Ari	23 11:20 Tau	21 23:22 Gem
25 18:27 Cap	26 04:52 Pis	25 15:05 Pis	26 03:27 Tau	25 16:28 Gem	24 07:24 Can
27 18:12 Aqu	28 04:54 Ari	27 15:47 Ari	28 07:48 Gem	27 23:50 Can	26 17:46 Leo
29 17:26 Pis		29 17:36 Tau	30 15:11 Can	30 10:07 Leo	29 06:13 Vir
31 18:11 Ari		31 22:08 Gem			

Jul 1979	Aug 1979	Sep 1979	Oct 1979	Nov 1979	Dec 1979
01 19:07 Lib	02 22:05 Sag	01 11:33 Cap	03 00:23 Pis	01 10:09 Ari	02 23:02 Gem
04 05:56 Sco	05 02:22 Cap	03 13:59 Aqu	05 00:28 Ari	03 11:16 Tau	05 04:01 Can
06 12:55 Sag	07 03:28 Aqu	05 14:03 Pis	07 00:44 Tau	05 13:26 Gem	07 12:08 Leo
08 16:07 Cap	09 03:05 Pis	07 13:29 Ari	09 03:07 Gem	07 18:23 Can	09 23:32 Vir
10 16:59 Aqu	11 03:10 Ari	09 14:12 Tau	11 09:08 Can	10 03:14 Leo	12 12:28 Lib
12 17:23 Pis	13 05:21 Tau	11 17:53 Gem	13 19:11 Leo	12 15:19 Vir	15 00:07 Sco
14 18:57 Ari	15 10:40 Gem	14 01:26 Can	16 07:50 Vir	15 04:16 Lib	17 08:36 Sag
16 22:42 Tau	17 19:16 Can	16 12:24 Leo	18 20:44 Lib	17 15:29 Sco	19 13:54 Cap
19 04:59 Gem	20 06:28 Leo	19 01:15 Vir	21 08:02 Sco	19 23:56 Sag	21 17:12 Aqu
21 13:40 Can	22 19:10 Vir	21 14:10 Lib	23 17:08 Sag	22 06:01 Cap	23 19:50 Ari
24 00:29 Leo	25 08:13 Lib	24 01:53 Sco	26 00:11 Cap	24 10:36 Aqu	25 22:40 Ari
26 13:00 Vir	27 20:12 Sco	26 11:35 Sag	28 05:16 Aqu	26 14:17 Pis	28 02:07 Tau
29 02:05 Lib	30 05:38 Sag	28 18:39 Cap	30 08:28 Pis	28 17:16 Ari	30 06:32 Gem
31 13:45 Sco		30 22:48 Aqu		30 19:54 Tau	

Jan 1980	Feb 1980	Mar 1980	Apr 1980	May 1980	Jun 1980
01 12:29 Can	02 15:20 Vir	03 10:39 Lib	02 05:21 Sco	01 22:21 Sag	02 19:29 Aqu
03 20:47 Leo	05 04:03 Lib	05 23:22 Sco	04 16:34 Sag	04 07:14 Cap	05 00:09 Pis
06 07:47 Vir	07 16:45 Sco	08 10:37 Sag	07 01:42 Cap	06 14:03 Aqu	07 03:23 Ari
08 20:37 Lib	10 03:18 Sag	10 19:01 Cap	09 07:59 Aqu	08 18:33 Pis	09 05:29 Tau
11 08:54 Sco	12 10:11 Cap	12 23:45 Aqu	11 11:06 Pis	10 20:44 Ari	11 07:22 Gem
13 18:16 Sag	14 13:19 Aqu	15 01:10 Pis	13 11:40 Ari	12 21:24 Tau	13 10:29 Can
15 23:51 Cap	16 13:54 Pis	17 00:40 Ari	15 11:11 Tau	14 22:07 Gem	15 16:21 Leo
18 02:24 Aqu	18 13:43 Ari	19 00:12 Tau	17 11:41 Gem	17 00:51 Can	18 01:46 Vir
20 03:33 Pis	20 14:35 Tau	21 01:47 Gem	19 15:11 Can	19 07:13 Leo	20 13:54 Lib
22 04:51 Ari	22 17:58 Gem	23 06:55 Can	21 22:51 Leo	21 17:31 Vir	23 02:26 Sco
24 07:31 Tau	25 00:34 Can	25 15:57 Leo	24 10:11 Vir	24 06:10 Lib	25 13:01 Sag
26 12:10 Gem	27 10:09 Leo	28 03:51 Vir	26 23:09 Lib	26 18:36 Sco	27 20:45 Cap
28 19:02 Can	29 21:52 Vir	30 16:48 Lib	29 11:34 Sco	29 05:04 Sag	30 02:03 Aqu
31 04:08 Leo				31 13:14 Cap	

Jul 1980	Aug 1980	Sep 1980	Oct 1980	Nov 1980	Dec 1980
02 05:48 Pis	02 16:55 Tau	01 01:49 Gem	02 19:56 Leo	01 12:17 Vir	01 07:12 Lib
04 08:46 Ari	04 20:09 Gem	03 06:39 Can	05 06:18 Vir	04 00:31 Lib	03 19:59 Sco
06 11:30 Tau	07 01:12 Can	05 14:21 Leo	07 18:29 Lib	06 13:18 Sco	06 07:57 Sag
08 14:33 Gem	09 08:23 Leo	08 00:30 Vir	10 07:14 Sco	09 01:25 Sag	08 18:11 Cap
10 18:44 Can	11 17:54 Vir	10 12:21 Lib	12 19:37 Sag	11 12:14 Cap	11 02:35 Aqu
13 01:02 Leo	14 05:31 Lib	13 01:05 Sco	15 06:36 Cap	13 21:09 Aqu	13 09:03 Pis
15 10:10 Vir	16 18:14 Sco	15 13:27 Sag	17 14:53 Aqu	16 03:20 Pis	15 13:21 Ari
17 21:54 Lib	19 06:08 Sag	17 23:44 Cap	19 19:31 Pis	18 06:21 Ari	17 15:36 Tau
20 10:32 Sco	21 15:10 Cap	20 06:30 Aqu	21 20:43 Ari	20 06:51 Tau	19 16:40 Gem
22 21:41 Sag	23 20:32 Aqu	22 09:27 Pis	23 19:55 Tau	22 06:27 Gem	21 18:03 Can
25 05:44 Cap	25 22:43 Pis	24 09:38 Ari	25 19:17 Gem	24 07:18 Can	23 21:33 Leo
27 10:34 Aqu	27 23:10 Ari	26 08:53 Tau	27 21:00 Can	26 11:22 Leo	26 04:32 Vir
29 13:11 Pis	29 23:40 Tau	28 09:21 Gem	30 02:38 Leo	28 19:36 Vir	28 15:04 Lib
31 14:53 Ari		30 12:46 Can			31 03:35 Sco

Jan 1981	Feb 1981	Mar 1981	Apr 1981	May 1981	Jun 1981
02 15:41 Sag	01 10:36 Cap	03 03:50 Aqu	01 18:40 Pis	01 06:57 Ari	01 16:49 Gem
05 01:41 Cap	03 17:55 Aqu	05 08:12 Pis	03 20:25 Ari	03 06:59 Tau	03 16:39 Can
07 09:12 Aqu	05 22:21 Pis	07 09:48 Ari	05 20:04 Tau	05 06:01 Gem	05 18:42 Leo
09 14:42 Pis	08 01:01 Ari	09 10:23 Tau	07 19:47 Gem	07 06:17 Can	08 00:25 Vir
11 18:43 Ari	10 03:10 Tau	11 11:42 Gem	09 21:33 Can	09 09:39 Leo	10 09:54 Lib
13 21:44 Tau	12 05:50 Gem	13 15:05 Can	12 02:36 Leo	11 16:54 Vir	12 21:54 Sco
16 00:17 Gem	14 09:42 Can	15 21:02 Leo	14 10:55 Vir	14 03:23 Lib	15 10:31 Sag
18 03:07 Can	16 15:10 Leo	18 05:19 Vir	16 21:37 Lib	16 15:37 Sco	17 22:20 Cap
20 07:20 Leo	18 22:33 Vir	20 15:30 Lib	19 09:38 Sco	19 04:13 Sag	20 08:35 Aqu
22 14:02 Vir	21 08:11 Lib	23 03:13 Sco	21 22:14 Sag	21 16:19 Cap	22 16:43 Pis
24 23:45 Lib	23 19:54 Sco	25 15:50 Sag	24 10:30 Cap	24 03:00 Aqu	24 22:18 Ari
27 11:47 Sco	26 08:28 Sag	28 03:51 Cap	26 20:56 Aqu	26 11:04 Pis	27 01:16 Tau
30 00:11 Sag	28 19:45 Cap	30 13:14 Aqu	29 03:56 Pis	28 15:43 Ari	29 02:21 Gem
				30 17:10 Tau	

Jul 1981	Aug 1981	Sep 1981	Oct 1981	Nov 1981	Dec 1981
01 02:57 Can	01 18:54 Vir	02 21:09 Sco	02 16:59 Sag	01 12:45 Cap	01 07:08 Aqu
03 04:47 Leo	04 02:23 Lib	05 09:23 Sag	05 05:48 Cap	04 00:50 Aqu	03 17:15 Pis
05 09:25 Vir	06 12:57 Sco	07 21:48 Cap	07 17:00 Aqu	06 09:51 Pis	05 23:48 Ari
07 17:41 Lib	09 01:22 Sag	10 07:58 Aqu	10 00:32 Pis	08 14:38 Ari	08 02:31 Tau
10 05:01 Sco	11 13:19 Cap	12 14:33 Pis	12 04:01 Ari	10 15:45 Tau	10 02:30 Gem
12 17:34 Sag	13 22:56 Aqu	14 17:55 Ari	14 04:43 Tau	12 15:00 Gem	12 01:40 Can
15 05:19 Cap	16 05:34 Pis	16 19:30 Tau	16 04:41 Gem	14 14:37 Can	14 02:08 Leo
17 15:01 Aqu	18 09:49 Ari	18 20:59 Gem	18 05:52 Can	16 16:32 Leo	16 05:37 Vir
19 22:25 Pis	20 12:43 Tau	20 23:39 Can	20 09:34 Leo	18 21:52 Vir	18 12:57 Lib
22 03:43 Ari	22 15:18 Gem	23 04:08 Leo	22 16:04 Vir	21 06:32 Lib	20 23:38 Sco
24 07:18 Tau	24 18:16 Can	25 10:28 Vir	25 00:56 Lib	23 17:36 Sco	23 12:10 Sag
26 09:41 Gem	26 22:09 Leo	27 18:40 Lib	27 11:37 Sco	26 06:00 Sag	26 00:59 Cap
28 11:41 Can	29 03:31 Vir	30 04:52 Sco	29 23:48 Sag	28 18:52 Cap	28 12:53 Aqu
30 14:20 Leo	31 11:02 Lib				30 23:00 Pis

Jan 1982	Feb 1982	Mar 1982	Apr 1982	May 1982	Jun 1982
02 06:32 Ari	02 20:20 Gem	02 01:49 Gem	02 13:36 Leo	01 23:44 Vir	02 21:11 Sco
04 11:02 Tau	04 22:17 Can	04 04:48 Can	04 18:18 Vir	04 06:32 Lib	05 08:30 Sag
06 12:49 Gem	06 23:49 Leo	06 07:50 Leo	07 00:26 Lib	06 15:23 Sco	07 21:11 Cap
08 13:01 Can	09 02:15 Vir	08 11:27 Vir	09 08:32 Sco	09 02:16 Sag	10 10:07 Aqu
10 13:21 Leo	11 07:01 Lib	10 16:33 Lib	11 19:06 Sag	11 14:49 Cap	12 21:43 Pis
12 15:37 Vir	13 15:15 Sco	13 00:16 Sco	14 07:40 Cap	14 03:43 Aqu	15 06:19 Ari
14 21:16 Lib	16 02:44 Sag	15 11:02 Sag	16 20:17 Aqu	16 14:45 Pis	17 11:06 Tau
17 06:45 Sco	18 15:35 Cap	17 23:46 Cap	19 06:19 Pis	18 22:03 Ari	19 12:34 Gem
19 18:59 Sag	21 03:14 Aqu	20 11:52 Aqu	21 12:22 Ari	21 01:21 Tau	21 12:13 Can
22 07:50 Cap	23 12:08 Pis	22 21:01 Pis	23 14:59 Tau	23 01:54 Gem	23 11:57 Leo
24 19:24 Aqu	25 18:17 Ari	25 02:36 Ari	25 15:48 Gem	25 01:38 Can	25 13:36 Vir
27 04:49 Pis	27 22:31 Tau	27 05:39 Tau	27 16:43 Can	27 02:26 Leo	27 18:29 Lib
29 11:58 Ari		29 07:44 Gem	29 19:09 Leo	29 05:43 Vir	30 03:01 Sco
31 17:03 Tau		31 10:09 Can		31 12:02 Lib	

Jul 1982	Aug 1982	Sep 1982	Oct 1982	Nov 1982	Dec 1982
02 14:24 Sag	01 09:35 Cap	02 16:10 Pis	02 08:05 Ari	03 00:22 Gem	02 10:58 Can
05 03:14 Cap	03 22:16 Aqu	05 00:23 Ari	04 13:09 Tau	05 01:58 Can	04 11:26 Leo
07 16:02 Aqu	06 09:23 Pis	07 06:26 Tau	06 16:39 Gem	07 04:10 Leo	06 13:32 Vir
10 03:35 Pis	08 18:20 Ari	09 10:57 Gem	08 19:39 Can	09 07:39 Vir	08 18:10 Lib
12 12:48 Ari	11 01:00 Tau	11 14:18 Can	10 22:44 Leo	11 12:45 Lib	11 01:34 Sco
14 18:59 Tau	13 05:21 Gem	13 16:46 Leo	13 02:08 Vir	13 19:42 Sco	13 11:26 Sag
16 22:03 Gem	15 07:40 Can	15 18:57 Vir	15 06:22 Lib	16 04:51 Sag	15 23:15 Cap
18 22:46 Can	17 08:40 Leo	17 22:02 Lib	17 12:20 Sco	18 16:20 Cap	18 12:11 Aqu
20 22:35 Leo	19 09:40 Vir	20 03:32 Sco	19 21:02 Sag	21 05:20 Aqu	21 00:55 Pis
22 23:19 Vir	21 12:22 Lib	22 12:29 Sag	22 08:37 Cap	23 17:41 Pis	23 11:33 Ari
25 02:44 Lib	23 18:20 Sco	25 00:31 Cap	24 21:35 Aqu	26 03:06 Ari	25 18:36 Tau
27 09:57 Sco	26 04:10 Sag	27 13:20 Aqu	27 09:11 Pis	28 08:31 Tau	27 21:48 Gem
29 20:47 Sag	28 16:40 Cap	30 00:18 Pis	29 17:24 Ari	30 10:36 Gem	29 22:12 Can
	31 05:23 Aqu		31 22:03 Tau		31 21:33 Leo

Jan 1983	Feb 1983	Mar 1983	Apr 1983	May 1983	Jun 1983
02 21:49 Vir	01 09:47 Lib	02 23:50 Sco	01 16:19 Sag	01 11:00 Cap	02 19:41 Pis
05 00:44 Lib	03 14:31 Sco	05 07:14 Sag	04 02:29 Cap	03 23:08 Aqu	05 06:58 Ari
07 07:15 Sco	05 23:28 Sag	07 18:28 Cap	06 15:05 Aqu	06 11:42 Pis	07 15:04 Tau
09 17:13 Sag	08 11:32 Cap	10 07:29 Aqu	09 03:30 Pis	08 22:16 Ari	09 19:37 Gem
12 05:25 Cap	11 00:40 Aqu	12 19:46 Pis	11 13:36 Ari	11 05:35 Tau	11 21:32 Can
14 18:26 Aqu	13 13:01 Pis	15 06:00 Ari	13 20:58 Tau	13 10:03 Gem	13 22:21 Leo
17 07:02 Pis	15 23:45 Ari	17 14:04 Tau	16 02:14 Gem	15 12:48 Can	15 23:37 Vir
19 18:07 Ari	18 08:30 Tau	19 20:19 Gem	18 06:13 Can	17 15:01 Leo	18 02:36 Lib
22 02:35 Tau	20 14:51 Gem	22 00:52 Can	20 09:26 Leo	19 17:36 Vir	20 07:59 Sco
24 07:39 Gem	22 18:31 Can	24 03:43 Leo	22 12:11 Vir	21 21:11 Lib	22 15:54 Sag
26 09:28 Can	24 19:46 Leo	26 05:18 Vir	24 15:04 Lib	24 02:17 Sco	25 02:08 Cap
28 09:10 Leo	26 19:49 Vir	28 06:48 Lib	26 19:04 Sco	26 09:27 Sag	27 14:06 Aqu
30 08:35 Vir	28 20:30 Lib	30 09:56 Sco	29 01:28 Sag	28 19:06 Cap	30 02:51 Pis
				31 06:59 Aqu	

Jul 1983	Aug 1983	Sep 1983	Oct 1983	Nov 1983	Dec 1983
02 14:46 Ari	01 07:36 Tau	02 02:52 Can	01 12:54 Leo	01 23:30 Lib	01 09:40 Sco
05 00:05 Tau	03 14:42 Gem	04 04:47 Leo	03 14:15 Vir	04 01:53 Sco	03 14:56 Sag
07 05:41 Gem	05 18:08 Can	06 04:36 Vir	05 14:42 Lib	06 06:08 Sag	05 22:27 Cap
09 07:50 Can	07 18:37 Leo	08 04:13 Lib	07 16:06 Sco	08 13:30 Cap	08 08:38 Aqu
11 07:54 Leo	09 17:49 Vir	10 05:49 Sco	09 20:20 Sag	11 00:10 Aqu	10 20:52 Pis
13 07:43 Vir	11 17:51 Lib	12 11:07 Sag	12 04:29 Cap	13 12:40 Pis	13 09:16 Ari
15 09:10 Lib	13 20:43 Sco	14 20:33 Cap	14 15:59 Aqu	16 00:36 Ari	15 19:32 Tau
17 13:37 Sco	16 03:33 Sag	17 08:45 Aqu	17 04:40 Pis	18 10:06 Tau	18 02:23 Gem
19 21:31 Sag	18 13:58 Cap	19 21:29 Pis	19 16:18 Ari	20 16:45 Gem	20 06:02 Can
22 08:10 Cap	21 02:25 Aqu	22 09:10 Ari	22 01:47 Tau	22 21:10 Can	22 07:44 Leo
24 20:26 Aqu	23 15:09 Pis	24 19:12 Tau	24 09:10 Gem	25 00:19 Leo	24 09:01 Vir
27 09:10 Pis	26 03:07 Ari	27 03:24 Gem	26 14:46 Can	27 03:01 Vir	26 11:18 Lib
29 21:20 Ari	28 13:37 Tau	29 09:24 Can	28 18:50 Leo	29 05:56 Lib	28 15:26 Sco
	30 21:48 Gem		30 21:32 Vir		30 21:43 Sag

Jan 1984	Feb 1984	Mar 1984	Apr 1984	May 1984	Jun 1984
02 06:07 Cap	03 11:21 Pis	01 17:29 Pis	02 23:55 Tau	02 16:01 Gem	01 05:53 Can
04 16:30 Aqu	06 00:03 Ari	04 06:06 Ari	05 10:04 Gem	04 23:25 Can	03 10:19 Leo
07 04:33 Pis	08 12:04 Tau	06 18:08 Tau	07 17:59 Can	07 04:42 Leo	05 13:27 Vir
09 17:14 Ari	10 21:38 Gem	09 04:29 Gem	09 23:01 Leo	09 08:02 Vir	07 16:03 Sco
12 04:35 Tau	13 03:20 Can	11 11:47 Can	12 01:11 Vir	11 09:54 Lib	09 18:48 Sco
14 12:40 Gem	15 05:09 Leo	13 15:21 Leo	14 01:29 Lib	13 11:22 Sco	11 22:26 Sag
16 16:47 Can	17 04:32 Vir	15 15:47 Vir	16 01:41 Sco	15 13:50 Sag	14 03:48 Cap
18 17:50 Leo	19 03:39 Lib	17 14:52 Lib	18 03:43 Sag	17 18:43 Cap	16 11:40 Aqu
20 17:36 Vir	21 04:44 Sco	19 14:49 Sco	20 09:10 Cap	20 02:55 Aqu	18 22:17 Pis
22 18:07 Lib	23 09:21 Sag	21 17:40 Sag	22 18:26 Aqu	22 14:07 Pis	21 10:39 Ari
24 21:03 Sco	25 17:48 Cap	24 00:35 Cap	25 06:25 Pis	25 02:39 Ari	23 22:37 Tau
27 03:12 Sag	28 05:01 Aqu	26 11:08 Aqu	27 19:02 Ari	27 14:13 Tau	26 08:03 Gem
29 12:12 Cap		28 23:37 Pis	30 06:30 Tau	29 23:22 Gem	28 14:09 Can
31 23:10 Aqu		31 12:13 Ari			30 17:30 Leo

Jul 1984	Aug 1984	Sep 1984	Oct 1984	Nov 1984	Dec 1984
02 19:27 Vir	01 04:03 Lib	01 16:29 Sag	01 05:27 Cap	02 07:49 Pis	02 03:41 Ari
04 21:26 Lib	03 06:03 Sco	03 22:54 Cap	03 14:02 Aqu	04 20:20 Ari	04 16:19 Tau
07 00:28 Sco	05 10:29 Sag	06 08:11 Aqu	06 01:19 Pis	07 08:53 Tau	07 03:23 Gem
09 05:02 Sag	07 17:24 Cap	08 19:24 Pis	08 13:50 Ari	09 20:10 Gem	09 11:56 Can
11 11:22 Cap	10 02:25 Aqu	11 07:46 Ari	11 02:28 Tau	12 05:31 Can	11 18:08 Leo
13 19:41 Aqu	12 13:12 Pis	13 20:32 Tau	13 14:13 Gem	14 12:33 Leo	13 22:35 Vir
16 06:10 Pis	15 01:27 Ari	16 08:25 Gem	16 00:00 Can	16 17:07 Vir	16 01:51 Lib
18 18:25 Ari	17 14:12 Tau	18 17:35 Can	18 06:40 Leo	18 19:29 Lib	18 04:27 Sco
21 06:51 Tau	20 01:31 Gem	20 22:48 Leo	20 09:56 Vir	20 20:30 Sco	20 06:58 Sag
23 17:09 Gem	22 09:19 Can	23 00:19 Vir	22 10:32 Lib	22 21:34 Sag	22 10:20 Cap
25 23:43 Can	24 13:00 Leo	24 23:41 Lib	24 10:08 Sco	25 00:17 Cap	24 15:47 Aqu
28 02:41 Leo	26 13:33 Vir	26 23:04 Sco	26 10:43 Sag	27 06:05 Aqu	27 00:18 Pis
30 03:29 Vir	28 12:57 Lib	29 00:31 Sag	28 14:04 Cap	29 15:32 Pis	29 11:48 Ari
	30 13:23 Sco		30 21:12 Aqu		

Jan 1985	Feb 1985	Mar 1985	Apr 1985	May 1985	Jun 1985
01 00:36 Tau	02 05:58 Can	01 15:22 Can	02 10:25 Vir	01 21:22 Lib	02 07:33 Sag
03 11:59 Gem	04 11:02 Leo	03 21:28 Leo	04 10:54 Lib	03 21:17 Sco	04 08:34 Cap
05 20:17 Can	06 13:09 Vir	05 23:42 Vir	06 10:11 Sco	05 20:56 Sag	06 11:51 Aqu
08 01:28 Leo	08 14:11 Lib	07 23:47 Lib	08 10:17 Sag	07 22:11 Cap	08 18:46 Pis
10 04:39 Vir	10 15:49 Sco	09 23:47 Sco	10 12:56 Cap	10 02:37 Aqu	11 05:23 Ari
12 07:13 Lib	12 19:08 Sag	12 01:28 Sag	12 19:03 Aqu	12 10:55 Pis	13 18:10 Tau
14 10:07 Sco	15 00:26 Cap	14 05:54 Cap	15 04:30 Pis	14 22:25 Ari	16 06:44 Gem
16 13:48 Sag	17 07:36 Aqu	16 13:10 Aqu	17 16:17 Ari	17 11:23 Tau	18 17:21 Can
18 18:28 Cap	19 16:37 Pis	18 22:50 Pis	20 05:12 Tau	20 00:00 Gem	21 01:31 Leo
21 00:38 Aqu	22 03:42 Ari	21 10:19 Ari	22 18:00 Gem	22 11:04 Can	23 07:32 Vir
23 09:01 Pis	24 16:26 Tau	23 23:06 Tau	25 05:25 Can	24 19:53 Leo	25 11:47 Lib
25 20:04 Ari	27 05:10 Gem	26 12:01 Gem	27 14:09 Leo	27 02:06 Vir	27 14:37 Sco
28 08:52 Tau		28 23:13 Can	29 19:24 Vir	29 05:40 Lib	29 16:30 Sag
30 21:00 Gem		31 06:51 Leo		31 07:07 Sco	

Jul 1985	Aug 1985	Sep 1985	Oct 1985	Nov 1985	Dec 1985
01 18:22 Cap	02 12:33 Pis	01 05:41 Ari	01 00:34 Tau	02 08:30 Can	02 00:59 Leo
03 21:35 Aqu	04 21:42 Ari	03 17:27 Tau	03 13:35 Gem	04 19:03 Leo	04 09:13 Vir
06 03:39 Pis	07 09:40 Tau	06 06:26 Gem	06 01:58 Can	07 02:18 Vir	06 14:33 Lib
08 13:19 Ari	09 22:31 Gem	08 18:09 Can	08 11:33 Leo	09 05:51 Lib	08 16:56 Sco
11 01:43 Tau	12 09:27 Can	11 02:27 Leo	10 17:09 Vir	11 06:31 Sco	10 17:13 Sag
13 14:22 Gem	14 16:57 Leo	13 06:52 Vir	12 19:12 Lib	13 05:52 Sag	12 17:00 Cap
16 00:54 Can	16 21:15 Vir	15 08:34 Lib	14 19:13 Sco	15 05:53 Cap	14 18:15 Aqu
18 08:25 Leo	18 23:43 Lib	17 09:17 Sco	16 19:06 Sag	17 08:25 Aqu	16 22:49 Pis
20 13:29 Vir	21 01:51 Sco	19 10:40 Sag	18 20:35 Cap	19 14:41 Pis	19 07:36 Ari
22 17:10 Lib	23 04:36 Sag	21 13:49 Cap	21 00:54 Aqu	22 00:42 Ari	21 19:40 Tau
24 20:16 Sco	25 08:24 Cap	23 19:11 Aqu	23 08:27 Pis	24 13:06 Tau	24 08:44 Gem
26 23:12 Sag	27 13:31 Aqu	26 02:50 Pis	25 18:46 Ari	27 02:07 Gem	26 20:43 Can
29 02:20 Cap	29 20:24 Pis	28 12:42 Ari	28 06:59 Tau	29 14:23 Can	29 06:44 Leo
31 06:25 Aqu			30 19:58 Gem		31 14:43 Vir

Jan 1986	Feb 1986	Mar 1986	Apr 1986	May 1986	Jun 1986
02 20:45 Lib	01 06:19 Sco	02 14:51 Sag	03 03:11 Aqu	02 14:29 Pis	01 04:42 Ari
05 00:44 Sco	03 09:31 Sag	04 17:55 Cap	05 09:03 Pis	04 23:00 Ari	03 15:44 Tau
07 02:47 Sag	05 12:01 Cap	06 21:42 Aqu	07 17:11 Ari	07 09:58 Tau	06 04:26 Gem
09 03:42 Cap	07 14:35 Aqu	09 02:48 Pis	10 03:36 Tau	09 22:25 Gem	08 17:15 Can
11 05:01 Aqu	09 18:32 Pis	11 10:03 Ari	12 15:50 Gem	12 11:17 Can	11 05:11 Leo
13 08:39 Pis	12 01:20 Ari	13 20:03 Tau	15 04:41 Can	14 23:14 Leo	13 15:17 Vir
15 16:02 Ari	14 11:37 Tau	16 08:22 Gem	17 16:09 Leo	17 08:44 Vir	15 22:37 Lib
18 03:13 Tau	17 00:16 Gem	18 21:04 Can	20 00:23 Vir	19 14:40 Lib	18 02:36 Sco
20 16:11 Gem	19 12:38 Can	21 07:38 Leo	22 04:50 Lib	21 17:02 Sco	20 03:35 Sag
23 04:14 Can	21 22:24 Leo	23 14:39 Vir	24 06:15 Sco	23 16:57 Sag	22 03:00 Cap
25 13:47 Leo	24 04:57 Vir	25 18:22 Lib	26 06:16 Sag	25 16:15 Cap	24 02:50 Aqu
27 20:51 Vir	26 09:07 Lib	27 20:05 Sco	28 06:41 Cap	27 17:00 Aqu	26 05:12 Pis
30 02:09 Lib	28 12:06 Sco	29 21:20 Sag	30 09:05 Aqu	29 20:54 Pis	28 11:34 Ari
		31 23:25 Cap			30 21:53 Tau

Jul 1986	Aug 1986	Sep 1986	Oct 1986	Nov 1986	Dec 1986
03 10:31 Gem	02 06:03 Can	01 01:08 Leo	03 01:02 Lib	01 14:19 Sco	01 02:08 Sag
05 23:19 Can	04 17:26 Leo	03 10:05 Vir	05 04:35 Sco	03 15:19 Sag	03 01:28 Cap
08 10:55 Leo	07 02:44 Vir	05 16:33 Lib	07 06:47 Sag	05 15:49 Cap	05 01:22 Aqu
10 20:49 Vir	09 10:04 Lib	07 21:11 Sco	09 08:52 Cap	07 17:28 Aqu	07 03:48 Pis
13 04:39 Lib	11 15:35 Sco	10 00:40 Sag	11 11:45 Aqu	09 21:29 Pis	09 09:48 Ari
15 09:58 Sco	13 19:17 Sag	12 03:28 Cap	13 16:03 Pis	12 04:14 Ari	11 19:09 Tau
17 12:34 Sag	15 21:22 Cap	14 06:07 Aqu	15 22:13 Ari	14 13:24 Tau	14 06:41 Gem
19 13:10 Cap	17 22:44 Aqu	16 09:27 Pis	18 06:35 Tau	17 00:26 Gem	16 19:09 Can
21 13:18 Aqu	20 00:52 Pis	18 14:33 Ari	20 17:14 Gem	19 12:45 Can	19 07:43 Leo
23 14:59 Pis	22 05:27 Ari	20 22:25 Tau	23 05:36 Can	22 01:24 Leo	21 19:30 Vir
25 20:02 Ari	24 13:35 Tau	23 09:12 Gem	25 18:01 Leo	24 12:45 Vir	24 05:04 Lib
28 05:10 Tau	27 01:00 Gem	25 21:44 Can	28 04:19 Vir	26 20:58 Lib	26 11:06 Sco
30 17:18 Gem	29 13:39 Can	28 09:38 Leo	30 11:04 Lib	29 01:13 Sco	28 13:20 Sag
		30 18:57 Vir			30 12:55 Cap

Jan 1987	Feb 1987	Mar 1987	Apr 1987	May 1987	Jun 1987
01 11:54 Aqu	02 02:09 Ari	01 12:37 Ari	02 12:16 Gem	02 07:38 Can	01 03:25 Leo
03 12:36 Pis	04 08:52 Tau	03 18:11 Tau	04 23:33 Can	04 20:06 Leo	03 15:55 Vir
05 16:50 Ari	06 19:22 Gem	06 03:26 Gem	07 12:03 Leo	07 08:06 Vir	06 02:24 Lib
08 01:12 Tau	09 07:54 Can	08 15:23 Can	09 23:27 Vir	09 17:28 Lib	08 09:06 Sco
10 12:38 Gem	11 20:21 Leo	11 03:54 Leo	12 08:05 Lib	11 23:09 Sco	10 11:53 Sag
13 01:18 Can	14 07:25 Vir	13 14:54 Vir	14 13:40 Sco	14 01:41 Sag	12 12:05 Cap
15 13:44 Leo	16 16:44 Lib	15 23:33 Lib	16 17:01 Sag	16 02:36 Cap	14 11:45 Aqu
18 01:14 Vir	19 00:04 Sco	18 05:56 Sco	18 19:21 Cap	18 03:42 Aqu	16 12:54 Pis
20 11:08 Lib	21 05:09 Sag	20 10:32 Sag	20 21:45 Aqu	20 06:23 Pis	18 16:55 Ari
22 18:30 Sco	23 07:57 Cap	22 13:48 Cap	23 01:01 Pis	22 11:22 Ari	21 00:08 Tau
24 22:35 Sag	25 09:09 Aqu	24 16:18 Aqu	25 05:40 Ari	24 18:38 Tau	23 09:54 Gem
26 23:42 Cap	27 10:07 Pis	26 18:45 Pis	27 12:06 Tau	27 03:55 Gem	25 21:22 Can
28 23:17 Aqu		28 22:12 Ari	29 20:42 Gem	29 14:58 Can	28 09:51 Leo
30 23:24 Pis		31 03:46 Tau			30 22:33 Vir

Jul 1987	Aug 1987	Sep 1987	Oct 1987	Nov 1987	Dec 1987
03 09:54 Lib	02 01:09 Sco	02 17:04 Cap	02 01:51 Aqu	02 13:39 Ari	02 01:05 Tau
05 18:02 Sco	04 06:47 Sag	04 18:22 Aqu	04 03:39 Pis	04 18:02 Tau	04 08:13 Gem
07 22:05 Sag	06 08:52 Cap	06 18:37 Pis	06 05:35 Ari	07 00:15 Gem	06 17:19 Can
09 22:43 Cap	08 08:37 Aqu	08 19:34 Ari	08 08:57 Tau	09 09:09 Can	09 04:39 Leo
11 21:49 Aqu	10 08:01 Pis	10 22:57 Tau	10 15:03 Gem	11 20:44 Leo	11 17:29 Vir
13 21:36 Pis	12 09:09 Ari	13 05:54 Gem	13 00:30 Can	14 09:28 Vir	14 05:39 Lib
16 00:00 Ari	14 13:37 Tau	15 16:21 Can	15 12:33 Leo	16 20:47 Lib	16 14:40 Sco
18 06:04 Tau	16 21:58 Gem	18 04:49 Leo	18 01:05 Vir	19 04:46 Sco	18 19:33 Sag
20 15:32 Gem	19 09:18 Can	20 17:12 Vir	20 11:49 Lib	21 09:16 Sag	20 21:07 Cap
23 03:12 Can	21 21:57 Leo	23 03:58 Lib	22 19:41 Sco	23 11:32 Cap	22 21:20 Aqu
25 15:49 Leo	24 10:23 Vir	25 12:30 Sco	25 00:56 Sag	25 13:13 Aqu	24 22:10 Pis
28 04:25 Vir	26 21:35 Lib	27 18:48 Sag	27 04:32 Cap	27 15:40 Pis	27 01:05 Ari
30 15:58 Lib	29 06:49 Sco	29 23:08 Cap	29 07:26 Aqu	29 19:35 Ari	29 06:36 Tau
	31 13:23 Sag		31 10:19 Pis		31 14:28 Gem

Jan 1988	Feb 1988	Mar 1988	Apr 1988	May 1988	Jun 1988
03 00:16 Can	01 18:05 Leo	02 13:05 Vir	01 08:04 Lib	01 01:39 Sco	01 20:58 Cap
05 11:47 Leo	04 06:54 Vir	05 01:31 Lib	03 18:25 Sco	03 08:52 Sag	03 23:33 Aqu
08 00:35 Vir.	06 19:35 Lib	07 12:26 Sco	06 02:28 Sag	05 13:54 Cap	06 02:00 Pis
10 13:16 Lib	09 06:41 Sco	09 20:58 Sag	08 08:19 Cap	07 17:36 Aqu	08 05:03 Ari
12 23:39 Sco	11 14:35 Sag	12 02:31 Cap	10 12:10 Aqu	09 20:38 Pis	10 09:02 Tau
15 05:58 Sag	13 18:36 Cap	14 05:07 Aqu	12 14:24 Pis	11 23:23 Ari	12 14:14 Gem
17 08:15 Cap	15 19:25 Aqu	16 05:42 Pis	14 15:47 Ari	14 02:21 Tau	14 21:18 Can
19 08:02 Aqu	17 18:44 Pis	18 05:45 Ari	16 17:31 Tau	16 06:31 Gem	17 06:57 Leo
21 07:27 Pis	19 18:35 Ari	20 07:05 Tau	18 21:10 Gem	18 13:05 Can	19 19:02 Vir
23 08:30 Ari	21 20:50 Tau	22 11:20 Gem	21 04:04 Can	20 22:51 Leo	22 07:56 Lib
25 12:36 Tau	24 02:41 Gem	24 19:26 Can	23 14:33 Leo	23 11:11 Vir	24 18:57 Sco
27 20:01 Gem	26 12:11 Can	27 06:53 Leo	26 03:15 Vir	25 23:49 Lib	27 02:17 Sag
30 06:11 Can	29 00:12 Leo	29 19:48 Vir	28 15:36 Lib	28 10:05 Sco	29 06:00 Cap
				30 16:57 Sag	

Jul 1988	Aug 1988	Sep 1988	Oct 1988	Nov 1988	Dec 1988
01 07:30 Aqu	01 17:53 Ari	02 08:11 Gem	01 22:38 Can	03 04:01 Vir	03 00:55 Lib
03 08:33 Pis	03 20:24 Tau	04 15:36 Can	04 08:30 Leo	05 17:03 Lib	05 12:50 Sco
05 10:37 Ari	06 01:42 Gem	07 02:14 Leo	09 10:03 Lib	08 04:46 Sco	07 21:55 Sag
07 14:26 Tau	08 09:51 Can	09 14:47 Vir	11 21:57 Sco	10 14:05 Sag	10 04:06 Cap
09 20:16 Gem	10 20:26 Leo	12 03:50 Lib	14 07:57 Sag	12 21:12 Cap	12 08:25 Aqu
12 04:08 Can	13 08:45 Vir	14 16:06 Sco	16 15:44 Cap	15 02:36 Aqu	14 11:53 Pis
14 14:11 Leo	15 21:51 Lib	17 02:25 Sag	18 21:04 Aqu	17 06:33 Pis	16 15:03 Ari
17 02:17 Vir	18 10:11 Sco	19 09:44 Cap	20 23:58 Pis	19 09:12 Ari	18 18:10 Tau
19 15:21 Lib	20 19:54 Sag	21 13:43 Aqu	23 00:58 Ari	21 11:02 Tau	20 21:42 Gem
22 03:12 Sco	23 01:48 Cap	23 14:51 Pis	25 01:22 Tau	23 13:12 Gem	23 02:34 Can
24 11:41 Sag	25 04:04 Aqu	25 14:30 Ari	27 02:55 Gem	25 17:19 Can	25 09:57 Leo
26 16:07 Cap	27 04:01 Pis	27 14:29 Tau	29 07:28 Can	28 00:51 Leo	27 20:27 Vir
28 17:25 Aqu	29 03:29 Ari	29 16:43 Gem	31 16:02 Leo	30 11:58 Vir	30 09:08 Lib
30 17:23 Pis	31 04:22 Tau				

Jan 1989	Feb 1989	Mar 1989	Apr 1989	May 1989	Jun 1989
01 21:33 Sco	02 23:29 Cap	02 08:57 Cap	03 01:36 Pis	02 11:50 Ari	02 22:02 Gem
04 07:11 Sag	05 02:51 Aqu	04 13:36 Aqu	05 01:50 Ari	04 11:55 Tau	05 00:16 Can
06 13:14 Cap	07 03:52 Pis	06 14:59 Pis	07 01:07 Tau	06 12:03 Gem	07 05:27 Leo
08 16:31 Aqu	09 04:17 Ari	08 14:37 Ari	09 01:30 Gem	08 14:19 Can	09 14:28 Vir
10 18:31 Pis	11 05:44 Tau	10 14:25 Tau	11 04:57 Can	10 20:22 Leo	12 02:30 Lib
12 20:35 Ari	13 09:22 Gem	12 16:16 Gem	13 12:30 Leo	13 06:29 Vir	14 15:10 Sco
14 23:35 Tau	15 15:39 Can	14 21:27 Can	15 23:39 Vir	15 19:06 Lib	17 02:12 Sag
17 03:56 Gem	18 00:32 Leo	17 06:12 Leo	18 12:30 Lib	18 07:47 Sco	19 10:41 Cap
19 09:56 Can	20 11:34 Vir	19 17:39 Vir	21 01:13 Sco	20 18:51 Sag	21 16:56 Aqu
21 18:02 Leo	23 00:04 Lib	22 06:23 Lib	23 12:38 Sag	23 03:53 Cap	23 21:36 Pis
24 04:32 Vir	25 12:56 Sco	24 19:10 Sco	25 22:14 Cap	25 11:00 Aqu	26 01:05 Ari
26 17:00 Lib	28 00:29 Sag	27 06:53 Sag	28 05:32 Aqu	27 16:12 Pis	28 03:45 Tau
29 05:48 Sco		29 16:25 Cap	30 10:03 Pis	29 19:25 Ari	30 06:08 Gem
31 16:29 Sag		31 22:44 Aqu		31 20:59 Tau	

Jul 1989	Aug 1989	Sep 1989	Oct 1989	Nov 1989	Dec 1989
02 09:19 Can	03 07:18 Vir	02 01:47 Lib	01 20:52 Sco	03 02:46 Cap	02 17:41 Aqu
04 14:37 Leo	05 18:27 Lib	04 14:22 Sco	04 09:28 Sag	05 12:08 Aqu	05 00:47 Pis
06 23:04 Vir	08 07:04 Sco	07 02:50 Sag	06 20:44 Cap	07 18:24 Pis	07 05:11 Ari
09 10:29 Lib	10 19:01 Sag	09 13:12 Cap	09 05:06 Aqu	09 21:08 Ari	09 06:59 Tau
11 23:08 Sco	13 04:16 Cap	11 20:01 Aqu	11 09:37 Pis	11 21:09 Tau	11 07:15 Gem
14 10:30 Sag	15 09:58 Aqu	13 23:07 Pis	13 10:42 Ari	13 20:19 Gem	13 07:49 Can
16 19:01 Cap	17 12:46 Pis	15 23:38 Ari	15 09:53 Tau	15 20:51 Can	15 10:41 Leo
19 00:35 Aqu	19 13:59 Ari	17 23:22 Tau	17 09:19 Gem	18 00:45 Leo	17 17:18 Vir
21 04:06 Pis	21 15:10 Tau	20 00:15 Gem	19 11:09 Can	20 08:53 Vir	20 03:44 Lib
23 06:40 Ari	23 17:38 Gem	22 03:50 Can	21 16:46 Leo	22 20:24 Lib	22 16:17 Sco
25 09:10 Tau	25 22:13 Can	24 10:43 Leo	24 02:14 Vir	25 09:12 Sco	25 04:36 Sag
27 12:14 Gem	28 05:11 Leo	26 20:32 Vir	26 14:10 Lib	27 21:29 Sag	27 15:10 Cap
29 16:31 Can	30 14:29 Vir	29 08:14 Lib	29 02:55 Sco	30 08:26 Cap	29 23:37 Aqu
31 22:41 Leo			31 15:22 Sag		

Jan 1990	Feb 1990	Mar 1990	Apr 1990	May 1990	Jun 1990
01 06:10 Pis	01 19:27 Tau	01 01:42 Tau	01 12:49 Can	01 00:08 Leo	01 23:30 Lib
03 10:56 Ari	03 22:12 Gem	03 03:37 Gem	03 17:49 Leo	03 07:17 Vir	04 11:21 Sco
05 14:04 Tau	06 01:26 Can	05 07:02 Can	06 01:41 Vir	05 17:27 Lib	06 23:59 Sag
07 16:02 Gem	08 05:51 Leo	07 12:24 Leo	08 11:44 Lib	08 05:22 Sco	09 12:11 Cap
09 17:52 Can	10 12:13 Vir	09 19:46 Vir	10 23:17 Sco	10 17:55 Sag	11 23:08 Aqu
11 21:02 Leo	12 21:09 Lib	12 05:08 Lib	13 11:47 Sag	13 06:20 Cap	14 07:59 Pis
14 02:57 Vir	15 08:33 Sco	14 16:24 Sco	16 00:14 Cap	15 17:29 Aqu	16 13:54 Ari
16 12:16 Lib	17 21:06 Sag	17 04:55 Sag	18 10:52 Aqu	18 01:53 Pis	18 16:42 Tau
19 00:15 Sco	20 08:29 Cap	19 17:00 Cap	20 17:56 Pis	20 06:31 Ari	20 17:15 Gem
21 12:43 Sag	22 16:52 Aqu	22 02:30 Aqu	22 20:58 Ari	22 07:42 Tau	22 17:10 Can
23 23:27 Cap	24 21:49 Pis	24 08:08 Pis	24 21:03 Tau	24 07:00 Gem	24 18:25 Leo
26 07:25 Aqu	27 00:16 Ari	26 10:16 Ari	26 20:12 Gem	26 06:34 Can	26 22:41 Vir
28 12:50 Pis		28 10:27 Tau	28 20:39 Can	28 08:29 Leo	29 06:46 Lib
30 16:34 Ari		30 10:42 Gem		30 14:07 Vir	

Jul 1990	Aug 1990	Sep 1990	Oct 1990	Nov 1990	Dec 1990
01 18:00 Sco	03 02:08 Cap	01 20:50 Aqu	01 13:42 Pis	02 05:32 Tau	01 16:23 Gem
04 06:35 Sag	05 12:18 Aqu	04 04:05 Pis	03 17:42 Ari	04 05:06 Gem	03 15:28 Can
06 18:39 Cap	07 19:54 Pis	06 08:23 Ari	05 19:06 Tau	06 05:07 Can	05 16:00 Leo
09 05:06 Aqu	10 01:12 Ari	08 10:55 Tau	07 19:47 Gem	08 07:23 Leo	07 19:38 Vir
11 13:29 Pis	12 04:54 Tau	10 13:04 Gem	09 21:29 Can	10 12:47 Vir	10 02:59 Lib
13 19:36 Ari	14 07:41 Gem	12 15:52 Can	12 01:16 Leo	12 21:08 Lib	12 13:27 Sco
15 23:28 Tau	16 10:12 Can	14 19:51 Leo	14 07:20 Vir	15 07:38 Sco	15 01:43 Sag
18 01:31 Gem	18 13:11 Leo	17 01:18 Vir	16 15:26 Lib	17 19:38 Sag	17 14:34 Cap
20 02:43 Can	20 17:33 Vir	19 08:33 Lib	19 01:23 Sco	20 08:31 Cap	20 02:58 Aqu
22 04:28 Leo	23 00:16 Lib	21 18:05 Sco	21 13:08 Sag	22 21:06 Aqu	22 13:47 Pis
24 08:17 Vir	25 09:55 Sco	24 05:51 Sag	24 02:02 Cap	25 07:31 Pis	24 21:44 Ari
26 15:18 Lib	27 21:57 Sag	26 18:35 Cap	26 14:13 Aqu	27 14:06 Ari	27 02:08 Tau
29 01:38 Sco	30 10:22 Cap	29 05:53 Aqu	28 23:21 Pis	29 16:37 Tau	29 03:26 Gem
31 13:59 Sag			31 04:14 Ari		31 03:02 Can

Jan 1991	Feb 1991	Mar 1991	Apr 1991	May 1991	Jun 1991
02 02:54 Leo	02 20:02 Lib	02 06:03 Lib	03 07:58 Sag	03 03:54 Cap	01 23:41 Aqu
04 04:56 Vir	05 04:00 Sco	04 13:08 Sco	05 20:19 Cap	05 16:50 Aqu	04 11:35 Pis
06 10:32 Lib	07 15:22 Sag	06 23:34 Sag	08 08:58 Aqu	08 04:04 Pis	06 20:24 Ari
08 19:58 Sco	10 04:15 Cap	09 12:12 Cap	10 19:17 Pis	10 11:34 Ari	09 01:12 Tau
11 08:05 Sag	12 16:16 Aqu	12 00:30 Aqu	13 01:49 Ari	12 15:07 Tau	11 02:36 Gem
13 21:00 Cap	15 01:58 Pis	14 10:10 Pis	15 05:05 Tau	14 16:02 Gem	13 02:16 Can
16 09:04 Aqu	17 09:11 Ari	16 16:37 Ari	17 06:41 Gem	16 16:14 Can	15 02:10 Leo
18 19:23 Pis	19 14:24 Tau	18 20:40 Tau	19 08:17 Can	18 17:30 Leo	17 04:02 Vir
21 03:27 Ari	21 18:10 Gem	20 23:36 Gem	21 11:04 Leo	20 21:00 Vir	19 09:00 Lib
23 09:00 Tau	23 20:56 Can	23 02:27 Can	23 15:29 Vir	23 03:07 Lib	21 17:18 Sco
25 12:06 Gem	25 23:12 Leo	25 05:43 Leo	25 21:36 Lib	25 11:41 Sco	24 04:15 Sag
27 13:23 Can	28 01:50 Vir	27 09:40 Vir	28 05:33 Sco	27 22:20 Sag	26 16:49 Cap
29 14:04 Leo		29 14:49 Lib	30 15:41 Sag	30 10:40 Cap	29 05:47 Aqu
31 15:44 Vir		31 22:01 Sco			

Jul 1991	Aug 1991	Sep 1991	Oct 1991	Nov 1991	Dec 1991
01 17:50 Pis	02 16:31 Tau	01 03:02 Gem	02 14:58 Leo	03 04:12 Lib	02 16:32 Sco
04 03:33 Ari	04 20:54 Gem	03 06:19 Can	04 17:44 Vir	05 10:08 Sco	05 01:32 Sag
06 09:51 Tau	06 22:47 Can	05 08:13 Leo	06 21:00 Lib	07 18:21 Sag	07 12:40 Cap
08 12:42 Gem	08 23:09 Leo	07 09:35 Vir	09 01:59 Sco	10 05:15 Cap	10 01:26 Aqu
10 13:03 Can	10 23:34 Vir	09 11:51 Lib	11 09:57 Sag	12 18:05 Aqu	12 14:18 Pis
12 12:35 Leo	13 01:51 Lib	11 16:42 Sco	13 21:09 Cap	15 06:32 Pis	15 01:06 Ari
14 13:12 Vir	15 07:33 Sco	14 01:14 Sag	16 10:03 Aqu	17 16:07 Ari	17 08:09 Tau
16 16:33 Lib	17 17:10 Sag	16 13:02 Cap	18 21:52 Pis	19 21:49 Tau	19 11:21 Gem
18 23:40 Sco	20 05:33 Cap	19 01:57 Aqu	21 06:33 Ari	22 00:22 Gem	21 11:55 Can
21 10:15 Sag	22 18:26 Aqu	21 13:20 Pis	23 11:55 Tau	24 01:25 Can	23 11:39 Leo
23 22:55 Cap	25 05:51 Pis	23 21:55 Ari	25 15:09 Gem	26 02:37 Leo	25 12:23 Vir
26 11:48 Aqu	27 15:00 Ari	26 03:59 Tau	27 17:37 Can	28 05:11 Vir	27 15:37 Lib
28 23:34 Pis	29 21:59 Tau	28 08:25 Gem	29 20:20 Leo	30 09:46 Lib	29 22:03 Sco
31 09:19 Ari		30 11:58 Can	31 23:46 Vir		

Jan 1992	Feb 1992	Mar 1992	Apr 1992	May 1992	Jun 1992
01 07:29 Sag	02 14:08 Aqu	03 09:10 Pis	a02 03:03 Ari	01 19:09 Tau	02 11:58 Can
03 19:08 Cap	05 02:50 Pis	05 20:06 Ari	04 11:17 Tau	04 00:28 Gem	04 13:35 Leo
06 07:58 Aqu	07 14:14 Ari	08 05:04 Tau	06 17:32 Gem	06 04:09 Can	06 15:28 Vir
08 20:51 Pis	09 23:35 Tau	10 12:03 Gem	08 22:18 Can	08 07:07 Leo	08 18:33 Lib
11 08:22 Ari	12 06:07 Gem	12 16:49 Can	11 01:45 Leo	10 09:56 Vir	10 23:26 Sco
13 16:59 Tau	14 09:30 Can	14 19:20 Leo	13 04:09 Vir	12 13:05 Lib	13 06:28 Sag
15 21:54 Gem	16 10:15 Leo	16 20:13 Vir	15 06:10 Lib	14 17:15 Sco	15 15:49 Cap
17 23:26 Can	18 09:47 Vir	18 20:55 Lib	17 09:09 Sco	16 23:21 Sag	18 03:18 Aqu
19 22:56 Leo	20 10:05 Lib	20 23:19 Sco	19 14:40 Sag	19 08:12 Cap	20 15:59 Pis
21 22:22 Vir	22 13:11 Sco	23 05:12 Sag	21 23:40 Cap	21 19:43 Aqu	23 04:02 Ari
23 23:42 Lib	24 20:25 Sag	25 15:07 Cap	24 11:38 Aqu	24 08:24 Pis	25 13:28 Tau
26 04:31 Sco	27 07:32 Cap	28 03:44 Aqu	27 00:19 Pis	26 19:52 Ari	27 19:13 Gem
28 13:19 Sag	29 20:33 Aqu	30 16:23 Pis	29 11:13 Ari	29 04:16 Tau	29 21:42 Can
31 01:07 Cap				31 09:19 Gem	

Jul 1992	Aug 1992	Sep 1992	Oct 1992	Nov 1992	Dec 1992
01 22:15 Leo	02 08:17 Lib	03 00:49 Sag	02 17:28 Cap	01 12:42 Aqu	01 09:22 Pis
03 22:37 Vir	04 11:15 Sco	05 10:05 Cap	05 04:52 Aqu	04 01:12 Pis	03 21:48 Ari
06 00:27 Lib	06 17:56 Sag	07 22:08 Aqu	07 17:37 Pis	06 13:18 Ari	06 08:16 Tau
08 04:53 Sco	09 04:00 Cap	10 10:55 Pis	10 05:35 Ari	08 23:18 Tau	08 15:36 Gem
10 12:16 Sag	11 16:06 Aqu	12 23:02 Ari	12 15:48 Tau	11 06:49 Gem	10 20:05 Can
12 22:15 Cap	14 04:50 Pis	15 09:46 Tau	15 00:08 Gem	13 12:19 Can	12 22:47 Leo
15 10:02 Aqu	16 17:11 Ari	17 18:39 Gem	17 06:35 Can	15 16:23 Leo	15 00:55 Vir
17 22:44 Pis	19 04:09 Tau	20 00:58 Can	19 11:00 Leo	17 19:28 Vir	17 03:33 Lib
20 11:06 Ari	21 12:35 Gem	22 04:18 Leo	21 13:27 Vir	19 22:02 Lib	19 07:19 Sco
22 21:35 Tau	23 17:36 Can	24 05:08 Vir	23 14:40 Lib	22 00:51 Sco	21 12:42 Sag
25 04:44 Gem	25 19:15 Leo	26 04:55 Lib	25 16:04 Sco	24 05:00 Sag	23 20:04 Cap
27 08:08 Can	27 18:47 Vir	28 05:44 Sco	27 19:28 Sag	26 11:37 Cap	26 05:42 Aqu
29 08:39 Leo	29 18:11 Lib	30 09:33 Sag	30 02:17 Cap	28 21:18 Aqu	28 17:27 Pis
31 08:01 Vir	31 19:38 Sco				31 06:06 Ari

Jan 1993	Feb 1993	Mar 1993	Apr 1993	May 1993	Jun 1993
02 17:29 Tau	01 11:14 Gem	03 02:16 Can	01 14:21 Leo	03 01:20 Lib	01 10:22 Sco
05 01:41 Gem	03 16:56 Can	05 05:40 Leo	03 16:10 Vir	05 01:57 Sco	03 13:01 Sag
07 06:10 Can	05 18:51 Leo	07 05:52 Vir	05 15:55 Lib	07 03:34 Sag	05 17:26 Cap
09 07:49 Leo	07 18:29 Vir	09 04:46 Lib	07 15:32 Sco	09 07:50 Cap	08 00:39 Aqu
11 08:20 Vir	09 17:58 Lib	11 04:39 Sco	09 17:09 Sag	11 15:43 Aqu	10 10:56 Pis
13 09:30 Lib	11 19:23 Sco	13 07:33 Sag	11 22:23 Cap	14 02:50 Pis	12 23:13 Ari
15 12:41 Sco	14 00:07 Sag	15 14:27 Cap	14 07:35 Aqu	16 15:23 Ari	15 11:18 Tau
17 18:30 Sag	16 08:19 Cap	18 00:52 Aqu	16 19:32 Pis	19 03:16 Tau	17 21:11 Gem
20 02:46 Cap	18 19:04 Aqu	20 13:10 Pis	19 08:14 Ari	21 13:07 Gem	20 04:05 Can
22 13:00 Aqu	21 07:11 Pis	23 01:51 Ari	21 20:07 Tau	23 20:37 Can	22 08:26 Leo
25 00:47 Pis	23 19:50 Ari	25 13:58 Tau	24 06:26 Gem	26 02:03 Leo	24 11:18 Vir
27 13:27 Ari	26 08:10 Tau	28 00:47 Gem	26 14:45 Can	28 05:46 Vir	26 13:45 Lib
30 01:36 Tau	28 18:51 Gem	30 09:13 Can	28 20:39 Leo	30 08:18 Lib	28 16:37 Sco
			30 23:59 Vir		30 20:28 Sag

Jul 1993	Aug 1993	Sep 1993	Oct 1993	Nov 1993	Dec 1993
03 01:48 Cap	01 16:36 Aqu	02 21:20 Ari	02 16:12 Tau	01 10:12 Gem	01 02:16 Can
05 09:14 Aqu	04 02:43 Pis	05 10:08 Tau	05 04:26 Gem	03 20:24 Can	03 09:32 Leo
07 19:09 Pis	06 14:38 Ari	07 22:15 Gem	07 14:41 Can	06 04:06 Leo	05 14:43 Vir
10 07:10 Ari	09 03:22 Tau	10 07:36 Can	09 21:33 Leo	08 08:47 Vir	07 18:03 Lib
12 19:36 Tau	11 14:46 Gem	12 12:51 Leo	12 00:35 Vir	10 10:42 Lib	09 20:04 Sco
15 06:06 Gem	13 22:46 Can	14 14:20 Vir	14 00:47 Lib	12 11:00 Sco	11 21:39 Sag
17 13:07 Can	16 02:43 Leo	16 13:44 Lib	16 00:00 Sco	14 11:21 Sag	14 00:05 Cap
19 16:47 Leo	18 03:41 Vir	18 13:15 Sco	18 00:23 Sag	16 13:34 Cap	16 04:51 Aqu
21 18:24 Vir	20 03:35 Lib	20 14:53 Sag	20 03:41 Cap	18 19:07 Aqu	18 12:58 Pis
23 19:39 Lib	22 04:27 Sco	22 19:53 Cap	22 10:48 Aqu	21 04:27 Pis	21 00:18 Ari
25 22:00 Sco	24 07:45 Sag	25 04:18 Aqu	24 21:17 Pis	23 16:29 Ari	23 13:03 Tau
28 02:12 Sag	26 13:57 Cap	27 15:12 Pis	27 09:38 Ari	26 05:13 Tau	26 00:45 Gem
30 08:26 Cap	28 22:41 Aqu	30 03:28 Ari	29 22:20 Tau	28 16:47 Gem	28 09:46 Can
	31 09:18 Pis				30 15:59 Leo

Jan 1994	Feb 1994	Mar 1994	Apr 1994	May 1994	Jun 1994
01 20:14 Vir	02 07:49 Sco	01 14:43 Sco	02 03:37 Cap	01 16:34 Aqu	02 18:30 Ari
03 23:30 Lib	04 11:14 Sag	03 16:53 Sag	04 09:45 Aqu	04 00:46 Pis	05 07:13 Tau
06 02:28 Sco	06 16:01 Cap	05 21:23 Cap	06 18:50 Pis	06 12:00 Ari	07 20:02 Gem
08 05:34 Sag	08 22:16 Aqu	08 04:14 Aqu	09 06:08 Ari	09 00:50 Tau	10 07:21 Can
10 09:16 Cap	11 06:22 Pis	10 13:09 Pis	11 18:47 Tau	11 13:43 Gem	12 16:28 Leo
12 14:25 Aqu	13 16:48 Ari	12 23:58 Ari	14 07:47 Gem	14 01:26 Can	14 23:16 Vir
14 22:03 Pis	16 05:19 Tau	15 12:26 Tau	16 19:40 Can	16 10:57 Leo	17 03:47 Lib
17 08:41 Ari	18 18:04 Gem	18 01:28 Gem	19 04:44 Leo	18 17:30 Vir	19 06:20 Sco
19 21:21 Tau	21 04:26 Can	20 12:53 Can	21 09:57 Vir	20 20:54 Lib	21 07:32 Sag
22 09:33 Gem	23 10:47 Leo	22 20:38 Leo	23 11:40 Lib	22 21:50 Sco	23 08:37 Cap
24 18:54 Can	25 13:27 Vir	25 00:13 Vir	25 11:19 Sco	24 21:43 Sag	25 11:09 Aqu
27 00:38 Leo	27 14:06 Lib	27 00:46 Lib	27 10:48 Sag	26 22:16 Cap	27 16:44 Pis
29 03:39 Vir		29 00:14 Sco	29 12:04 Cap	29 01:18 Aqu	30 02:06 Ari
31 05:33 Lib		31 00:41 Sag		31 08:02 Pis	

Jul 1994	Aug 1994	Sep 1994	Oct 1994	Nov 1994	Dec 1994
02 14:22 Tau	01 11:04 Gem	02 15:36 Leo	02 06:39 Vir	02 20:19 Sco	02 07:13 Sag
05 03:12 Gem	03 22:22 Can	04 20:33 Vir	04 08:56 Lib	04 19:46 Sag	04 06:43 Cap
07 14:17 Can	06 06:30 Leo	06 22:56 Lib	06 09:22 Sco	06 20:02 Cap	06 07:51 Aqu
09 22:43 Leo	08 11:42 Vir	09 00:25 Sco	08 09:47 Sag	08 22:48 Aqu	08 12:23 Pis
12 04:48 Vir	10 15:06 Lib	11 02:25 Sag	10 11:43 Cap	11 05:03 Pis	10 21:03 Ari
14 09:14 Lib	12 17:55 Sco	13 05:44 Cap	12 16:09 Aqu	13 14:43 Ari	13 08:55 Tau
16 12:34 Sco	14 20:53 Sag	15 10:42 Aqu	14 23:18 Pis	16 02:43 Tau	15 21:59 Gem
18 15:09 Sag	17 00:17 Cap	17 17:31 Pis	17 08:55 Ari	18 15:40 Gem	18 10:24 Can
20 17:30 Cap	19 04:33 Aqu	20 02:29 Ari	19 20:34 Tau	21 04:20 Can	20 21:12 Leo
22 20:38 Aqu	21 10:27 Pis	22 13:47 Tau	22 09:27 Gem	23 15:32 Leo	23 06:00 Vir
25 01:56 Pis	23 18:54 Ari	25 02:41 Gem	24 22:15 Can	26 00:08 Vir	25 12:27 Lib
27 10:30 Ari	26 06:12 Tau	27 15:11 Can	27 09:04 Leo	28 05:22 Lib	27 16:17 Sco
29 22:12 Tau	28 19:06 Gem	30 00:55 Leo	29 16:20 Vir	30 07:21 Sco	29 17:45 Sag
	31 06:59 Can		31 19:46 Lib		31 17:58 Cap

Jan 1995	Feb 1995	Mar 1995	Apr 1995	May 1995	Jun 1995
02 18:39 Aqu	01 08:05 Pis	02 23:29 Ari	01 16:58 Tau	01 11:52 Gem	02 19:16 Leo
04 21:49 Pis	03 14:12 Ari	05 08:49 Tau	04 04:48 Gem	04 00:44 Can	05 05:45 Vir
07 04:56 Ari	06 00:08 Tau	07 20:54 Gem	06 17:39 Can	06 12:54 Leo	07 13:12 Lib
09 15:57 Tau	08 12:42 Gem	10 09:39 Can	09 05:15 Leo	08 22:33 Vir	09 17:03 Sco
12 04:57 Gem	11 01:16 Can	12 20:27 Leo	11 13:38 Vir	11 04:30 Lib	11 17:50 Sag
14 17:19 Can	13 11:31 Leo	15 03:54 Vir	13 18:20 Lib	13 06:53 Sco	13 17:05 Cap
17 03:36 Leo	15 18:51 Vir	17 08:18 Lib	15 20:13 Sco	15 06:59 Sag	15 16:52 Aqu
19 11:39 Vir	18 00:00 Lib	19 10:52 Sco	17 20:51 Sag	17 06:36 Cap	17 19:13 Pis
21 17:53 Lib	20 03:55 Sco	21 12:57 Sag	19 21:53 Cap	19 07:39 Aqu	20 01:28 Ari
23 22:32 Sco	22 07:12 Sag	23 15:31 Cap	22 00:37 Aqu	21 11:39 Pis	22 11:34 Tau
26 01:36 Sag	24 10:10 Cap	25 19:09 Aqu	24 05:50 Pis	23 19:12 Ari	25 00:02 Gem
28 03:26 Cap	26 13:14 Aqu	28 00:17 Pis	26 13:40 Ari	26 05:46 Tau	27 12:55 Can
30 05:03 Aqu	28 17:16 Pis	30 07:25 Ari	28 23:52 Tau	28 18:06 Gem	30 01:01 Leo
				31 06:59 Can	

Jul 1995	Aug 1995	Sep 1995	Oct 1995	Nov 1995	Dec 1995
02 11:34 Vir	01 01:23 Lib	01 16:56 Sag	01 01:10 Cap	01 13:17 Pis	01 00:50 Ari
04 19:54 Lib	03 07:29 Sco	03 19:44 Cap	03 03:59 Aqu	03 19:20 Ari	03 09:39 Tau
07 01:18 Sco	05 11:14 Sag	05 21:47 Aqu	05 07:35 Pis	06 03:35 Tau	05 20:34 Gem
09 03:37 Sag	07 12:52 Cap	08 00:07 Pis	07 12:41 Ari	08 13:54 Gem	08 08:44 Can
11 03:43 Cap	09 13:28 Aqu	10 04:13 Ari	09 20:04 Tau	11 01:56 Can	10 21:24 Leo
13 03:21 Aqu	11 14:46 Pis	12 11:21 Tau	12 06:09 Gem	13 14:36 Leo	13 09:25 Vir
15 04:37 Pis	13 18:40 Ari	14 21:47 Gem	14 18:19 Can	16 02:01 Vir	15 19:08 Lib
17 09:22 Ari	16 02:24 Tau	17 10:15 Can	17 06:45 Leo	18 10:17 Lib	18 01:06 Sco
19 18:19 Tau	18 13:39 Gem	19 22:19 Leo	19 17:11 Vir	20 14:40 Sco	20 03:13 Sag
22 06:22 Gem	21 02:23 Can	22 08:01 Vir	22 00:15 Lib	22 15:56 Sag	22 02:46 Cap
24 19:15 Can	23 14:12 Leo	24 14:49 Lib	24 04:06 Sco	24 15:49 Cap	24 01:51 Aqu
27 07:06 Leo	25 23:50 Vir	26 19:20 Sco	26 05:56 Sag	26 16:15 Aqu	26 02:44 Pis
29 17:11 Vir	28 07:14 Lib	28 22:30 Sag	28 07:14 Cap	28 18:58 Pis	28 07:05 Ari
	30 12:51 Sco		30 09:23 Aqu		30 15:20 Tau

Jan 1996	Feb 1996	Mar 1996	Apr 1996	May 1996	Jun 1996
02 02:29 Gem	03 09:45 Leo	01 16:46 Leo	02 21:26 Lib	02 12:42 Sco	01 01:42 Sag
04 14:55 Can	05 21:22 Vir	04 04:12 Vir	05 03:56 Sco	04 16:05 Sag	03 02:29 Cap
07 03:30 Leo	08 07:29 Lib	06 13:40 Lib	07 08:21 Sag	06 17:54 Cap	05 02:44 Aqu
09 15:28 Vir	10 15:34 Sco	08 21:05 Sco	09 11:30 Cap	08 19:39 Aqu	07 04:19 Pis
12 01:54 Lib	12 20:57 Sag	11 02:32 Sag	11 14:09 Aqu	10 22:28 Pis	09 08:22 Ari
14 09:29 Sco	14 23:29 Cap	13 06:07 Cap	13 17:00 Pis	13 03:00 Ari	11 15:10 Tau
16 13:25 Sag	16 23:59 Aqu	15 08:15 Aqu	15 20:42 Ari	15 09:24 Tau	14 00:15 Gem
18 14:07 Cap	19 00:09 Pis	17 09:50 Pis	18 02:05 Tau	17 17:47 Gem	16 11:07 Can
20 13:15 Aqu	21 01:58 Ari	19 12:15 Ari	20 09:54 Gem	20 04:15 Can	18 23:21 Leo
22 13:02 Pis	23 07:08 Tau	21 16:58 Tau	22 20:24 Can	22 16:27 Leo	21 12:06 Vir
24 15:36 Ari	25 16:13 Gem	24 00:59 Gem	25 08:43 Leo	25 04:58 Vir	23 23:37 Lib
26 22:16 Tau	28 04:10 Can	26 12:05 Can	27 20:48 Vir	27 15:32 Lib	26 07:53 Sco
29 08:41 Gem		29 00:36 Leo	30 06:26 Lib	29 22:30 Sco	28 12:01 Sag
31 21:10 Can		31 12:14 Vir			30 12:47 Cap

Jul 1996	Aug 1996	Sep 1996	Oct 1996	Nov 1996	Dec 1996
02 12:05 Aqu	02 23:04 Ari	01 12:19 Tau	01 04:01 Gem	02 09:15 Leo	02 06:10 Vir
04 12:07 Pis	05 03:32 Tau	03 19:07 Gem	03 13:13 Can	04 21:56 Vir	04 18:22 Lib
06 14:41 Ari	07 11:48 Gem	06 05:29 Can	06 01:11 Leo	07 09:28 Lib	07 03:38 Sco
08 20:43 Tau	09 22:57 Can	08 17:53 Leo	08 13:48 Vir	09 18:01 Sco	09 08:58 Sag
11 05:52 Gem	12 11:28 Leo	11 06:28 Vir	11 01:00 Lib	11 23:26 Sag	11 11:15 Cap
13 17:07 Can	15 00:07 Vir	13 17:50 Lib	13 09:45 Sco	14 02:43 Cap	13 12:14 Aqu
16 05:31 Leo	17 11:54 Lib	16 03:19 Sco	15 16:07 Sag	16 05:14 Aqu	15 13:44 Pis
18 18:16 Vir	19 21:50 Sco	18 10:30 Sag	17 20:37 Cap	18 07:59 Pis	17 16:55 Ari
21 06:13 Lib	22 04:48 Sag	20 15:12 Cap	19 23:50 Aqu	20 11:33 Ari	19 22:09 Tau
23 15:42 Sco	24 08:21 Cap	22 17:39 Aqu	22 02:22 Pis	22 16:11 Tau	22 05:17 Gem
25 21:23 Sag	26 09:11 Aqu	24 18:43 Pis	24 04:50 Ari	24 22:19 Gem	24 14:14 Can
27 23:17 Cap	28 08:49 Pis	26 19:45 Ari	26 08:11 Tau	27 06:37 Can	27 01:08 Leo
29 22:47 Aqu	30 09:15 Ari	28 22:23 Tau	28 13:34 Gem	29 17:29 Leo	29 13:44 Vir
31 22:00 Pis			30 21:56 Can		

Jan 1997	Feb 1997	Mar 1997	Apr 1997	May 1997	Jun 1997
01 02:31 Lib	02 04:50 Sag	01 12:00 Sag	02 03:58 Aqu	01 12:50 Pis	02 00:38 Tau
03 13:01 Sco	04 08:44 Cap	03 17:38 Cap	04 05:42 Pis	03 14:59 Ari	04 04:54 Gem
05 19:27 Sag	06 09:21 Aqu	05 19:54 Aqu	06 06:19 Ari	05 17:04 Tau	06 11:02 Can
07 21:54 Cap	08 08:34 Pis	07 19:57 Pis	08 07:20 Tau	07 20:20 Gem	08 19:57 Leo
09 22:00 Aqu	10 08:29 Ari	09 19:33 Ari	10 10:27 Gem	10 02:12 Can	11 07:42 Vir
11 21:51 Pis	12 10:56 Tau	11 20:37 Tau	12 17:02 Can	12 11:32 Leo	13 20:34 Lib
13 23:21 Ari	14 16:52 Gem	14 00:48 Gem	15 03:21 Leo	14 23:43 Vir	16 07:50 Sco
16 03:39 Tau	17 02:12 Can	16 08:50 Can	17 15:59 Vir	17 12:26 Lib	18 15:38 Sag
18 10:52 Gem	19 13:52 Leo	18 20:07 Leo	20 04:36 Lib	19 23:11 Sco	20 20:02 Cap
20 20:28 Can	22 02:38 Vir	21 08:59 Vir	22 15:18 Sco	22 06:50 Sag	22 22:20 Aqu
23 07:49 Leo	24 15:22 Lib	23 21:35 Lib	24 23:31 Sag	24 11:51 Cap	25 00:08 Pis
25 20:26 Vir	27 02:56 Sco	26 08:41 Sco	27 05:32 Cap	26 15:20 Aqu	27 02:38 Ari
28 09:20 Lib		28 17:39 Sag	29 09:50 Aqu	28 18:18 Pis	29 06:23 Tau
30 20:47 Sco		31 00:06 Cap		30 21:17 Ari	

Jul 1997	Aug 1997	Sep 1997	Oct 1997	Nov 1997	Dec 1997
01 11:35 Gem	02 10:26 Leo	01 04:26 Vir	03 11:57 Sco	02 04:26 Sag	01 18:38 Cap
03 18:32 Can	04 22:14 Vir	03 17:29 Lib	05 22:42 Sag	04 12:30 Cap	03 23:57 Aqu
06 03:44 Leo	07 11:16 Lib	06 06:09 Sco	08 07:03 Cap	06 18:33 Aqu	06 04:07 Pis
08 15:21 Vir	09 23:50 Sco	08 16:53 Sag	10 12:29 Aqu	08 22:34 Pis	08 07:23 Ari
11 04:20 Lib	12 09:44 Sag	11 00:23 Cap	12 14:59 Pis	11 00:43 Ari	10 10:00 Tau
13 16:19 Sco	14 15:42 Cap	13 04:10 Aqu	14 15:25 Ari	13 01:45 Tau	12 12:35 Gem
16 01:02 Sag	16 17:58 Aqu	15 04:59 Pis	16 15:16 Tau	15 03:04 Gem	14 16:25 Can
18 05:45 Cap	18 18:01 Pis	17 04:25 Ari	18 16:26 Gem	17 06:32 Can	16 22:57 Leo
20 07:29 Aqu	20 17:45 Ari	19 04:21 Tau	20 20:45 Can	19 13:37 Leo	19 08:59 Vir
22 08:00 Pis	22 18:57 Tau	21 06:38 Gem	23 05:09 Leo	22 00:32 Vir	21 21:34 Lib
24 09:03 Ari	24 22:56 Gem	23 12:32 Can	25 16:58 Vir	24 13:28 Lib	24 10:06 Sco
26 11:53 Tau	27 06:10 Can	25 22:12 Leo	28 06:04 Lib	27 01:42 Sco	26 20:07 Sag
28 17:04 Gem	29 16:18 Leo	28 10:26 Vir	30 18:15 Sco	29 11:28 Sag	29 02:48 Cap
31 00:38 Can		30 23:32 Lib			31 06:58 Aqu

Jan 1998	Feb 1998	Mar 1998	Apr 1998	May 1998	Jun 1998
02 09:56 Pis	02 21:24 Tau	02 05:00 Tau	02 19:09 Can	02 09:48 Leo	01 03:20 Vir
04 12:43 Ari	05 01:09 Gem	04 07:14 Gem	05 02:35 Leo	04 19:46 Vir	03 15:16 Lib
06 15:52 Tau	07 06:57 Can	06 12:26 Can	07 13:24 Vir	07 08:18 Lib	06 04:05 Sco
08 19:42 Gem	09 14:56 Leo	08 20:45 Leo	10 02:04 Lib	09 21:09 Sco	08 15:34 Sag
11 00:42 Can	12 01:09 Vir	11 07:34 Vir	12 14:55 Sco	12 08:47 Sag	11 00:50 Cap
13 07:45 Leo	14 13:16 Lib	13 19:57 Lib	15 02:52 Sag	14 18:38 Cap	13 08:02 Aqu
15 17:30 Vir	17 02:12 Sco	16 08:50 Sco	17 13:04 Cap	17 02:30 Aqu	15 13:31 Pis
18 05:43 Lib	19 13:55 Sag	18 20:55 Sag	19 20:41 Aqu	19 08:03 Pis	17 17:22 Ari
20 18:33 Sco	21 22:29 Cap	21 06:43 Cap	22 01:05 Pis	21 11:05 Ari	19 19:47 Tau
23 05:24 Sag	24 03:10 Aqu	23 13:01 Aqu	24 02:30 Ari	23 12:06 Tau	21 21:26 Gem
25 12:39 Cap	26 04:42 Pis	25 15:42 Pis	26 02:08 Tau	25 12:26 Gem	23 23:38 Can
27 16:27 Aqu	28 04:42 Ari	27 15:49 Ari	28 01:55 Gem	27 13:58 Can	26 04:03 Leo
29 18:08 Pis		29 15:07 Tau	30 03:56 Can	29 18:37 Leo	28 11:53 Vir
31 19:21 Ari		31 15:37 Gem			30 23:04 Lib

Jul 1998	Aug 1998	Sep 1998	Oct 1998	Nov 1998	Dec 1998
03 11:44 Sco	02 07:47 Sag	01 02:22 Cap	02 23:23 Pis	01 11:27 Ari	02 21:29 Gem
05 23:23 Sag	04 17:17 Cap	03 09:20 Aqu	05 00:32 Ari	03 11:12 Tau	04 21:28 Can
08 08:27 Cap	06 23:31 Aqu	05 12:48 Pis	06 23:57 Tau	05 10:11 Gem	06 23:55 Leo
10 14:52 Aqu	09 03:04 Pis	07 13:53 Ari	08 23:43 Gem	07 10:39 Can	09 06:20 Vir
12 19:22 Pis	11 05:10 Ari	09 14:16 Tau	11 01:48 Can	09 14:32 Leo	11 16:42 Lib
14 22:44 Ari	13 07:04 Tau	11 15:40 Gem	13 07:24 Leo	11 22:36 Vir	14 05:16 Sco
17 01:33 Tau	15 09:45 Gem	13 19:19 Can	15 16:31 Vir	14 09:57 Lib	16 17:47 Sag
19 04:18 Gem	17 13:55 Can	16 01:47 Leo	18 04:01 Lib	16 22:40 Sco	19 04:54 Cap
21 07:43 Can	19 20:00 Leo	18 10:51 Vir	20 16:36 Sco	19 11:12 Sag	21 14:16 Aqu
23 12:48 Leo	22 04:21 Vir	20 21:56 Lib	23 05:15 Sag	21 22:45 Cap	23 21:44 Pis
25 20:33 Vir	24 15:01 Lib	23 10:21 Sco	25 17:04 Cap	24 08:43 Aqu	26 03:03 Ari
28 07:13 Lib	27 03:25 Sco	25 23:04 Sag	28 02:44 Aqu	26 16:13 Pis	28 06:04 Tau
30 19:43 Sco	29 15:54 Sag	28 10:29 Cap	30 08:58 Pis	28 20:33 Ari	30 07:22 Gem
		30 18:53 Aqu		30 21:52 Tau	

Jan 1999	Feb 1999	Mar 1999	Apr 1999	May 1999	Jun 1999
01 08:15 Can	02 01:37 Vir	01 10:04 Vir	02 12:48 Sco	02 07:35 Sag	01 02:05 Cap
03 10:31 Leo	04 09:55 Lib	03 18:34 Lib	05 01:07 Sag	04 20:11 Cap	03 13:36 Aqu
05 15:48 Vir	06 21:05 Sco	06 05:21 Sco	07 13:38 Cap	07 07:39 Aqu	05 23:00 Pis
08 00:52 Lib	09 09:37 Sag	08 17:45 Sag	10 00:24 Aqu	09 16:15 Pis	08 05:07 Ari
10 12:47 Sco	11 21:09 Cap	11 05:53 Cap	12 07:34 Pis	11 20:52 Ari	10 07:43 Tau
13 01:22 Sag	14 05:56 Aqu	13 15:31 Aqu	14 10:46 Ari	13 21:56 Tau	12 07:48 Gem
15 12:28 Cap	16 11:39 Pis	15 21:30 Pis	16 11:08 Tau	15 21:07 Gem	14 07:14 Can
17 21:11 Aqu	18 15:06 Ari	18 00:12 Ari	18 10:39 Gem	17 20:39 Can	16 08:07 Leo
20 03:39 Pis	20 17:29 Tau	20 01:08 Tau	20 11:27 Can	19 22:36 Leo	18 12:11 Vir
22 08:24 Ari	22 19:53 Gem	22 02:05 Gem	22 15:05 Leo	22 04:14 Vir	20 20:10 Lib
24 11:52 Tau	24 23:08 Can	24 04:33 Can	24 22:03 Vir	24 13:28 Lib	23 07:17 Sco
26 14:29 Gem	27 03:44 Leo	26 09:22 Leo	27 07:45 Lib	27 01:04 Sco	25 19:50 Sag
28 16:57 Can		28 16:34 Vir	29 19:12 Sco	29 13:37 Sag	28 08:11 Cap
30 20:15 Leo		31 01:49 Lib			30 19:19 Aqu

Jul 1999	Aug 1999	Sep 1999	Oct 1999	Nov 1999	Dec 1999
03 04:34 Pis	01 16:46 Ari	02 05:24 Gem	01 13:31 Can	02 04:06 Vir	01 17:28 Lib
05 11:21 Ari	03 21:08 Tau	04 08:09 Can	03 17:13 Leo	04 11:56 Lib	04 03:35 Sco
07 15:21 Tau	05 23:56 Gem	06 11:29 Leo	05 22:39 Vir	06 21:45 Sco	06 15:27 Sag
09 17:00 Gem	08 01:52 Can	08 15:56 Vir	08 05:51 Lib	09 09:14 Sag	09 04:13 Cap
11 17:27 Can	10 03:55 Leo	10 22:15 Lib	10 15:01 Sco	11 21:59 Cap	11 16:58 Aqu
13 18:26 Leo	12 07:21 Vir	13 07:08 Sco	13 02:18 Sag	14 10:44 Aqu	14 04:17 Pis
15 21:38 Vir	14 13:23 Lib	15 18:34 Sag	15 15:02 Cap	16 21:20 Pis	16 12:29 Ari
18 04:19 Lib	16 22:39 Sco	18 07:12 Cap	18 03:16 Aqu	19 03:57 Ari	18 16:45 Tau
20 14:29 Sco	19 10:30 Sag	20 18:37 Aqu	20 12:32 Pis	21 06:26 Tau	20 17:39 Gem
23 02:47 Sag	21 22:59 Cap	23 02:51 Pis	22 17:41 Ari	23 06:14 Gem	22 16:53 Can
25 15:07 Cap	24 09:48 Aqu	25 07:33 Ari	24 19:25 Tau	25 05:29 Can	24 16:32 Leo
28 01:54 Aqu	26 17:49 Pis	27 09:51 Tau	26 19:33 Gem	27 06:18 Leo	26 18:34 Vir
30 10:27 Pis	28 23:09 Ari	29 11:21 Gem	28 20:09 Can	29 10:10 Vir	29 00:14 Lib
	31 02:40 Tau		30 22:46 Leo		31 09:35 Sco

Jan 2000	Feb 2000	Mar 2000	Apr 2000	May 2000	Jun 2000
02 21:31 Sag	01 17:09 Cap	02 13:13 Aqu	01 08:12 Pis	01 00:54 Ari	01 16:35 Gem
05 10:23 Cap	04 05:30 Aqu	04 23:29 Pis	03 15:21 Ari	03 04:54 Tau	03 16:30 Can
07 22:52 Aqu	06 16:01 Pis	07 06:54 Ari	05 19:29 Tau	05 06:23 Gem	05 16:45 Leo
10 09:58 Pis	09 00:17 Ari	09 12:01 Tau	07 21:58 Gem	07 07:14 Can	07 18:57 Vir
12 18:48 Ari	11 06:20 Tau	11 15:45 Gem	10 00:15 Can	09 09:01 Leo	09 23:58 Lib
15 00:37 Tau	13 10:22 Gem	13 18:51 Can	12 03:15 Leo	11 12:40 Vir	12 07:54 Sco
17 03:25 Gem	15 12:45 Can	15 21:43 Leo	14 07:18 Vir	13 18:27 Lib	14 18:17 Sag
19 04:01 Can	17 14:11 Leo	18 00:48 Vir	16 12:35 Lib	16 02:16 Sco	17 06:26 Cap
21 03:58 Leo	19 15:53 Vir	20 04:57 Lib	18 19:35 Sco	18 12:09 Sag	19 19:25 Aqu
23 05:07 Vir	21 19:21 Lib	22 11:17 Sco	21 04:57 Sag	21 00:01 Cap	22 07:51 Pis
25 09:09 Lib	24 01:57 Sco	24 20:42 Sag	23 16:46 Cap	23 12:59 Aqu	24 17:55 Ari
27 17:00 Sco	26 12:09 Sag	27 08:50 Cap	26 05:41 Aqu	26 01:07 Pis	27 00:18 Tau
30 04:17 Sag	29 00:45 Cap	29 21:33 Aqu	28 17:05 Pis	28 10:07 Ari	29 02:59 Gem
				30 15:02 Tau	

Jul 2000	Aug 2000	Sep 2000	Oct 2000	Nov 2000	Dec 2000
01 03:09 Can	01 13:27 Vir	02 05:54 Sco	01 22:49 Sag	03 06:40 Aqu	03 03:22 Pis
03 02:37 Leo	03 15:31 Lib	04 14:07 Sag	04 09:41 Cap	05 19:12 Pis	05 14:16 Ari
05 03:19 Vir	05 21:04 Sco	07 01:46 Cap	06 22:33 Aqu	08 05:02 Ari	07 21:26 Tau
07 06:46 Lib	08 06:29 Sag	09 14:43 Aqu	09 10:35 Pis	10 11:11 Tau	10 00:50 Gem
09 13:47 Sco	10 18:43 Cap	12 02:34 Pis	11 19:51 Ari	12 14:27 Gem	12 01:48 Can
12 00:05 Sag	13 07:42 Aqu	14 12:00 Ari	14 02:06 Tau	14 16:21 Can	14 02:08 Leo
14 12:27 Cap	15 19:41 Pis	16 19:05 Tau	16 06:19 Gem	16 18:18 Leo	16 03:29 Vir
17 01:26 Aqu	18 05:43 Ari	19 00:22 Gem	18 09:37 Can	18 21:15 Vir	18 07:00 Lib
19 13:43 Pis	20 13:30 Tau	21 04:15 Can	20 12:42 Leo	21 01:34 Lib	20 13:11 Sco
22 00:09 Ari	22 18:54 Gem	23 07:00 Leo	22 15:52 Vir	23 07:32 Sco	22 21:57 Sag
24 07:43 Tau	24 21:59 Can	25 09:02 Vir	24 19:30 Lib	25 15:32 Sag	25 08:53 Cap
26 12:01 Gem	26 23:16 Leo	27 11:22 Lib	27 00:23 Sco	28 01:57 Cap	27 21:25 Aqu
28 13:30 Can	28 23:55 Vir	29 15:29 Sco	29 07:40 Sag	30 14:25 Aqu	30 10:26 Pis
30 13:24 Leo	31 01:32 Lib		31 18:01 Cap		

Jan 2001	Feb 2001	Mar 2001	Apr 2001	May 2001	Jun 2001
01 22:13 Ari	02 20:55 Gem	02 03:36 Gem	02 17:53 Leo	02 02:16 Vir	02 14:55 Sco
04 06:56 Tau	05 00:00 Can	04 08:24 Can	04 19:46 Vir	04 04:50 Lib	04 20:57 Sag
06 11:43 Gem	07 00:20 Leo	06 10:30 Leo	06 20:57 Lib	06 08:00 Sco	07 05:22 Cap
08 13:09 Can	08 23:35 Vir	08 10:44 Vir	08 23:01 Sco	08 13:05 Sag	09 16:19 Aqu
10 12:44 Leo	10 23:45 Lib	10 10:48 Lib	11 03:46 Sag	10 21:09 Cap	12 04:53 Pis
12 12:26 Vir	13 02:50 Sco	12 12:42 Sco	13 12:20 Cap	13 08:19 Aqu	14 17:02 Ari
14 14:05 Lib	15 10:01 Sag	14 18:16 Sag	16 00:10 Aqu	15 21:00 Pis	17 02:38 Tau
16 19:02 Sco	17 20:58 Cap	17 04:01 Cap	18 12:59 Pis	18 08:40 Ari	19 08:42 Gem
19 03:35 Sag	20 09:53 Aqu	19 16:35 Aqu	21 00:17 Ari	20 17:29 Tau	21 11:41 Can
21 14:56 Cap	22 22:44 Pis	22 05:27 Pis	23 08:56 Tau	22 23:11 Gem	23 12:55 Leo
24 03:43 Aqu	25 10:19 Ari	24 16:43 Ari	25 15:11 Gem	25 02:42 Can	25 13:58 Vir
26 16:38 Pis	27 20:05 Tau	27 01:50 Tau	27 19:49 Can	27 05:11 Leo	27 16:10 Lib
29 04:34 Ari		29 09:00 Gem	29 23:24 Leo	29 07:37 Vir	29 20:28 Sco
31 14:20 Tau		31 14:22 Can		31 10:41 Lib	

Jul 2001	Aug 2001	Sep 2001	Oct 2001	Nov 2001	Dec 2001
02 03:13 Sag	03 05:53 Aqu	02 00:32 Pis	01 19:07 Ari	02 21:12 Gem	02 10:30 Can
04 12:21 Cap	05 18:29 Pis	04 12:57 Ari	04 06:00 Tau	05 03:43 Can	04 14:15 Leo
06 23:33 Aqu	08 07:04 Ari	07 00:17 Tau	06 15:11 Gem	07 08:33 Leo	06 17:11 Vir
09 12:04 Pis	10 18:22 Tau	09 09:40 Gem	08 22:19 Can	09 11:48 Vir	08 19:56 Lib
12 00:35 Ari	13 02:58 Gem	11 16:09 Can	11 02:54 Leo	11 13:53 Lib	10 23:09 Sco
14 11:12 Tau	15 07:54 Can	13 19:15 Leo	13 04:58 Vir	13 15:45 Sco	13 03:29 Sag
16 18:25 Gem	17 09:25 Leo	15 19:39 Vir	15 05:26 Lib	15 18:51 Sag	15 09:47 Cap
18 21:56 Can	19 08:53 Vir	17 19:00 Lib	17 06:02 Sco	18 00:39 Cap	17 18:42 Aqu
20 22:42 Leo	21 08:19 Lib	19 19:27 Sco	19 08:46 Sag	20 09:54 Aqu	20 06:09 Pis
22 22:28 Vir	23 09:50 Sco	21 23:02 Sag	21 15:10 Cap	22 21:51 Pis	22 18:44 Ari
24 23:07 Lib	25 14:58 Sag	24 06:47 Cap	24 01:26 Aqu	25 10:20 Ari	25 06:12 Tau
27 02:16 Sco	28 00:01 Cap	26 18:04 Aqu	26 13:55 Pis	27 21:05 Tau	27 14:38 Gem
29 08:43 Sag	30 11:47 Aqu	29 06:49 Pis	29 02:14 Ari	30 05:03 Gem	29 19:40 Can
31 18:15 Cap			31 12:47 Tau		31 22:09 Leo

Jan 2002	Feb 2002	Mar 2002	Apr 2002	May 2002	Jun 2002
02 23:34 Vir	01 08:44 Lib	02 18:51 Sco	01 06:48 Sag	03 04:43 Aqu	01 23:37 Pis
05 01:23 Lib	03 10:35 Sco	04 21:54 Sag	03 11:57 Cap	05 15:45 Pis	04 11:50 Ari
07 04:41 Sco	05 15:20 Sag	07 04:47 Cap	05 21:06 Aqu	08 04:21 Ari	07 00:06 Tau
09 09:57 Sag	07 23:08 Cap	09 14:55 Aqu	08 08:57 Pis	10 16:31 Tau	09 10:28 Gem
11 17:18 Cap	10 09:14 Aqu	12 02:56 Pis	10 21:40 Ari	13 03:04 Gem	11 18:14 Can
14 02:41 Aqu	12 20:52 Pis	14 15:33 Ari	13 09:55 Tau	15 11:33 Can	13 23:39 Leo
16 13:59 Pis	15 09:25 Ari	17 04:00 Tau	15 20:56 Gem	17 17:52 Leo	16 03:23 Vir
19 02:34 Ari	17 21:57 Tau	19 15:19 Gem	18 06:00 Can	19 22:00 Vir	18 06:10 Lib
24 00:27 Gem	20 08:49 Gem	22 00:06 Can	20 12:20 Leo	22 00:18 Lib	20 08:42 Sco
26 06:16 Can	22 16:15 Can	24 05:12 Leo	22 15:34 Vir	24 01:38 Sco	22 11:42 Sag
28 08:31 Leo	24 19:36 Leo	26 06:44 Vir	24 16:22 Lib	26 03:19 Sag	24 16:01 Cap
30 08:40 Vir	26 19:47 Vir	28 06:04 Lib	26 16:16 Sco	28 06:54 Cap	26 22:35 Aqu
	28 18:47 Lib	30 05:21 Sco	28 17:13 Sag	30 13:34 Aqu	29 08:00 Pis
			30 21:02 Cap		

Jul 2002	Aug 2002	Sep 2002	Oct 2002	Nov 2002	Dec 2002
01 19:48 Ari	03 03:46 Gem	01 21:13 Can	01 11:57 Leo	02 01:28 Lib	01 11:15 Sco
04 08:15 Tau	05 12:01 Can	04 02:36 Leo	03 14:52 Vir	04 01:10 Sco	03 11:58 Sag
06 19:00 Gem	07 16:27 Leo	06 04:16 Vir	05 14:52 Lib	06 01:01 Sag	05 13:39 Cap
09 02:36 Can	09 18:03 Vir	08 03:57 Lib	07 13:58 Sco	08 02:58 Cap	07 17:53 Aqu
11 07:07 Leo	11 18:38 Lib	10 03:48 Sco	09 14:21 Sag	10 08:26 Aqu	10 01:45 Pis
13 09:41 Vir	13 20:00 Sco	12 05:44 Sag	11 17:44 Cap	12 17:41 Pis	12 12:57 Ari
15 11:39 Lib	15 23:25 Sag	14 10:47 Cap	14 00:51 Aqu	15 05:37 Ari	15 01:43 Tau
17 14:12 Sco	18 05:15 Cap	16 18:54 Aqu	16 11:06 Pis	17 18:23 Tau	17 13:42 Gem
19 18:01 Sag	20 13:16 Aqu	19 05:17 Pis	18 23:13 Ari	20 06:24 Gem	19 23:29 Can
21 23:25 Cap	22 23:10 Pis	21 17:10 Ari	21 11:56 Tau	22 16:47 Can	22 06:48 Leo
24 06:39 Aqu	25 10:47 Ari	24 05:54 Tau	24 00:17 Gem	25 00:59 Leo	24 12:05 Vir
26 16:04 Pis	27 23:31 Tau	26 18:26 Gem	26 11:09 Can	27 06:41 Vir	26 15:53 Lib
29 03:38 Ari	30 11:44 Gem	29 05:01 Can	28 19:19 Leo	29 09:54 Lib	28 18:41 Sco
31 16:16 Tau			30 23:59 Vir		30 21:01 Sag

Jan 2003	Feb 2003	Mar 2003	Apr 2003	May 2003	Jun 2003
01 23:42 Cap	02 19:54 Pis	02 03:25 Pis	03 08:20 Tau	03 03:27 Gem	01 21:27 Can
04 03:56 Aqu	05 05:44 Ari	04 13:29 Ari	05 21:23 Gem	05 15:41 Can	04 07:24 Leo
06 10:56 Pis	07 17:58 Tau	07 01:36 Tau	08 09:35 Can	08 01:46 Leo	06 14:50 Vir
08 21:14 Ari	10 06:44 Gem	09 14:36 Gem	10 18:53 Leo	10 08:30 Vir	08 19:29 Lib
11 09:47 Tau	12 17:18 Can	12 02:11 Can	13 00:06 Vir	12 11:42 Lib	10 21:39 Sco
13 22:07 Gem	15 00:04 Leo	14 10:06 Leo	15 01:41 Lib	14 12:14 Sco	12 22:12 Sag
16 07:55 Can	17 03:22 Vir	16 13:52 Vir	17 01:17 Sco	16 11:43 Sag	14 22:38 Cap
18 14:29 Leo	19 04:48 Lib	18 14:43 Lib	19 00:51 Sag	18 12:03 Cap	17 00:41 Aqu
20 18:32 Vir	21 06:09 Sco	20 14:38 Sco	21 02:20 Cap	20 15:00 Aqu	19 05:56 Pis
22 21:22 Lib	23 08:45 Sag	22 15:33 Sag	23 06:57 Aqu	22 21:40 Pis	21 15:05 Ari
25 00:08 Sco	25 13:10 Cap	24 18:47 Cap	25 15:01 Pis	25 07:58 Ari	24 03:14 Tau
27 03:25 Sag	27 19:24 Aqu	27 00:50 Aqu	28 01:54 Ari	27 20:32 Tau	26 16:12 Gem
29 07:29 Cap		29 09:25 Pis	30 14:26 Tau	30 09:31 Gem	29 03:51 Can
31 12:44 Aqu		31 20:04 Ari			

Jul 2003	Aug 2003	Sep 2003	Oct 2003	Nov 2003	Dec 2003
01 13:12 Leo	02 06:47 Lib	02 18:31 Sag	02 03:21 Cap	02 19:51 Pis	02 10:55 Ari
03 20:15 Vir	04 10:12 Sco	04 21:51 Cap	04 07:46 Aqu	05 05:02 Ari	04 22:29 Tau
06 01:20 Lib	06 13:10 Sag	07 02:14 Aqu	06 14:20 Pis	07 16:28 Tau	07 11:25 Gem
08 04:43 Sco	08 16:02 Cap	09 08:06 Pis	08 23:07 Ari	10 05:14 Gem	10 00:10 Can
10 06:48 Sag	10 19:23 Aqu	11 16:08 Ari	13 22:44 Gem	12 18:09 Can	12 11:40 Leo
12 08:21 Cap	13 00:18 Pis	14 02:49 Tau	16 11:40 Can	15 05:47 Leo	14 21:06 Vir
14 10:38 Aqu	15 07:59 Ari	16 15:31 Gem	18 22:41 Leo	17 14:35 Vir	17 03:46 Lib
16 15:13 Pis	17 18:52 Tau	19 04:07 Can	21 06:01 Vir	19 19:41 Lib	19 07:19 Sco
18 23:19 Ari	20 07:40 Gem	21 14:02 Leo	23 09:27 Lib	21 21:23 Sco	21 08:16 Sag
21 10:47 Tau	22 19:44 Can	23 20:04 Vir	25 10:09 Sco	23 21:03 Sag	23 07:55 Cap
23 23:42 Gem	25 04:48 Leo	25 22:49 Lib	27 09:55 Sag	25 20:31 Cap	25 08:13 Aqu
26 11:22 Can	27 10:26 Vir	27 23:52 Sco	29 10:37 Cap	27 21:48 Aqu	27 11:09 Pis
28 20:16 Leo	29 13:41 Lib	30 00:57 Sag	31 13:41 Aqu	30 02:25 Pis	29 18:08 Ari
31 02:26 Vir	31 16:00 Sco				

Jan 2004	Feb 2004	Mar 2004	Apr 2004	May 2004	Jun 2004
01 05:01 Tau	02 14:02 Can	03 09:17 Leo	02 02:45 Vir	01 18:02 Lib	02 07:52 Sag
03 17:57 Gem	05 00:49 Leo	05 17:17 Vir	04 07:52 Lib	03 20:38 Sco	04 07:12 Cap
06 06:38 Can	07 09:02 Vir	07 22:30 Lib	06 10:24 Sco	05 21:08 Sag	06 07:10 Aqu
08 17:38 Leo	09 15:12 Lib	10 02:02 Sco	08 11:50 Sag	07 21:16 Cap	08 09:38 Pis
11 02:37 Vir	11 19:57 Sco	12 04:57 Sag	10 13:33 Cap	09 22:46 Aqu	10 15:48 Ari
13 09:37 Lib	13 23:35 Sag	14 07:51 Cap	12 16:32 Aqu	12 02:51 Pis	13 01:36 Tau
15 14:32 Sco	16 02:13 Cap	16 11:10 Aqu	14 21:23 Pis	14 10:02 Ari	15 13:43 Gem
17 17:17 Sag	18 04:27 Aqu	18 15:26 Pis	17 04:24 Ari	16 19:56 Tau	18 02:37 Can
19 18:24 Cap	20 07:26 Pis	20 21:28 Ari	19 13:42 Tau	19 07:46 Gem	20 15:04 Leo
21 19:11 Aqu	22 12:45 Ari	23 06:09 Tau	22 01:09 Gem	21 20:34 Can	23 02:09 Vir
23 21:28 Pis	24 21:29 Tau	25 17:34 Gem	24 13:55 Can	24 09:06 Leo	25 10:49 Lib
26 03:05 Ari	27 09:21 Gem	28 06:22 Can	27 02:14 Leo	26 19:51 Vir	27 16:12 Sco
28 12:45 Tau	29 22:11 Can	30 18:06 Leo	29 11:59 Vir	29 03:22 Lib	29 18:15 Sag
31 01:18 Gem				31 07:08 Sco	

Jul 2004	Aug 2004	Sep 2004	Oct 2004	Nov 2004	Dec 2004
01 18:02 Cap	02 04:34 Pis	03 00:15 Tau	02 18:54 Gem	01 14:52 Can	01 10:49 Leo
03 17:22 Aqu	04 07:59 Ari	05 10:23 Gem	05 06:53 Can	04 03:31 Leo	03 23:00 Vir
05 18:26 Pis	06 15:25 Tau	07 22:50 Can	07 19:22 Leo	06 14:59 Vir	06 08:45 Lib
07 23:03 Ari	09 02:32 Gem	10 11:05 Leo	10 06:00 Vir	08 23:22 Lib	08 14:43 Sco
10 07:50 Tau	11 15:19 Can	12 21:16 Vir	12 13:32 Lib	11 04:05 Sco	10 16:54 Sag
12 19:44 Gem	14 03:29 Leo	15 04:53 Lib	14 18:10 Sco	13 05:56 Sag	12 16:42 Cap
15 08:40 Can	16 13:49 Vir	17 10:25 Sco	16 20:58 Sag	15 06:33 Cap	14 16:10 Aqu
17 20:55 Leo	18 22:09 Lib	19 14:29 Sag	18 23:06 Cap	17 07:38 Aqu	16 17:24 Pis
20 07:43 Vir	21 04:36 Sco	21 17:35 Cap	21 01:37 Aqu	19 10:37 Pis	18 21:51 Ari
22 16:38 Lib	23 09:08 Sag	23 20:09 Aqu	23 05:13 Pis	21 16:10 Ari	21 05:51 Tau
24 23:08 Sco	25 11:46 Cap	25 22:55 Pis	25 10:24 Ari	24 00:15 Tau	23 16:31 Gem
27 02:47 Sag	27 13:08 Aqu	28 02:57 Ari	27 17:37 Tau	26 10:25 Gem	26 04:37 Can
29 03:57 Cap	29 14:33 Pis	30 09:23 Tau	30 03:10 Gem	28 22:10 Can	28 17:13 Leo
31 03:54 Aqu	31 17:46 Ari				31 05:32 Vir

Jan 2005	Feb 2005	Mar 2005	Apr 2005	May 2005	Jun 2005
02 16:18 Lib	01 06:50 Sco	02 18:29 Sag	01 03:47 Cap	02 14:42 Pis	01 00:07 Ari
04 23:59 Sco	03 12:20 Sag	04 22:11 Cap	03 06:31 Aqu	04 18:35 Ari	03 06:19 Tau
07 03:44 Sag	05 14:32 Cap	06 23:49 Aqu	05 08:45 Pis	07 00:01 Tau	05 14:35 Gem
09 04:11 Cap	07 14:27 Aqu	09 00:32 Pis	07 11:28 Ari	09 07:28 Gem	08 00:46 Can
11 03:07 Aqu	09 14:00 Pis	11 02:03 Ari	09 15:49 Tau	11 17:20 Can	10 12:39 Leo
13 02:50 Pis	11 15:21 Ari	13 06:05 Tau	11 22:54 Gem	14 05:16 Leo	13 01:21 Vir
15 05:26 Ari	13 20:17 Tau	15 13:43 Gem	14 09:02 Can	16 17:45 Vir	15 12:58 Lib
17 12:05 Tau	16 05:17 Gem	18 00:43 Can	16 21:16 Leo	19 04:29 Lib	17 21:23 Sco
19 22:23 Gem	18 17:12 Can	20 13:16 Leo	19 09:26 Vir	21 11:48 Sco	20 01:44 Sag
22 10:41 Can	21 05:54 Leo	23 01:10 Vir	21 19:26 Lib	23 15:38 Sag	22 02:52 Cap
24 23:20 Leo	23 17:44 Vir	25 10:59 Lib	24 02:25 Sco	25 17:11 Cap	24 02:36 Aqu
27 11:23 Vir	26 03:58 Lib	27 18:29 Sco	26 06:46 Sag	27 18:10 Aqu	26 03:02 Pis
29 22:12 Lib	28 12:20 Sco	29 23:56 Sag	28 09:32 Cap	29 20:09 Pis	28 05:51 Ari
			30 11:53 Aqu		30 11:44 Tau

Jul 2005	Aug 2005	Sep 2005	Oct 2005	Nov 2005	Dec 2005
02 20:25 Gem	01 12:52 Can	02 19:55 Vir	02 14:23 Lib	01 07:28 Sco	03 01:42 Cap
05 07:07 Can	04 01:09 Leo	05 07:51 Lib	05 00:03 Sco	03 13:55 Sag	05 03:36 Aqu
07 19:10 Leo	06 13:53 Vir	07 18:09 Sco	07 07:27 Sag	05 18:17 Cap	07 05:44 Pis
10 07:56 Vir	09 02:08 Lib	10 02:02 Sag	09 12:43 Cap	07 21:30 Aqu	09 09:01 Ari
12 20:08 Lib	11 12:34 Sco	12 06:56 Cap	11 16:05 Aqu	10 00:22 Pis	11 13:45 Tau
15 05:50 Sco	13 19:47 Sag	14 09:02 Aqu	13 18:05 Pis	12 03:22 Ari	13 19:59 Gem
17 11:34 Sag	15 23:12 Cap	16 09:25 Pis	15 19:39 Ari	14 07:02 Tau	16 04:01 Can
19 13:26 Cap	17 23:38 Aqu	18 09:43 Ari	17 22:04 Tau	16 12:10 Gem	18 14:17 Leo
21 12:56 Aqu	19 22:52 Pis	20 11:47 Tau	20 02:44 Gem	18 19:42 Can	21 02:38 Vir
23 12:12 Pis	21 23:01 Ari	22 17:06 Gem	22 10:40 Can	21 06:09 Leo	23 15:25 Lib
25 13:22 Ari	24 01:57 Tau	25 02:10 Can	24 21:48 Leo	23 18:40 Vir	26 02:03 Sco
27 17:54 Tau	26 08:42 Gem	27 14:02 Leo	27 10:27 Vir	26 06:57 Lib	28 08:43 Sag
30 02:01 Gem	28 18:56 Can	30 02:44 Vir	29 22:14 Lib	28 16:32 Sco	30 11:35 Cap
	31 07:13 Leo			30 22:32 Sag	

Jan 2006	Feb 2006	Mar 2006	Apr 2006	May 2006	Jun 2006
01 12:15 Aqu	01 22:46 Ari	01 09:19 Ari	01 23:49 Gem	01 15:17 Can	02 20:16 Vir
03 12:44 Pis	04 01:31 Tau	03 10:22 Tau	04 06:14 Can	04 00:17 Leo	05 09:07 Lib
05 14:44 Ari	06 07:32 Gem	05 14:37 Gem	06 16:24 Leo	06 12:19 Vir	07 20:40 Sco
07 19:08 Tau	08 16:33 Can	07 22:37 Can	09 04:58 Vir	09 01:10 Lib	10 05:05 Sag
10 01:58 Gem	11 03:44 Leo	10 09:41 Leo	11 17:46 Lib	11 12:24 Sco	12 10:19 Cap
12 10:49 Can	13 16:13 Vir	12 22:23 Vir	14 05:08 Sco	13 20:56 Sag	14 13:32 Aqu
14 21:30 Leo	16 05:08 Lib	15 11:12 Lib	16 14:19 Sag	16 02:58 Cap	16 16:05 Pis
17 09:48 Vir	18 17:10 Sco	17 22:58 Sco	18 21:13 Cap	18 07:19 Aqu	18 18:53 Ari
19 22:48 Lib	21 02:37 Sag	20 08:42 Sag	21 01:55 Aqu	20 10:39 Pis	20 22:22 Tau
22 10:27 Sco	23 08:15 Cap	22 15:35 Cap	23 04:43 Pis	22 13:23 Ari	23 02:49 Gem
24 18:37 Sag	25 10:14 Aqu	24 19:21 Aqu	25 06:12 Ari	24 16:00 Tau	25 08:47 Can
26 22:31 Cap	27 09:56 Pis	26 20:32 Pis	27 07:27 Tau	26 19:19 Gem	27 17:08 Leo
28 23:09 Aqu		28 20:31 Ari	29 09:58 Gem	29 00:33 Can	30 04:14 Vir
30 22:32 Pis		30 21:00 Tau		31 08:51 Leo	

Jul 2006	Aug 2006	Sep 2006	Oct 2006	Nov 2006	Dec 2006
02 17:04 Lib	01 13:07 Sco	02 14:34 Cap	02 03:24 Aqu	02 15:46 Ari	02 01:26 Tau
05 05:12 Sco	03 23:13 Sag	04 18:14 Aqu	04 05:33 Pis	04 16:05 Tau	04 03:05 Gem
07 14:13 Sag	06 05:19 Cap	06 18:57 Pis	06 05:32 Ari	06 16:46 Gem	06 06:00 Can
09 19:24 Cap	08 07:47 Aqu	08 18:23 Ari	08 05:04 Tau	08 19:45 Can	08 11:51 Leo
11 21:46 Aqu	10 08:11 Pis	10 18:30 Tau	10 06:06 Gem	11 02:33 Leo	10 21:30 Vir
13 22:59 Pis	12 08:22 Ari	12 20:59 Gem	12 10:20 Can	13 13:17 Vir	13 09:59 Lib
16 00:38 Ari	14 09:59 Tau	15 02:53 Can	14 18:37 Leo	16 02:14 Lib	15 22:42 Sco
18 03:44 Tau	16 14:06 Gem	17 12:14 Leo	17 06:15 Vir	18 14:46 Sco	18 09:10 Sag
20 08:37 Gem	18 21:02 Can	20 00:06 Vir	19 19:19 Lib	21 01:15 Sag	20 16:39 Cap
22 15:27 Can	21 06:33 Leo	22 13:05 Lib	22 07:54 Sco	23 09:25 Cap	22 21:48 Aqu
25 00:24 Leo	23 18:07 Vir	25 01:54 Sco	24 18:53 Sag	25 15:40 Aqu	25 01:43 Pis
27 11:35 Vir	26 07:01 Lib	27 13:15 Sag	27 03:46 Cap	27 20:20 Pis	27 05:03 Ari
30 00:27 Lib	28 19:55 Sco	29 22:01 Cap	29 10:16 Aqu	29 23:29 Ari	29 08:08 Tau
	31 06:59 Sag		31 14:10 Pis		31 11:16 Gem

Jan 2007	Feb 2007	Mar 2007	Apr 2007	May 2007	Jun 2007
02 15:14 Can	01 05:14 Leo	02 21:31 Vir	01 15:42 Lib	01 10:40 Sco	02 15:09 Cap
04 21:14 Leo	03 14:33 Vir	05 09:24 Lib	04 04:35 Sco	03 22:47 Sag	04 23:15 Aqu
07 06:17 Vir	06 02:14 Lib	07 22:16 Sco	06 16:56 Sag	06 09:20 Cap	07 05:23 Pis
09 18:14 Lib	08 15:08 Sco	10 10:36 Sag	09 03:35 Cap	08 17:47 Aqu	09 09:26 Ari
12 07:07 Sco	11 03:00 Sag	12 20:34 Cap	11 11:22 Aqu	10 23:31 Pis	11 11:29 Tau
14 18:10 Sag	13 11:41 Cap	15 02:51 Aqu	13 15:38 Pis	13 02:18 Ari	13 12:24 Gem
17 01:49 Cap	15 16:34 Aqu	17 05:30 Pis	15 16:47 Ari	15 02:48 Tau	15 13:45 Can
19 06:15 Aqu	17 18:30 Pis	19 05:42 Ari	17 16:11 Tau	17 02:33 Gem	17 17:25 Leo
21 08:48 Pis	19 19:06 Ari	21 05:15 Tau	19 15:51 Gem	19 03:37 Can	20 00:45 Vir
23 10:52 Ari	21 20:03 Tau	23 06:06 Gem	21 17:50 Can	21 07:56 Leo	22 11:42 Lib
25 13:28 Tau	23 22:41 Gem	25 09:48 Can	23 23:37 Leo	23 16:25 Vir	25 00:26 Sco
27 17:09 Gem	26 03:47 Can	27 17:03 Leo	26 09:23 Vir	26 04:15 Lib	27 12:23 Sag
29 22:16 Can	28 11:29 Leo	30 03:26 Vir	28 21:44 Lib	28 17:10 Sco	29 22:04 Cap
				31 05:06 Sag	

Jul 2007	Aug 2007	Sep 2007	Oct 2007	Nov 2007	Dec 2007
02 05:23 Aqu	02 20:42 Ari	01 05:35 Tau	02 16:56 Can	01 04:48 Leo	03 06:00 Lib
04 10:52 Pis	04 23:15 Tau	03 07:29 Gem	04 22:26 Leo	03 12:43 Vir	05 18:30 Sco
06 14:56 Ari	07 02:01 Gem	05 11:07 Can	07 07:02 Vir	05 23:47 Lib	08 07:10 Sag
08 17:53 Tau	09 05:36 Can	07 16:59 Leo	09 17:57 Lib	08 12:17 Sco	10 18:50 Cap
10 20:09 Gem	11 10:41 Leo	10 01:09 Vir	12 06:13 Sco	11 00:58 Sag	13 05:01 Aqu
12 22:39 Can	13 18:02 Vir	12 11:30 Lib	14 18:57 Sag	13 13:00 Cap	15 13:14 Pis
15 02:43 Leo	16 04:03 Lib	14 23:36 Sco	17 07:02 Cap	15 23:29 Aqu	17 18:52 Ari
17 09:39 Vir	18 16:12 Sco	17 12:20 Sag	19 16:51 Aqu	18 07:14 Pis	19 21:38 Tau
19 19:53 Lib	21 04:43 Sag	19 23:51 Cap	21 23:02 Pis	20 11:24 Ari	21 22:14 Gem
22 08:17 Sco	23 15:19 Cap	22 08:17 Aqu	24 01:24 Ari	22 12:19 Tau	23 22:18 Can
24 20:29 Sag	25 22:34 Aqu	24 12:55 Pis	26 01:06 Tau	24 11:30 Gem	25 23:51 Leo
27 06:21 Cap	28 02:34 Pis	26 14:23 Ari	28 00:11 Gem	26 11:07 Can	28 04:43 Vir
29 13:13 Aqu	30 04:24 Ari	28 14:17 Tau	30 00:49 Can	28 13:23 Leo	30 13:36 Lib
31 17:40 Pis		30 14:34 Gem		30 19:43 Vir	

Jan 2008	Feb 2008	Mar 2008	Apr 2008	May 2008	Jun 2008
02 01:31 Sco	03 09:51 Cap	01 18:32 Cap	02 20:54 Pis	02 10:51 Ari	02 22:06 Gem
04 14:12 Sag	05 19:09 Aqu	04 04:24 Aqu	05 00:27 Ari	04 11:58 Tau	04 21:16 Can
07 01:42 Cap	08 01:46 Pis	06 10:52 Pis	07 01:19 Tau	06 11:18 Gem	06 22:00 Leo
09 11:13 Aqu	10 06:17 Ari	08 14:23 Ari	09 01:26 Gem	08 11:02 Can	09 02:01 Vir
11 18:44 Pis	12 09:33 Tau	10 16:14 Tau	11 02:43 Can	10 13:09 Leo	11 09:54 Lib
14 00:23 Ari	14 12:19 Gem	12 17:54 Gem	13 06:28 Leo	12 18:47 Vir	13 20:52 Sco
16 04:12 Tau	16 15:12 Can	14 20:37 Can	15 13:06 Vir	15 03:46 Lib	16 09:19 Sag
18 06:30 Gem	18 18:51 Leo	17 01:03 Leo	17 22:09 Lib	17 14:58 Sco	18 21:51 Cap
20 08:05 Can	21 00:06 Vir	19 07:24 Vir	20 09:00 Sco	20 03:18 Sag	21 09:33 Aqu
22 10:20 Leo	23 07:44 Lib	21 15:44 Lib	22 21:07 Sag	22 15:55 Cap	23 19:31 Pis
24 14:48 Vir	25 18:05 Sco	24 02:06 Sco	25 09:46 Cap	25 03:51 Aqu	26 02:48 Ari
26 22:34 Lib	28 06:21 Sag	26 14:10 Sag	27 21:26 Aqu	27 13:37 Pis	28 06:50 Tau
29 09:34 Sco		29 02:42 Cap	30 06:10 Pis	29 19:52 Ari	30 08:03 Gem
31 22:07 Sag		31 13:33 Aqu		31 22:18 Tau	

Jul 2008	Aug 2008	Sep 2008	Oct 2008	Nov 2008	Dec 2008
02 07:53 Can	02 20:59 Vir	01 11:44 Lib	01 04:26 Sco	02 11:12 Cap	02 06:44 Aqu
04 08:15 Leo	05 02:27 Lib	03 20:01 Sco	03 15:13 Sag	05 00:01 Aqu	04 18:22 Pis
06 11:03 Vir	07 11:25 Sco	06 07:10 Sag	06 03:48 Cap	07 10:42 Pis	07 02:43 Ari
08 17:30 Lib	09 23:10 Sag	08 19:44 Cap	08 16:02 Aqu	09 17:25 Ari	09 06:52 Tau
11 03:34 Sco	12 11:41 Cap	11 07:19 Aqu	11 01:31 Pis	11 20:05 Tau	11 07:34 Gem
13 15:49 Sag	14 22:55 Aqu	13 16:04 Pis	13 07:07 Ari	13 20:11 Gem	13 06:40 Can
16 04:19 Cap	17 07:46 Pis	15 21:39 Ari	15 09:31 Tau	15 19:52 Can	15 06:22 Leo
18 15:39 Aqu	19 14:09 Ari	18 00:56 Tau	17 10:26 Gem	17 21:07 Leo	17 08:35 Vir
21 01:07 Pis	21 18:37 Tau	20 03:16 Gem	19 11:40 Can	20 01:12 Vir	19 14:22 Lib
23 08:22 Ari	23 21:48 Gem	22 05:48 Can	21 14:34 Leo	22 08:19 Lib	21 23:36 Sco
25 13:14 Tau	26 00:18 Can	24 09:13 Leo	23 19:39 Vir	24 17:53 Sco	24 11:12 Sag
27 15:55 Gem	28 02:50 Leo	26 13:52 Vir	26 02:47 Lib	27 05:13 Sag	26 23:55 Cap
29 17:12 Can	30 06:18 Vir	28 20:05 Lib	28 11:47 Sco	29 17:47 Cap	29 12:42 Aqu
31 18:22 Leo			30 22:40 Sag		

Jan 2009	Feb 2009	Mar 2009	Apr 2009	May 2009	Jun 2009
01 00:27 Pis	01 22:08 Tau	01 03:33 Tau	01 16:30 Can	01 00:55 Leo	01 15:16 Lib
03 09:49 Ari	04 02:14 Gem	03 07:58 Gem	03 19:32 Leo	03 04:36 Vir	03 22:43 Sco
05 15:45 Tau	06 04:05 Can	05 11:07 Can	05 23:01 Vir	05 09:51 Lib	06 08:23 Sag
07 18:11 Gem	08 04:43 Leo	07 13:24 Leo	08 03:22 Lib	07 16:47 Sco	08 19:59 Cap
09 18:14 Can	10 05:38 Vir	09 15:34 Vir	10 09:23 Sco	10 01:49 Sag	11 08:52 Aqu
11 17:41 Leo	12 08:32 Lib	11 18:46 Lib	12 18:00 Sag	12 13:08 Cap	13 21:31 Pis
13 18:33 Vir	14 14:50 Sco	14 00:22 Sco	15 05:26 Cap	15 02:01 Aqu	16 07:51 Ari
15 22:29 Lib	17 05:04 Sag	16 09:21 Sag	17 18:18 Aqu	17 14:16 Pis	18 14:20 Tau
18 06:19 Sco	19 13:24 Cap	18 21:18 Cap	20 05:54 Pis	19 23:30 Ari	20 17:00 Gem
20 17:29 Sag	22 02:06 Aqu	21 10:05 Aqu	22 14:08 Ari	22 04:40 Tau	22 17:12 Can
23 06:17 Cap	24 12:59 Pis	23 21:07 Pis	24 18:46 Tau	24 06:34 Gem	24 16:50 Leo
25 18:56 Aqu	26 21:23 Ari	26 05:02 Ari	26 21:02 Gem	26 06:58 Can	26 17:46 Vir
28 06:11 Pis		28 10:09 Tau	28 22:38 Can	28 07:44 Leo	28 21:24 Lib
30 15:24 Ari		30 13:36 Gem		30 10:17 Vir	

Jul 2009	Aug 2009	Sep 2009	Oct 2009	Nov 2009	Dec 2009
01 04:18 Sco	02 08:07 Cap	01 03:42 Aqu	03 09:20 Ari	02 00:44 Tau	01 14:23 Gem
03 14:10 Sag	04 21:07 Aqu	03 15:57 Pis	05 16:33 Tau	04 04:52 Gem	03 16:01 Can
06 02:07 Cap	07 09:34 Pis	06 02:14 Ari	07 21:46 Gem	06 07:42 Can	05 17:07 Leo
08 15:02 Aqu	09 20:22 Ari	08 10:17 Tau	10 01:47 Can	08 10:22 Leo	07 19:05 Vir
11 03:43 Pis	12 04:49 Tau	10 16:16 Gem	12 05:02 Leo	10 13:30 Vir	09 22:46 Lib
13 14:39 Ari	14 10:25 Gem	12 20:19 Can	14 07:45 Vir	12 17:22 Lib	12 04:31 Sco
15 22:29 Tau	16 13:13 Can	14 22:39 Leo	16 10:29 Lib	14 22:23 Sco	14 12:24 Sag
18 02:41 Gem	18 13:57 Leo	16 23:55 Vir	18 14:22 Sco	17 05:21 Sag	16 22:31 Cap
20 03:51 Can	20 14:01 Vir	19 01:26 Lib	20 20:48 Sag	19 15:00 Cap	19 10:38 Aqu
22 03:27 Leo	22 15:12 Lib	21 04:52 Sco	23 06:38 Cap	22 03:10 Aqu	21 23:41 Pis
24 03:22 Vir	24 19:16 Sco	23 11:42 Sag	25 19:07 Aqu	24 16:06 Pis	24 11:38 Ari
26 05:25 Lib	27 03:15 Sag	25 22:18 Cap	28 07:44 Pis	27 03:10 Ari	26 20:25 Tau
28 10:55 Sco	29 14:43 Cap	28 11:05 Aqu	30 17:56 Ari	29 10:33 Tau	29 01:13 Gem
30 20:09 Sag		30 23:25 Pis			31 02:45 Can

Jan 2010	Feb 2010	Mar 2010	Apr 2010	May 2010	Jun 2010
02 02:41 Leo	02 13:42 Lib	02 00:31 Lib	02 16:52 Sag	02 09:59 Cap	01 05:07 Aqu
04 02:52 Vir	04 16:55 Sco	04 02:11 Sco	05 01:06 Cap	04 20:51 Aqu	03 17:32 Pis
06 04:58 Lib	07 00:03 Sag	06 07:35 Sag	07 12:49 Aqu	07 09:33 Pis	06 05:49 Ari
08 09:59 Sco	09 10:42 Cap	08 17:12 Cap	10 01:47 Pis	09 21:28 Ari	08 15:40 Tau
10 18:09 Sag	11 23:23 Aqu	11 05:41 Aqu	12 13:30 Ari	12 06:47 Tau	10 22:10 Gem
13 04:53 Cap	14 12:22 Pis	13 18:43 Pis	14 22:54 Tau	14 13:17 Gem	13 01:50 Can
15 17:16 Aqu	17 00:30 Ari	16 06:31 Ari	17 06:07 Gem	16 17:45 Can	15 03:54 Leo
18 06:16 Pis	19 10:54 Tau	18 16:29 Tau	19 11:38 Can	18 21:06 Leo	17 05:40 Vir
20 18:35 Ari	21 18:46 Gem	21 00:28 Gem	21 15:41 Leo	20 23:58 Vir	19 08:13 Lib
23 04:39 Tau	23 23:28 Can	23 06:15 Can	23 18:24 Vir	23 02:49 Lib	21 12:13 Sco
25 11:11 Gem	26 01:08 Leo	25 09:38 Leo	25 20:16 Lib	25 06:17 Sco	23 18:09 Sag
27 14:01 Can	28 00:52 Vir	27 10:57 Vir	27 22:28 Sco	27 11:15 Sag	26 02:21 Cap
29 14:10 Leo		29 11:21 Lib	30 02:35 Sag	29 18:43 Cap	28 12:51 Aqu
31 13:23 Vir		31 12:41 Sco			

Jul 2010	Aug 2010	Sep 2010	Oct 2010	Nov 2010	Dec 2010
01 01:09 Pis	02 08:12 Tau	01 00:19 Gem	02 18:20 Leo	01 03:51 Vir	02 14:43 Sco
03 13:43 Ari	04 16:53 Gem	03 06:50 Can	04 20:00 Vir	03 05:19 Lib	04 17:59 Sag
06 00:28 Tau	06 21:49 Can	05 09:45 Leo	06 19:52 Lib	05 06:15 Sco	06 23:15 Cap
08 07:50 Gem	08 23:22 Leo	07 09:53 Vir	08 19:52 Sco	07 08:27 Sag	09 07:30 Aqu
10 11:38 Can	10 23:00 Vir	09 09:01 Lib	10 22:08 Sag	09 13:36 Cap	11 18:40 Pis
12 12:54 Leo	12 22:42 Lib	11 09:21 Sco	13 04:16 Cap	11 22:31 Aqu	14 07:14 Ari
14 13:15 Vir	15 00:26 Sco	13 12:51 Sag	15 14:22 Aqu	14 10:23 Pis	16 18:48 Tau
16 14:24 Lib	17 05:33 Sag	15 20:29 Cap	18 02:51 Pis	16 22:58 Ari	19 03:37 Gem
18 17:41 Sco	19 14:16 Cap	18 07:34 Aqu	20 15:22 Ari	19 10:04 Tau	21 09:22 Can
20 23:48 Sag	22 01:37 Aqu	20 20:14 Pis	23 02:29 Tau	21 18:45 Gem	23 12:50 Leo
23 08:38 Cap	24 14:10 Pis	23 08:46 Ari	25 11:47 Gem	24 01:13 Can	25 15:14 Vir
25 19:37 Aqu	27 02:49 Ari	25 20:16 Tau	27 19:14 Can	26 06:01 Leo	27 17:37 Lib
28 07:59 Pis	29 14:34 Tau	28 06:10 Gem	30 00:38 Leo	28 09:33 Vir	29 20:49 Sco
30 20:41 Ari		30 13:45 Can		30 12:15 Lib	

Jan 2011	Feb 2011	Mar 2011	Apr 2011	May 2011	Jun 2011
01 01:20 Sag	01 23:21 Aqu	01 05:14 Aqu	02 11:15 Ari	02 05:58 Tau	03 08:36 Can
03 07:38 Cap	04 10:23 Pis	03 16:46 Pis	04 23:45 Tau	04 17:08 Gem	05 15:03 Leo
05 16:07 Aqu	06 22:45 Ari	06 05:13 Ari	07 11:21 Gem	07 02:31 Can	07 19:33 Vir
08 02:56 Pis	09 11:21 Tau	08 17:51 Tau	09 21:01 Can	09 09:35 Leo	09 22:30 Lib
10 15:22 Ari	11 22:20 Gem	11 05:30 Gem	12 03:36 Leo	11 13:58 Vir	12 00:33 Sco
13 03:36 Tau	14 05:48 Can	13 14:28 Can	14 06:40 Vir	13 15:56 Lib	14 02:38 Sag
15 13:22 Gem	16 09:14 Leo	15 19:32 Leo	16 06:59 Lib	15 16:32 Sco	16 05:58 Cap
17 19:28 Can	18 09:39 Vir	17 20:53 Vir	18 06:19 Sco	17 17:23 Sag	18 11:47 Aqu
19 22:15 Leo	20 09:01 Lib	19 20:03 Lib	20 06:49 Sag	19 20:15 Cap	20 20:44 Pis
21 23:10 Vir	22 09:28 Sco	21 19:17 Sco	22 10:24 Cap	22 02:31 Aqu	23 08:23 Ari
23 23:58 Lib	24 12:45 Sag	23 20:45 Sag	24 17:58 Aqu	24 12:22 Pis	25 20:52 Tau
26 02:15 Sco	26 19:31 Cap	26 01:57 Cap	27 04:57 Pis	27 00:36 Ari	28 07:55 Gem
28 06:54 Sag		28 10:59 Aqu	29 17:32 Ari	29 13:01 Tau	30 16:12 Can
30 14:03 Cap		30 22:37 Pis		31 23:56 Gem	

Jul 2011	Aug 2011	Sep 2011	Oct 2011	Nov 2011	Dec 2011
02 21:42 Leo	01 08:41 Vir	01 18:48 Sco	01 04:41 Sag	01 22:07 Aqu	01 14:44 Pis
05 01:15 Vir	03 10:04 Lib	03 21:03 Sag	03 08:15 Cap	04 07:17 Pis	04 01:50 Ari
07 03:53 Lib	05 11:57 Sco	06 02:03 Cap	05 15:17 Aqu	06 19:01 Ari	06 14:33 Tau
09 06:31 Sco	07 15:20 Sag	08 09:41 Aqu	08 01:13 Pis	09 07:45 Tau	09 02:52 Gem
11 09:46 Sag	09 20:37 Cap	10 19:26 Pis	10 12:56 Ari	11 20:09 Gem	11 13:25 Can
13 14:13 Cap	12 03:47 Aqu	13 06:49 Ari	13 01:34 Tau	14 07:18 Can	13 21:47 Leo
15 20:29 Aqu	14 12:53 Pis	15 19:24 Tau	15 14:14 Gem	16 16:16 Leo	16 03:58 Vir
18 05:12 Pis	17 00:01 Ari	18 08:05 Gem	18 01:37 Can	18 22:18 Vir	18 08:06 Lib
20 16:24 Ari	19 12:35 Tau	20 18:52 Can	20 10:05 Leo	21 01:16 Lib	20 10:33 Sco
23 04:57 Tau	22 00:52 Gem	23 01:55 Leo	22 14:40 Vir	23 01:58 Sco	22 12:03 Sag
25 16:33 Gem	24 10:30 Can	25 04:49 Vir	24 15:49 Lib	25 01:57 Sag	24 13:47 Cap
28 01:11 Can	26 16:08 Leo	27 04:51 Lib	26 15:09 Sco	27 03:04 Cap	26 17:14 Aqu
30 06:15 Leo	28 18:13 Vir	29 04:05 Sco	28 14:45 Sag	29 07:01 Aqu	28 23:45 Pis
	30 18:25 Lib		30 16:38 Cap		31 09:47 Ari

Jan 2012	Feb 2012	Mar 2012	Apr 2012	May 2012	Jun 2012
02 22:15 Tau	01 19:13 Gem	02 15:07 Can	01 08:35 Leo	03 02:03 Lib	01 12:31 Sco
05 10:43 Gem	04 06:03 Can	04 23:17 Leo	03 13:52 Vir	05 02:19 Sco	03 12:33 Sag
07 21:04 Can	06 13:23 Leo	07 03:26 Vir	05 15:32 Lib	07 01:39 Sag	05 12:31 Cap
10 04:35 Leo	08 17:32 Vir	09 04:50 Lib	07 15:18 Sco	09 01:59 Cap	07 14:16 Aqu
12 09:44 Vir	10 19:54 Lib	11 05:24 Sco	09 15:12 Sag	11 05:02 Aqu	09 19:21 Pis
14 13:28 Lib	12 22:01 Sco	13 06:53 Sag	11 17:01 Cap	13 11:41 Pis	12 04:20 Ari
16 16:33 Sco	15 00:56 Sag	15 10:23 Cap	13 21:47 Aqu	15 21:45 Ari	14 16:21 Tau
18 19:28 Sag	17 05:03 Cap	17 16:11 Aqu	16 05:37 Pis	18 10:02 Tau	17 05:23 Gem
20 22:40 Cap	19 10:28 Aqu	20 00:05 Pis	18 15:58 Ari	20 23:05 Gem	19 17:33 Can
23 02:52 Aqu	21 17:31 Pis	22 09:57 Ari	21 04:04 Tau	23 11:30 Can	22 03:47 Leo
25 09:11 Pis	24 02:47 Ari	24 21:43 Tau	23 17:04 Gem	25 22:11 Leo	24 11:42 Vir
27 18:27 Ari	26 14:28 Tau	27 10:42 Gem	26 05:41 Can	28 06:05 Vir	26 17:15 Lib
30 06:27 Tau	29 03:26 Gem	29 23:06 Can	28 16:09 Leo	30 10:45 Lib	28 20:32 Sco
			30 23:02 Vir		30 22:03 Sag

Jul 2012	Aug 2012	Sep 2012	Oct 2012	Nov 2012	Dec 2012
02 22:51 Cap	01 09:56 Aqu	02 05:37 Ari	01 23:26 Tau	03 07:42 Can	03 01:56 Leo
05 00:25 Aqu	03 13:58 Pis	04 15:40 Tau	04 11:45 Gem	05 19:38 Leo	05 11:50 Vir
07 04:28 Pis	05 20:58 Ari	07 04:09 Gem	07 00:45 Can	08 04:34 Vir	07 18:35 Lib
09 12:13 Ari	08 07:27 Tau	09 16:48 Can	09 11:54 Leo	10 09:35 Lib	09 21:50 Sco
11 23:30 Tau	10 20:10 Gem	12 03:00 Leo	11 19:23 Vir	12 11:10 Sco	11 22:21 Sag
14 12:25 Gem	13 08:27 Can	14 09:30 Vir	13 23:01 Lib	14 10:52 Sag	13 21:42 Cap
17 00:31 Can	15 18:04 Leo	16 12:55 Lib	16 00:06 Sco	16 10:36 Cap	15 21:52 Aqu
19 10:12 Leo	18 00:33 Vir	18 14:46 Sco	18 00:25 Sag	18 12:10 Aqu	18 00:48 Pis
21 17:24 Vir	20 04:45 Lib	20 16:34 Sag	20 01:40 Cap	20 16:54 Pis	20 07:42 Ari
23 22:38 Lib	22 07:53 Sco	22 19:20 Cap	22 05:02 Aqu	23 01:11 Ari	22 18:24 Tau
26 02:29 Sco	24 10:50 Sag	24 23:32 Aqu	24 10:59 Pis	25 12:17 Tau	25 07:12 Gem
28 05:17 Sag	26 13:58 Cap	27 05:23 Pis	26 19:30 Ari	28 00:58 Gem	27 20:06 Can
30 07:29 Cap	28 17:38 Aqu	29 13:13 Ari	29 06:15 Tau	30 13:54 Can	30 07:45 Leo
	30 22:30 Pis		31 18:39 Gem		

Jan 2013	Feb 2013	Mar 2013	Apr 2013	May 2013	Jun 2013
01 17:34 Vir	02 12:00 Sco	01 17:33 Sco	02 05:35 Cap	01 14:20 Aqu	02 06:33 Ari
04 01:09 Lib	04 15:44 Sag	03 21:10 Sag	04 08:41 Aqu	03 18:25 Pis	04 15:53 Tau
06 06:08 Sco	06 17:54 Cap	06 00:13 Cap	06 13:00 Pis	06 01:03 Ari	07 03:31 Gem
08 08:27 Sag	08 19:16 Aqu	08 03:01 Aqu	08 19:02 Ari	08 10:09 Tau	09 16:15 Can
10 08:45 Cap	10 21:20 Pis	10 06:18 Pis	11 03:22 Tau	10 21:21 Gem	12 04:57 Leo
12 09:01 Aqu	13 01:52 Ari	12 11:17 Ari	13 14:12 Gem	13 09:56 Can	14 16:25 Vir
14 10:50 Pis	15 10:08 Tau	14 19:08 Tau	16 02:49 Can	15 22:36 Leo	17 01:17 Lib
16 16:07 Ari	17 21:48 Gem	17 06:08 Gem	18 15:12 Leo	18 09:31 Vir	19 06:37 Sco
19 01:36 Tau	20 10:44 Can	19 18:45 Can	21 01:06 Vir	20 17:06 Lib	21 08:29 Sag
21 14:04 Gem	22 22:10 Leo	22 06:49 Leo	23 07:23 Lib	22 20:53 Sco	23 08:08 Cap
24 02:59 Can	25 06:51 Vir	24 15:48 Vir	25 10:24 Sco	24 21:48 Sag	25 07:26 Aqu
26 14:19 Leo	27 13:00 Lib	26 21:30 Lib	27 11:31 Sag	26 21:28 Cap	27 08:32 Pis
28 23:26 Vir		29 00:52 Sco	29 12:21 Cap	28 21:48 Aqu	29 13:07 Ari
31 06:35 Lib		31 03:12 Sag		31 00:31 Pis	

Jul 2013	Aug 2013	Sep 2013	Oct 2013	Nov 2013	Dec 2013
01 21:43 Tau	03 04:29 Can	01 23:59 Leo	01 18:51 Vir	02 17:34 Sco	02 06:30 Sag
04 09:21 Gem	05 16:57 Leo	04 10:42 Vir	04 02:58 Lib	04 20:13 Sag	04 06:49 Cap
06 22:13 Can	08 03:56 Vir	06 19:11 Lib	06 08:31 Sco	06 21:43 Cap	06 06:53 Aqu
09 10:47 Leo	10 13:07 Lib	09 01:43 Sco	08 12:20 Sag	08 23:29 Aqu	08 08:34 Pis
11 22:11 Vir	12 20:16 Sco	11 06:35 Sag	10 15:16 Cap	11 02:36 Pis	10 13:06 Ari
14 07:39 Lib	15 01:03 Sag	13 09:55 Cap	12 17:59 Aqu	13 07:39 Ari	12 20:40 Tau
16 14:22 Sco	17 03:24 Cap	15 12:04 Aqu	14 21:05 Pis	15 14:49 Tau	15 06:40 Gem
18 17:53 Sag	19 04:06 Aqu	17 13:58 Pis	17 01:18 Ari	18 00:07 Gem	17 18:16 Can
20 18:38 Cap	21 04:43 Pis	19 16:57 Ari	19 07:26 Tau	20 11:23 Can	20 06:47 Leo
22 18:06 Aqu	23 07:13 Ari	21 22:34 Tau	21 16:14 Gem	22 23:56 Leo	22 19:18 Vir
24 18:22 Pis	25 13:14 Tau	24 07:34 Gem	24 03:35 Can	25 12:09 Vir	25 06:16 Lib
26 21:30 Ari	27 23:08 Gem	26 19:24 Can	26 16:11 Leo	27 21:58 Lib	27 13:56 Sco
29 04:43 Tau	30 11:32 Can	29 07:56 Leo	29 03:43 Vir	30 04:01 Sco	29 17:36 Sag
31 15:41 Gem			31 12:20 Lib		31 18:00 Cap

Jan 2014	Feb 2014	Mar 2014	Apr 2014	May 2014	Jun 2014
02 17:02 Aqu	01 03:44 Pis	02 15:40 Ari	01 05:20 Tau	03 06:12 Can	02 01:43 Leo
04 16:58 Pis	03 04:54 Ari	04 19:12 Tau	03 11:48 Gem	05 17:55 Leo	04 14:19 Vir
06 19:45 Ari	05 09:47 Tau	07 02:38 Gem	05 21:39 Can	08 06:23 Vir	07 01:59 Lib
09 02:24 Tau	07 18:43 Gem	09 13:33 Can	08 09:49 Leo	10 17:18 Lib	09 10:36 Sco
11 12:26 Gem	10 06:32 Can	12 02:08 Leo	10 22:06 Vir	13 01:05 Sco	11 15:21 Sag
14 00:24 Can	12 19:14 Leo	14 14:16 Vir	13 08:32 Lib	15 05:43 Sag	13 17:04 Cap
16 13:00 Leo	15 07:25 Vir	17 00:44 Lib	15 16:19 Sco	17 08:11 Cap	15 17:27 Aqu
19 01:22 Vir	17 18:22 Lib	19 09:12 Sco	17 21:42 Sag	19 09:57 Aqu	17 18:25 Pis
21 12:42 Lib	20 03:32 Sco	21 15:38 Sag	20 01:27 Cap	21 12:18 Pis	19 21:26 Ari
23 21:42 Sco	22 10:10 Sag	23 20:02 Cap	22 04:17 Aqu	23 16:01 Ari	22 03:03 Tau
26 03:11 Sag	24 13:49 Cap	25 22:38 Aqu	24 06:54 Pis	25 21:27 Tau	24 11:05 Gem
28 05:03 Cap	26 14:54 Aqu	28 00:10 Pis	26 10:00 Ari	28 04:47 Gem	26 21:05 Can
30 04:32 Aqu	28 14:52 Pis	30 01:53 Ari	28 14:23 Tau	30 14:13 Can	29 08:42 Leo
			30 20:56 Gem		

Jul 2014	Aug 2014	Sep 2014	Oct 2014	Nov 2014	Dec 2014
01 21:23 Vir	03 02:55 Sco	01 17:16 Sag	01 04:40 Cap	01 16:36 Pis	01 01:13 Ari
04 09:41 Lib	05 10:16 Sag	03 22:13 Cap	03 07:59 Aqu	03 18:53 Ari	03 05:14 Tau
06 19:32 Sco	07 13:36 Cap	05 23:57 Aqu	05 09:23 Pis	05 21:33 Tau	05 10:28 Gem
09 01:22 Sag	09 13:51 Aqu	07 23:46 Pis	07 10:06 Ari	08 01:45 Gem	07 17:34 Can
11 03:23 Cap	11 12:55 Pis	09 23:33 Ari	09 11:44 Tau	10 08:38 Can	10 03:14 Leo
13 03:06 Aqu	13 13:01 Ari	12 01:17 Tau	11 15:51 Gem	12 18:44 Leo	12 15:18 Vir
15 02:40 Pis	15 15:58 Tau	14 06:25 Gem	13 23:30 Can	15 07:07 Vir	15 04:04 Lib
17 04:07 Ari	17 22:41 Gem	16 15:24 Can	16 10:29 Leo	17 19:29 Lib	17 14:50 Sco
19 08:43 Tau	20 08:45 Can	19 03:09 Leo	18 23:07 Vir	20 05:30 Sco	19 21:53 Sag
21 16:36 Gem	22 20:49 Leo	21 15:53 Vir	21 11:10 Lib	22 12:17 Sag	22 01:23 Cap
24 02:59 Can	25 09:32 Vir	24 03:58 Lib	23 21:08 Sco	24 16:30 Cap	24 02:51 Aqu
26 14:54 Leo	27 21:53 Lib	26 14:28 Sco	26 04:39 Sag	26 19:22 Aqu	26 04:06 Pis
29 03:36 Vir	30 08:51 Sco	28 22:49 Sag	28 10:02 Cap	28 22:03 Pis	28 06:35 Ari
31 16:08 Lib			30 13:51 Aqu		30 10:56 Tau

Jan 2015	Feb 2015	Mar 2015	Apr 2015	May 2015	Jun 2015
01 17:08 Gem	02 17:40 Leo	01 23:34 Leo	03 07:07 Lib	03 01:46 Sco	01 18:38 Sag
04 01:07 Can	05 05:45 Vir	04 11:57 Vir	05 19:03 Sco	05 11:11 Sag	04 00:49 Cap
06 11:03 Leo	07 18:43 Lib	07 00:51 Lib	08 05:07 Sag	07 18:15 Cap	06 05:01 Aqu
08 22:57 Vir	10 07:04 Sco	09 13:08 Sco	10 12:45 Cap	09 23:21 Aqu	08 08:15 Pis
11 11:56 Lib	12 16:45 Sag	11 23:29 Sag	12 17:43 Aqu	12 02:52 Pis	10 11:13 Ari
13 23:42 Sco	14 22:22 Cap	14 06:39 Cap	14 20:11 Pis	14 05:13 Ari	12 14:15 Tau
16 07:59 Sag	17 00:11 Aqu	16 10:12 Aqu	16 20:59 Ari	16 07:02 Tau	14 17:50 Gem
18 12:02 Cap	18 23:47 Pis	18 10:56 Pis	18 21:31 Tau	18 09:27 Gem	16 22:51 Can
20 12:58 Aqu	20 23:13 Ari	20 10:28 Ari	20 23:28 Gem	20 13:56 Can	19 06:22 Leo
22 12:47 Pis	23 00:29 Tau	22 10:40 Tau	23 04:25 Can	22 21:42 Leo	21 16:58 Vir
24 13:32 Ari	25 04:53 Gem	24 13:23 Gem	25 13:13 Leo	25 08:51 Vir	24 05:40 Lib
26 16:37 Tau	27 12:50 Can	26 19:45 Can	28 01:07 Vir	27 21:41 Lib	26 17:56 Sco
28 22:36 Gem		29 05:47 Leo	30 14:02 Lib	30 09:32 Sco	29 03:20 Sag
31 07:08 Can		31 18:11 Vir			

Jul 2015	Aug 2015	Sep 2015	Oct 2015	Nov 2015	Dec 2015
01 09:09 Cap	01 22:35 Pis	02 09:02 Tau	01 20:03 Gem	02 15:48 Leo	02 10:09 Vir
03 12:20 Aqu	03 23:24 Ari	04 11:48 Gem	04 00:23 Can	05 02:22 Vir	04 23:33 Lib
05 14:22 Pis	06 01:29 Tau	06 17:39 Can	06 08:31 Leo	07 15:13 Lib	07 11:24 Sco
07 16:37 Ari	08 05:39 Gem	09 02:36 Leo	08 19:50 Vir	10 04:01 Sco	09 22:23 Sag
09 19:49 Tau	10 12:08 Can	11 13:55 Vir	11 08:45 Lib	12 15:13 Sag	12 06:46 Cap
12 00:16 Gem	12 20:52 Leo	14 02:40 Lib	13 21:37 Sco	15 00:20 Cap	14 12:57 Aqu
14 06:13 Can	15 07:45 Vir	16 15:42 Sco	16 09:17 Sag	17 07:23 Aqu	16 17:44 Pis
16 14:15 Leo	17 20:22 Lib	19 03:30 Sag	18 18:51 Cap	19 12:20 Pis	18 21:25 Ari
19 00:47 Vir	20 09:23 Sco	21 12:31 Cap	21 01:36 Aqu	21 15:11 Ari	21 00:12 Tau
21 13:22 Lib	22 20:39 Sag	23 17:50 Aqu	23 05:17 Pis	23 16:25 Tau	23 02:30 Gem
24 02:06 Sco	25 04:20 Cap	25 19:42 Pis	25 06:21 Ari	25 17:15 Gem	25 05:26 Can
26 12:22 Sag	27 08:02 Aqu	27 19:28 Ari	27 06:07 Tau	27 19:26 Can	27 10:31 Leo
28 18:46 Cap	29 08:50 Pis	29 18:56 Tau	29 06:24 Gem	30 00:48 Leo	29 18:58 Vir
30 21:39 Aqu	31 08:32 Ari		31 09:10 Can		